Early Families of OTSEGO COUNTY
New York

Volume 1

Martha Reamy

HERITAGE BOOKS
2007

HERITAGE BOOKS
AN IMPRINT OF HERITAGE BOOKS, INC.

Books, CDs, and more—Worldwide

For our listing of thousands of titles see our website at
www.HeritageBooks.com

Published 2007 by
HERITAGE BOOKS, INC.
Publishing Division
65 East Main Street
Westminster, Maryland 21157-5026

Copyright © 1995 Martha Reamy

All rights reserved. No part of this book may be reproduced or transmitted in any form or by any means, electronic or mechanical, including photocopying, recording or by any information storage and retrieval system without written permission from the author, except for the inclusion of brief quotations in a review.

International Standard Book Number: 978-1-58549-660-0

INTRODUCTION

Otsego County in central New York is bounded on the north by the counties of Oneida, Herkimer and Montgomery; on the east by Schoharie; on the south by Delaware; and on the west by Chenango and Madison Counties. It was originally part of Albany County. In 1772 Tryon County was set off from Albany County; in 1784 the name Tryon was changed to Montgomery and in 1791 Otsego was set off from Montgomery with Cooperstown as its county seat.

Before the coming of the white man, this area was the hunting ground of the famous Indian league called by the English the "Six Nations," though the French applied to them the general term "Iroquois." The first whites to come into contact with the tribes of this confederacy were the French, and they were here "in the upper Susquehanna valley" in 1616. They came as explorers and then as traders. In 1738 the first grant of land to white settlers was made and consisted of about 8,000 acres, located in the northeast part of the present county of Otsego. In 1769 surveyors arrived.

The first grant was made by George Clark, the lieutenant governor of New York, to four men - John Lindesay, Jacob Roseboom, Lenelet Ganesvoort and Sybrant VanSchaick. The originator and leader of the settlement, Mr. Lindesay, was a Scotchman, a man of wealth and culture. Their settlement was at Cherry Valley.

There was much history made in the area that is today Otsego County, and that history is contained in numerous books on the region.

Below is a list of all the villages and post offices in the county, reproduced here from *Otsego County, New York; Geographical and Historical* ... by Edwin F. Bacon, 1902 in an effort to aid researchers.

Villages & Postoffices

NAME	TOWNSHIP
Bourne	Exeter
Bowerstown	Middlefield
Brighton	Richfield
Burlington	Burlington
Burlington Flats	Burlington
Center Valley	Cherry Valley
Chase	Hartwick
Chaseville	Maryland
Clintonville	Hartwick
Cherry Valley	Cherry Valley
Colliersville	Milford
Cooperstown	Otsego
Cooperstown Junction	Milford
Decatur	Decatur
East Springfield	Springfield
East Worcester	Worcester
Edmeston	Edmeston
Elk Creek	Maryland

Exeter	Exeter
Fly Creek	Otsego
Garrattsville	New Lisbon
Gilbertswille	Butternuts
Hartwick	Hartwick
Hartwick Seminary	Hartwick
Hope Factory	Otsego
Hyde Park	Hartwick
Ketchum	Pittsfield
Laurens	Laurens
Lena	New Lisbon
Lentsville	Middlefield
Maple Grove	Morris
Maple Valley	Westford
Maryland	Maryland
Middlefield	Middlefield
Middlefield Center	Middlefield
Middle Village	Springfield
Milford	Milford
Milford Center	Milford
Monticello	Richfield
Morris	Morris
Mount Vision	Laurens
New Lisbon	New Lisbon
North Edmeston	Edmeston
Oaksville	Otsego
Oneonta	Oneonta
Oneonta Plains	Oneonta
Otego	Otego
Otsdawa	Otego
Patent	Burlington
Phoenix Mills	Middlefield
Pierstown	Otsego
Pittsfield	Pittsfield
Plainfield Center	Plainfield
Pleasant Brook	Roseboom
Portlandville	Milford
Richfield Springs	Richfield
Roseboom	Roseboom
Salt Springville	Cherry Valley
Schenevus	Maryland
Schuyler Lake	Exeter
Snowdon	Otsego
South Edmeston	Edmeston
South Harwick	Hartwick
South Valley	Roseboom
South Worcester	Worcester
Springfield	Springfield
Springfield Center	Springfield

Stetsonville	New Lisbon
Toddsville	Hartwick
Unadilla	Unadilla
Unadilla Center	Unadilla
Uandailla Forks	Plainfield
Welcome	New Lisbon
Wells Bridge	Unadilla
West Burlington	Burlington
West Edmeston	Edmeston
West Exeter	Exeter
Westford	Westford
West Laurens	Laurens
West Oneonta	Oneonta
Westville	Westford
Wharton	Burlington
Worcester	Worcester

REFERENCES

A = *History of Otsego County, New York* . . . by D. Hamilton Hurd.

AA = *American Ancestry: Giving the Name & Descent, in the Male Line, of Americans Whose Ancestors Settled in the United States Previous to the Declaration of Independence, A. D. 1776, Vol. XII* pub. by Joel Munsell's Sons, Baltimore, Genealogical Publishing Co., 1968.

Barbour Collection of CT.

BOWENY = *10,000 Vital Records of Eastern New York, 1777-1835* by Fred Bowman.

BR = *Biographical Review . . . Biographical Sketches of the Leading Citizens of Otsego County, New York*, Boston, Biographical Review Publishing Co., 1893.

BUC = "Otsego County, New York Cemetery Inscriptions," by Harry E. Bolton, *New England Genealogic & Historic Register*, Oct. 1944.

CCD = Records of Christ's Church in The Town of Duanesburgh [Butternuts], beginning in 1775.

CENT = *A History of Cooperstown* including "The Chronicles of Cooperstown" by James Fenimore Cooper, "The History of Cooperstown" *1839-1886* by Samuel M. Shaw and "The History of Cooperstown" *1886-1020* by Walter R. Littell, 1929.

CH1 = *History of Cherry Valley from 1740 to 1898* by John Sawyer.

COP1 = *A History of Cooperstown*. LH4367?

CPC = Cooperstown Presbyterian Church [Records], Otsego Co., NY 1800 to 1863

CUT1 = *Genealogical and Family History of Central New York* by William Richard Cutter, A.M., Lewis Historical Pub. Co., 1912. [Also consulted was his volumes on Western NY.]

CVC = LDS Manuscript of two pages, "List of Cherry Valley Residents Who Were Moved to Cherry Valley Cemetery c. 1864 from Private or the "Old" Cemeteries."

CWNY = *Genealogical & Family History of Northern New York, Volume I*, Lewis Historical Pub. Co., 1910

DARPI = National Daughters of the American Revolution, *Patriot Index.*

EXC = "Inscriptions in Exeter Center Cemetery in The Town of Exeter, Otsego Co., New York," in *New England Genealogic & Historic Register*, Oct. 1957, copied by Harry E. Bolton.

F = *History of Otego* by Stuart Banyar Blakely, 1907.

G = *A Centennial Offering, Being a Brief History of Cooperstown* . . . by Hon. Isaac N. Arnold, edited by S. M. Shaw, pub. Cooperstown, NY 1886.

GBC1 = *Records of Christ Church at Cooperstown, Otsego County, N.Y.* copied by Gertrude A. Barber, New York, 1933.

GBM = *Marriages From Jan. 4, 1841 - July 9, 1862 Taken from the Otsego Herald & Western Advertiser* compiled by Gertrude A. Barber, 1939.

GBW = *Abstracts of Wills of Otsego County, N.Y. from 1794 - 1824* copied & compiled by Gertrude A. Barber, 1941.

GH = *Otsego County, New York, Geographical & Historical* . . . by Edwin F. Bacon, Oneonta, NY 1902; republished Pipe Creek Publishing, Mt. Airy, MD 1992.

MOHAWK = *Compendium of Early Mohawk Valley Families* by Maryly B. Penrose, 1990, Genealogical Publishing Co.

NASH = *Record of Births & Baptisms, 1797-1827, Kept by Rev. Daniel Nash, Christ Church, Cooperstown, Otsego County, N.Y.* compiled by Gertrude A. Barber, New York, 1935.

NEGHR/NER = New England Genealogical & Historical *Register.*

NYB&G = New York Biographial & Genealogical Society publication.

OB = *A Collection of Abstracts from Otsego Co., New York Newspaper Obituaries 1808-1875* compiled by Gertrude Audrey Barber, Pipe Creek Publishing, Mt. Airy, MD, 1993.

ONE/D = *A History of Oneonta: from its earliest settlement* . . . by Dudley M. Campbell.

RS = *Richfield Springs & Vicinity* . . . by A. S. Barnes & Co., NY, 1874.

SCR = Guardianship Records from the Otsego County Court

SPR = *The History of Springfield* by Kate M. Gray, 1938, Pub. by Gen. James Clinton Chapter No. 640, Daughters of American Revolution.

TAG = *The American Genealogist*

UN/UNA = *The Pioneers of Unadilla Village* by Francis Whiting Halsey, sold by the vestry of St. Matthew's Church, Unadilla, NY 1902.

WILL = *Emma Willard and Her Pupils or Fifty Years of Troy Female Seminary, 1822-1872* edited by Mrs. A. W. Fairbanks, 1898.

3CONG = *Third Congregational Church Records, 1800-1825, Worcester, NY* [original records]

All entries marked [P] indicate that a portrait appears in the text. All portraits included here were taken from *History of Otsego County, New York* . . . by D. Hamilton Hurd. All land-owner maps were taken from *Atlas of Otsego County, New York* . . . F. W. Beers, 1868. These old books were obtained from a variety of sources available to the public: The Latter Day Saints Family History Libraries, the Michigan Microform Corp., and the American Genealogical Lending Library in Bountiful, Utah.

PREFACE

This is the second volume featuring early families of New York state. The first volume was for Orange County, was published also by Pipe Creek, and is available from them.

It is the intention of the editor in this series to bring some order to the genealogical research chaos found in New York state. Fellow researchers have frequently confided to me their dread of searching for a New York ancestor after finding lines in the orderly records of New England. The manner of record keeping in New York state, with few published town records compared to New England, leads to frustration.

I have long been fascinated with turn-of-the century local histories-- sometimes referred to as mugbooks. Their wealth of genealogical information, undocumented and in unindexed tomes, are frustrating for researchers to use.

In this volume I have taken a number of such sources and combined the lineage data found therein. In cases where information found disagrees among volumes, conflicting data has been added in brackets [].

The lineages presented here are for the most part from undocumented sources and should be checked against primary records. This information should be used as clues for further investigation, but in some cases they may be the only surviving references available. No attempt was made to correct the spelling of names; all are as they were found.

In this volume, with the assistance of Beverly McGuire and Genevieve Coleman, many of these families have been traced back to the immigrant ancestor. Full documentation is given in the list of references that follow each family entry.

Several volumes are planned for Otsego County and the last volume will probably contain leftover records that can not be connected to lineages given.

Martha Reamy
Waipio, Hawaii
January 1995

ABELL, ROBERT A., b. 23 Oct. 1829, m. 1850 **Ann Lucinda Rockwell**, d/o **Anson** and **Hannah F. (Coye) Rockwell**. [See Rockwell family entry.] Res. Chicago. Children:
i.   **Eleanor Bryant**, b. Gilbertsville, NY 27 Aug. 1851; m. Dec. 1867 **George L. Tount**. She d. Anamosa, IA in 1877.
ii.   **Frances H.**, b. Gilbertsville 2 Oct. 1852; m. 1870 **Charles P. Stacy**, res. Chicago, IL in 1892.
[*A Genealogy of the Families of John Rockwell of Stamford, Conn. 1641*... by James Broughton, 1903.]

ADAMS, ABNER (Capt.), b. in Brooklyn, CT, reared and m. in CT, removed to Otsego Co. in 1793. He located at the town of Hartwick in what is now (1893) School District No. 13, where he lived two years. After that time he relocated in District No. 14, where he d. in 1857. He filled various town offices and for 28 years was Assessor for the Town of Hartwick. He m. **Desire Ashcraft** who d. in 1844. **Abner** was a soldier of the Revolution. Their dau., **Lucy**, m. **George M. Augur** of Town of Hartwick. [See Augur family entry.]
[BR:639-40]

ADAMS, LEVI[9] (*David*[8] *of MA & CT; Jonathan*[7] *of MA; Thomas*[6] *of England & MA; Henry*[5] *of England & MA; Richard*[4] *of England; Henry*[3] *of England; John*[2] *of England; Robert*[1] *of England*) Levi was b. 18 Nov. 1728 in Canterbury, CT; d. 1816 in Hartwick, s/o **David Adams** (b. Chelmsford, MA) and **Dorcas Paine** his wife, d/o **Elisha** and **Rebecca (Doane) Paine**. Levi was a soldier of the Revolution; served as private and corporal in **Capt. Timothy Backus'** company, **Col. John Douglas'** CT regiment. He removed to Pawlet, VT in 1782, wither several of his family had gone. In 1811 [1790?] settled in Milford, NY [mistakenly identified as "Hardwick, Oswego Co." in Adams Genealogy, p. 91]; carpenter who built many pioneer homes in the area. He was one of Town of Hartwick's first pathmasters/fence viewers. He m. **Margaret Perkins** (1729-1827) on 26 Dec. 1752. Children, all b. in Canterbury, CT:
i.   **Lucy**, b. 23 March 1753.
10 ii.   **Levi Jr.**
iii.   **David**, b. 2 March 1756, d. at Westford 31 May 1833. Identified as <u>Captain</u>.
vi.   **Margaret**, b. 20 Dec. 1758.
v.   **Margaret**, b. 17 Jan. 1760.
vi.   **John**, b. 16 Dec. 1762. Could be the **John Adams** who d. 24 Nov. 1810 at Fly Creek.
vii. **Joanna**, b. 4 Aug. 1764.
viii. **Asahel**, b. 4 Aug. 1764.
ix.   **Asenath**, b. 11 March 1767.
x.   **Lydia**.

LEVI ADAMS JR.[10] b. 14 Feb. 1754 in Canterbury, CT, d. 26 Dec. 1833 in Ripley, Chautauqua, NY. He received a pension in 1833 for service in the Revolutionary War as a private in the CT and VT troops. Although one source says he was born in CT, the DAR lineage book says he was born in Dutchess Co., NY. He m. **Hannah Pettingall** (1753-1835) 9 Aug. 1771 in Canterbury, CT. [LDS Ancestral File says he d. at Ripley, Chautauqua Co., NY 26 Dec. 1833 and **Hannah** at the same place on 3 March 1835.] Children, first three b. Canterbury, next five b. Pawlet, VT:

i. **Ezra**, b. 23 Nov. 1773; was supervisor of Otego, of which Oneonta was a part, in 1809-13.
ii. **Lucy**, b. 24 May 1776.
iii. **Polly**, b. c. 1782; d. 21 Oct. 1875 in Otego; m. **Joseph Mumford**.
iv. **Ruby**, b. 11 May 1783.
v. **Oren**, b. 21 Jan. 1785.
vi. **Hannah**, b. 21 Sept. 1787.
vii. **Levi**, b. 30 Oct. 1790. [LDS Ancestral File says he d. 3 March 1844 at Ripley, Chautauqua Co., NY.]
viii. **Ores**, b. 3 June 1793. Is probably the **Orrin Adams** referred to in DAR Lineage #149608 who m. **Fannie Lee** (1787-1832). This source states that their son, **Orrin Adams Jr.** (1819-1894, m. 1844 **Clarissa Smith** (1826-1904) and that their dau., **Clarissa Adams** (1857-1927) was the 2nd wife of **Mortimer M. Lee** (1846-1931).
ix. **John**, b. 27 Nov. 1794, Milford, NY; d. 28 Sept. 1872, Ripley, Chautauqua Co., NY. He could be the **John Adams** of Milford who m. 3 April 1823 to **Sarah Lane** of Hartwick.
x. **Henry**, b. 17 June 1796, Milford, NY.

[A:160, 192; DARPI; OB; NEGHR 7:39-40; *History of Concord, Shattuck; A Genealogical History of Henry Adams* by Andrew N. Adams, Rutland, VT, 1898, pp. 1-5; DAR Lineage #149608 & 09; BOWENY; Barbour Collection]

AINSWORTH, DARIUS[4] (*Nathan*[3] *CT, Edward*[2] *MA & CT, Edward*[1] *England & MA*) b. 8 [18] Sept. 1738, d. 21 March 1818 at Burlington, NY; served as a corporal from CT in the Revolution and res. at Woodstock. He was s/o **Nathan Ainsworth** and wife **Huldah Peake** of Woodstock, CT who m. there on 14 April 1736. Darius m. 20 Dec. [July] 1759 **Mary Child** who was b. Woodstock, CT 6 Aug. 1740, d/o **Samuel Child** and **Keziah Hutchings** of Killingly. She also d. Burlington on 18 Oct. 1812. He and wife **Mary** bur. at the old cemetery at Burlington. Children, all b. Woodstock:

i. **Cyril**, b. 28 Aug. 1760; soldier in the Revolutionary War. "Was trepanned by **Dr. Albigence Waldo**." He d. 8 Nov. 1782.
ii. **Huldah**, b. 16 Oct. 1763; m. 12 June 1783 **James Wheeler** of Scituate, RI who was s/o **James Wheeler Jr.** and **Abigial**.
iii. **Stephen**, b. 10 Jan. 1767, m. **Deborah Bolton** of Ashford CT.
iv. **Sarepta**, b. 30 Nov. 1768; m. 18 Sept. 1788 **Willard Bugbee** who was b. in Woodstock, CT 19 Jan. 1766 and d. 21 July 21 1844. He was s/o **William Bugbee** and **Elizabeth Franklin**, both of Woodstock. **Sarepta** d. 4 Aug. 1851.
v. **Lois**, b. 30 Aug. 1770; m. 12 Jan. 1797 **Ezra Bartlett** of Ashford who was b. in 1834, d. 1855, s/o **Daniel Bartlett** and **Sarah**

	Cutler. Several children, none res. at Otsego Co.
vi.	---, b. 8 March 1773, d. young.
vii.	**Levi,** b. 13 Nov. 1774, m. 16 Oct. 1805 **Elizabeth Hayward**; d. in State Prison.
4 viii.	**Darius.**
ix.	**Polly,** b. 27 June 1778; m. 1st 19 Feb. 1795 **Loammi Stone,** m. 2nd --- **Arnold** of Burlington Flats, NY.
x.	**Luther,** b. Oct. 1781, d. 16 Aug. 1848 in Providence. On 24 April 1815 he m. **Mary Westcott** who was b. 1777 and d. 20 Aug. 1857.
xi.	**Alice,** b. 6 March 1780.

DARIUS AINSWORTH[4] b. 3 Sept. 1776, d. 4 Jan. 1844; m. **Elizabeth Howard** 16 Oct. 1805. She was b. 1788 and d. 21 Feb. 1845. The family is bur. in West Bloomfield Cemetery, near Volney, Oswego Co., NY, where he lived. Children, all b. in Burlington, NY:

i.	**Ira,** b. 1807, d. 1848.
ii.	**Stephen Howard,** b. 6 March 1809.
iii.	**Mary Ann,** b. 1811, d. 1834.
iv.	**Eliza,** b. 1815; d. 1833.

[BUC6:356; DARPI; *Genealogies of Woodstock Families*; *Genealogy of the Ainsworth Families in America* by Francis J. Parker, 1894; NER:98:356]

ALEXANDER, ELIPHAS, s/o **Simeon Alexander Jr.,** was b. 8 March 1764; res. Northfield, MA and Burlington, NY. **Simeon** was b. 26 May 1722 and d. 19 Feb. 1801 in Northfield, MA and in 1776 he joined the local Committee of Safety. His wife was **Sarah Howe. Eliphas** m. 20 June 1791 **Asenath Foote,** d/o **Obed Foote** and **Mary Todd.** [See Foote family entry.] She was b. 19 Sept. 1762 and d. of palsey in Burlington 18 Nov. 1813. In 1849 **Eliphas** was res. in Syracuse. Children:

i.	**Laura,** b. 4 July 1792 in Brattleboro, VT; d. 8 July 1842; res. Moravia, NY, unm.
ii.	**Almira,** b. 21 March 1794 in Northfield, MA; d. 11 June 1835 Moravia, unm.
iii.	**Amanda,** b. 26 Nov. 1795 in Northfield, MA; m. 20 Jan. 1818 **William Henry Alexander.**
iv.	**Mary Ann,** b. 12 July 1797 in Gill, MA; m. **Isaac Watts Sinkker** at Moravia, NY 24 Feb. 1820. Res. Brasher, NY.
v.	**Eliphaz [Eliphas],** b. 17 April 1799 in Burlington, NY; d. there 9 Oct. 1802.
vi.	**Lydia,** b. 1 April 1801 in Burlington; d. in Moravia, NY 3 Jan. 1835.
vii.	**Sarah,** b. 8 May 1804; m. 16 Oct. 1844 **William Smart** of Brockville, Canada.
v.	**Caleb.**
vii.	**Francis Elizabeth.**

[*Foote Family, Comprising the Genealogy & History of Nathaniel Foote of Wethersfield, CT and His Descendants* by Abram W. Foote, 1907; *Massachusetts Soldiers & Sailors in the Revolution*; *History of Western Massachusetts* by J. G.

Holland, 1855; DARPI.]

ALMY, WANTON [WALTER][7] (*William*[6] *of MA, RI & NY, John*[5] *of RI, William*[4] *of RI, Christopher*[3] *of RI, Christopher*[2] *of RI, William*[1] *of England, MA & RI*) **Wanton/Walter** was s/o **William** and **Elizabeth (Green) Almy** of Portsmith, RI, Freetown, Bristol Co., MA (1796) and Middleburgh, NY (1805-1822). His grandmother was a **Wanton**, "but apparently he disliked the name" and early changed it to **Walter**. **Wanton/Walter** was b. 16 April 1786 and d. at Toddsville, Otsego Co., NY 5 Nov. 1868; physician of Toddsville. He studied medicine under **Dr. John C. Moeller** at Sharon and m. his tutor's sister, **Juliana Moeller**, b. c. 1789, d. 9 Jan. 1865, d/o **Rev. Henry Moeller**, Lutheran minister from Germany, and wife **Julia Ann Zetwitz** nee **Ritter**. It is related that **Walter** bought a burial vault "at the foot of the hill in his meadow, overlooking the field and the Oaks Creek," where he is buried with his daughter. When alive **Dr. Almy** used to sit in the doorway of the vault and smoke evenings. "**Mrs. Almy** dreaded it, and made her son promise that if she died first he would, after his father's death, move her body to her family burying ground at Sharon; this, in due time, he did, and she lies there with the **Mullers**." **Juliana** was blind for many years and d. in 1863, from which time the doctor's health commenced gradually to decline. Children:

    i.   **Edmund James**, b. 6 March 1813, d. 17 July 1871; physician of Cooperstown & Toddsville; m. 23 Feb. 1836 **Augusta Maria Todd** who d. 26 Dec. 1884, aged 67 years, d/o **Lemuel Todd**. In his obituary **Edmund** is described as "an ingenuous and eccentric man," a little obstinate and perhaps blunt in his approach to medical and other problems.

    ii.   **Maria Sophia**, b. 2 July 1814, d. 1 Dec. 1891; m. 15 Aug. 1829, **Dr. Freeborn Garretson Thrall** who was b. 3 June 1810, d. 26 May 1877, s/o **Roger Thrall** and **Sarah Reynolds**. He res. Cooperstown and on retirement removed to Cleveland, OH.

    iii.   **Juliana**, b. 2 Aug. 1816, d. 26 July 1852, bur. Toddsville, NY; m. Feb. 1834 **Deane K. Fenner**.

8   iv.   **Henry Augustus**, b. 30 June 1819.

    v.   **William Walton**, b. 30 June 1819, d. 14 Jan. 1827.

    vi.   **Henrietta Jeanette**, b. 17 April 1827, d. 31 July 1880. She m. 23 June 1847 **Andrew H. Todd**, b. 21 June 1824, d. 25 Nov. 1884 in Paducah, KY. **Andrew** was s/o **Ira** and **Sarah Todd**. Family lived briefly in Minonk, IL, then to Chicago, where **Andrew** had a feed mill on South Water St.

HENRY AUGUSTUS ALMY[8], b. 30 June 1819, d. Rutland, IL 30 Aug. 1871. Doctor of Otsego Co. NY & Rutland, IL. He m. at Sharon, Schoharie Co., NY on 30 Sept. 1846, **Joanna Beekman TenEyck** d/o **Dr. Harmon Hoffman TenEyck** and wife **Maria Beekman**. **Joanna** b. 24 Oct. 1821, d. 11 April 1891. Family res. in four small towns in Otsego Co. until 1865 when they removed to Rutland, IL. Children:

    i.   **Joanna Maria**, b. Schuyler Lake, Otsego Co., 4 July 1847, d. Walport, OR. She m. 1st 2 July 1867, **Maurice Fitch**, m. 2nd

	Richard Grogan.
ii.	**Frances Janet**, b. Toddsville, NY 3 June 1849, d. Rutland IL. She m. **Dr. William O. Ensign**.
iii.	**William Hoffman**, b. Middlefield Centre, 20 April 1851, d. 20 Dec. 1941 in Streator, IL as the result of a fall. He m. 10 Feb. 1878, **Mary Louise Shull** who was b. Marcus Hook, PA on 11 Feb. 1854 and d. 4 April 1903, bur. Sterling, IL. She was d/o **Frederick Augustus Shull** and **Sarah Mustin Barger**. They had children, all b. in IL.
iv.	**Henry Beekman**, b. Middlefield Center on 8 June 1854; d. Rutland, IL 13 Sept. 1874.
v.	**Mary Linn**, b. Middlefield Center 25 Sept. 1856, d. Waldport, OR. She m. **John A. C. Nye** who was b. 13 April 1849.
vi.	**Walter Duryea**, b. Hartwick 6 March 1862, d. Oakland, CA 17 May 1923; m. **Alice Elizabeth Bowdish** in Carroll, IA on 10 April 1883. She was b. in MI 1865, d. San Leandro, CA in 1946.

The "English Ancestry of William Almy of Portsmouth, Rhode Island" is an article featured in the *New England Register*, Volume 71, 1917.

[*Henry Augustus Almy, His Descendants & Lineage From The Immigrant William Almy* by Lloyd Huber Almy, 1956; OB]

ARMSTRONG, AZARIAH[3] (*Hopestill*[2] *MA, James*[1] *MA*) b. 1 April 1776 at Bennington, VT; settler of Plainfield who came to this place from VT in 1812. He was the s/o **Hopestale [Hopestill] Armstrong**, a farmer who had removed from CT to VT about the time of his mar., and his wife **Lydia Haynes**. [Groton, MA vital records gives the mar. of **Hopestill Armstrong** to **Prudence M. Bailey** of Groton, 1 Jan. 1838.] **Hopestill** b. 10 April 1746, 27 Feb. 1797 [1-26-1806 at VT] at Franklin, MA. **Azariah** was a mail carrier and removed from VT to the town of Plainfield, Otsego Co. with his wife **Avis Wing** shortly after their mar. c. 1812. She was of White Creek, Washington Co., NY. He d. 1855 and left a family of six sons and one daughter. Avis had d. in 1848. Children:

	i.	**Ominda**, b. 9 June 1788; m. **Chester Cowen**, both now (1893) dec'd. They left a dau. **Finnet** who m. **Simon Hubbard**.
	ii.	**Farrand S.**, m. **Sarah Wilcox**; dec'd. by 1878. Both dec'd. in 1893 reference. They left one dau.
	iii.	**Hopestill**, m. **Margaret Washburne**, dec'd. by 1878. Left a son, **Azariah**.
	iv.	**Morey W.**, res. on part of old farm; m. **Patience Clark** & has one son, **Floyd**.
2	v.	**Solomon**.
	vi.	**Gethro [Jethro] Gray**, d. aged 22.
	vii.	**David M.**, dec'd. by 1878. Left daughters **Nellie, Iris** and **Morey E.** [1893 ref. states he is living on the old homestead; m. **Elizabeth Taylor** and had by her 8 children, four of whom are living.]
	viii.	**Azariah**, physician. Could be the **Azariah Armstrong** shown in the IGI as marrying **Hannah Eldred** in Winfield, Herkimer Co., NY on 23 Sept. 1858. [BR says an **Azariah** d. aged 14.]

ix.   Charles H., dec'd. by 1878.

SOLOMON ARMSTRONG[2] [P], farmer, b. 16 Nov. 1819 at Plainfield; 1876 & 77 Town Supervisor; 1848 [age 27] m. **Louisa M.**, d/o **Epaphras** and **Caroline (Morse) Taylor** of Plainfield, who was b. 1828. The Taylors had four sons and five daus., Mrs. Armstrong was the third child. After five years of mar., the Armstrong family removed to Plainfield Center and bought the **Loomis** farm, now occupied by their son. Dairy farmer. Members of Freewill Baptist Church. "Mr. Armstrong is one of the best men in his county, honest, upright and intelligent, and both he and his wife are highly esteemed." Children of **Solomon** and **Louisa**:
   i.   **Solomon Eugene**, res. on old farm; m. **Minnie Goodyear** of Cedar Lake by whom he has 3 daus.: **Edith, May** and **Avis**.
   ii.   **Clara B.**, m. **Edwin Worden**.
[A:293, 298; IGI, GMB; GH1:49; BR:459-60; Groton, MA Vital Records; DARPI]

AUGUR, PETER[4] (*John*[3] *CT, John*[2] *CT, Robert*[1] *England & CT*), b. 12 June 1750 at North Branford, CT, s/o **John** and **Rachel (Barnes) Augur**. He m. 19 Feb. 1784 to **Chlorana Blakeslee** who d. 22 [29?] Oct. 1817; she was d/o **Oliver**. Peter d. 29 Dec. 1837 at North Branford. Children:
	i.	**Leverett**, b. 24 Dec. 1784; m. **Sophia Hoadley**, bapt. 22 Oct. 1796, d/o **Ralph** and **Deborah (Frisbie) Hoadley**. He d. 7 April 1873 and she 10 Jan. 1864, both at West Pittsfield, MA in the Shaker Community, which they had joined in 1818. He was a shoemaker. Left three children.
5	ii.	**Peter**, b. 21 Nov. 1786.
5	iii.	**Edward Blakeslee**, b. 19 July 1788.
	vi.	**Lorana** [Lorena/Lorene], b. 2 [or 20] July 1790; m. --- **Clark**.
	v.	**Harriet**, b. 14 May 1792; m. **Lummis Brockett**.
	vi.	**Harvey**, b. 13 July 1794.
	vii.	**Reuel**, b. 9 July 1796.
	viii.	**Lucinda**, b. 24 May 1798.
	ix.	**Elsie**, b. 15 March 1800; d. 6 Feb. 1821.
	x.	**Elizabeth**, b. 19 March 1801; d. 26 Oct. 1883 at Shaker Village, West Pittsfield, MA.
	xi & xii.	Twins b. 1 Jan. 1806; d. 2 Jan. 1806.
	xiii.	**George M.**, b. 10 June 1807.
	xiv.	**Adaline**, b. 20 July 1810; d. 23 July 1813.

PETER AUGUR JR[5], was a carpenter & joiner and followed that trade in CT until 1812, when with his 2nd wife he removed to Hartwick, Otsego Co., settled in what is now School District No. 16. In 1826 he accompanied his brother-in-law [**Gad** and **Asher Blakeslee**, mar. to sisters of Peter's wife] to OH and was employed by them to assist in clearing land. After one year, to save money, he walked back to NY. In 1836 he sold his NY farm and purchased another, in what is now District No. 13, where he lived until his death on 10 March 1864. He m. 1st **Ruth Rogers** who was b. 31 Nov. 1788 & d. in 1808 in childbirth. She was d/o **Ebenezer** by his 2nd wife, **Ruth (Blakeslee)**. Peter m. 2nd **Matty Latin**, b. 1785 in Plymouth, CT,

d/o **Luke Lattin**; she d. 29 Aug. 1860 at Hartwick, NY. **Peter** d. 10 [12] March 1864 and bur. at Hartwick Hill. He had lived the last years of his life with his son **Gideon**. Children:
   i.   **Mary Ruth**, b. 14 Aug. 1808, at Northford, brought up by her grandparents; m. 7 April 1825 **William H. DeGroat**. She d. 6 March 1824, aged 18 and left on edau., **Mary Adella DeGroat**.
      Children by 2nd wife:
   ii.   **Minerva**, b. 2 April 1812 at Hartwick, NY; m. 9 May 1838 **Horace Beckley**, s/o **Jason** and **Clarissa (Dart) Beckley**. She d. 7 Oct. 1882; he d. 9 March 1890 at Hartwick. Four children.
   iii.   **Adaline**, b. 12 April 1814, Hartwick; d. 20 Dec. 1838.
6   iv.   **George Morrell**, b. 26 April 1816 at Hartwick.
   v.   **John Wells**, b. 10 Feb. 1819, Hartwick; m. 19 Aug. 1846 **Betsey Temple** who d. 8 Nov. 1891. **John** d. 7 July 1894 at Otsego, NY. He was a farmer and was Commissioner of Highways. No children.

GEORGE MORRELL AUGUR[6] was b. in Town of Hartwick, 26 April 1816. At the time of his mar. (25 April 1839) he located on his father's homestead, where he lived until 1851 when he purchased a farm in School District No. 13, where he res. a number of years. He then removed to the village of Hartwick and lived there retired the rest of his life. He m. **Diana Upham**, b. Town of Otego 7 Jan. 1820, d/o **Sylvanus Upham**, who was b. in Town of Milford, NY. **Diana** d. 20 Jan. 1887 at Hartwick. **Sylvanus** removed to Chemung Co., NY, where he d. **Sylvanus**' wife was **Lucy Adams**, b. also in the town of Hartwick, d/o Capt. **Abner Adams** who was b. in Brooklyn, CT., as was his father, another **Abner**, a Revolutionary soldier. The **Adams** family removed to Hartwick c. 1794. [See Adams family entry.] **Diana** d. 20 June 1887. Children:
7   i.   **Charles M.**
   ii.   **Adeline**, m. 13 Jan. 1864 **James E. Todd**; he b. 20 Jan. 1836, s/o **Orange** and **Ann Todd**. **James** is a farmer of Unadilla. She member of Baptist Church. Several children.
   iii.   **Austin Henry**, m. 19 [or 9] Feb. 1870, **Mary Farmer** who was b. 27 July 1847, d/o **William** and **Ann (Whitewell) Farmer**. They res. at Otsego and have one child, **Monroe Farmer Augur**, b. 30 Oct. 1874.
   iv.   **Abner E.**, b. 29 March 1857; d. 11 April 1872.
   v.   **George McClellan**, m. 13 Dec. 1882, **Elizabeth Barney** who was b. 13 Feb. 1860, d/o **William** and **Ann Elizabeth (Farmer) Barney**. He is proprietor of a hardware store at Hartwick, where he was postmaster under Cleveland's administration; also justice of the peace.

CHARLES MORRELL AUGUR[7] was b. Town of Hartwick 17 March 1840. Except for one year of teaching when he was 20, he has been a farmer all his life, involved in general farming and dairying. In 1890 he erected a cheese factory on his farm in the Susquehanna Valley, one mile from Hartwick Seminary. He m. in Oct. 1864 to **Ellen L. Chase** who was b. in Town of Hartwick, d/o **Nathan Chase** who was b. in CT and wife **Olive**

Bowen. His father, **Comfort Chase**, was also b. in that state, the s/o **Benjamin Comfort Chase**. He, **Comfort**, came to Otsego Co. with his wife & three children c. 1805; settled in the Town of Hartwick. His wife was **Mercy Murdock**. Members of the Baptist Church. Children:

    i.   **Frank Allen**, physician; m. 21 April 1891 **Elenora Reynolds** d/o **James Henry and Elizabeth Ann (Roselle) Reynolds**. Grad. College of Physicians & Surgeons, Baltimore, MD, as an M.D. in March 1886. Practiced ten years in Westchester Co., NY at Bedford; since then res. Orange Co. at Pine Bush. Episcopal.

    ii.   **Maurice Edwin**, merchant at Hyde Park, Otsego Co.; m. 5 May 1894, **Mary Ellen Ward**, b. 1874, d/o **Leonard** and **Mary Ellen (Gilday) Ward**. Episcopal, served in the Civil War. Has one son, **Henry Dorr**, b. 21 Aug. 1896 at Hartwick.

    iii.   **Abner Adams**, farms with his father, d. 3 Aug. 1897, aged c. 26.

    iv.   **Adeline Jeanette**; m. 12 Feb. 1899 **Claude Alexander Burnside**, b. 19 Apri l1876; s/o **Ephraim** and **Ella Melissa (Applebee) Burnside**. Res. Utica, NY, have two daus.

    v.   **Bessie Caroline**, m. 6 Dec. 1900 **Charles N. Todd**, who was b. 1 March 1871, s/o **Andrew** and **Nancy (Wentworth)**. Farmer at Hartwick, specializes in keeping bees, with over 100 swarms. Family are members of the Lutheran Church.

EDWARD BLAKESLEE AUGUR[5], b. 19 July 1788; m. 8 Sept. 1814 **Irene Comstock** who was b. 15 Jan. 1784; d. 5 Dec. 1841, d/o **Martin Luther** and **Hannah (Taylor) Comstock**, formerly of Litchfield. Edward d. 16 Sept. 1866 at Hartwick, NY. He was a seaman early in life and later settled on the farm bought of his father-in-law, on which his son, **Frederick T.**, now (1904) resides. Children, b. Hartwick, NY:

    i.   **Hannah Elizabeth**, b. 18 Jan. 1816; m. **Nathan Chase** [see Chase entry].

    ii.   **William Henry**, b. 30 Jan. 1819; m. 25 Oct. 1848 **Phebe C. Hunter** at Middlefield, NY. He d. 25 Jan. 1865 at Hartwick and left one son, **Samuel Henry**, b. 25 June 1858 at Hartwick, d. 4 Nov. 1873.

    iii.   **Edward Blakeslee**, b. 18 Jan. 1821; d. 10 Dec. 1849.

    iv.   **Maria Janette**, b. 23 Dec. 1823; m. 3 April 1850 **Michael Rich** of Hartwick. He d. 2 Jan. 1874 and she 23 Sept. 1853. The left one son, **Edward Blakeslee Rich**, b. 25 Aug. 1853; d. in Jan. 1875 at Hartwick.

6   v.   **Frederick Taylor**.

FREDERICK TAYLOR AUGUR[6], b. 28 July 1826; m. 28 Jan. 1851 **Emeline Bowdish**, b. 22 Dec. 1827 and d. 24 May 1904; d/o **John R.** and **Betsey (Keynon) Bowdish**. Frederick is a farmer of Hartwick (1904), a member of the Episcopal Church. Children, all b. Hartwick:

    i.   **Amelia Maria**, b. 22 July 1855, physician, grad. from the Woman's Medical College at Chicago in April 1882, practising at Binghamton, NY.

7   ii.   **George Milton**, b. 7 June 1859.

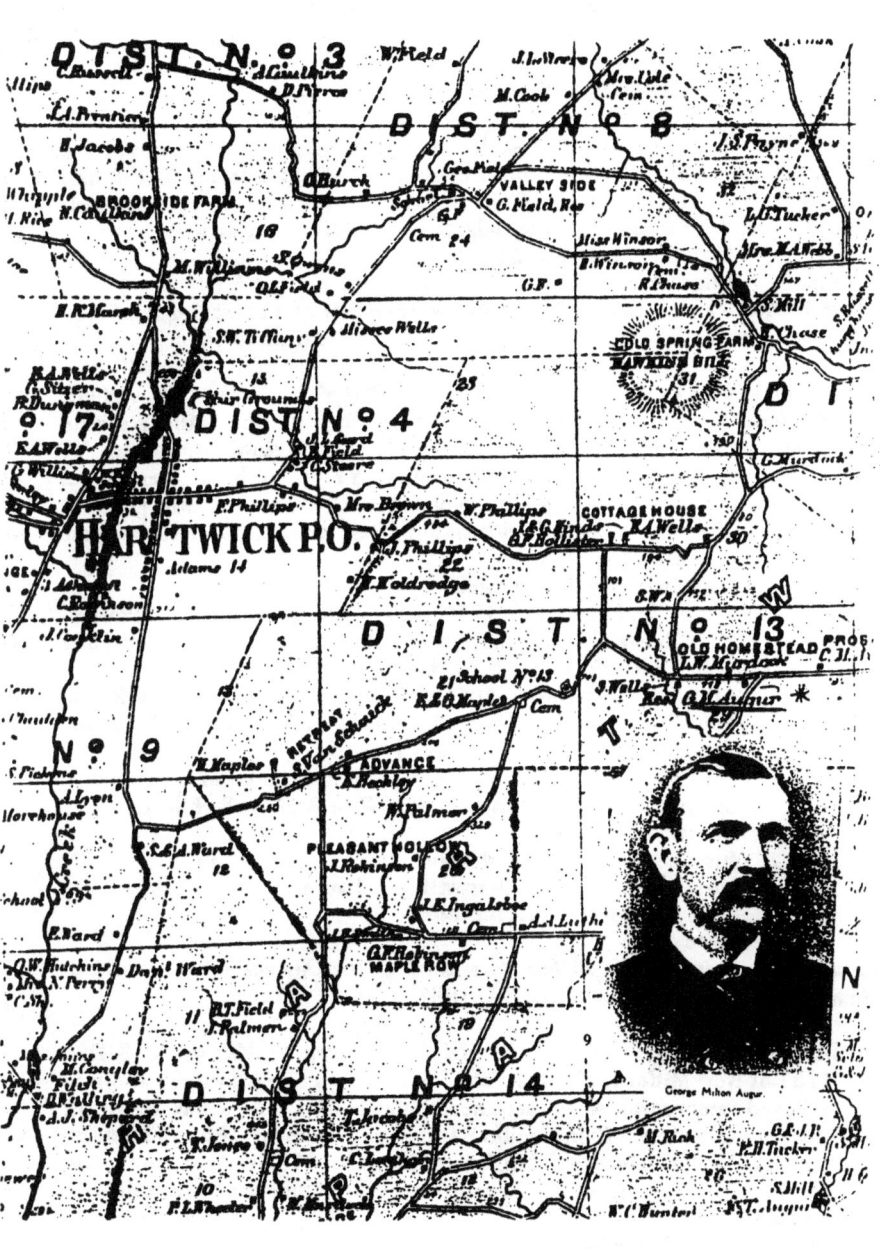

7   iii.   **Frederick Linn**, b. 12 June 1867.

GEORGE MILTON AUGUR[7] m. 9 Feb. 1881, **Jane Maples Wells** who was b. 7 Feb. 1863, d/o **Edwin A.** and **Lucinda (Maples) Wells**. He is a farmer; in 1892 purchased land near Hartwick where he now res. Member of the Christian Church. Child:
  i.   **Ernest Wells**, b. 24 May 1896 at Hartwick.

FREDERICK LINN AUGUR[7] m. 20 March 1889, **Dora McKennan** who was b. 19 May 1866, d/o **John** and **Elizabeth B. (Burlingham) McKennan**. He is a farmer and res. on old homestead at Hartwick, NY, formerly occupied by his father and grandgather. Children, b. Hartwick:
  i.   **Marion Amelia**, b. 28 Feb. 1890.
  ii.   **Charlotte Janette**, b. 24 April 1903.

[*Family History and Genealogy of the Descendants of Robert Augur of New Haven Colony* by Edwin P. Augur, 1904; OB; GBC1; BR:639-40]

AYLESWORTH, JAMES[5] (*James*[4] *VT & RI, Philip*[3] *RI, Arthur*[2] *RI, Arthur*[1] *England/Wales*), s/o **James** and **Lois (Harrington)**, (his father's second wife). **James** (Jr.) b. & m. in RI **Margaret Harrington**, res. Pownal, VT and removed in middle life to New Lisbon, NY, where he d. of erysipelas of the head, and is bur. in old "Mount Vision" Cemetery. **Margaret** d. either at the home of **Nathan Stanton** in West Amboy, NY or at the home of her dau. **Amy**. Children:
  i.   **Benjamin**, res. near Pownal, VT.
  ii.   **Isaac Clark**, b. 2 May 1777; m. **Theodosia Billings**, res. Pownal, VT, Geauga Co., OH and (1842 to Lee Co., IL, where **Theodosia** d. in 1850 and **Isaac** d. 1851. Seven children.
  iii.   **Amy**, m. **Nathaniel Gardner**, res. New Lisbon. She d. 2 Jan. 1863, he d. April 1858, aged 80; both bur. in Old Mount Vision Cemetery. [See Gardner family.]
  iv.   **Lois**, m. **William Barton**, res. Chautaugua, Co., NY.
  v.   **Lovina**, m. **Nathan Stanton**, res. West Amboy; 8 children.
  vi.   **Justus**.
  vii.   **Justin**, twin of **Justus**; d. unm.
  viii. **Martha**, m. **Caleb Aspenwall**, res. Laurens.
  ix.   **Polly**, m. **Daniel Harrington**.
  x.   **Mercy**.

[*Boston Transcript* #3168; *Arthur Aylesworth & His Descendants in America*, Homer E. Aylesworth, Providence, RI, 1887]

BABBITT, ELKANAH[5] (*Elkanah*[4,3,2] *MA & CT, Edward*[1] *MA*) was b. 3 Dec. 1737 at New Milford, CT; d. 9 Feb. 1807. He was s/o **Elkanah**[4] who it is believed removed to "somewhere near Cooperstown, NY" before his death and wife **Obedience Prindle**, d/o **Samuel** and **Dorothy (Plum) Prindle**. **Elkanah**[5] was at Lanesboro, MA for awhile and c. 1788 removed to the Fly Creek, NY area. He was a Revolutionary War veteran. His wife was **Rachel** ---. Children:
6   i.   **Stephen**.

6	ii.	**Warren**, b. 18 June 1774.
	iii.	**Annis**, m. **Ensign Rexford** and had child **Electa** who m. --- **Kibby**, and had two daus., **Nancy** and **Marcia**. Res. Otsego Co.
	iv.	**David**, b. c. 1766. Farmer in Lanesboro, MA, d. 1816 there, leaving wife **Naomi** and several children. His son **Semi**, b. 1788 in Cheshire, MA, d. 1860 in Fleming, NY, res. for a time in Otsego Co. **Semi** served in the War of 1812 and secured land in Cayuga Co. He m. 13 March 1789, **Nancy Luther**.

BABBITT, STEPHEN[6] of Otsego was thought to have b. in CT and was one of the earliest settlers of Hartwick & Town of Otsego in 1790. **Stephen** was b. 1765 and d. 12 April 1827. He m. **Sally Head**, also a native of New England, b. 1778 and d. 17 Sept. 1837. **Stephen** made his will 7 April 1827 and in it named wife **Sarah** and children:

7	i.	**David**, b. 1796.
7	ii.	**Josiah**.
7	iii.	**Stephen**, b. 3 April 1806.
	iv.	**William H.** [not named as a child in 2nd source]
	v.	**Reuben**.
	vi.	**Mary** m. **Rossell Barney**.
	vii.	**Margaret**, m. --- **Bishop**.

Other possible children, but noted as "probably incorrect:" **William, Truman, Linda** and **Maude**.

DAVID BABBITT[7] b. May 1794; d. 17 March 1867. He trained as a shoemaker, but seldom practiced this trade. He removed from Otsego Co. to Rushford, NY c. 1838. It was said that in personal appearance he was strikingly like Thomas Jefferson. He served in the War of 1812 from Otsego Co., for which he received bounty land. A detailed biography of him appears in *The Babbitt Family History, 1643-1900*. He m. **Lucy Shipman**, b. 1794/5, d. 3 June 1873. Both are bur. in Podonque Cemetery, Rushford. Children:

	i.	**Sally**, b. 1820, d. 2 Aug. 1853; m. **Lowell Farwell** who d. 8 Feb. 1863, aged 37 years. They had **Darius, Milo, Henry, Almeda** and **Florence** [Farwell].
	ii.	**Horace**, b. 1824.
	iii.	**William**, b. 1828.
	iv.	**Lemyra**, b. 1833, d. 13 March 1858; school teacher.
	v.	**Albert**, b. 1835; killed 21 July 1861 at Bull Run, the first from Alleghany Co., NY to die in the war.
	vi.	**Milo**, res. Syracuse, NY.
	vii.	**Lucy Ann**.

JOSIAH BABBITT[7], b. 2 Oct. 1823 [1798] at Town of Hartwick. He inherited one-third of the family homestead & d. there in 1853; farmer; in 1820 ensign in 2nd Regiment of Infantry of the county. He m. **Melinda Baker**, of a New England family. Children:

	i.	**Albert**, b. 1821; d. 15 Dec. 1830.
8	ii.	**Chester**, b. Town of Hartwick 2 Oct. 1823.

	iii.	**Amanda,** b. 1825, d. 16 July 1905; m. 1848 **Amos Mathewson.** [See Mathewson family entry.]
	iv.	**Sarah,** b. 1827; d. 3 May 1828.
8	v.	**Reuben,** b. 27 Sept. 1837.

CHESTER BABBITT[8] res. with his parents until 1850, when he joined the '49ers and went to California. From there he traveled to Sidney, Australia to visit the gold fields of that country. From there to London, England and back to the U.S. Took up farming on the homestead until 1883, when he took up res. in Geary Co., KS. After six years he returned to the homestead in Otsego Co. He was highly esteemed for his frank, friendly disposition, and well-know rectitude of character. He m. 20 June 1855 to **Mary Field** who was b. in Hartwick 19 Oct. 1826. [See Field family entry.] **Chester** d. 25 May 1909. No children.

REUBEN BABBITT[8] d. 29 Dec. 1896. He res. in Otsego Co. until 1867 when he settled in DeRuyter, NY. Mar. 15 Sept. 1858 **Emogene Field** d/o **William** and **Amorett (Yates) Field** who was b. 22 June 1838. Children:

	i.	**Herman Albert,** b. 15 Dec. 1859; m. **Eva Jane Bailey** 25 Dec. 1888. She was b. 3 April 1864. Their children: **Chester Harvey** b. 6 Nov. 1889; **Grace May,** b. 29 Aug. 1892 and **Orlin Holmes Babbitt,** b. 8 Aug. 1896.
	ii.	**Amber Melinda,** b. 14 Sept. 1861; m. **Erumett Nash** 18 March 1887, who was b. 12 April 1853. Children: **William Penn Nash** b. 10 May 1890 and **Josephine** b. 23 Dec. 1898.
9	iii.	**Noyes Reuben,** b. 22 April 1864; res. in NY, KS, MO, IL and finally in St. John's, OR.

STEPHEN BABBITT[7] b. 3 April 1806 in Otsego Co., d. 19 March 1857. He settled in Pike, Wyoming Co. and m. 14 Nov. 1829 **Fannie Bliss,** d/o **Eleazer** and **Clarissa (Boardman) Bliss,** who was b. 22 Jan. 1814 and d. 19 Nov. 1896. They had several children.

WARREN BABBITT[6] was b. 18 June 1774; d. 4 July 1847 at Fly Creek. He was a farmer and distiller. When he converted to Methodism he destroyed his distillery and liquor. He res. in Fly Creek and is bur. in Old Chapple Burial Ground there. He m. in Amenia, NY **Sally Delano,** d/o **Benjamin** and **Sarah (Clark) Delano.** She was b. 2 June 1778; d. 2 Jan. 1861. Children:

	i.	**Anna,** b. 8 Aug. 1799 [14 Sept. 1797], d. 5 Sept. 1867 in Fly Creek. She m. **James Johnson** 7 Aug. 1814. [See Johnson family entry.]
	ii.	**Clarissa,** b. 7 Sept. 1801; m. 1st --- **Thorpe** and had one child, **Earl** who m. **Abbie Steinburg** and had no children. All res. Fly Creek. Clarissa m. 2nd **John Thompson** and had **Sarah** m. **Truman Ellinwood** of Brooklyn, NY. They had one child, **Mamie,** who d. young. The second child of **Clarissa** and **John Thompson** was **Eunice** who m. **Elon Denio** of Auburn, NY.
7	iii.	**Daniel,** b. 4 May 1804.

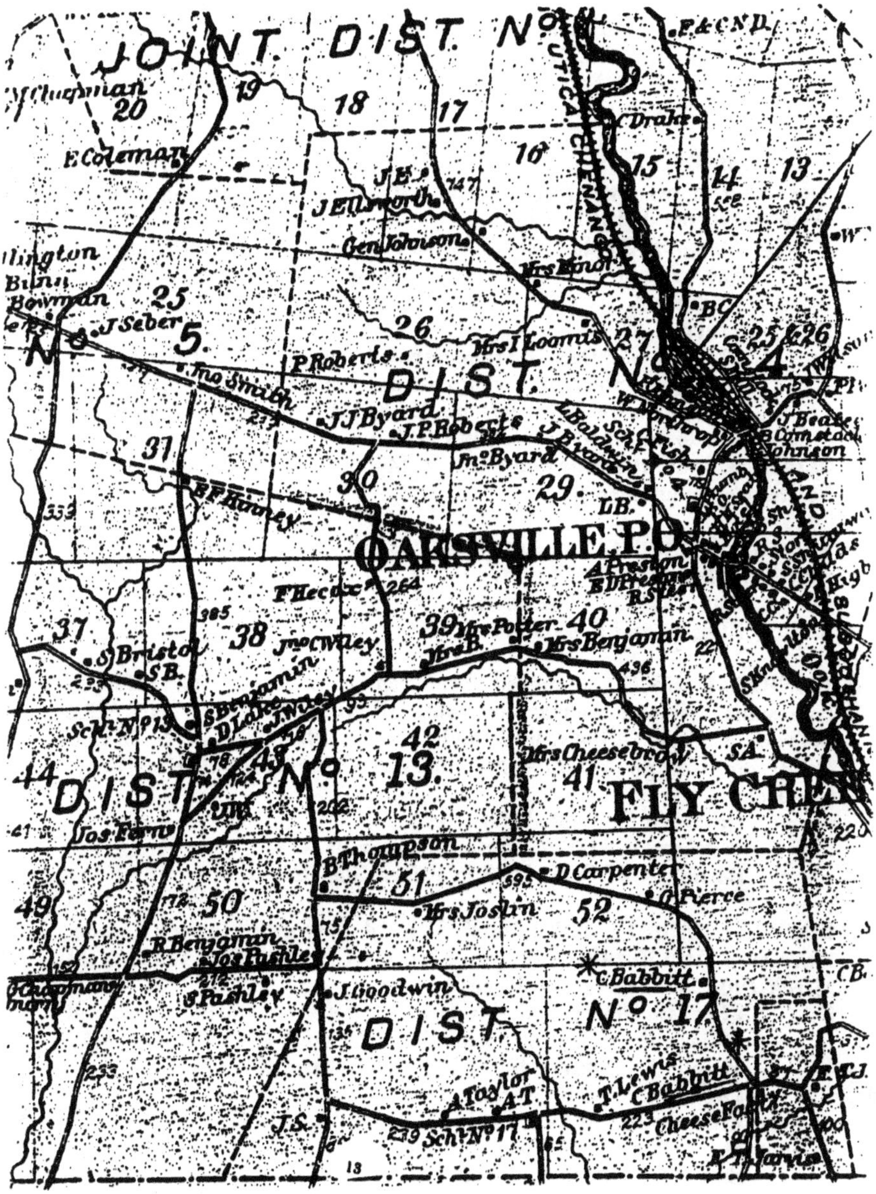
JOINT DIST No
OAKSVILLE P.O.
FLY CRE
DIST No 13
DIST No 17
DIST
UTICA CHENANGO
E Coleman
J Ellsworth
Gen Johnson
J Seber
P Roberts
Jno Smith
J J Byard
J P Roberts
Jno Byard
B F Kinney
Mrs Potter
Mrs Benjaman
Mrs Cheesebrow
S Bristol
B Thompson
D Carpenter
Mrs Joslin
C Babbitt
J Goodwin
R Benjaman
Jos Pashley
S Pashley
A Taylor
T Lewis
Cheese Fact
Sch No 17
A Preston
C Drake
Jno C Wiley

	iv.	**Eunice**, b. 12 Sept. 1807; d. 12 Sept. 1879. Res. Fly Creek and m. **Daniel Carpenter** there and had (1) **Ervin**, m. **Jane Wheeler** in Fly Creek and had **Clarence** and **Ada**; and (2) **Maria** m. **Schuyler O'Brien**; no children.
	v.	**Nancy Maria**, b. 11 Dec. 1809; m. **Rev. Charles Mead**; res. Fly Creek, no children.
7	vi.	**Roswell**, b. 22 March 1813.
	vii.	**Orrin**, b. 16 Feb. 1816; d. 13 Sept. 1884. He m. **Mary Putnam** and had children **Albert** and **Cora**; Cora m. --- **Luce**.

DANIEL BABBITT[7], b. 4 May 1804 in Otsego Co., d. 14 March 1884; shoemaker in his early years. He m. 1st **Anna Woodward**, d/o **Abijah Woodward**; she d. 1844. Children:

	i.	**Susan**, b. 30 March 1827; d. 22 Feb. 1878; m. **Dwight Chapman** and had one dau., **Nellie May**, who m. **Ira Thompson**.
8	ii.	**Andrew J.**
8	iii.	**Warren**.
	iv.	**Charles**, b. 2 Dec. 1834; m. **Sarah Green** in 1853. For a time he was a carpenter, but gave up the profession because of bad health. Carried on his father's farm. He had three children who did not live to adulthood. Res. Fly Creek.

Daniel[7] m. 2nd **Catherine Popple**, b. 30 March 1827 and d. 22 Feb. 1878. No children mentioned here.

ANDREW J. BABBITT[8] m. **Jane Barrs** and in 1912 res. in Oneonta [sic] with dau. **Mrs. Spencer**. Children:
i. **Anna**, m. **Kron Spencer**.
ii. **Ella**, m. and d. soon after.

WARREN BABBITT[8], removed from Schuyler's Lake, Otsego Co. to Painesville, OH and then to Conneaut, OH where he died. Mar. **Alice Doty**, d/o **George W. Doty**, in Schuyler Lake c. 1856. She was b. 22 Oct. 1838, d/o **George Washington** and **Katherine (Monmouth) Doty**. Children:
i. **Hattie**, b. 30 Sept. 1858.
ii. **William**, b. 11 Oct. 1865 in Painesville, OH.
iii. **Daniel**, b. 27 Sept. 1872 in Painesville, OH; unm.

ROSWELL BABBITT[7] b. 29 March 1813; d. May 1899 in New Lisbon. Farmer; m. **Ann Elizabeth Brown**, b. in Fly Creek 22 Dec. 1819; d. 29 March 1903 in Oneonta. Children:

	i.	**Franklin Henry**, b. 5 May 1842; m. **Delia Trowbridge**; removed to Danville, IL and had: **Blanche** b. 24 April 1863; **Bertha**, d. 19 March 1873; **Harry D.**, b. 1871, electrician of NY City.
8	ii.	**Lucien Emory**, b. 30 April 1844 in Exeter.
	iii.	**Ellen Lydia**, b. 29 Aug. 1847, d. 24 Aug. 1908; res. Dixon, IL. Mar. **Albert McKenney** and had children.
	iv.	**Emma Charlotte**, b. 2 Aug. 1849; m. **Dwight Chapman** and had **Sarah Beth** b. 9 Oct. 1886, d. 18 Jan. 1893. Emma res. in

  Auburn, NY.
v. **Otis H.**, b. 19 March 1854; studied medicine and practiced in Auburn and Cooperstown and held many public service offices. Methodist Episcopal. He m. **Emma Wentworth Luce** in Hartwick 23 Oct. 1878 and had one child, **Emma Blanche**, b. 5 Oct. 1881. She m. **George Denman** 12 June 1901.
vi. **Grace May**, b. 9 Oct. 1862; m. **Robert George** in New Lisbon; no children.

LUCIAN BABBITT[6] res. in Oneonta; m. 13 Nov. 1881 **Sarah A. Verry**. Children:
i. **Frank A.**, b. 25 Dec. 1884; d. 25 Sept. 1886.
ii. **Frederick D.**, b. 7 Jan. 1886; d. 23 Sept. 1886.
iii. **Lorena E.**, b. 30 Jan. 1887.
iv. **Charles H.**, b. 5 Aug. 1888.
v. **Harriet A.**, b. 10 July 1890.
vi. **Amy L.**, b. 30 July 1892; d. 18 Jan. 1897.
vii. **Morton L.**, b. 9 Nov. 1894.
viii. **Marian E.**, b. 4 July 1896.
ix. **Otis E.**, b. 16 June 1898.
x. **James F.**, b. 17 April 1900.

[GBW; BR:219-20; *The Babbitt Family History, 1643-1900* by William B. Browne, 1912; OB]

BABCOCK, JONAS[1] came with his brother **Samuel** [see entry below] from Berkshire, MA to Otsego Co. in 1795 and settled in Westford. They were both soldiers of the Revolution. **Jonas** was counted in the 1840 census in Westford, aged 76 and Revolutionary veteran. They were joined by their father **Josiah** in 1799. In the Worcester Congregational Church baptism records **Jonas**' death on 27 Dec. 1847 and his family were bapt. on these dates:
i. **Fannella**, bapt. 8 Jan. 1801.
ii. **Onill**, bapt. 8 Jan. 1801.
iii. **Betsey**, bapt. 8 Jan. 1801.
iv. **Hiram**, bapt. 8 Jan. 1801.
v. **Almira**, bapt. 8 Jan. 1801.
vi. **Chester**, bapt. 8 Jan. 1801.
vii. **Pamela**, bapt. 14 June 1802.
2 viii. **Enoch**, bapt. 6 May 1804.
ix. **Semantha**, bapt. 18 Oct. 1806.
xi. **Olive**, bapt. Nov. 1809; d. 20 Aug. 1853.

ENOCH BABCOCK's household baptisms in Westford Third Congregational Church:
i. **Louisa**, bapt. 4 May 1828.
ii. **Amelia Augusta**, bapt. 2 Jan. 1830.
iii. **John Barton**, bapt. 10 Sept. 1831.
[GH1:82; 3CONG]

BABCOCK, ROGER[5] (*William[4] of CT, Ebenezer[3] of CT, Ebenezer[2] of MA, Capt. Robert[1] of England & MA*) was living at Coventry, CT at the time of the taking of the first federal census in 1790. He had in his family two males under sixteen and three females. He was a pioneer settler of Burlington, Otsego Co., and cleared a farm there in the wilderness; later settled at South New Berlin, Chenango Co., NY, where he followed farming and blacksmithing to the end of his life. He d. 11 May 1836, aged 79. His wife, **Thankful**, d. 9 March 1822, aged 66 years. Both are bur. at Burlington Flats. Children:
    i.   **Chester**, b. 31 March 1790 at Burlington; supervisor of New Berlin, blacksmith. He m. **Sarah G. Fox** and had nine children. Their dau. **Betsey** d. 17 March 1819, aged 17 years and is bur. at Exeter, NY.
    ii.   **Roger**.
6   iii.   **Alva**.
    iv.   **Elizabeth** m. **Minerva Cushman**. [This man was named "Minerva."]
At least four other children and probably more; based on the 1790 census.

ALVA BABCOCK[6], b. Burlington 19 April 1799, d. in South Berlin 1 March 1867, where he had removed when a young man. Blacksmith, accounted an expert craftsman, especially in the art of tempering axes and other edge tools. He was energetic and industrious, and raised a large family. He served as a justice of the peace and supervisor for South New Berlin. Baptist. He m. 1st 22 April 1828, **Rebecca Hubbell**, b. 8 March 1808, d. 18 Feb. 1836. He m. 2d, 9 April 1837, **Isabelle Foote Pratt**, b. 19 June 1807, d. 16 Aug. 1857. By his first wife he had:
    i.   **Charles B.**
    ii.   **Hobart**.
    iii.   **Grove L.**
    By his second wife he had:
    iv.   **Linn [P]**.
    v.   **Sidney Smith**.
    vi.   **Adrian**.
    vii.   **Francis Ray**.
[CUT1:3:1215-18; NER101:230; EXC:309]

BABCOCK, SAMUEL[1], brother of **Jonas** above, and s/o **Josiah**, was noted as "colonel" in his obituary and of Westford, d. 25 Sept. 1836, age 75; Revolutionary War veteran. A Mrs. **Sylvina Babcock** joined the Third Congregational Church of Worcester by letter on 15 Nov. 1800; baptism records give the following children:
    i.   **Anna**, oldest dau., "dedicates herself to God in baptism. The administrator was a Methodist minister." No date given.
    i.   **Erastus**, bapt. 8 Jan. 1801.
    ii.   **Daniel**, bapt. 8 Jan. 1801. He could be the **Dan Babcock** who m. 20 Sept. 1842 at Maryland, NY to **Joanna Low**.
2   iii.   **Harvey**, bapt. 8 Jan. 1801.
    iv.   **Sylvina**, bapt. 8 Jan. 1801.

v. **Artemas**, bapt. 8 Jan. 1801.
vi. **Richardson**, bapt. 8 Jan. 1801.
vii. **Cyrus**, bapt. 8 Jan. 1801.
viii. **Alexander Hamilton**, bapt. 2 June 1805.
ix. **Electa**, bapt. Oct. 1807.

HARVEY BABCOCK[2]'s household according to Worcester Congregational Church records (below). He removed from the church in June 1831; joined 13 Sept. 1812.
i. **Julia Ann Frances**, bapt. 1811.
ii. **Mary Jane**, bapt. Nov. 1813.
iii. **Harrison Grey Otis**, bapt. 31 Dec. 1815.
iv. **Eliza Marie**, bapt. 1819.
v. **John Hervey** [sic], bapt. 20 May 1821. Probably the **John H. Babcock** who m. at Cooperstown on 2 Aug. 1842 to **Lucia M. Gregory**.
[3CONG; OB; GBM]

BABCOCK, WILLIAM DELOS, b. 26 April 1817; d. 26 July 1889. He was s/o **Joshua** and **Clarissa** his wife. William m. **Cornelia A. Rockwell**, on 4 Nov. 1841 at Butternuts. She was d/o **Ashbel R.** and **Caty (Shaw) Rockwell**. [See Rockwell family entry.] Children, all b. Gilbertsville:
i. **Mary Elizabeth**, b. 7 Sept. 1842, where she d. 18 Dec. 1857.
ii. **Russell Prentice**, b. 1 Jan. 1845; not mar., res. Chicago in 1892.
iii. **Frank Ruggles**, b. 18 July 1846; d. there 22 Oct. 1868.
iv. **Sarah Adell**, b. 4 Oct. 1849; d. there 17 May 1876.
[*A Genealogy of the Families of John Rockwell of Stamford, Conn. 1641* ... by James Boughton, 1903; GBM]

BACKUS, HEMAN[1], b. in VT in 1798 and removed to Chenango Co., NY with his parents when a lad. He m. a **Miss Buck** by whom he had seven children. She d. in the prime of life and he m. 2nd **Laura Goodrich**, by whom he had four children. At the time of his death (1882), these children were living:
i. **Rebecca**, m. **Allen Burgess**.
ii. **Sally**, m. **Thomas Fuller**.
2 iii. **Solomon**.
iv. **Leonard**, retired farmer of town of Pittsfield, Otsego Co., nearly 70 years of age (1893).
v. **Hiram**, farmer of Pittsfield.
vi. **John**, farmer res. New Lisbon, Otsego Co.
vii. **Julia**, m. **C. Furman**, res. near Beaver Dam, WI.
viii. **Maria**, m. **Ansel Angel** of Coontown, NY.
ix. **Lisetta**, m. **Halsey Williams**.
x. **Harriet**, m. **Clinton Stone**, farmer of town of Pittsfield.
xi. **Harrison**, farmer of Pittsfield.

SOLOMON BACKUS[2] m. **Betsy Angel** of Chenango Co., who was b. 1823, a d/o **Jonathan Angel** of RI who came to Chenango Co. in 1808. Soon after their marriage, **Solomon** and wife settled in town of Pittsfield, buying a small farm of fifty acres, where they lived until the spring of 1857 when they sold it and purchased a larger farm. They sold this farm in 1859 and for the next two years rented in Chenango Co., removing 1861 to another farm in Otsego Co. Then they bought 144 acres in Town of Morris, where they lived until removing to Town of Pittsfield, where he lived for the rest of his life, dying 1886. **Betsy** d. in 1884, aged 61. Children:

3   i.   **Ora O.**
    ii.   **Mary**, m. **Samuel Morse**, cheese manufacturer near Hartwick.
    iii.   **Allen.**

ORA O. BACKUS[3] farmer of District No. 2, Town of Pittsfield was b. in that town in June 1850. He has lived at his present home since age 17, with the exception of 1874 and 1875 when he worked in a cheese factory. He m. 18 Oct. 1876 to **Clara Wing**, b. in Morris in 1857, a d/o **Walter A. Wing.** Children:
    i.   **Heman W.**, b. c. 1883.
    ii.   **Stanley S.**, b. c. 1882.
    iii.   **Walter A.**, b. c. 1890.
[BR:565-6]

BAKER, HARVEY[6] (*Thomas*[5] *NH & NY, Capt. Gideon*[4] *NH & NY, Gideon*[3] *NH, Gideon*[2]*, Joshua*[1] *England & MA*) was b. in "the old town of Lisle, Broome County (formerly Tioga Co.), New York" 16 Oct. 1818. He was the 4th s/o **Thomas and Lois (Munson) Baker**, who m. 14 Oct. 1810 at Munson's Mills (now Upper Lisle), Broome Co. **Lois** was b. 6 Oct. 1790 in town of Goshen, Litchfield Co., CT, d/o **Moses Munson** and **Julia** his wife, who res. in Broome Co. and later in the City of Rochester, NY. [This source gives background material on the Munson family of CT.] **Thomas Baker** and **Lois** removed with them to Rochester. During their time there the War of 1812 broke out and **Thomas Baker** volunteered to serve and was among those who defended Sackett's Harbor in 1813-14. After eight years in Rochester, **Thomas Baker** moved his family back to Broome County, where son Harvey was born. **Harvey** is described as a "large, rugged boy..." who learned to read by the age of five. He was a farmer, business man, mechanic, millwright, carpenter and foundry operator. He res. for a time in Genesee, (Allegany Co.) NY with his brother **Hollister**, at Marcellus, Onondaga Co., NY and various other work locations. In 1841 he was contracted to work at in Colliersville, Otsego Co., and established himself in that county at that time. He became a citizen of Oneonta, his father, mother and younger brother [**Enos**] also setting up their residence there. On 6 March 1846 **Harvey** m. **Betsy Rose**, 2nd d/o **Nathan** and **Deborah (Morehouse) Rose**, of the town of Maryland in Otsego Co.; both were still living in 1893. Children:
    i.   **Helen**, b. 26 March 1849; still (1893) res. with parents, unm.
7   ii.   **Charles H.**, b. 19 Dec. 1853.

CHARLES H. BAKER[7] m. **Emma Birdsall**, 2nd d/o **Harvey** and **Jane Birdsall** of Oneonta, 22 May 1872. Children:

i.	Harry J., b. 13 Oct. 1873.
ii.	Fred M., b. 25 May 1876.
iii.	Merton H., b. 6 April 1880.
iv.	Louise M., b. 5 Jan. 1885.
v.	Clarence A., b. 23 Sept. 1888.

[BR:9; ONE:49, 142, 144]

BARNES, PHILIP[1] b. 22 June 1798 in Groton, CT [BR says a native of VT and of NH ancestry]; to Otsego with father in 1823. He m. **Jane T. Wallace** there in 1828. She was b. in Dutchess Co., NY of Scotch ancestry. He d. aged 78, she aged 76. Members of the Baptist Church. Children:

	i.	Mary Elvira, b. 15 Nov. 1829.
2	ii.	Simeon R., b. 1831/2.
	iii.	Pembroke S.
	iv.	Aaron.
	v.	Dennison R., b. 1836.
	vi.	Jerry F.
	vii.	Rebecca R.
	viii.	Helen Amelia, b. 1844
	ix.	Julia.
	x.	Jennie L., b. Maryland, NY 15 Nov. 1829; m. there 17 Jan. 1852 to **Amos Daniel Spencer**. [See Spencer family entry.] She d. 3 May 1908.

SIMEON R. BARNES[2] b. Town of Maryland, NY 18 Aug. 1831; grad. 1852 from NY Conf. Seminary at Charlotteville, Schoharie Co.; teacher in Delaware Co., NY. 1853 back to Maryland & manufacturer of shashes and blinds; in 1855 became a partner of **Francis M. Fox** [manufactured building supplies] April 1867 moved business to Colliersville, Town of Milford. He m. 1st in the Town of Milford, 11 Oct. 1853 **Margaret J.**, d/o **Stephen** and **Nancy Platt**, originally from CT, early settlers of town of Maryland, NY. **Margaret** was b. in Maryland, NY 14 Dec. 1833 and d. 7 Oct. 1888, aged 54, at Colliersville. **Simeon**[2] held town offices; director of the Wilbur National Bank of Oneonta; members of the Universalist Church of Colliersville and Maryland, NY. In 1893 he was living retired in a palatial home on Ford Ave., Oneonta, which he erected in 1891. Children by 1st mar.:

i.	Charles P., b. Maryland, NY 4 Dec. 1854; d. 15 Jan. 1872.
ii.	Frank Leslie, b. Maryland 6 Aug. 1858. Left a widow and one child, now (1893) living in Delaware Co.

SIMEON BARNES[2] m. 2nd Mrs. **Mary S. (Spencer) Rowe**, who was b. & raised in Otsego Co. Her first husband, **George Rowe**, d. in the prime of life leaving two children, **Grace** and **Spencer**, now (1893) both living with their mother and stepfather. They attend the Universalist Church.

[A:199; BR:696-97; *Herbert E. Spencer, His Ancestors & Descendants* by Floyd Mallory Shumway, NY City, 1964. Typescript found in LDS collection.]

Mrs. Margaret J. Barnes

Hon. S. R. Barnes

Residence of Hon. S. R. Barnes, Colliersville, Otsego Co., N.Y.

BARNUM, ABIAH[1] was b. 1742, d. 1842; "old settler" of Middlefield; Revolutionary War soldier. He m. **Orpha Hamilton, d/o Capt. Silas Hamilton,** on 23 Oct. 1763. They moved from CT to Otsego Co., later removing to Seneca Co., NY where he died, aged about 80. [An **Abiah Barnum** of Cooperstown d. 5 Feb. 1879, aged 76.] He had five children; those thus far located:

    i.   **Abiah Jr.,** b. 14 April 1766, m. **Sibel** --- 5 Feb. 1789.
2 ii.   **Lewis.**

LEWIS BARNUM[2] came from CT with his family; he m. **Lucy Jones,** a d/o **Thomas** and **Sarah Jones** [Sarah d. 28 Aug. 1830, aged 82]. **Lewis** was the first town clerk of the Town of Middlefield and was a justice of the peace. He served in the Revolutionary War and was of Middlefield when he made his will 28 Sept. 1842 [d. 7 March 1843]. In it he named his first wife **Lucy** and his second wife **Catherine** and children. He d. on his farm 31 [sic] Feb. 1847, "the farm upon with **Harry G. Barnum** now [1893] lives." **Lucy** was b. 12 Feb. 1790 & d. 25 Oct. 1830.

3 i.   **Henry C.**
    ii.   **Evander W.**
    iii.   **Jonas.**
    iv.   **Lewis Jr.**
    v.   **Abram C.**
    vi.   **Sylvester W.**
    vii.   **Betsey D.**
    viii. **Lucy.**
    ix.   **Jane.**
    x.   **Sarah.**
    xi.   **Isabella.**
    xii.   **Syvil R.,** m. **Daniel H. Chase** at Middlefield on 23 Sept. 1841.

HARRY G. [sic] BARNUM[3] was not named as such in the will transcript above. He is probably the **Henry C. Barnum** named as the first son of **Lewis.** Reference BR:283 says that **Harry G.** was one of seven children, "two of whom still survive," but does not name any other child. **Harry G.** was b. 4 Dec. 1821. 29 Dec. 1847 he m. **Clarinda Lent,** who was b. in Herkimer Co. 8 May 1827, a d/o **Daniel** and **Margaret (Grosbeck) Lent** and granddau. of **Abram** and **Christina (Storms) Lent** of Washington Co., NY & later Herkimer Co. The Lent family were from Holland; farmers. **Daniel Lent** was b. in 1791 in Washington Co. and d. 13 Dec. 1847, aged 56. **Harry** is a farmer, member of the Presbyterian Church. He served as Commissioner of Highways for 25 years & Assessor 3 years. On the death of his father, he bought out the 11 other heirs and obtained the home farm. Children:

    i.   **Daniel A.,** b. 18 Feb. 1849; m. **Cora Smith,** has one son, **Lewis,** b. 15 May 1883.
    ii.   **Harry E.,** b. 22 March 1851, living at home.

[GBW; GBM; BR:283-4; Barbour Collection; DARPI; A:186; OB; Danbury CT Vital Records]

BARRETT, BENJAMIN[4] (*Oliver*[3] *MA & NY, Joseph*[2] *MA [Thomas?*[2] *MA], Joseph*[1] *[Humphrey?*[1] *England & CT]*) b. 16 Jan. 1770 s/o **Oliver** and **Anna (Fiske) Barrett** of Westford, MA. Oliver was called out as a Minute Man in the Revolutionary War and was killed at Stillwater, near Saratoga, NY. **Anna [Annah]** was d/o Lt. **Beneezer Fiske** and 2nd wife **Bethia Muzzy** of Lexington, MA. Anna was b. 20 July 1735 and m. **Oliver Barrett** of Concord on 24 Oct. 1754; they settled at Chelmsford. Their son **Benjamin** m. **Betsey Gerrish** d/o **Samuel** of Westminster Co., MD where **Betsey** was b. 10 Nov. 1774, a d/o **Samuel** and **Harriet Gerish**, natives of MA. Benjamin and Betsey came to Springfield from MA in March 1811; a second source says he came from Wilton, NH. He was a farmer, tanner and currier and d. at Springfield 31 Oct. 1844. He had 11 children, 4 received a college education and 3 were clergymen. In 1893 only **George** had survived. Children:

    i.   **Samuel**, b. in Royalston, MA 11 Aug. 1795. Grad. Harvard College in class of 1818 & in 1822 from Harvard Divinity School. He d. 24 June 1866, leaving a wife and family of eight children. Unitarian.

    ii.   **Gerrish (Rev.)**, b. in Royalston, MA 4 July 1797, grad. Union College in 1824; Presbyterian. He d. 2 Sept. 1857, leaving three children, one dying in infancy. The eldest is a physician in Philadelphia and the second eldest a Presbyterian minister at Colorado Springs. [Neither named.]

    iii.   **Betsey**, b. Royalston, MA 11 Jan. 1800, d. at one month.

    iv.   **Benjamin Jr.**, b. Royalston, MA 21 Oct. 1801, d. 1852 leaving one child. Res. Springfield, NY.

    v.   **Oliver**, b. Wilton, NH, 26 Oct. 1803, a tanner & farmer until 1867 when he sold out and removed to Suffern, Rockland Co., NY and in 1870 removed to New London, CT, where he d. in 1873, leaving six children and aged 70 years.

    vi.   **Betsy**, b. Wilton, NH 24 Aug. 1805, d. 9 July 1806.

    vii.   **Almira**, b. Wilton NH 27 Aug. 1808, m. at Springfield, NY 19 Oct. 1832 to **George W. Cleveland**, M.D. of Waterville, Oneida Co., NY. She d. 11 March 1886, leaving three children.

5   viii.   **Fiske**, b. Wilton, NH 21 June 1810.

    ix.   **William**, b. 18 Nov. 1812 in Springfield, NY, grad. Union College in Schenectady, NY in medicine. Studied law with Col. **William Baker** at Otsego Co. He d. 17 March 1872 at Binghamton.

    viii.   **Fiske (Rev.)** [II], b. Springfield, NY 1 March 1816, d. 21 Nov. 1880. Grad. of Union College 1842, settled Lexington, MA Sept. 1849; resigned 1852 and later res. Scituate and Stoneham. He m. 8 June 1853 **Ann E. T. Henchman**, d/o **David** of Boston. Ordained Unitarian minister. He d. 25 Nov. 1879, leaving two daus.

5   iv.   **George**.

GEORGE BARRETT[5], b. in Springfield, NY 19 Sept. 1818, tanner & currier; in 1845 settled in Roseboom (Cherry Valley at that time) and on 15 Jan. 1851 m. **Elizabeth O. Gilchrist**, d/o **Daniel F.** and **Mary (Chase)**

Gilchrist. **Elizabeth** was b. in Springfield 9 June 1821. **George** retired in 1882 and has since "lived a life of comparative ease at his country seat." He is listed as a businessman, owner of South Valley Tannery, Town of Roseboom in the 1872/3 *Gazetteer of Otsego County*, his tannery located about one mile west of South Valley post office, "employs five hands, consumes from 125 to 150 cords of hemlock bark, and from 100 to 125 cords of wood per annum, and turns out about 8,000 sides of leather annually." He has served in public office as Loan Commissioner and Supervisor. They had only one child:

 i. **Samuel G.**, b. 20 March 1853, merchant of South Valley. He m. **Clara R. Griffin** 20 Jan. 1878, who was b. 12 July 1857. They had one child, **Mabel H.**, b. 30 Dec. 1879 in Mexico, MO, where Samuel d. 18 July 1881 of disease. Before going to MO he was in business with his father, afterward followed farming and mercantile business.

REV. FISKE BARRETT[5] b. at Springfield, NY [NH] 1 March 1816 91810]; d. 21 Nov. 1880. He grad. Union College, 1842 and entered the ministry. He was settled at Lexington, MA in Sept. 1849 & resigned in 1852. He subsequently res. at Scituate and Stoneham; m. 8 June 1853 **Ann E. T. Henchman**, d/o **David** of Boston. [No mention of children.]
[*History of Lexington, MA*, Hudson, 1913; NEGHR:42:260-61; SPR:190; DARPI; A:319; BR:775-6; OB]

BENEDICT [BENEDICK], HEZEKIAH[4] (*James*[3] *CT, James*[2] *NY & CT, Thomas*[1] *MA, Long Island, NY, CT & England*) was s/o **James Benedict** and wife **Mary Andrus** of Danbury, CT. Hezekiah was was a royalist in the Revolution and after the war removed to Town of Maryland, Otsego Co. His wife was **Hannah Judd**. Hezekiah made his will 4 Feb. 1807. Children:

 i. **Jemima**, m. --- **Elmer**.
 ii. **Hannah**, m. **Abel Benedict**.
 iii. **Asahel**, b. 1749; d. 1802. He m. 25 Nov. 1773, **Lydia Dibble**, widow of **Timothy Taylor**. Asahel lived and d. at Danbury and left two children.
 iv. **Elijah**.
 v. **Hezekiah**, b. 16 March 1754; m. 30 Jan. 1777, **Huldah Hall**, d/o **Ebenezer**. Probably a Revolutionary War soldier, he removed to OH and d. 16 March 1831 at Braceville, OH leaving seven children.
 vi. **John**, named in his father's will as dec'd.
5 vii. **David**.
 viii. **James**, b. 29 May 1761; d. 1843 Stoney Hill, Danbury. He m. **Rhoda Dibble**, d/o **Samuel** on 11 Dec. 1784.
 ix. **Obadiah**, bapt. Bethel 25 Sept. 1765.
 x. **Dorcas**, d. unm.

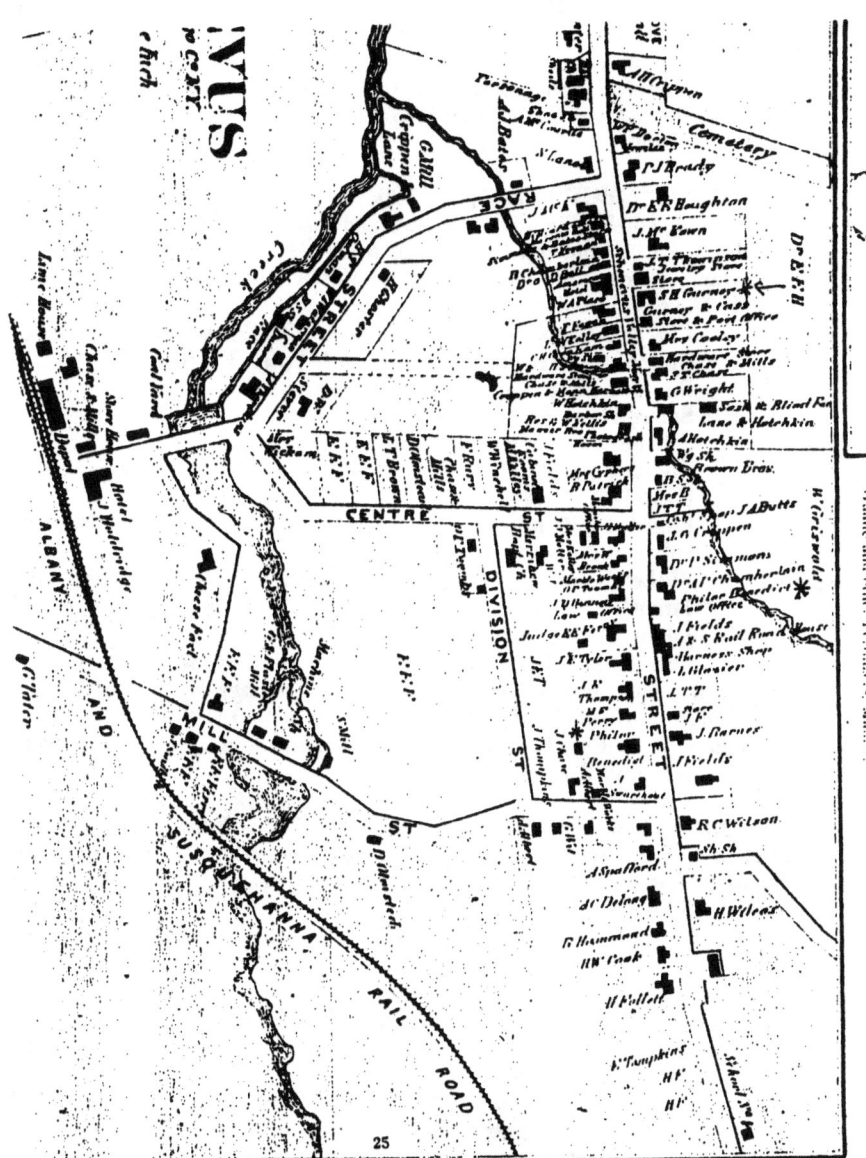

DAVID BENEDICT[5] b. c. 1760; m. 17 Oct. 1782 **Deborah Dibble** who d. 14 Aug. 1804. He left Danbury, CT settled Town of Maryland, NY c. 1803 and became large landowner. His father followed him to this place one year later and died here. **David** kept tavern in 1805 and prior to **David** it was kept by his brother **Obadiah**. **David** made his will 9 Jan. 1826 (d. 7 March 1826) and in it named his wife **Betsey** [sic] and children:

    i.   **Amiel**, d. young, not in his father's will.
    ii.   **Clarissa**, b. 29 March 178(5?); m. --- **Bostwick**.
6 i.   **Philor**.

PHILOR BENEDICT[6] b. 14 April 1790; m. 7 July 1811 **Rebecca Chase**, b. 1790, d. 1861. She was d/o **Josiah** and **Hannah (Goddard) Chase** of Danbury, CT. **Philor** left Danbury at the age of 14 and settled in Town of Maryland, Otsego Co. He d. there 16 March 1849. **Rebecca** d. 2 Oct. 1861. Their children:

    i.   **Clarissa C.**, b. 16 Jan. 1814; m. 1832 **Elkanah Boardman** s/o **Ephraim Boardman** and **Elizabeth Yale**. **Clarissa** d. 1833.
    ii.   **David E.**, b. 8 Sept. 1816; dec'd. by 1878.
    iii. **Sarah A.**, b. 29 Aug. 1820; m. 9 Sept. 1840 **Seth H. Chase**, res. Schenevus. She was widowed by 1878.
    iv. **Elvira B.**, b. 22 May 1824; m. 2 Sept. 1845 **Nathan Clark**, res. IL 1878.
    v.   **Emily**, b. 30 July 1828; m. 5 Feb. 1851 **Lysander W. Kelley**; both dec'd. by 1878.
    vi. **Philor**, b. 26 July 1832; m. 16 Jan. 1859 **Mary A. Murphy**, d/o **Timothy**. Attorney of village of Schenevus; present D.A. of county (1878). Had a son, **Philor T.**, b. 1 Oct. 1860.
    vii. **Ada A.**, b. 3 June 1835; m. 29 April 1858 **M. M. Clark**.

[A:177; GBW; *The Compendium of American Genealogy* by Virkus, V. 5; *McCall-Tidwell & Allied Families* by Ettie Tidwell McCall, 1931; *The Story of The Benedicts . . .* by Lyle L. Benedict, n.d.; *The Genealogy of the Benedicts in America* by Henry M. Benedict, 1870; OB.]

BILYEA, JOHN[1], b. 6 Sept. 1796, d. 12 [13?] Dec. 1863 at Edmeston. Built the first tannery in Edmeston. He m. **Deborah Ann May**, d/o **Harmon** and **Sarah (Monroe) May**, b. 11 Dec. 1808 at Burlington. [See May family entry.] Children:

2 i.   **Foster Harmon**.
2 ii.   **Homer C.**.

FOSTER HARMON BILYEA[2] b. 15 July 1841 at Edmeston; m. 25 Oct. 1870 **Mina Thompson** who was b. 10 Aug. 1845. In 1912 res. Unadilla. Child:

    i.   **Carl Thompson**, b. 18 April 1877 at Edmeston; m. 13 Nov. 1909 **Ann Elizabeth Hess** who was b. 1 Nov. 1885. Res. Cleveland, OH.

HOMER C. BILYEA[2] b. 20 Jan. 1847, Fayetteville, NY; m. 11 Sept. 1873 **Ida May Bassett** who was b. 18 June 1855. In 1912 res. Fayetteville. Child:

    i.   **J. Glenn**, b. 11 May 1882, Edmeston; m. 12 Sept. 1906 **Harriet Louise Roberts** who was b. 1 Sept. 1886. Res. Syracuse, NY.
[*Genealogy of Josiah Munroe, Revolutionary Soldier, Who Died in the Service of the Continental Army at Valley Forge* ... by G. S. Northrup, 1912; A:144]

BLOOMFIELD, JONATHAN (DEACON)[1] emigrated from NJ in 1790 and settled in Town of Warren, Herkimer Co., NY. He was b. 25 Aug. 1735; d. 1810, s/o **Joseph Bloomfield** and **Eunice Dunham** his wife. Jonathan served in the Revolutionary War from NJ and built the sawmill on Ocquionis Creek known as Bloomfield Mill. He m. 1st **Elizabeth Wood** and 2nd **Anna** ---. About 1800, accompanied by his wife and "large family" he removed to Herkimer Co., NY. He is described as a very industrious man. BR702 gives his wife's maiden name as **Eunice Bloomfield**. Children identified to date:

    i.   **Samuel**, occupied his father's farm until his death 23 Dec. 1866, aged 84 y, 4 m. He left two sons and three daus. Member of Presbyterian Church.
2 ii.   **Joseph**.

JOSEPH BLOOMFIELD[2], b. NJ; d. 26 July 1862, aged 72. His encounter with a bear at the age of nine is recounted in this first source. He m. **Hannah Abbott** who was b. in CT, d/o **Danford Abbott** and wife **Mary Allen**, both also b. CT. Mary's father was **Amasa Allen**, b. CT & a pioneer settler of the Town of Warren. **Hannah** d. at Richfield Springs in 1885. Children:

3 i.   **Allen**, now (1878) res. of Richfield Springs.
   ii.   **David C.**, a civil engineer, accidentally shot while sporting in the woods on his father's farm in the summer of 1854, aged 28.

ALLEN BLOOMFIELD[3] b. in the town of Warren, Herkimer Co., NY. At the age of 19 he began teaching. He inherited the home farm which his grandfather had improved, upon which he resided and farmed until 1873. He then removed to Richfield Springs. He became a director in the First National Bank and in the Mohawk Valley National Bank; President of the Waiontha Knitting Co. of Richfield Springs & other business enterprises. He m. in 1846 to **Rosalinda E. Bell**, b. in the town of Warren, a d/o **Henry Bell**. She d. in 1881 and Allen m. 2nd in 1883 to **Annette Ford**, b. in Richfield Springs, a d/o **Isaac** and **Lydia Ford**. Child:
    i.   **Charles W.**, m. **Libbie McCready** and they have two sons: **Allen** and **Russell**.
[RS:115-16; DARPI; BR702-03]

BOARDMAN, LEVI[6] (*Ephraim*[5] *CT, Ephraim*[4] *CT, Isaac*[3] *CT, Isaac*[2] *CT, Samuel*[1] *England, MA, CT*) of Maryland, NY was probably b. in Bristol, CT 5 March 1776, s/o **Ephraim Boardman** who was b. in CT in 1748 and d. 24 July 1813 in NY and wife **Rhoda Andrews**. Ephraim served as a private in the Revolutionary war from NY. Levi m. 9 Aug. 1797 **Elizabeth Yale**, b. 12 Nov. 1777, d/o **Abel** and **Sarah (Jerome) Yale** of Bristol, CT. They removed to Hillsdale, NY and in 1810 to Maryland, Otsego Co. In

1850 they removed to North Orwell, PA, where their sons **Ephraim** and **Edward** had already settled. **Levi** d. there 16 March 1862; **Elizabeth** on 7 Jan. 1860. **Levi** was a farmer and a cooper. Children:

	i.	**Amanda**, b. 27 Aug. 1798; m. **Richard Hoose**, res. Maryland, NY; seven children.
	ii.	**Lois**, b. 13 April 1800; m. **Samuel Cass** and had nine children, res. Schenevus, Otsego Co. Three sons, **Byron, David O.** and **Anson B.** served in the Civil War.
7	iii.	**Levi Yale**.
	iv.	**Elkanah**, b. 16 Jan. 1804; m. 1st at Maryland, NY 15 Jan. 1832, **Caroline Benedict**; m. 2nd **Eliza Gunn**; one dau. **Mrs. Annis Simmons** of Westfield, PA.
	v.	**Polly**, b. 10 Aug. 1805; m. 1st 4 July 1833 **David Brown**, 2nd **Col. Lemuel Davenport**, res. Elkland, PA.
	vi.	**Abel**, b. Oct. 3, 1807, d. 21 Oct. 1807.
	vii.	**Ephraim** [Twin of **Abel**] b. 3 Oct. 1807; m. **Leafy Seaver**, d/o **Daniel** of Maryland, NY. **Leafy** was b. 14 Oct. 1799 in Maryland and d. 7Sept. 1871. **Ephraim** d. 1 Oct. 1856; res. North Orwell, PA.
	viii.	**Eliza**, b. 1 May 1809; m. **David Howard**; d. 1899, no children, res. Schenevus.
	ix.	**William**, b. 26 May 1811; m. 1st 4 July 1833, **Hannah Wright** who d. c. 1875, 2nd **Mrs. Silence Hartshorn**, widow of **Samuel**. Res. eight years in Chahtam, Tioga Co., PA and then returned to Otsego Co., where he was a farmer and stock raiser. About 1857 he removed to North Orwell, PA where he d. 4 June 1891. Three children: **Elizabeth** wife of E. W. **Bushnell** of Rome, PA; **Triphena** m. a **Mr. Bushnell** of Rome, PA; and **Edward Y.** who m. **Ruby Hannah Frisbie** & res. Corning, NY.
	x.	**Anson**, b. 16 April 1813; d. 28 July 1825.
	xi.	**Philetus (Dr.)**, b. 5 Jan. 1816; m. **Submit E. Leach**. Physician in Kingston, WI; one son, **Anson Philetus**, b. 24 Sept. 1846; m. **Mattie E. Warner**, res. Watertown, WI.
	xii.	**Ransom Jerome**, b. 19 April 1818; m. **Charlotte Brown** 8 March 1843. She was b. 20 May 1828 in Westfield, Tioga Co., PA, d/o **George S. Brown**. **Ransom** d. 29 Jan. 1889. Res. Freeland, Saginaw Co., MI.
	xiii.	**Verus Nelson**, b. 8 March 1820; m. **Eliza Hill** who was b. in Chatham, PA 18 May 1823, d/o **Burdick Hill**. **Verus** d. 14 Aug. 1864, in the hospital while serving in the Civil War.
	xiv.	**Edward**, b. 10 April 1822; m. **Maryette Chamberlain** 31 Oct. 1841. Res. North Orwell, PA.

BOARDMAN, LEVI YALE[7] b. 21 Jan. 1802; m. 22 Nov. 1827 **Hannah Goddard** and res. Schenevus; supervisor in 1846. She was b. 6 May 1805, d/o **Edward** and **Hannah (Mann) Goddard** of Maryland, NY. She d. 14 Oct. 1865; he d. 15 Feb. 1882. Children:

i.	**Edward**, b. 15 Aug. 1828; m. 30 June 1870 **Elizabeth Parks**; res. Philadelphia, where he d. 21 April 1881. Their children were res.

ii. **Levi,** b. 25 Oct. 1830; m. 8 May 1860 **Mary E. Perry,** res. Schenevus; d. 27 April 1872, aged 41; had served as town supervisor. Children: **Edward** who m. L. E. **Hartwell** and had one son, **Yale**; and **William,** unm. in 1895.
iii. **Eliza,** b. 16 April 1836; m. 13 Nov. 1856 **Samuel H. Gurney,** postmaster of Schenevus 20 years & justice of the peace who d. 9 Oct. 1889. They had one dau., **Patience,** who m. **Leon D. Smith,** editor of the Schenevus *Monitor*.

[A:170, 177; OB; *Boardman Genealogy, 1525-1895 of the English Home and Ancestry of Samuel Boreman of Wethersfield, Conn. and Thomas Boreman of Ipswich, Mass.* by William F. J. Boardman, 1895; GBM.]

BOTSFORD, MARTIN, Martha --- his wife is probably the same **Martha Botsford** b. 5 Oct. 1799, bapt. at Cooperstown 30 Dec. 1804. Their children, bapt. 27 1805:
i. **Amos,** b. 6 Oct. 1800.
ii. **Charles Granderson,** b. 7 July 1802.
iii. **Martin,** d. 1854, bur. in lot "of **Amos S. Botsford,** his brother" in Cherry Valley Cemetery.

[NASH1; CVC]

BOTSFORD, VINE^1, wife **Jerusha** ---, their first four children bapt. at Cooperstown 7 Jan. 1798 along with **York,** a negro boy who was b. 2 May 1786:
i. **Caleb Baldwin,** b. 2 Oct. 1787.
ii. **Jerushann,** b. 26 Oct. 1789.
iii. **Elisha,** b. 11 April 1792.
iv. **Gideon,** b. 5 Jan. 1794.
v. **Annis,** b. 27 May and bapt. 21 July 1799.
2 vi. **Daniel.**

DANIEL BOTSFORD^2 b. 29 April and bapt. 19 June 1803; m. 19 Sept. 1827 to **Phebe Rockwell** [see Rockwell family entry], d/o **Ezra Rockwell** and **Annie Griffin** his wife of Butternuts. She d. at Scranton, PA 1 Feb. 1891; he d. 22 April 1882. Children, b. Butternuts:
i. **Ezra V.,** b. 30 Aug. 1829; m. 1st **Caroline L. Rockwell** in 1850; 2nd **Frances A. Brown**; res. at Sherburn, NY in 1892. One child, **Marcus R.,** b. Scranton, PA 1868; d. there in 1872.
ii. **Henry,** b. 5 Sept. 1831; res. Sherburn, NY in 1892.
iii. **Helen Eliza,** b. 2 July 1837; m. 25 May 1865, **Thomas K. Cope,** b. in Burmah, Asia. She d. at Butternuts 6 April 1878. [See Cope family entry.]
iv. **Caroline E.,** b. 8 July 1840; m. 27 Nov. 1872 **Arthur Hitchcock,** res. Scranton, PA in 1892. Children b. Scranton: **William B.** and **Robert B.**
v. **Marcus D.,** b. 25 Aug. 1842; m. 19 Feb. 1873 **Annie R. White**; res. Sherburn, NY in 1892.

[*A Genealogy of the Families of John Rockwell, of Stamford, Conn. 1641* ... by

James Boughton, 1903; NASH1]

BROWN, ASA[1] b. Stonington, CT, came with his brother **Oliver** [afterward a judge in Oneida Co.] to Madison Co., NY at an early day. "A few years later" he removed to Richfield, Otsego Co., where he d. aged 98. He m. **Lucy Dow**, cousin to **Lorenzo Dow** the famous preacher. **Lucy** was b. in Sterling CT. Children:
- i. **Lucy D.**, aged aged 40.
- ii. **Deborah**, m. **P. Brewer**.
- iii. **Mercy**, m. **L. McCullen**.
- iv. **Sarah**, m. **Benjamin Brewer**.
- v. **Asa**, m. **Louisa Wilbur**.
- vi. **Wheeler**, m. **Lucy A. Merchant**.
- vii. **Rebecca**, m. **Charles Wheeler**.
- viii. **Maria**, m. **Joseph Robinson**; still living in 1893. [All of her siblings dec'd. by that date except **Emeline**. See Robinson family entry.]
- ix. **Benjamin**, m. **Dolly Barstow**.
- x. **Martha**, m. **John Wheeler**.
- xi. **Emeline**, m. **John Wheeler**; still living in 1893.

[BR:600-02]

BRYAN, FOWLER P.[7] (*Samuel*[6] *CT, Richard*[5] *CT, Richard*[4] *CT, Richard*[3] *CT, Richard*[2] *CT, Alexander*[1] *England & Ct*) b. 12 Oct. 1783 in Washington, CT; d. 26 Oct. 1821 in Unadilla, NY and was bur. there on 29 Oct. 1821. **Fowler** was the s/o **Samuel Bryan** and wife **Sarah Platt** of Milford, CT. He m. **Amanda Giddings**, b. c. 1797 in New Milford, CT. Children:
- i. **Esther**.
- ii. **Alexander**.

[*History of the Towns of New Milford and Bridgewater, CT* by Samuel Orcutt, 1882, p. 89; UNA:44]

BUNDY, PETER (CAPT.)[1] came from Montgomery, MA with his family and settled in Otego with **Col. Elisha Bundy**, his brother, in 1787 [1777]. **Elisha**, b. 6 Oct. 1760 in CT, d. 5 Oct. 1826 in OH [he was a pioneer of Bundysburg, OH]; m. **Abigail French**. **Elisha** served in the Revolution as a private from MA; his son **Elisha Jr.** res. on the east side of the creek where **Henry Doliver** lives (1907). "**Elisha Bundy** (b. Oct. 1760-d. 1824 or '25, Bundysburg, Ohio." He was involved in lumbering early in the county. **Peter**[1], b. 11 Sept. 1754 in CT, d. 7 April 1822 in NY. He also served in the Revolution. They were s/o **Peter Bundy** and wife **Priscilla Prentice**, both of Preston, CT. The brothers first visited Otsego Co. with **William Cooper**. **Peter** moved his large family of young children and wife to Otsego, his wife in a wood-shod sled drawn by a small pair of oxen. He was accompanied by **Deacon Asahel Packard** and others, they having to "cut their way" a portion of the route traveled, before and after reaching the valley of the Charlotte. **Peter** kept a public house at that place on the site now (1878) occupied by dwelling of **Henry Bundy** and he also erected a saw mill on the west branch of the Otsdawa, near its junction with the east branch. **Peter** was a large landowner and in 1814 he purchased his Otsdawa property from **Isaac Edson** and **Moses Bundy** occupied the farm and built the stone house c. 1841. He was of Otego when he made his will 10 Dec. 1824 [first source gives his date of death as 1822]; proved in 1832. One source says he d. aged 68 and his wife at the age of 70. Members of the Baptist Church. **Peter** moved on to the property now owned by **William VanName** (1907), which he bought from **Ransom Hunt**, along with sons **Stephen** and **Gilbert**. His wife **Barsheba (Avery)** also made her will the same day and hers was proved the same day, 17 July 1832. Children mentioned in wills:

2 i.   **Levi.**
    ii.   **Ephraim**, res. on what is known (1907) as the **Edwin Root** place.
2 iii. **James.**
    iv. **David S.**, m. **Sophia Birdsall** and has a son, **Menzo**.
    v.   **Moses**. Is probably the **Moses** who is noted as an early settler of Laurens.
    vi. **Stephen A.**
    vii. **Gilbert S.**, one of the first trustees of Old School or Primative Baptist Church, organized 1857.
    viii. **Eunice**, m. --- **French**. **Wyram French** was involved in early lumber industry in Otsego Co., perhaps he is the husband of **Eunice**. Another early French settler was **James French** who shows up in T. R. Austin's day book for purchases in 1811/12.
    ix. **Rebekah**, m. --- **Shepard**.
    x.   **Sally**.
    xi. **Julia**.
    xii. **Marilla**. Early school teacher of Otego.
    xiii. **Peter Jr.**, not mentioned in wills of his parents; removed to Alleghany Co. to engage in lumbering. He served in Town of Otego as one of the first overseers of the highways.

LEVI BUNDY[2] of Otego made his will 12 May 1842 and in it named his wife **Sarah**, his brother **Moses**, his nephew **David B. Shepard**. **Stephen A.** and **Gilbert S. Bundy**, witnesses.

JAMES BUNDY[2], b. near Springfield, MA, aged two when his parents removed to Town of Otego in 1787, and d. at the age of 54. First clerk of Primative Baptist Church, organized 1857. Settled where **King J. Hatheway** now (1907) lives. About 1857 his son **Peter** was living on the place now (1907) owned and occupied by **John J. Enderlin**. "He was an ironsided man, who took a backbone farm and made it good." He m. in Town of Otego to **Polly Oberheiser** who was b. at East Albany, Rensselaer Co., but reared in Town of Otego, where her paretns moved when she was young. Her parents were **Conrad** and **Mary (Story) Oberheiser** and they d. in Steuben Co. **Polly** d. on the Bundy homestead at age nearly 96. She was mother to twelve children, eight sons and four daus. Their son **JAMES BUNDY**[3] was b. 24 May 1821; lumberman and farmer. He m. in Cobleskill, Schoharie Co. to **Emma Coonley**, who was b. and raised there. The family are Old School Baptists. Children:

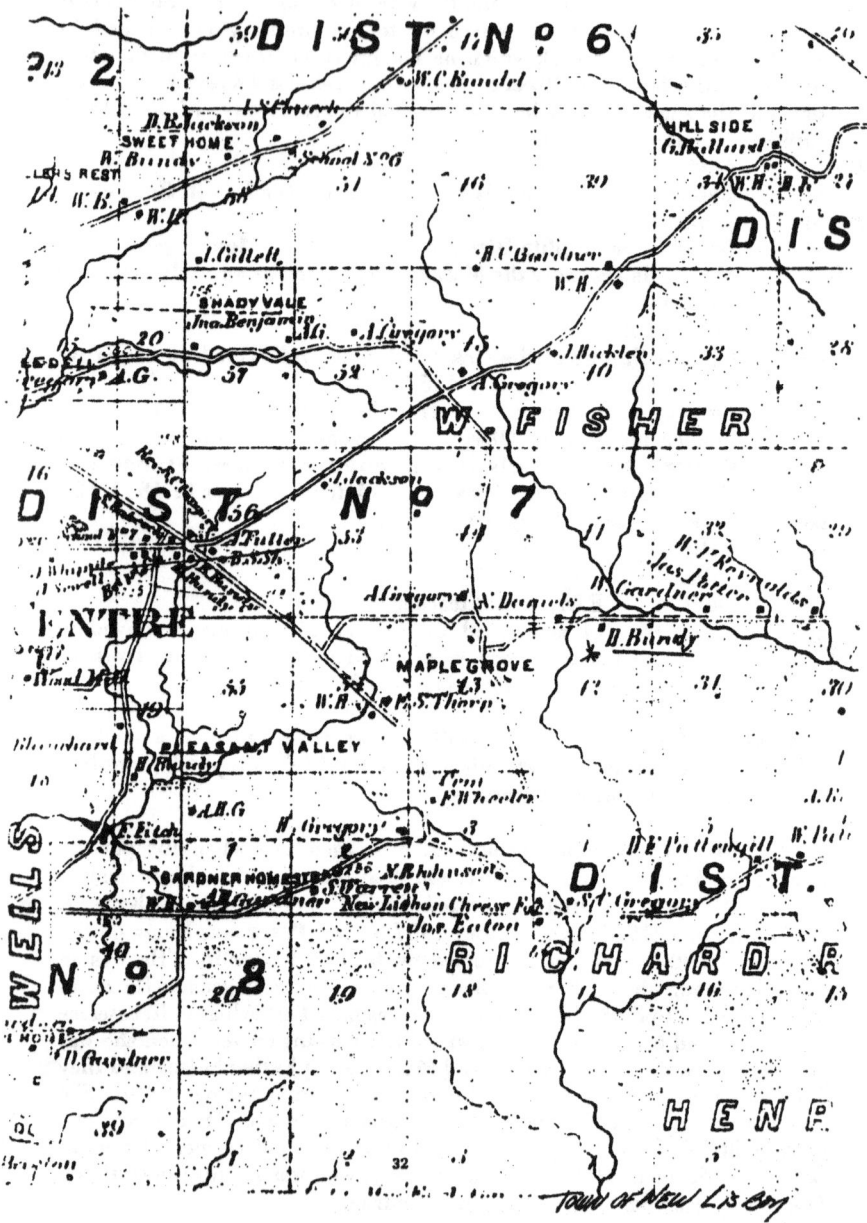

i. **Delilah**, d. aged 23.
ii. **John L.**, d. aged 15.
iii. **Greeley**, m. & res. N. Platte, NE.
iv. **Herman S.**, m. and res. Elmira, NY.
v. **Myron H.**, m. and res. on old homestead.
vi. **Bertha**, m. **Arthur P. Clark**, dentist.
vii. **James L.**, unm. (1893) & res. at home.

[F:54, 78-80, 92, 110, 117, 128, 130-31, 137; GH1:64; GBW; A:170, 239-40; DARPI; Barbour Collection; BR:538-39]

BURDICK, AMOS[5] (*Amos*[4], *Samuel Hubbard*[3] *RI*, *Thomas*[2], *Robert*[1]) of Plainfield, NY was s/o **Amos** (1741-1803) and **Elizabeth (Nichols) Burdick**, b. 1762. Amos m. **Phebe Covey**, b. 1766, d. 1849. He made his will 7 July 1837; probated in 1840. In it he named his children, below. **John** and **Syllia Davis** of Brookfield were witnesses.
i. **David**, b. 1802, d. 1881 in Plainfield; m. 1st 1824, **Lucy Green**.
ii. **Phebe**.
iii. **Marilla**.
iv. **Nancy**.
v. **Lois**.
vi. **Cyrena**.

[GBW; *American Compendium of First Families of America*, Vol. 6, by Virkus.]

CAMPBELL, JAMES[1], of a family from Argyleshire, Scotland to Ireland to America in the late 1700's. He was b. in 1690, Londonderry, Ulster, Scotland, s/o **William Campbell** and wife --- **McClean** of Londonderry, Ulster, Ireland. James landed in Boston in 1728 and settled in Londonderry, NH, one of the first to settle c. 1740 at Butternuts [Cherry Valley]. He m. 2nd wife **Sarah Simpson** [Sarah (Simpson) Thompson], b. 1696 in Londonderry, Ireland, who d. 1773, aged 79. James d. 1770 aged 80. Children:
2 i. **Robert**.
2 ii. **Samuel**.
iii. **Charles Henry**, b. 1785, d. 1849. He m. 1811 **Evelina Coleman Stone**, b. 1791, d. 1859.

ROBERT CAMPBELL[2] b. 20 Aug. 1735, Londonderry, NH; m. **Margaret Shannon**, b. 10 Jan. 1741 in Schodak, NY. [DARPI gives his birth as 20 Aug. 1735 in NY, d. 6 Aug. 1777.] He served as a first lt. from NY in the Revolution. Children, b. Cherry Valley, NY:
i. **Sarah**, b. c. 1767.
ii. **Jeanette**, b. 5 Nov. 1775; m. **Everet Lansing** of Rensselaer County and lived there.
iii. **Samuel R.**, b. 11 July 1775; m. **Sarah Mynderse**, b. 26. Oct. 1789; res. Rensselaer Co.

COL. SAMUEL CAMPBELL[2], b. 25 April 1738, Londonderry, NH and brought to Cherry Valley in 1741; m. **Jane Cannon**, d/o **Matthew**, b. Jan. 1743 in Antrim, Ireland [Matthew b. at Giant's Causeway, Ireland] and d.

1836. **Samuel** d. 1824, aged 86. He was a patriot of the Revolution, a member of the Tryon Co. Minutemen and County Committee of Safety, and in 1802 a member of the assembly. In 1777 the settlers of Cherry Valley took refuge in his house on account of its size and elevated position and threw up an embankment of earth and logs, including the house and barns. He had had not only been an officer in command of the battle of Oriskany in that year, but both he and **Major Samuel Clyde** had been especially conspicuous for their bravery. It is because of this, it is believed, that Cherry Valley was the target of Indian attacks. He was not at home at the time and Mrs. Campbell and the four children were taken prisoner [11 Nov. 1778]. When the house was attacked, it was defended vigorously by her father, who was wounded and the family captured with the exception of one child who was concealed by the negro nurse. **Mrs. Cannon** because of her age and enfeebled condition could not keep up with the captured party and was killed and left by the wayside. The families of **John Moore** and **Samuel Campbell** were not released until the close of the war. In 1783 **General Washington** accompanied by **Gov. George Clinton** and others visited Cherry Valley on their tour of the state and visited with **Col. Campbell**. On the site of his home his great-grandchildren have built a summer home. The children, below, held a reunion on 15 Dec. 1860, the 60th wedding anniversary of their parents. The group had been separated for 28 years, scattered from the St. Lawrence to the Isthmus and California. Children, b. Cherry Valley:

	i.	**William**, b. 28 Dec. 1768; m. **Sabrina Crafts**, b. 1776 at Cherry Valley, and d. there 30 Jan. 1830. They had one dau., **Judith Sabrina**, b. 1813. **William** was one of the first elected Trustees of the Village of Cherry Valley in 1812.
	ii.	**Eleanor**, b. 11 Nov. 1770; m. **Samuel Dickson** of Cherry Valley and had several children. [See Dickson entry.]
3	iii.	**James S.**, b. 9 Nov. 1772; only surviving sibling in 1862. At that time he was a res. on the old homestead in vigorous health and faculties seemingly unimpaired.
3	iv.	**Matthew**.
	v.	**Samuel S.**, b. 16 June 1777; m. **Elizabeth Griffin**, b. c. 1780 at Cherry Valley. They had: **Alonzo** b. 1802; **Jane** b. 1804, **Almira** b. c. 1806, **Samuel G.** b. c. 1808, **Sarah** b. c. 1810, **Sabrina** b. c. 1812.
3	vi.	**Robert**.

JAMES S. CAMPBELL[3] m. **Sarah**, d/o **Col. Elderkin** of Windham, CT and settled in Cherry Valley, one of the original settlers in 1741 he came with a group of Scots-Irish from Londonderry, NH. He d. in 1869, aged 97, the last survivor of the Cherry Valley Indian Massacre. A child aged 6 at the time, he was carried to Canada and adopted into an Indian family. Children, b. Cherry Valley.

	i.	**Alfred E.**, b. 1802. Could be the **Rev. Alfred Campbell** who m. **Betsey Hughs** in Hartwick on 16 Oct. 1831.
	ii.	**Mary Ann**, b. 20 Feb. 1804; m. **Erastus Crafts**, b. 1780.
	iii.	**Hon. (Dr.) William W. [P]**, b. Cherry Valley 10 June 1806;

author, Surveyor-General of NY State, d. 27 Oct. 1844; his wife, **Mariah Starkweather**, b. 1808, d. 1830. He wrote *Annals of Tryon County, Life of DeWitt Clinton* and other works and served as circuit judge, judge of the supreme court and member of Congress.

4   iv.   **George W.**, b. 28 May 1810.
       v.   **Samuel B.**, b. 1812.
       vi.   **Henry James**, b. 23 Nov. 1815.
4   vii   **John Cannon**, b. 19 Aug. 1817.
       viii.   **Augustus**, b. 1819.

GEORGE W. CAMPBELL[4] aged 42, carpenter, was enumerated in the 1850 Census and he and his wife **Catherine**, aged 41; both are listed as "deaf and dumb." The children in their household per this census were:
   i.   **Jane Ann**, aged 7 in 1850.
   ii.   **James L.**, aged 5 in 1850.
   iii.   **Elizabeth**, aged one month [or 6 months] in 1850.
[See top of Cherry Valley map found with Clyde family.]

JOHN CANNON CAMPBELL[4] b. in Cherry Valley in 1817. As a young worked with his uncle **William Campbell**, Surveyor General of NY State. Studied engineering and worked on the Croton aqueduct, worked in GA building roads for a time and worked with the Hudson River Railroad in their tunnel through the highlands near West Point. He later worked on the Panama Railroad, which proved too trying for his constitution and he resigned this position in 1853. On his return to the north, he m. **Sarah M. Campbell**, a descendant of a Revolutionary officer and a cousin. He next built a road west of Indianapolis and in 1863 was with the Racine & Mississippi Railroad as General Superintendent. He returned to NY and gave his attention to hydraulic engineering. In 1887 to San Francisco, where he met with a severe accident which finally resulted in his death. He d. in NY in March 1890. He was bur. in Cherry Valley. His children:
   i.   **Mrs. Montgomery H. Throop.**
   ii.   **Mrs. Clarence C. Howard.**
   iii.   **Mrs. William Henry Macy.**
   iv.   **Marion.**
   v.   **Bessie B.**, d. previous to her father.

MATTHEW CAMPBELL[3], b. 6 Jan. 1775, d. aged 70 and his wife, **Deborah Putnam**, b. 3 Feb. 1778 at Pomfret, CT, d. also aged 70. Children, all b. Cherry Valley:
   i.   **Jane**, b. 23 April 1797.
   ii.   **Aaron Putnam**, b. 24 Aug. 1801.
   iii.   **Elizabeth**, b. 10 Jan. 1803; m. **Hiram Flint** [see Flint family entry].
4   iv.   **Samuel.**
   v.   **Dewitt Clinton**, b. 7 May 1808; m. **Mary Jones.**
   vi.   **Sarah**, b. 5 March 1813; m. **Frederick E. Goodsell** on 7 June 1832 at Cherry Valley; he of Bridgewater, NY.

4   vii.   **Brayton Allen,** b. 4 June 1816.
       viii.   **Deborah,** b. 20 Feb. 1818.
       xi.   **Matthew,** b. 19 April 1822.

SAMUEL CAMPBELL[4] b. 6 Jan. 1806; m. **lcynthia Meeks** of Otsego, b. 3 March 1812. They had two children b. in Otsego Co., **Sarah Meeks** and **Eugene Milton Campbell,** b. 10 June 1844. He had res. for many years in NY City, a prominent lawyer, having amassed a large fortune. He returned to Cherry Valley and was a res. of that place at the time of the taking of the 1850 census. His age given as 44, lawyer with real estate valued at $11,600. Also in his household is **Sarah Campbell,** aged 38 and children (all b. NY):
     i.   **Sarah,** aged 17 in 1850.
     ii.   **Ellen,** aged 13 in 1850.
     iii.   **Samuel,** aged 8 in 1850.
     iv.   **Howard,** aged 3 in 1850.
     v.   **Josephine,** aged 1 in 1850.
Also in his household are **Deborah Campbell,** aged 35; **Ruth Putnam,** aged 63, b. CT; **Hannah Putnam,** aged 65, b. CT; **Ellen Crane,** aged 24, b. Ireland; and **Ann Blonk,** aged 18, b. Ireland. All those not otherwise noted were b. in NY.

BRAYTON ALLEN CAMPBELL[4] was a res. of Cherry Valley at the time of the taking of the 1850 census. He is listed as aged 34, lawyer, real estate valued at $4,000. His wife is **Matilda,** aged 27. Children, all b. in NY as was wife **Matilda:**
     i.   **Frederick,** aged 5 in 1850.
     ii.   **Clarence,** aged 1 month in 1850.
Also in their household and enumerated were **Caroline Nicklas,** aged 16; **John Platner,** aged 30, male; **Domenick Flaty,** aged 16 and b. in Ireland; **Peggy Mabey** aged 20, b. Ireland; **Mary Flaty,** aged 19, b. Ireland.

ROBERT CAMPBELL[3], b. 16 Sept. 1781 [1782] in Cherry Valley; m. **Rachel Pomeroy,** b. 1781, d/o **Robert Pomeroy** (1809-70) and wife **Helen Starkweather.** Rachel d. at Cooperstown 3 Dec. 1856. **Robert** grad. Union College and became a res. of Cooperstown in 1802. He was the first president of the Otsego County Bank of Cooperstown, incorporated in 1830 and an attorney. He was known far and near as an honest lawyer. He made his will at Cooperstown 11 Feb. 1845 and d. 30 Aug. 1847 at that place. In his will he mentioned his wife and children, and **Dr. Charles D. Brayton** of Cleveland. Children:
     i.   **Robert Pomeroy Campbell,** bapt. at Cooperstown Jan. 1840.
     ii.   **Julia C.,** b. Cooperstown, 1830 m. **Levi C. Turner,** lawyer, Col. of the US Army and Judge Advocate of the War Dept. She lived for years in Cleveland, OH, but returned to Cooperstown where she d. 1892.

[A:120-21, 138-39; CH1:19, 77, 115, 129; GH1:35; OB; GBM; BR: 271-2; *American Compendium,* Vol. I, p. 924-25; BR:804-5; DARPI; WILL:49; GBM; COP1:153-54]

CAMPBELL, JOHN³ (*John² Scotland & MA, Rev. John¹ Scotland & MA*) was one of the first settlers of the Town of Milford, Otsego Co. He came from Oxford, Worcester Co., MA; had served in the Revolutionary War as a young man and took part in the Battle of Bunker Hill. He d. full of years and honors. **John³** was the grandson of **Rev. John Campbell¹** who came to America very early in the 18th century; the first Congregational minister in Oxford, MA from 1721 to the year of his death, 1761. He was b. in the north of Scotland and came of a prominent Scottish family. He was the first of his family to come to America. His eldest son, **John²** m. and res. in Oxford; he left America and started to return to Scotland, but "as no further trace of him could ever be found, it is believed that the ship in which he embarked to cross the ocean went down." After the Revolution **John³** moved to Otsego Co. On their way from MA their son **Sylvanus** was b. in VT. **John³** m. 1st **Martha Marsh** and after their children grew up, he removed to Tioga Co., NY and d. there at an advanced age. The only other child of his first mar. named here is:

GILBERT E. CAMPBELL⁴ b. in Milford, Otsego Co. in 1809. In 1830 he removed to what is now the village of Oneonta (then part of Milford, known as Milfordville). He res. there until his death in 1883. Farmer; "he had always been a good, kind man in all relations of life, was a noble character, and a deep thinker." Member of the Baptist Church. He m. in Oneonta to **Lovina Lindsley**; she d. in Otsego Co. 5 Sept. 1891, aged c. 83. She was a d/o **Joseph Lindsley**, physician of Otsego Co., the first to practice in Oneonta, coming to that place in 1807 from Cherry Valley. Children:

i. **Loomis J.**, b. 1839 & reared in Oneonta. He was a scholar and was one of the collaborators on Worcester's Quarto Dictionary. He "brought out" several school books, among them the Franklin Readers. Ass't. editor of the international edition of Webster's Unabridged Dictionary and other works. Res. Oneonta, retired in 1893.

ii. **Lavina**, m. **Rev. Lorin Babcock**, res. Minneapolis, MN. He a Baptist clergyman and businessman.

iii. **Dudley M.**, student & farmer; instructor in mathematics at Fergusonville Academy 1857-58. A lawyer by education, author of a history of Oneonta and numerous newspaper articles.

iv. **Mary L.**, m. **Matthew Herrington**, res. Oneonta. He a tinner by trade.

v. **Caroline**, m. **Rev. George Remington**, Baptist clergyman of North Colebrook, Litchfield Co., CT.

vi. **Ada C.**, res. with her brother on the old homested.

[BR:519-21]

CARLEY, EBENEZER⁶ (*Joseph⁵ MA & VT, Peter⁴ MA, Bartholomew³ MA, Henry² England & MA, William¹ England & MA*) s/o **Joseph Carley** and wife **Sarah Washburn** of Leicester and Spencer, MA, b. at Leicester 12 Feb. 1767. **Joseph**, b. c. 1716; d. 7 March 1808 in VT, also served in the Revolution from MA. After the Revolutionary War he removed to Unadilla, NY, whence he removed c. 1800 to Marathon, Cortland Co., NY, as the second family to locate in that town. He served as captain in the local

militia. He m. **Joanna Swift**, b. 1764, d. 13 May 1831. He d. at Martahon 12 July 1814. His children, named in his will.
7   i.   **Alanson.**
   ii.   **Orrin.**
   iii.   **Rachel**, m. **Silas Wilder.**
   iv.   **Eleanor**, m. **John Smith.**
   v.   **Ellen.**
   vi.   **Hannah**, m. **Nathan Herring.**
   vii. **Hepsibath.**
   viii. **Polly**, m. **Miles Ransom.**

ALANSON CARLEY[7], b. 6 June 1797 in Unadilla, d. at Marathon, NY 8 April 1879. He was aged two when his family removed to Marathon. Elected to the NY state assembly and served as county sheriff (1840). Buinessman and bank director. He m. in Feb. 1818 **Sally**, d/o **Thomas** and **Hester Cortright** of Broome Co., NY, b. 15 May 1799, d. 5 Oct. 1872. They left ten children.
[CUT1:3:1369-73; DARPI]

CARROLL, JOHN[6] (*Amos*[5] *MA, Nathaniel*[4,3,2] *MA, Robert*[1] *MA*) of Springfield, NY, was b. in Middleton, MA 1754, d. 1823. He m. 24 Nov. 1779 **Hannah Thayer.** Children, b. Thompson, CT and removed to Springfield, Otsego Co. with the family:
   i.   **Polly**, b. 20 March 1780; m. (int.) Dec. 1800 **Phineas Allen.**
   ii.   **Nancy**, b. 24 Nov. 1781.
   iii.   **Ezra**, b. 8 Dec. 1783, d. Springfield 22 Feb. 1844, aged 60.
   iv.   **Davis**, b. 25 Feb. 1786.
   v.   **Child** b. 15 April 1790.
   vi.   **John**, b. 9 July 1792; d. Springfield 1845, aged 52.
   vii. **Wotey [Waty]**, b. 28 Aug. 1793; m. **Francis Sammons**. After his death she lived in Fort Plain with her daus., dying there in 1884.
   viii. **Seneca**, b. 7 June 1799; d. 30 March 1800.
   ix.   **Lucinda**, b. 3 June 1801.
[*History of Woodstock, CT* by C. W. Bowen; SPR:239; OB.]

CARYL, ISAAC[8] (*Jonathan*[7], *Benjamin*[6], *Benjamin*[5], *Joseph*[4], *Nathaniel*[3], *Benjamin*[2], *Isaac*[1] *England, MA*), b. in Hopkinton, MA 19 April 1771, s/o **Jonathan Caryl**, who moved with his family when he was young to Chester, VT, and wife **Ann Clark** [their mar. intentions found in Hopkington Vital Records dated 28 Dec. 1752]. On 20 May 1792 **Isaac** m. **Susan Snell** at Chester by **Elder Aaron Leland.** She d. 26 Feb. 1807 and **Isaac** m. 2nd in 1808 at Chester to **Mary (Polly) Barnes**, who was b. 14 March 1774 at Chester, VT and they moved to Sharon, Schoharie Co., NY and thence to Worcester, NY in 1820 [1810]. **Mary** was d/o **Asa Barnes** and wife **Esther Richardson.** They occupied the farm later occupied by **William H. Ely**, where they erected a distillery and carried on a large farm. He was highly esteemed; a few years before his death moved to what is now Richmondville in Schoharie Co., where his two sons, **Moses** and **Joel**, were running a store in the village, which was then known as 'Carylville,' and where he d. 17 Sept. 1843. Children:

9 i. **John.**
 ii. **Isaac Jr.**, b. 8 Nov. 1794. Removed to Worcester, NY and later to NY City. He m. 13 Oct. 1816 to **Sarah Barnes** in Schoharie Co. He d. 11 Dec. 1872 at Anamosa, IA; she d. 22 Feb. 1857 in NY City. Several children. Their son **Isaac**, b. 1858, was murdered at Wendell Estate in Saddle River, NJ by a crazed coachman. This entire family bur. at Trinity Cemetery in NY City.
 iii. **Susan**, b. 28 Dec. 1796 at Chester; m. at Worcester to **William Gott**; three children: **Isaac, Mary D.** and **William L. Gott**. Susan m. 2nd **Samuel Witt** of Worcester and had two children: **John** and **Frances**, both mar. and res. in Nunda, Livingston Co., NY.
9 iv. **Leonard**.
 v. **Emily**, b. 20 April 1801 at Chester, d. aged 5.
 vi. **Moses**, b. 17 Aug. 1803; in business with brother **Joel** in Carylville; later West Richmondville NY. He d. in Seward, Schoharie Co. in 1869. In 1830 at Worcester, NY m. **Catherine Barney Crippen**, widow of **Silas Crippen Jr.**, s/o **Judge Silas Crippen**. She d. 1885. They had 3 children: **Elizabeth** b. 1832 d. 1848; **Moses Henry** b. 1836, d. 1911 and **Silas A.** b. 1839, d. 1872. **Moses Henry** m. 1st in 1858 to **Emily Wilsey** of Worcester, she b. 1841, d. 1865 and is bur. in Worcester. He was a colonel at the close of the Civil War and was aide-de-camp to **Gen. Grant** from 1862 to 1865.
 vii. **Joel**, b. 9 April 1806; d. 7 Nov. 1869, unm. Was associated with brother **Moses** in general store in West Richmondville, NY (earlier known as Carylville) for 30 years.

Children by 2nd wife, **Mary Barnes** who he m. 18 March 1808; she d. 21 June 1859 and is bur. with husband **Isaac** at West Richmondville, NY.
 viii. **Mary**, b. 31 Aug. 1809; m. **Elisha Rogers** of West Richmondville, where they res.
 ix. **Clarissa**, b. 1811; m. **John Jaycox** of Worcester and had **Lorenzo, Leonard, Samuel, Chester, Adelbert, John Henry, Anna Eliza, Amanda** and **Sally Jane**.
 x. **Louisa**, b. 12 Oct. 1812; m. **Amos Elmore**, res. Richmondville, New York Mills & later Utica.

JOHN CARYL[9], b. 1 Oct. 1792. Res. with his father; member of **Capt. Giles Kellog's** company of Artillery; enlisted in 1812 for two years. Was at the battle of Sacketts Harbor. In 1812 he m. **Hannah Lampman** who was b. in 1791 at Hoosack, NY. Removed to Worcester, Otsego Co. where he d. 18 June 1859; she d. 4 Nov. 1864. Both bur. at Worcester. Children:
i. **John Gibson**, b. 5 May 1813 in Sharon; merchant of Worcester. He m. **Christina Ann**, d/o **Samuel Smith** of Central Bridge, Schoharie Co., NY. Removed from Worcester to Central Bridge; farmer & merchant. Had 3 children: **Mary** b. 1863, **Anne** b.

39

	1866 and Ella b. 1868.
ii.	**Catherine M.**, b. 3 Feb. 1819.
iii.	**Joel**, b. 29 Sept. 1823. 1852 m. in Oswego, NY to **Catherine VanAlstyne**. He d. April 1859; bur. at Worcester, NY. [His obituary shows death date as 12 April 1860 at Worcester; aged 36.] Children: **Frank B.**, b. 1856; m. 1881 **Rose Bowen**, d. at Minneapolis, MN in 1932 and **Lillian**, b. 1858; m. 1875 **DeWitt Clinton Tiffany** of NY City; in 1935 she a widow res. Minneapolis, MN.
iv.	**Alvira C.**, b. 3 Dec. 1829.
v.	**Susan**, b. 1816, d. 1865.

LEONARD CARYL[9] b. 20 March 1799, Chester. At age 18 entered store of Caryl & Fulton at Stockbridge, VT. 1820 to Worcester. Later in partnership with **Dr. T. P. Fay**, merchant. Returned to Worcester in 1825 and at that place on 5 Oct. 1824 m. **Mary**, youngest d/o **Judge Silas Crippen**. She was b. Worcester 29 July 1800; her parents being among the earlist settlers of Otsego Co., originally from CT. Her brother **Philip** was the first child born of white parents in Otsego Co. She d. at Worcester 26 June 1854. In 1841 he built the large brick building now (1937) occupied by his son-in-law **William H. Ely**, the most expensive and finest buidling in Worcester. The same year he was elected to the Legislature. In 1837 he erected a hotel opposite his store. He was into banking & an early supporter of the railroad. Children:

i.	**Helen**, d. aged four.
ii.	**Mary Jane**, m. **J. Lasell Hayden** of Middlefield; removed to New York City where he became a partner in the dry goods jobbing business of **Herbert VanValkenbrugh** & Co. until the Civil War, when the firm was dissolved. **Mary Jane** d. of fever, leaving two sons **Lasell Jr.** [Lasselle Hayden] and **Louis O. Hayden**. Soon after their father d. at Elizabeth, NJ and their grandfather Caryl was made their guardian. **Louis Hayden** m. **Mary Dante** of East Worcester.
iii.	**Elizabeth Crippen**, m. **Dr. Benjamin C. Ely**, s/o **Dr. Sumner Ely** of Middletown; removed to Girard, Erie Co., PA. He was a druggist at that place; they have eight children; four sons and four daus.
iv.	**Ellen**, b. 12 Feb. 1834, m. **William Horace Ely** in 1855, brother of **Dr. Benjamin C.**, and was for many years in mercantile business in Clarksville, NY. They later moved to Worcester. She d. 21 Aug. 1917.
v.	**Julius Henry**, b. 24 Dec. 1827, merchant of Worcester and later removed to New York City and carried on real estate business. 1870 he m. in NY **Eliza**, d/o **Nelson Chase**, a niece and adopted dau. of **Madame Jumel**. They res. at the celebrated Jumel Mansion on Washington Heights. Both bur. at Trinity Churchyard in NY City. No children.

[*The Caryl Family in England and America* ... by Arthur S. Caryl; Hopkington, MA Vital Records; OB.]

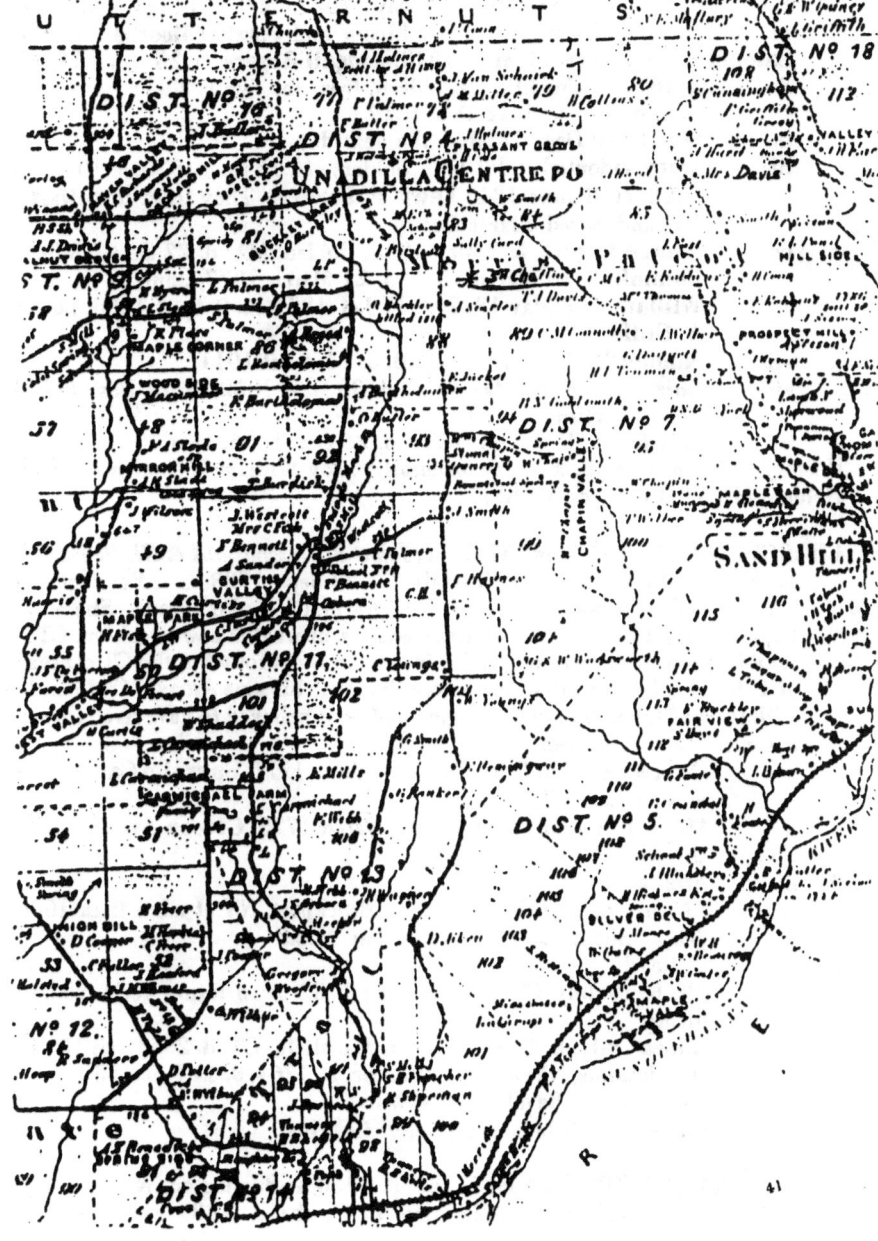

CHAFFIN, SAMUEL[4] (*Tilla[3] MA, Samuel MA[2], Robert[1] MA*) b. 5 May 1792 in Holden, MA, d. 17 July 1845 in Unadilla, NY [Delaware Co.], where he settled prior to 1830. He was the s/o **Tilla** and **Hannah (Mirick) Chaffin** of Holden, MA. **Tilla** was a Revolutionary soldier from militia of Hampshire & Worcester Cos., b. 14 May 1762 in MA, d. 1 Sept. 1838 also in Holden, MA. **Hannah** was d/o **Elisha** and **Persis (Moore) Mirick**. Samuel m. in Holden 14 April 1818, **Abigail Rogers**, b. 25 April 1795; d. 15 May 1879 in Unadilla. Children, from the family Bible:

 i. Son, b. 2 Dec., d. 18 Dec. 1819.
 ii. Son, b. 10 Dec., 1820; d. the next day.
 iii. Mary, [adopted child], b. in Holden, MA 16 Nov. 1820, d. 10 Nov. 1898; m. 8 June 1843 **Lewis P. LeSuer**. They lived in Belfast, NY, and raised a large family.
 iv. **George Rogers**, b. 3 May 1823, Holden, MA; d. 22 Sept. 1879.
 v. **Hannah**, b. 18 March 1825; d. 21 March 1877, unm.
 vi. **William**, b. 8 May 1827; d. 17 Jan. 1851; m. 9 April 1850, **Lucy A. Guild**.
 vii. **Samuel H.**, b. 17 April 1830; d. 11 April 1911.
 viii. **Abigail C.**, b. 14 May 1832; d. 30 Nov. 1852; m. 24 Nov. 1852 **Isaac Sterline**.
 ix. **Charles N.**, b. 9 Sept. 1837; d. 26 Oct. 1856, unm.

[*History of Robert Chaffin & His Descendants* . . . by William L. Chaffin, 1913; Holden, MA Vital Records; DARPI.]

CHURCH, JONATHAN[5] (*John[4] RT & CT, John[3] RI, Joseph[2] MA & RI, Richard[1] England & MA*) was bapt. in Killingly, CT 27 Sept. 1723; d. at Burlington, NY c. 1797; m. **Abigail Cady** of Killingly in 1747, d/o **James**. She was bapt. 29 May 1726; d. 1797. **James** was res. of what is now Brooklyn, CT, founding a church there in 1754. **Jonathan** is not found in the CT census of 1790, it is believed that just before that time his sons **Amasa**, **Cady** and **Willard** had taken him to Burlington and he is believed to have lived there c. seven years. Children:

 i. **Elizabeth**, b. 30 Feb. 1748, m. 5 June 1771, **Ephraim Campbell** of Mansfield CT.
 ii. **Mary**, b. 12 Jan. 1750; m. 15 March 1775, **Gideon Arnold**. No children.
6 iii. **Amasa**.
 iv. **Abigail**, b. 10 July 1756; d. in Brockport, NY at more than 100 years. She m. 26 Oct. 1780 **John Wood**.
6 v. **Willard**.
 vi. **Eli**, b. 19 July 1763; d. 22 June 1782 of an injury rec'd. while lifting.
 vii. **James Cady**, b. 7 Sept. 1765 at Mansfield, CT; d. 28 March 1855 at Columbus, NY; m. **Mary Porter**, b. 1764, d. 11 Feb. 1839. He served in the Revolutionary War.
 viii. **Clarissa**, b. 3 Jan., 1768; m. --- **Calkins**.

AMASA CHURCH[6], b. 23 Jan. 1755; d. 1838 at Burlington, NY. He m. **Mnetriphantham Allen** on 22 May 1777, she d. 1839 and was d/o

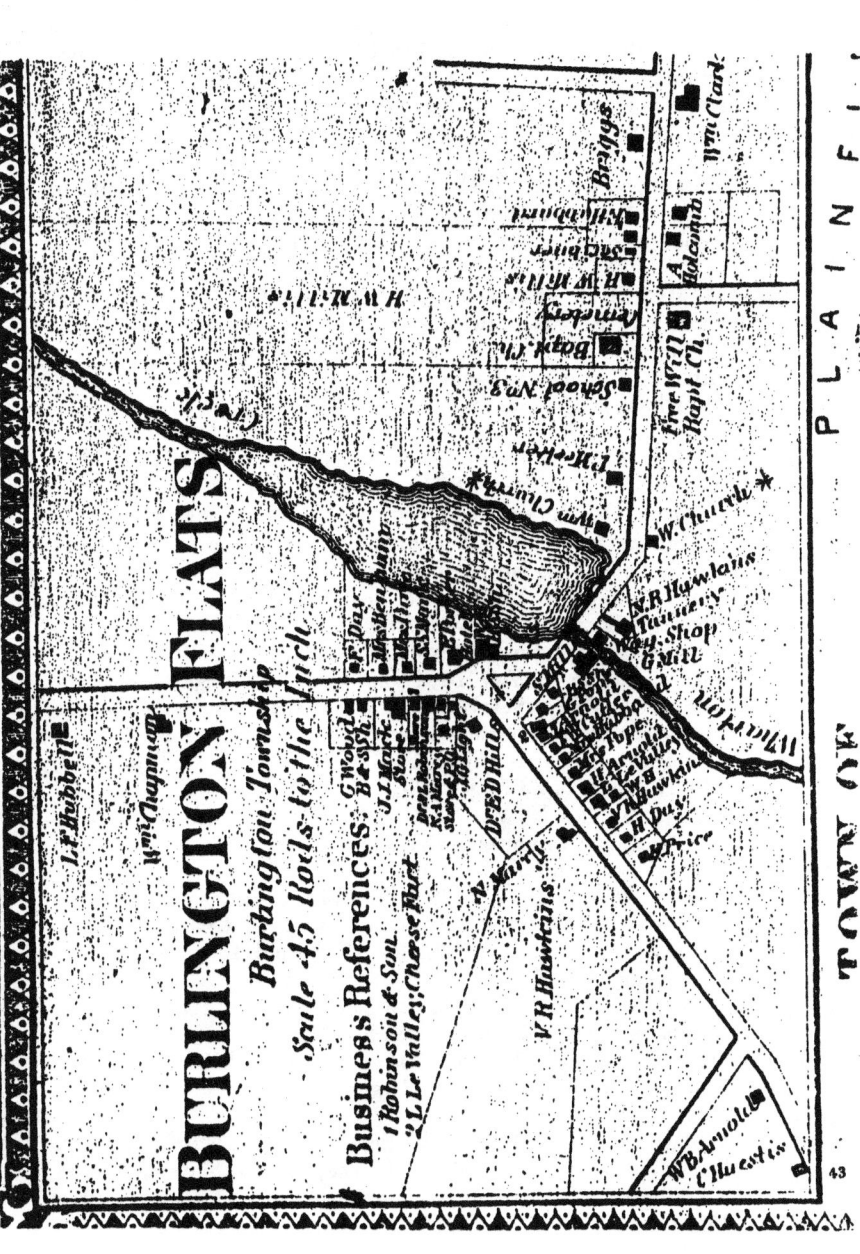

Hezekiah. All of their children were b. at Mansfield, CT. **Amasa** served in the Revolutionary War. In 1790 he and brothers **Willard** and **Cady** bought land in Otsego Co. of **Andrew Craig** of Burlington, NJ. Others who settled with them were **Hezekiah Allen**, father of **Amasa's** wife, and **Ephraim Campbell** and **Gideon Arnold**, who m. sisters of **Amasa**. Altogether they took up 656 1/2 acres. The others left Burlington after eight years, but **Amasa** and his wife d. there. Children:

7	i.	**William**.
7	ii.	**Origen**.
	iii.	**Abigail**, b. 18 (or 23) Oct. 1786; d. 25 Dec. 1858. She m. in 1803 to **Dea. Jonathan Sheldon**, a Presbyterian, b. 1780. They removed to Barre, NY and had seven children.

WILLIAM CHURCH[7] b. 18 June 1778 in Mansfield, CT; d. 22 April 1831 in Burlington, NY. He was m. twice, but no wives' names recorded in this source. Children:
- i. **Amasa**, d. young at Hammondsport, NY.
- ii. **Jonathan**, b. 1812; d. 28 Feb. 1870 at Delevan, WI, left children.

ORIGEN CHURCH[6] b. 22 Feb. 1782, Mansfield, CT; d. 14 Nov. 1874 at Burlington, NY. He m. 8 Nov. 1804 **Sarah Smith** who was b. 22 Dec. 1782; d. 31 Oct. 1870. He was eight years old when his father removed to Otsego Co., and he spent the rest of his life there, living at Exeter and Burlington. He bought his father's farm in 1831. Children:

- i. **Emily**, b. 5 Sept. 1805; d. 28 Nov. 1874; m. 13 March 1827, **Hiram Wilcox**, b. 11 Nov. 1804; d. 13 Aug. 1872. Their son Charles m. **Cornelia A. Church**, d/o Charles. The Wilcox family left Burlington in May 1844 and went to Cottage Grove, WI. After three years they removed to Butte des Morts, WI, where they spent the rest of their lives.
- ii. **Charles**, b. 2 March 1807; d. 22 May 1889; m. 10 Feb. 1833, **Almira Gere**, b. 23 Aug. 1808; d. 11 Nov. 1885.
- iii. **Abigail**, b. 5 (or 13) May 1809; d. 20 May 1891 at Fond du Lac, WI; m. **Zenas Chapman** who was b. 7 Sept. 1807; d. 18 July 1875 at Fond du Lac.
- iv. **Lucy**, b. 10 July 1811; d. 29 Sept. 1889 at Sheboygan Falls, WI; m. in NY state **Webster Balcom** and had a son, **George Webster Balcom**. She m. 2nd **Charles Cobb** and they removed to Sheboygan Falls, WI.
- v. **Nancy**, b. 16 Nov. 1813; d. 20 Jan. 1895; m. 13 Nov. 1838, **Albert Sumner Bolton**, who was b. 4 Nov. 1811.
- vi. **Mary**, b. 14 (or 24) Feb. 1816; d. 10 Feb. 1885; m. **Albert Lummis [Loomis]** who d. Burlington, NY; she m. 2nd **Asa W. Sprague** of Burlington.
- vii. **William**, b. 7 June 1818; d. 21 Sept. 1900; m. **Lorinda Osborn**, b. 14 Sept. 1820; d. 31 May 1901. They had no children. He was a Presbyterian clergyman, res. Burlington and adopted his niece **Ella Lummis**.

WILLARD CHURCH⁶, b. Mansfield, CT 7 Sept. 1758; d. 17 Sept. 1846 in Oakland, MI. He m. at Unadilla, June 1795 to **Sarah Davis**, d/o **Jonathan** and **Mehitable (Bowen) Davis** of Unadilla [now Butternuts Twp.]. She was b. in Oct. 1779. At the time of their mar. he was 37 and she 16. They lived in Burlington, NY for five years after their mar and he then bought a farm in Goshen, now Hopewell Center, NY. In 1812 they went to Ontario Twp., Wayne Co. where she d. in 1841 and he went to his dau. **Huldah Wood** in MI. He d. while visiting his dau. **Susan Hodges** at Oakland, MI. **Willard** served in the Revolutionary army and during his service he was taken prisoner and confined on the notorious prison ship *Jersey*, which lay in Wallabout Bay, New York Harbor, where the US Navy Yard is now. His venture into real estate in Otsego Co. was a disaster. It is certain that he lost everything. During the War of 1812, at his Ontario farm in 1814 he was seized by a detachment of British soldiers and carried on board the flasghip of a squadron which had come to seize stores at Pultneyville, eight miles from his farm. He was landed at Pultneyville the next day. He was an unusual character, not only a skeptic, but a strong opponent to religion. "He was quck tempered, passionate and often violent and when angered could use language more forcible than polite." One of his sons said that throughout his boyhood he felt a sense of fear in his presence. In later life he was wonderfully changed and his temper became subdued and sweetened. He was a hypochondriac in his earlier years, "filled with gloomy forebodings." His wife **Sarah** is described as a most happy, cheerful and courageous woman. She is bur. on the Ridge Road near their Lake shore farm. Children:

i. **Susan**, b. Sept. 1796, d. 2 Nov. 1867; m. 1815 **Darius Hodges** at Sempronius, NY.

ii. **Lorenzo**, b. 29 March 1799 in Burlington; taken in infancy to Hopewell & d. 27 June 1851 at Hudson, MI; m. 4 March 1819 at Ontario, NY, **Susan Halleck**.

iii. **Pharcellus**, b. 11 Sept. 1801 near Geneva, NY; d. 6 June 1886 at Tarrytown, NY; m. 13 May 1828 at Brandon, VT, **Clara Emily Conant**.

iv. **Volney**, b. 25 Feb. 1804 at Hopewell Center, NY; d. 22 Nov. 1893; m. at Whiting, VT 19 May 1831, **Harriet Bush**, b. Orwell, VT, 6 June 1813. He m. 2nd 5 Dec. 1861, **Mrs. Ellen (Fisher) Ingersoll**.

v. **Huldah**, b. 19 July 1806; d. 10 Aug. 1895; m. 12 May 1831, **Zebina Wood**.

vi. **Avolin**, b. 17 Sept. 1808 Hopewell Center; d. 11 May 1851; m. 10 Nov. 1836 at Macedonia, NY, **Mari Putnam**, b. 27 Oct. 1817. Their dau., **Elizabeth**, b. 19 Nov. 1837 in Ontario, NY, m. in Kalamazoo, MI 30 Sept. 1862 to **Cyrenius Gregory** who was b. 13 May 1819 at New Lisbon, Otsego Co. Res. Ithaca, MI.

vii. **Alonzo**, b. 1811, d. 1855; m. **Jane Ann Hicks**.

viii. **Leroy**, b. 8 June 1813; d. 25 Jan. 1898; m. 8 Sept. 1841, **Jane Ealick**.

ix. **Lafayette**, b. 16 July 1816; d. 2 Jan. 1907 at Alma, MI; m. 29 Jan. 1840, **Sophronia Benjamin**, b. 1824.

[*Descendants of Richard Church of Plymouth, MA* by John Church, 1913.]
BR:630-1

CHURCH, TITUS[1] (*Simeon*[4] *CT, Samuel*[3] *CT, Edward*[2] *CT, Richard*[1] *Eng. & CT*) was b. in Saybrook [Chester], CT 19 May 1745, s/o **Simeon Church**, b. CT and d. 7 Aug, 1792, aged 84. **Simeon's** wife was **Eunice** and she d. 16 July 1809, aged 90. **Titus** was one of six brothers, all served in the Revolutionary War. He m. 2nd **Mary Lowell**, she d. in May 1813, the first woman interred in Unadilla Cemetery; he d. in 1805 [1807] in Pawlet, VT. Children:

    i.   **Eunice**, b. 8 Sept. 1778; m. **Bethuel Huntley**, res. West Guillingburg, Can. [Canada?], near New Market.
    ii.   **Amy**, m. --- **Briggs**, res. Williamston, MA.
    iii.   **Lucy**, m. 1st --- **Smead** and 2nd --- **Benson**; res. Putney VT, Sacketts Harbor NY and Stillwater, NY; she d. Aug. 1818.
    iv.   **Polly [Mary]** b. 1780, d. 1824. She m. **Jehiel Clark**, b. 1773, d. 1850.
    v.   **Theodosia**, m. **Chester Darbe**, res. Perryburg, NY.
2 vi.   **Simeon**.

SIMEON CHURCH[2] b. 29 July 1783 in Pawlet, VT; d. 26 Feb. 1870. He was raised in Jamaica, NH and moved from there with his family to Pawlet, VT, and thence to Unadilla, Otsego Co. in 1808, accompanied by his mother and several families. He remained in Otsego Co. until his death on 26 Feb. 1870. In Nov. 1808 he m. **Anna Bushnell**, d/o **Capt. Abisha Bushnell**, and who d. 23 Aug. 1851. **Simeon** was an officer in the War of 1812. Baptist church members. Children:

    i.   **Henrietta**, b. 7 April 1810; d. 8 Oct. 1878. unm.
    ii.   **Anna Maria**, b. 17 April 1812, d. 31 Jan. 1843, unm.
    iii.   **Caroline**, b. Sept. 1814. m. **Hiram Willey** by whom she had six children, three living: **Norman B.**, 1st governor of the state of ND from 1891 to 1893 & later res. Blue Canyon, CA; **T. L.** res. Afton, NY and **Mrs. Phebe A. Black** of Auburn, KS. **Caroline** d. 1 April 1851.
3 iv.   **Eber Ferris**.
    v.   **Lucy**, b. 29 Feb. 1820, res. with bro. **Simeon**, unm. She d. 10 Feb. 1907.
    vi.   **Simeon**, b. Oct. 1822, reared to farming and for the past 63 years has lived upon his farm in Union School Dist. No. 4 (1893; unm. He d. 2 May 1905.
    vii.   **John W.**, b. 14 Oct. 1822; d. 14 Dec. 1822.
    viii.   **Titus**, b. 18 May 1826; d. Aug. 1828.
3 ix.   **Theodore Huntley**.

EBER FERRIS CHURCH[3], b. May 1817, one of the founders of the D. M. Ferry Seed Co. at Detroit, MI; a member of the company ten years. He m. Miss **E. A. Miller** of Unadilla, by whom he had:
    i.   **Mary**, m. **Jacob Hull** of Detroit.
    ii.   **Fred L.**, now (1893) res. at Norwalk, CT, in the hat trade.

THEODORE H. CHURCH[3], b. May 1830, teacher in the district and also taught vocal music some years. Served as an officer in the Western House

of Refuge at Rochester, NY one year; now (1893) engaged in book and stationary business at Topeka, KS. He m. **Sarah L. Blelock** of Rochester. Children:
- i. **Herbert B.**, banker of Boston, MA.
- ii. **Willard O.**, official of the Atchison, Topeka & Santa Fe Railroad Company, res. Wichita, KS.
- iii. **Mary Violet.**
- iv. **M. D.**
- v. **Alena.**

[BR:630-31; *Simeon Church of Chester, CT 1708-1792 & His Descendants* by Charles W. Church, 1914, Waterbury, CT]

CLARK, EDWARD[1], s/o **Nathan Clark** and wife --- **Nichols**, d/o **John Nichols [Nicholas]** of Waterbury, CT, was b. in Athens, Greene Co., NY 19 Dec. 1811. He studied law in the office of **Ambrose L. Jordan** at Hudson; in 1830 he was an attorney at that place and in 1833 he removed to Poughkeepsie, NY. Oct. 1835 m. **Caroline Jordon**, eldest d/o **Ambrose L. Jordan**, whose partner Edward became in 1837, in 1838 the office was removed to NY City where he was an attorney for and partner in the Singer Sewing Machine Co., for which **Edward** took stock as payment. In 1854 to Cooperstown where he purchased "Apple Hill" from **George A. Starkweather** and the family spent summers there; in 1869 he erected a handsome stone residence which he named "Fernleigh." He expended large sums of money in the erection of an elegant mansion and improvement of neighborhood property, giving steady employment to large numbers of local workers. **Caroline** d. 27 June 1874, aged 59, is bur. at Lakewood Cemetery. **Edward** d. 14 Oct. 1882, aged 71. Children:
- i. **Edward L.**
- ii. **Ambrose Jordan.**
- 3 iii. **Alfred Corning.**

ALFRED CORNING CLARK[3], b. 1843; d. 8 April 1896 of pneumonia. He was the last surviving child and inherited a large estate, including a controlling interest in the Singer Sewing Machine Co. He made his home at Fernleigh. He is described as modest and retiring in manner and habits; public-spirited, devout and helpful in church and other benevolent organizations; Protestant Episcopal. He traveled abroad extensively. He m. **Elizabeth Severin**, who m. as her 2nd husband the late **Bishop Henry C. Potter** of NY. Children:
- i. **Edward Severin.**
- ii. **Robert Sterling.**
- iii. **F. Ambrose.**
- 4 iv. **Stephen Carlton.**

STEPHEN CARLTON CLARK[4] b. at Cooperstown 29 Aug. 1882; grad. from Yale College in 1903 and from Columbia Law School, class of 1907. He makes his home at Fernleigh in Cooperstown; served as assemblyman from his Otsego district. Protestant Episcopal and a member of many NY City clubs. He has an office in the Singer Building in NY City. He m. 20 Feb.

1909, **Susan Vanderpoel**, d/o **Marcus T. Hun** [sic].
[G:161, 175; OB; A:280-82 [P]; CUT1:484-5]

CLARK, JARED[4] (*Nathaniel*[3] *CT, Daniel*[2] *CT, Daniel*[1] *England & CT*) b. 15 July 1729 at Lebanon, CT; d. 11 Sept. 1775. He was s/o **Nathaniel Clark** and wife **Hannah Kellogg**. Jared m. 12 Dec. 1754 **Mary Abell**, b. 24 Feb. 1736, d/o **Daniel Abel** and wife **Sarah Crane** of Lebanon. Jared d. 11 Sept. 1775, leaving a large family. She m. 2nd **Zebulon Metcalfe**, also from CT. About 1794 the Clark family removed to Pierstown, c. miles north of Cooperstown. Children, b. Lebanon, CT [Goshen Parish]:

	i.	**Philotha**, b. 1756; m. 1st Mr. **Tracy**, 2nd **Ezekiel Kellogg**.
	ii.	**Jared**, b. 1758.
	iii.	**Mary**, bapt. 11 Oct. 1761; m. **Darius Warren**.
	iv.	**Simon**, b. 11 Sept. 1763.
5	v.	**Abel**, bapt. 24 Nov. 1765; m. **Betsey Loomis**.
5	vi.	**Ambrose**, b. 1769.
	vii.	**Cyrus**, b. 18 April 1772 [twin]; m. 26 Jan. 1796, **Ann Fitch**, d/o **Harry**.
	viii.	**Cyrenus**, b. 18 April 1772; m. 19 Jan. 1797 **Rachel Tracy**.
	ix.	**Solomon**, res. on farm next to Kelloggs, where he d. in 1814. He m. a d/o **John Williams Sr.** & she d. aged 92. [Not named here.]

ABEL CLARK[5] of Otsego made his will 18 Dec. 1828; proved in 1832. **Ambrose Clark** was a witness. In it he named his wife **Betsey** and children:
  i.   **Joseph**.
  ii. **Daniel**.
  iii. **Sherman**.
  iv. **Eliza**.
  v.   **Marsha**.

AMBROSE CLARK[5] settled on a farm later owned by **Julius Warren**. He was noted for his probity and uprightedness and held the office of surrogate from 1808 to 1813. He was frequently consulted in the settlement of estates, as his experience and good judgment were considered valuable. He was also justice of the peace and his last years were spent in Fort Plain, where he d. at an advanced age. Children (all engaged in printing):
  i.   **Justin**, established 1st newspaper printed in Susquehanna Co., PA at Montrose. He d. in 1822, aged 27. On 13 Aug. 1815 he m. in Pierstown to **Lucy Williams** of that place.
  ii. **Israel**, pub. the *Watchtower* newspaper in Cooperstown 1814-1817 and later went to Albany to pub. the *Albany Register*. He d. at the home of **Thurlow Weed** in Rochester
  iii. **Harry**, d. in early manhood.
  iv. **Ambrose**. On 23 Oct. 1831 at Otsego, he is noted of Exeter and he m. **Mrs. Susan Williams**.

[*The Clark Genealogy: Some Descendants of Daniel Clark of Windsor, CT 1639-1913* by E. L. Walton, 1913; *Hartford Times*:5-10-1952 #B3762, #A-5952, 23 Feb. 1946, #7392, 7 Sept. 1946, #7473 28 Sept. 1940; *Early Lebanon, an*

48

Historical Address 4 July 1876 by Rev. Orlo D. Hine, pub. Hartford, 1880; GBM; G217; GBW]

CLYDE, SAMUEL (COL.)[1] b. Windham, Rockingham Co., NH 11 April 1732 of Scotch ancestry. His parents were **Daniel** and **Esther (Rankin) Clyde**, both b. in Scotland. They settled for a time in the North of Ireland and came to America, settling in what is now Windham (now a part of Londonderry), NH. In early manhood **Samuel** was a ship carpenter and went as far East as Cape Breton and Halifax. He began his military career on his return to NH when he raised a company of bateau men and rangers and received his commission in the field as captain from **Gen. Abercrombie**, then Commander-In-Chief of his Majesty's forces in America. In 1758 **Samuel** was appointed captain and served in the French and Indian War, which ended in 1762. He was member of the state assembly 1777-8 and sheriff of Montgomery [Otsego] Co., NY 1785-9, and the first Chairman of the Tryon Co. Committee of Safety. He m. in 1761 **Catharine Wasson**, niece of **Dr. Matthew Thornton**, signer of the Declaration of Independence. She was b. in Worcester, MA and her maternal grandfather, **James Thornton**, was one of the survivors of the historic siege of Londonderry in 1669. In 1762 the Clyde family removed to Cherry Valley, then in Tyrone Co., NY. The colonel was not at home at the time of the Indian massacre in Cherry Valley in 1788, but had gone early that morning to arrnage for the safety of his family. He served as captain in the 1st Regiment of Foot, Tyron County Militia and later as colonel of the 4th Regiment of Montgomery Co. His wife heard of the attack and took their seven children and a negro lad and hid them until rescue came. Their home was south of the fort and the homestead was later occupied by desc. **Capt. James D. Clyde** who served as a captain in the Civil War. **Col. Samuel** was a hero of the Revolution and participated in the battle of Oriskany. He was a farmer and d. 30 Nov. 1790. **Catherine** d. 31 May 1823. She is described as a true type of the American woman of the Revolution. The Cherry Valley massacre is said to have been foreshadowed in her dreams the preceding night. She lived to an advanced age. Children so far identified:

2   i.   **George C.**
2   ii.   **Joseph.**

HON. GEORGE C. CLYDE[2] [P] was b. in Cherry Valley 14 Oct. 1772 and d. 15 Oct. 1847 on the farm where he spent his life. He was bur. on the Clyde farm but later removed to Cherry Valley Cemetery. He studied law and practiced in Burlington until 1835 when he removed to Cooperstown. There he served as county clerk and in 1838 returned to Cherry Valley. On 4 June 1829 he m. at Ghent, NY **Catherine V. S. Dorr**, d/o **Dr. Russell Dorr** of Chatham, Columbia Co., NY and removed there in 1839; judge. In 1852 returned to Cherry Valley, where he d. 21 Dec. 1868, leaving his wife and one son. He is described as a "genial friend, a patriotic citizen, an excellent lawyer, an able counselor, a wise judge and an honest man."

GEORGE CLINTON CLYDE.

Reference BR:419-21 gives the name of the wife of **George** as **Martha Campbell** and makes no menton of **Catherine Dorr**. A **Catherine Clyde** d. at Cherry Valley 5 June 1828, aged 24. **Martha** was b. in 1782 and d. 5 Feb. 1833 of consumption. Her family were pioneer settlers in Otsego Co. from Londonderry, NH c. 1740. She d. 5 Feb. 1833, aged 51 and was bur. in Cherry Valley Cemetery. Their son according to this reference was: **LAFAYETTE CLYDE**[3] who was b. 27 Aug. 1812 and d. 12 Sept. 1849. In 1840 he m. **Frances A. Crafts**, who was b. in Cherry Valley 27 Nov. 1816, and d. 25 May 1851, was a d/o **Alfred** and **Hannah (Burbanks) Crafts**, natives of CT. Only two of five children of this mar. now (1893) survive (first two below):

4 i.   **James D.**
   ii.   **Eloise C.**, m. --- **Doubleday**, res. Binghamton, NY.
   iii.   **Catherine**, d. 5th of Jan. 1828, aged 24.

JAMES D. CLYDE[4], fatherless at age six, was brought up by an uncle, **George C. Clyde**, who became Clerk of Otsego Co., Judge of the Court of Common Pleas for Columbia Co. and a member of the Constitutional Convention of 1846. In 1852 Judge Clyde returned to Cherry Valley, where he d. 21 Dec. 1868. On 28 Sept. 1861 **James D.** enlisted in the war for the Union as a private in Company C, 44th NY Volunteers, in which he served four months. Discharged on account of ill health in Jan. and re-enlisting in Aug., 1862, he was commissioned First Lt. in Co. G., 121st NY Volunteer Infantry. He was again discharged in Nov. of that year and in Nov. 1863 he again reenlisted in Co. E, 76th NY Volunteers, and at the close of the was was mustered out as captain of Co. B, 76th NY Volunteers. He was taken prisoner at the Battle of the Wilderness and held ten months at Charleston, SC. He was exchanged at Columbia and returned home to Otsego Co. where he began the study of medicine. He opened a drug store at Binghamton and then removed to Cherry Valley, where he continued in business until 1891, when he retired to his ancestral acres.

Also bur. in the Clyde family plot in Cherry Valley Cemetery are **Julia Clyde Darby**, d/o **Col. Joseph** and **Margaret Clyde**. No dates of birth and/or death given. Originally bur. on Clyde farm and removed. A **Mrs. Margaret Clyde** of Cherry Valley d. 24 March 1829, aged 44.

COL. JOSEPH CLYDE[2], youngest s/o **Col. Samuel Clyde**, d. 2 Dec. 1869 aged 92 years. He was bur. on the family farm and later removed to Cherry Valley Cemetery to a lot owned by his nephew **George C. Clyde**. **Joseph's** wife was **Margaret Campbell** who d. 25 March 1829, aged 44. He was prominent in political affairs and occupied an excellent social position; was a member of the Constitutional Convention of 1821 and a Member of Assembly in 1828.
[CH1:9, 27, 89, 100, 123; GH1:36; A:120A, 120-21; GBM; BR:419-21; List of Cherry Valley burials, removed to Cherry Valley Cemetery from LDS film; OB.]

COLE, ALBERT B.[7] (*Abel*[6] *VT & NY, Benjamin*[5]*, Ebenezer*[4] *MA & VT, Benjamin*[3] *MA, Hugh*[2] *England & MA, James*[1] *England*) was b. in Exeter, NY in 1806;

d. 1870. He m. **Elizabeth Ross** in 1832 and had at least one child:
    i.   **Ernest B.** b. in Noblesville, IN 1846; m. 1874 **Sarah E. Dunn.**
[AA:7-6]

COLE, BYRON, s/o **Joseph Cole** who was b. in Columbia, Herkimer Co. and wife **Achsah Pearl** of Fairfield. [The LDS IGI gives the father of **Joseph Cole,** who was b. 7 Sept. 1795 in Winfield, NY as **Benjamin Cole** and his mother as "Iscar_ KEEP".] Byron was b. in Cedarville, Herkimer Co. 2 March 1830 and attended school to the age of 13 when his father died, and until the age of 23 **Byron** farmed and attended school as best he could. At that age, in company with two of his brothers, he bought a large farm in town of Columbia, Herkimer Co.; the three worked in partnership eight years when he sold out to his brothers. At that time he m. **Caroline Miller,** who was b. in Columbia 9 Oct. 1830. She is d/o **William J.** and **Nancy (Haner) Miller,** both b. in town of Columbia, NY. After their mar. they removed to the Town of Exeter, NY where he worked a farm for five years, after which he bought the place upon which he now (1893) lives in Richfield, District No. 3. Universalists. Children:
    i.   **Clayton,** res. Winfield, m. **Jeannie Bowen**; has three children: **Lee, Merton** and **Clyde.**
    ii.   **Carrie M.,** m. **Clark Getman,** has had four children, only one living in 1893, **Lynn.**
    iii.   **Blanch V.,** m. **William H. Dayger,** farmer of "the same town" [Richfield?]; one child, **Carrie.**
    iv.   **Florence,** dec'd. by 1893.
    v.   **Ada,** dec'd. by 1893.
    vi.   **William J.,** at home.
    vii.   **Emerson,** at home.
[BR:653-54]

COLE, DAVID[6] (*Elisha*[5] *NY, Elisha*[4] *MA & NY, Elisha*[3] *MA, William*[2] *MA, William Rappleye Cole*[1] *MA*) s/o **Elisha Cole** and wife **Charity Hazen** who m. in 1763; they were of Dutchess Co., NY & Carmel, Putnam Co., NY. His parents are bur. on the family plot on that farm. **Elisha** served as a private in the 7th Regiment, Dutchess Co. Militia. **David** was b. 1768; m. **Hannah Bangs** and res. Frederickstown, Dutchess Co. About 1800 he removed with his family to Edmeston, Otsego Co., where he d. 13 Feb. 1833; farmer. **Hannah** was b. 10 June 1779; d. 3 May 1842. "David and his wife left Dutchess Co. for Columbus, Chenango Co." Their son:
    i.   **Eli,** b. on their journey to Columbus.

David's brother **Elisha,** b. 8 Aug. 1776, m. 29 Oct. 1797 **Rebecca** b. 7 Dec. 1779, d/o **Joseph** and **Elizabeth (Townsend) Hopkins.** He d. 18 July 1851 and she d. 31 Dec. 1862. "He was a farmer and bought the Philipse farm. Upon this farm is the Gilead burying ground in which is bur. **Enoch Crosby,** the Revolutionary Spy, who is the "Harvey Birch" of Cooper's novel, *The Spy.*"
[*The Ancestors of William Rappleye Cole* by DeKilgore, 1956]

COLE, RICHARD² was b. in Butternuts in 1820; a s/o **Richard Cole¹** who was b. in Great Barrington, MA in 1784 and d. at his home in the Town of Butternuts in 1877. His father, **Capt. Cole**, came to Otsego Co. c. 1796 from MA. **Richard²** was the fourth of ten children, eight sons and two daus. He m. **Elizabeth Rockwell** in Dec. 1843 [then **Mrs. Elizabeth Gray**], d/o **Amos** and **Elizabeth (Emmons) Rockwell** of Butternuts. [See Rockwell family entry.] Richard was a farmer and cheesemaker, which he hauled to Catskill, on the Hudson, and thence down river to NY City. Children, b. Butternuts:

i.   **Mary E.**, b. 4 Feb. 1845; m. 7 Sept. 1874 **Alexander Brush**, res. at Spirit Lake, IA in 1892. One son & three daus.
ii.   **William R.**, B. 3 Sept. 1846; m. 20 Feb. 1869 **Mary Casterline**; d. TX 1872. Left two children, not named here.
iii.   **Emma L.** [Emily], b. 18 Feb. 1848; m. 30 Nov. 1869 **Joseph E. Tobey** of Gilbertsville [Butternuts] and res. there in 1892. Have three sons.
iv.   **Ida M.**, b. 3 Oct. 1849; m. 30 Nov. 1869 **Theodore Wallin** of Gilbertsville [Butternuts], res. there in 1892. Two sons & four daus.
v.   **Alice A.**, b. 2 Feb. 1852; m. 21 March 1887 **George H. Wallin**, d. Eugene City, OR 1890. No children.
vi.   **Jennie M.**, b. 23 March 1855; m. 7 Sept. 1874 **Charles H. Bryant**; res. Sioux City, IA in 1892. Two children, b. Gilbertsville, res. Sioux City: **William C. Bryant**, b. 1877; **Anita C.**, b. 1881.
vii.   **Hobart H.**, b. 30 May 1857; res. Gilbertsville [at home] in 1892, unm.
viii.   **Carrie**, b. 15 Jan. 1859; d. 16 Aug. 1860.

Richard³ m. 2nd **Saray Tobey**, b. in the area, a d/o **Elisha** and **Hannah (Hillman) Tobey**. Elisha originally of New Bedford, MA and Hannah from the Black River Country in NY. **Stephen Tobey**, the father of Elisha, came from MA to Otsego Co. c. 1804 and he left five children, three sons and two daus. Elisha d. 22 April 1877 at the age of 77; his wife d. aged 88 y, 3 m.
[*A Genealogy of the Families of John Rockwell, of Stamford, Conn. 1641* . . . by James Boughton, 1903; BR:616-17]

COLE, SISSON⁷ (*Hugh*⁶, ⁵, ⁴, ³ *MA & RI, James*², ¹ *England & MA*), b. Foster, RI 20 Jan. 1746; d. Richfield, NY 28 March 1845. He was s/o **Hugh Cole** and wife **Jane Sisson**, who moved their family from Swansea, MA to Scituate in 1750. Sisson rec'd. a pension in 1832 for service as a private in the RI Troops. He m. **Elizabeth Hunter**, b. 18 Jan. 1746, d. 12 Nov. 1842. He was a Revolutionary War soldier. Came to NY first on horseback to select a location for a home. He had a poplar stick with which he urged his beast along, and upon arriving in Otsego Co. and selecting a farm, he stuck the stick in the ground. It took root and grew to be an immense tree. He returned to RI and brought his family to Otsego by team. He lived upon his farm until he was nearly 90 years old; soldier of the Revolutionary

War. His wife lived to be nearly 96. Children:
- i. **Amey**, b. 3 May 1769; m. **Jonathan Cheney**.
- ii. **Nehemiah**, b. 18 Sept. 1771.
- iii. **Elizabeth**, b. 22 June 1773.
- iv. **Lillas**, b. 16 April 1775.
- v. **William**, b. 1776, d. 1863; m. **Patience Bucklin** (1767-1841); had at least one child, **Calvin**.
- vi. **James**, b. 16 Feb. 1778.
- 8 vii. **Eseck**, b. 12 April 1780.
- viii. **Thomas**, b. 14 March 1782; d. 18 May 1802, unm.
- ix. **Lucretia**, b. 20 Dec. 1787.

ESECK COLE[8] b. RI 1780; d. 1830. To Otsego Co. with his father in 1793 and lived here all his life. He d. aged 60, before the death of his father. He m. **Nancy Davis** (1784-1864) of RI whose father was an early settler in Otsego Co. He was of Richfield when he made his will 15 Sept. 1838; proved in 1845. In it he named his wife **Nancy** and children (below). **Mathewson** and **Rupel Eddy** of Richfield, executors.
- i. **Syson [Sisson]**.
- 9 ii. **Eseck**.
- iii. **LeRoy**.
- iv. **Abby [Abbie]**, b. 1805, d. 1901; m. **Charles Montague Bowen** (1806-1896).
- v. **Lucinda**.
- vi. **Lovina**.
- vii. **Nancy**, m. --- **Osborn**.
- viii. **Eliza**, m. --- **Green**.
- ix. **Paulina**.
- x. **Lucy**.

ESECK COLE[9], b. on the family farm 24 June 1817, and has always lived upon it, with the exception of 2 1/2 years spent in MI. He lived with his father until he died, and then went to live with his grandfather until his death. At that time the farm came into his possession, and in time he purchased the interests of the other heirs. His mother d. at the home of one of her daus., aged 83. At age 28 Eseck m. **Emeline O. Faulkner** who was b. 23 May 1817, a d/o **Joseph** and **Mary (Reynolds) Faulkner**. They m. 7 March 1816. **Joseph** was from Dutchess Co., NY and his wife from CT. They had two children: **Judson G.** and **Emeline O.** Children of Eseck and Emeline:
- i. **Menzo S.**, d. aged 33 years. A young man of exceedingly bright intellect, and was much given to study, so much so that his intense application unbalanced his mind, and doubtless shortened his life.
- ii. **Mary E.**, res. at home with her parents (1893) and is their help and solace in their declining years. Taught school in Herkimer and Otsego Cos.

[GBW; BR:433-34; *The Descendants of James Cole of Plymouth, 1633* by E. B. Cole, 1908; DAR #133165, 147983 & 157104; DARPI]

COLEMAN, SAMUEL[5] (*Job*[4] *MA, James*[3] *MA, Samuel*[2] *MA, James*[1] *England & MA*), b. [bapt.] Ashburnham, MA 10 Sept. 1769, d. 1857; s/o **Job** of Ipswich & Lunenburg, MA and wife **Elizabeth Martin** who m. 20 Feb. 1766 at Lunenburg. **Elizabeth** was the d/o **John** and **Elizabeth Martin** of Lunenburg and was b. 1744. **Job** was bapt. 11 Oct. 1741 and d. 2 Sept. 1805 in MA. He served as a private from MA in the Revolution. **Samuel** was a pioneer settler in Town of Springfield, Otsego Co. He erected a log cabin near Allen's Lake and returned to MA [CT?] to m. **Abigail [Nabby] Dole**, a cousin of the celebrated **Capt. Lawrence** of the War of 1812 and d/o **Parker Dole** and **Abigail Lawrence** his wife. **Abigail** b. 3 Oct. 1773 Shelburne, d. in Springfield, NY aged 82. **Samuel** d. on the homestead at the age of 90. He was the first president of the county Agricultural Society. It is said that he was a hardy, courageous, efficient pioneer who faced privations and hardships in opening up a farm. Children:

    i.   **Anson**, b. 17 March 1795, Richfield Springs, physician of Rochester; m. 8 Sept. 1819, **Catherine Kimball Rochester** d/o **Nathaniel Rochester**, founder of the City. **Anson** d. 17 July 1837 at Rochester.
    ii.   **Franklin**, farmer.
    iii.   **Homer**, farmer.
    iv.   **Horace**, farmer.
6   v.   **Hamilton**, b. Springfield, NY.
    vi.   **Caroline**.
    vii.   **Nelson**, farmer.
    viii.   **Charles Darwin**, attorney.

HAMILTON COLEMAN[6], taught school for a time and after his marriage purchased a farm joining that of his father and remained there until 1850, when he went to Louisville, KY after selling his farm. Not liking the country, he returned to the Town of Richfield, bought a farm and later became Town Supervisor. He m. **Nancy Sprague**, b. in Warren, Herkimer Co., NY; res. Danube, same county. Her father was a pioneer of that place and he d. about the time of **Nancy's** birth. Her mother later m. **John Kessler** and went to Palmyra, Wayne Co., taking **Nancy** with her. At the age of 12 **Nancy** returned to Springfield to live with her maternal grandmother, **Mary House**, and lived with her until her marriage. **Hamilton** d. Oct. 1886 at Richfield, aged 81; **Nancy** d. in Springfield Sept. 1886. Children:

    i.   **Norman J.**, attorney of New Albany, IN; later of St. Louis where he published a newspaper. Served as Commissioner of Agriculture under President **Cleveland**, the first to hold that office as a cabinet member. Also was Lt. Governor of MO. He m. **Clarissa Harlow Porter**. Their dau. **Laura Kate (Coleman) Liggett**'s obituary appears in NER 96:395. She was a member of the New England Society, b. 1860, d. 1942.
7   ii.   **Lester**.
    iii.   **Sophia**.
    iv.   **Harriet Cornelia**.

LESTER COLEMAN[7], b. Springfield, NY 27 Nov. 1828. After his marriage located in Town of Otsego. His wife was **Marietta Fake**, d/o **Joseph** and **Barbara Fake**. They m. 11 Nov. 1852; she was b. in Springfield. He is described as a "man of irreproachable character, of well-poised mind and unostentatious manner . . ." Children:
- i. **Ella S.**, m. **Sheldon H. Elderkin**; two children, **Jennie M.** and **Mary Elderkin**.
- ii. **Clara**, m. **Norman J. Quaif**.
- iii. **Arthur**, m. **Jennie Bliss**, he is a gardener & seedsman. Children: **Grace, Lester, Floyd** and **Blanche**.
- iv. **Hamilton**, clerk in the Dept. of the Interior, Washington, DC, m. **Gertrude Hines**. One child, **Gertrude**.

[SPR:186; *Boston Transcript* #8151 & 2507; *Ipswich Vital Records; Ashburnham Vital Records; The Early Records of the Town of Lunenburg [MA]; Early Inhabitants of Ipswich, MA*, Hammett; *Shelburne Vital Records*; OB; NEGHR96:395; DARPI; BR:634-5; *Boston Transcript* May 1920, #8151.]

COLEMAN, EDWARD[3] (*Dr. Noah*[2] *MA & NY, Noah*[1] *MA*) farmer, res. of Town Otsego, was b. in Morrisville, Madison Co., NY 30 Jan. 1821. **Dr. Noah Coleman, Edward's** father, served in Continental Army as a surgeon and in 1792 came to New York. **Noah** m. **Polly Tunnicliff**, b. in Warren, Herkimer Co., d/o Major **John Tunnicliff**, of English birth and res. of Exeter, NY; farmer and public house keeper. **Polly** d. at the home of her son **Edward** in her declining rears. **Edward** was about 14 when his parents came to settle in Town of Otsego. **Edward** studied medicine with **Dr. Pomeroy** of Cooperstown and after mar. removed to Morrisville and engaged in the drug business. Subsequently he went to Rochester and kept a hotel until 1833, when he returned to Otsego Co., and located on a part of the old farm that belonged to his father and which he inherited. Children [**Edward** and **Elizabeth** only survivors in 1893.]:
- i. **Noah T.**
- ii. **Maria.**
- iii. **Caroline.**
- iv. **Horatio.**
- 4 v. **Edward.**
- vi. **Asaph.**
- vii. **Elizabeth.** Now [1893] widow of **John H. Coolidge**; res. Minneapolis, MN.

EDWARD COLEMAN[4]'s early education was rec'd. in City of Rochester. He has been a farmer since he began life for himself. In 1853 located on the farm he now [1893] owns in Town of Otsego [although in this source he is named as "Dr. Coleman]. 6 Feb. 1854 he m. **Eliza Burk**, b. Exeter, NY, d/o **James Burk** who was b. in England, and **Maria Freeland**, b. in Harlem, d/o **James Freeland**. **Eliza's** grandmother was **Martha Bush** of Harlem. Children:
- i. **John E.**, m. **Carrie Lewis**.

[BR:811-12]

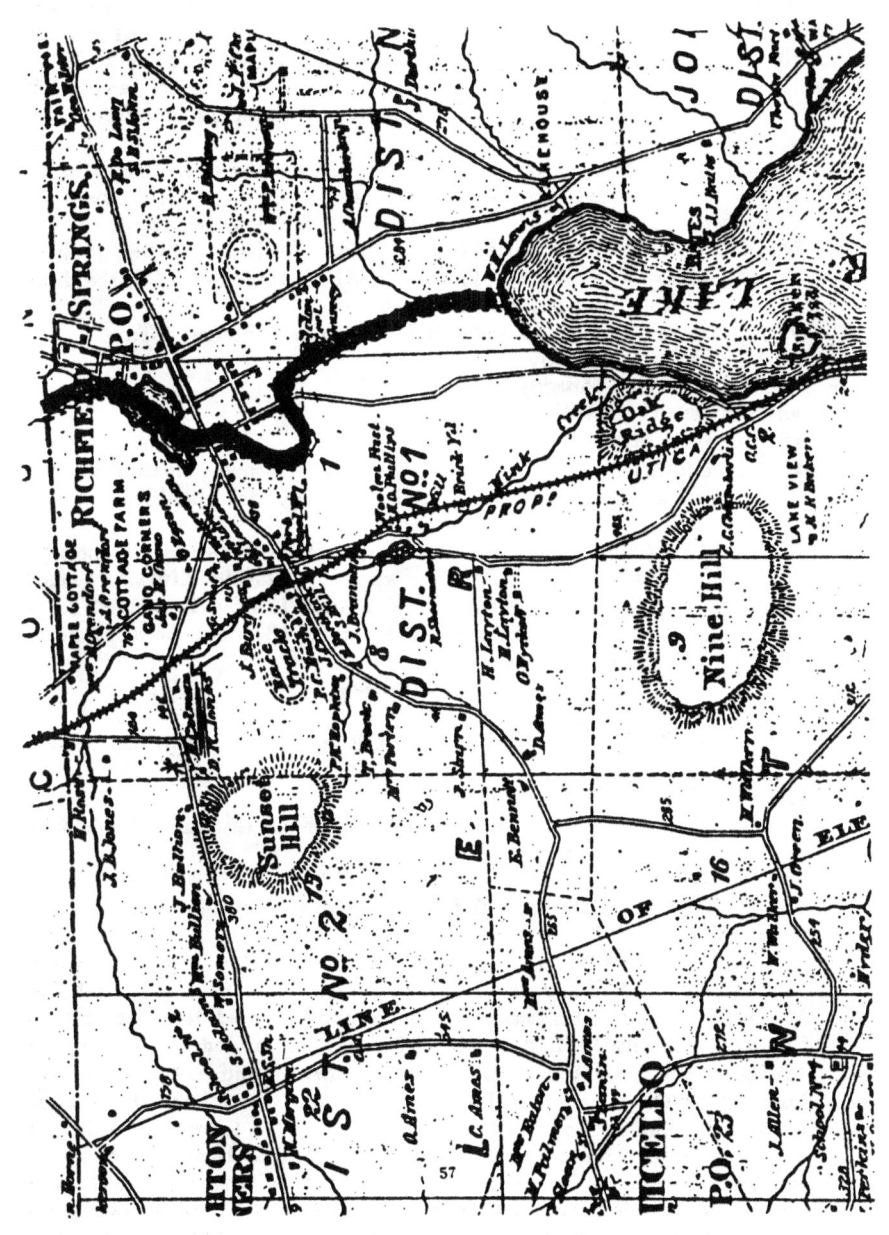

CONE, ZACHARIAH[5] (*Stephen*[4] *CT, Stephen*[3] *CT, Jared*[2] *CT, Daniel*[1] *Scotland & CT*), b. 23 Feb. 1739, East Haddom, CT, d. c. 1802; 3rd s/o **Stephen** (1706-1771) and **Susannah (Clark) Cone** of Bolton, CT who m. 21 Feb. 1723. Zachariah m. **Mary Gilbert**, settled in Hebron, CT. He served in the Revolution. They had 7 sons & 3 daus. Four (first four listed here) of their sons were among the first settlers of Unadilla, all dec'd. by 1878:

	i.	**Samuel**, b. 1766, m. **Susannah Hutchinson**; d. 10 Jan. 1848. Emigrated to GA in an early day, d. Atlanta [Rome, Floyd Co., GA] 10 Jan. 1848.
	ii.	**Caroline**, b. June 1768; m. **Jonathan Peters**; d. 19 Aug. 1853.
	iii.	**Frederick**, b. Dec. 1769 at Bolton, CT; m. **Lucy Williamson**; d. 4 March 1814. He d. New Marlboro, MA 4 March 1814.
	iv.	**Wealthy**, b. 26 April 1772; m. **Linden Hebbard** c. 1798 and they removed to Tioga Co., PA and in 1815 to Unadilla, NY where they both d. He was a farmer.
6	v.	**Zachariah Jr.**, b. 8 March 1774 Andover [Bolton], CT.
	vi.	**Molly**, b. 28 July 1776.
6	vii.	**Adonijah [Adanijah/Nijah]**, b. 1778.
6	viii.	**Daniel [David]**.
6	xi.	**Gardner**.
	x.	**Gilbert**, b. 1786, unm.; d. 15 Feb. 1858; farmer & manufacturer; was a member of the NY State Assembly. Res. Unadilla.

ZACHARIAH CONE JR.[6] settled in Hebron. He m. **Wealthy Kingsbury** 11 April 1804 in Coventry, CT. She was d/o **Nathaniel Kingsbury** and **Aseneth Daggett** and was b. in Andover 24 Oct. 1783, d. Batavia 25 July 1843. Zachariah was a soldier in the War of 1812 and he d. 14 July 1854 Batavia, NY. Children:

	i.	**Mary**, b. 1805; m. **Reuben Rowley**.
	ii.	**Walter**, b. 1807.
	iii.	**Hubbell**, b. 1809; m. **Mary Skilton**. He d. in Chicago before 1878.
	iv.	**Albert Gallatin**, b. 1811.
	v.	**Nathaniel K.**, b. 1813; m. **Adeline Brewer**; res. Valley Forge, PA & AL.
7	vi.	**Salmon Gardner**.
	vii.	**Harriet**, b. 181?, m. **William Phelps**; res. Philadelphia.

SALMON GARDNER CONE[7] b. 6 Aug. 1815, Hebron, CT; d. 19 April 1890, Unadilla, NY; bur. there in Greenwood Cemetery. He m. 1st 26 March 1843 **Mercy Ann Cone**, d/o **Gardner** and **Sarah Cone**. [See below.] She was b. 15 July 1826, d. 1 May 1847. Salmon m. 2nd. in Unadilla on 19 March 1862, **Julia Eleanor Fowler**, d/o **Hiram** and **Sarah (Austin) Fowler**, who was b. 12 April 1842 in Otego and d. 2 June 1921 at Unadilla where she is bur. in the Cone family plot at Evergreen Cemetery. Salmon was an educator who taught at East Hartford, Middle Haddam (1835-40) and was principal of the high school at Sag Harbor, Long Island, NY and later at New Castle, KY. He came to Unadilla in 1843, where he was a businessman and farmer. He was an extensive land owner in IL after the

Civil War. His res. was on the homestead on the Susquehanna River northeast of Village of Unadilla; held many local offices. Children:
  i.   **Sarah Alaska**, b. 21 July 1868, d. 25 Dec. 1943, bur. Deposit NY. She m. in Masonville, NY 11 Jan. 1893, **Clarence Ernest Vail**, s/o **Abraham** and **Elizabeth (McKinley) Vail**. He d. at Deposit & is bur. there.
  ii   **Solomon Fowler**, known as **Monte S.** or **M. S.**, b. Unadilla 12 Jan. 1874, m. in Oneonta 26 Sept. 1865 [1895?], **Bertha McKay** who was b. in Erieville, NY 9 May 1878, the d/o **Thomas** and **Sarah (Kelly) McKay**. They res. Unadilla, he d. there 24 Nov. 1950, she d. 15 Jan. 1939 at Evanston, IL while visiting dau. **Katherine**. Both bur. at family plot in Evergreen Cemetery, Unadilla. Children: **Katherine Sarah, Barbara Fowler** and **Montie Fowler Cone**.

DR. NIJAH [ADONIJAH/ADANIJAH] CONE[6] b. 18 July 1778 Hebron CT; came to Unadilla from CT in 1808 with his wife **Lydia Taylor**, d/o **Noadiah Taylor** and **Lydia Lewis** his wife, b. 16 April 1787 at Middle Haddam. Lydia and Nijah m. 10 April 1805 at Chatham, CT and she is now (1878) aged 91. [She d. 18 Dec. 1881 at Unadilla, NY.] He was a founder of St. Matthew's Episcopal Church and kept a public house; d. there 28 March 1862. Nijah was a noted physician with an extensive practice in Otsego, Chenango and Delaware counties of NY. He d. at Unadilla 28 May 1862. Children:
  i.   **Julia Ann**, b. 1806; m. --- **Bolles**; no issue; she d. 14 Feb. 1868.
7 ii.   **Lewis G.**

LEWIS G. CONE[7], b. Unadilla 27 Jan. 1808; m. **Elizabeth More** d/o **David More** and **Elizabeth Gould**, 21 Oct. 1818. Lewis was a farmer and removed with his father's family to Unadilla in 1810 and res. there until he d. 21 March 1884. Children:
  i.   **Frederick Lewis**, b. 1 Sept. 1853; merchant; unm. and res. in Unadilla.

DANIEL [DAVID] CONE[6], b. 1780 at Hebron, CT; m. 1st **Margaret Hall** of Haddam 10 July 1808, 2d **Hannah Taylor**, sister of **Lydia**, 11 Sept. 1828. Hannah was b. East Hampton, CT 23 Dec. 1799 and d. Middle Haddam 6 Jan. 1894. Daniel was a farmer and manufacturer. He removed to Uandilla in 1810 and held for many years the position of colonel of a regiment of NY Militia. Died 6 July 1842 and his obituary lists him as **Col. Daniel Cone** of Unadilla. GBW gives his name as **David Cone**. He made his will 19 Sept. 1840 and in it named family members. **George H.** and **Charles C. Noble**, witnesses. Child:
  i.   **Harriet**, b. 28 July 1813, m. **Thomas Hanford**; she d. 10 Nov. 1861 in Unadilla. [See Hanford family entry.]

GARDNER CONE[6], b. 6 April 1783 at Hebron, CT; m. **Sarah Ann Robertson** 20 Oct. 1806. She was b. 17 Oct. 1786. They removed to Unadilla in 1810 and both d. there; farmer. Child:

i. **Mercy A.**, b. 15 July 1824; m. **Salmon G. Cone**. She d. 1 May 1846; no issue. **Salmon** m. 2d **Julia E. Fowler** and he d. April 1890. **Salmon** was the s/o **Zachariah Cone** and wife **Wealthy Kingsbury** above. **Salmon** and 2nd wife **Julia** had children: [1]**Sarah Alaska Cone**; [2]**Solomon Fowler Cone** [known as **Montie S.** or **M.S.**]. [See above under **Salmon Gardner Cone**[7].]
[A:334, 351; UNA:89; OB; CUT1:2:739; DARPI. NOTE: The LDS Ancestral File has extensive data on this family before they came to Otsego Co., NY; *Some Account of the Cone Family in America* ... by William W. Cone, Topeka, KS, 1902; *Faulk-Cone & Allied Families* ... by Eleanor Faulk Cone, Gateway Press, Inc., 1983.]

COOK[E], CONSTANT[5] *(Joseph*[4] *RI, Joseph*[3] *RI, John*[2] *alias Butcher of England & RI, Thomas*[1] *alias Butcher (Bowcher) of England & RI)*, s/o **Joseph Cook** and wife **Hannah Peabody**, was b. 16 day, 4th month [June] 1724 at Newport, RI, d. c. 1800 at Springfield, NY. He m. at Dartmouth 12 April 1750, **Isabel Devol**, d/o **Joseph** and **Margaret (Potter) Devol**. **Isabel** was living in 1790 when she was named in the Bristol Co. will of her sister **Hannah Russell**. In 1746/7 **Constant** inherited from his grandfather the half òf the 19th Great Lot in Pocasset Purchase which would have been his father's had he lived; his uncle **William Cook** inherited the other half. 17 Nov. 1747 **Constant Cook**, of Newport, glazier, sold this land. He probably spent most of his early life in Newport and learned the trade of glazier from his step-father, **John Forrester**. On 4 Nov. 1754 **Constant** and family were given a certificate to remove from Newport to Middletown, RI. It is not clear where the family res. between 1758 and 1773, when he was of Dartmouth, but after the Revolution he removed to Springfield, Otsego Co. Most of his desc. spell the family name as **Cooke**. Children:

 i. **Joseph Russell**, b. c. 1751; m. **Mary Elliott**.
 ii. **Hannah**, b. c. 1753; m. **Benjamin Sawdy**.
 iii. **Thomas**, b. c. 1755; m. **Sarah Mitchell**.
 iv. **Benjamin**, b. c. 1757; family tradition claims that he went to sea and later settled in Bristol, England where he died. He may be the **Benjamin Cook** who enlisted 24 April 1777 and sailed from RI on the ship *Columbus*. A **Benjamin Cook** served in 1778 under **Capt. Hoysteed Hacker** of the sloop *Providence*.
 v. **Molly**, b. c. 1759; d. near Rochester, NY. She could be the **Mercy Cook** whose intentions of mar. with **Elisha Parker Jr.** of Freetown, both of them of Dartmouth, were published 17 Aug. 1778.
 vi. **Charles**, b. c. 1761, d. young.
 vii. **Philip**, b. 5 Nov. 1763; m. **Clarissa Hatch**.
6 viii. **Peabody**, b. c. 1767.
6 ix. **Abner**.
 x. **Paul**, b. 17 Oct. 1771; m. **Jerusha Hatch**.

PEABODY COOK of Springfield made his will 7 Dec. 1846; proved in 1849. In it he named his wife **Mary (Picard)** and children:
 i. **Nelson**.

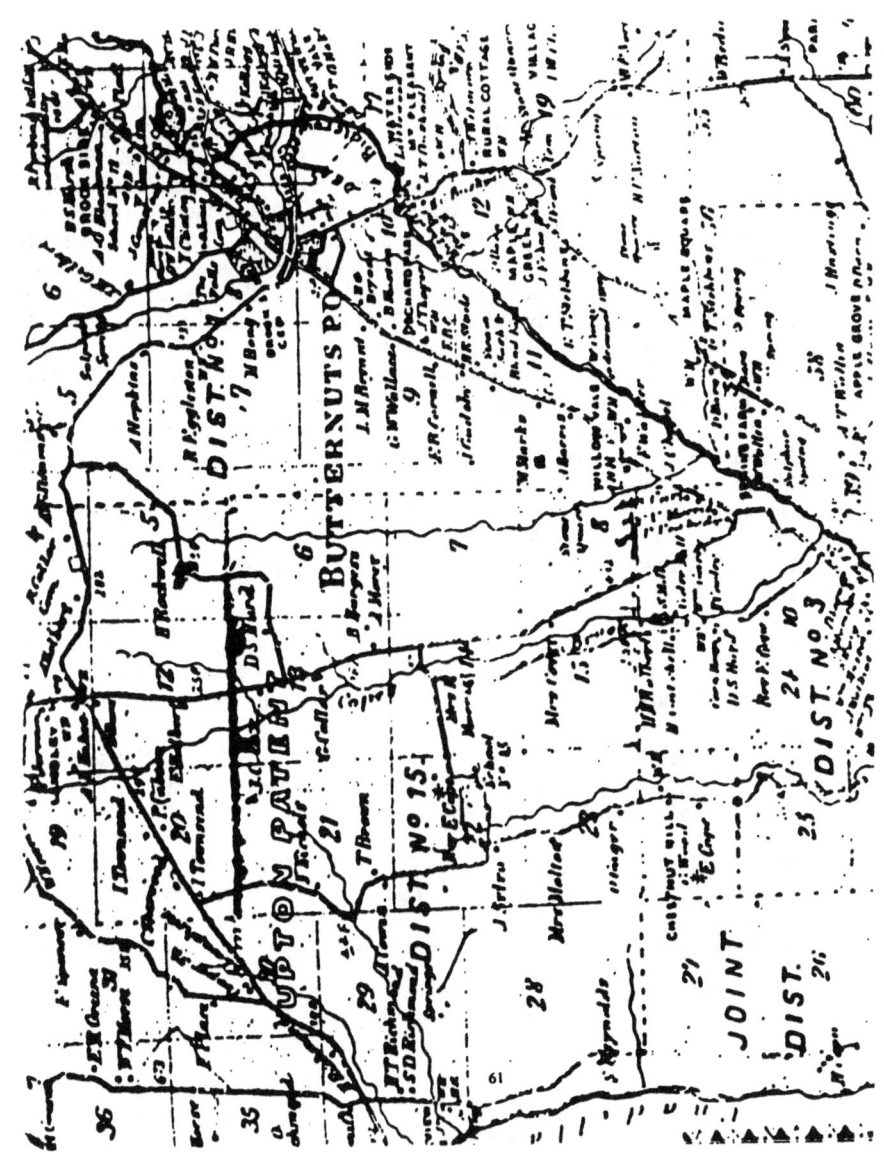

ii.	Ann M., m. William C. Stewart.
iii.	Clarissa, m. Joseph Herkimer.
iv.	Lucy, m. --- Wilcox.
v.	Susan, m. --- Monk.
vi.	Phebe, m. Henry Conklin.
vii.	Mary, m. --- Conine.
viii.	Elizabeth, m. Joseph Elwood.

ABNER COOK[6], b. Dartmouth, MA 6 Oct. 1768/69, settled in the northern part of the present town of Springfield, Otsego Co. in 1788; he the first in the family to visit Springfield to look for a place to settle. After a few years (1800) he moved to the farm on the turnpike later occupied by **Thomas Cook**, which he purchased from **John Kelly**. **Abner** was the first "pettifogger" in the town. It is said that he possessed a quick perception, coupled with sound judgment and indomitable will which caused him to be sought ofter by the early litigants. **Abner** was granted a license to sell sprits in Springfield, renting the tavern of **Paul Keyes** from Nov. of that year. He m. **Susanna Mattison** at White Creek, NY 22 Jan. 1789. She was b. 3 Feb. 1771 at Shaftsbury, VT & d. East Springfield 16 July 1841, aged 70 y, 5 m, 13 d. She was the d/o **Thomas** and **Susanna (Doolittle) Mattison** of VT. **Abner** d. on the homestead farm in East Springfield 18 March 1853. Both are bur. at the General Cemetery at Springfield Center, NY, to which their graves were moved from their homestead farm cemetery. Children all b. Springfield:

	i.	**Susanna**, b. 26 Nov. 1790; m. **Rufus Conant**.
7	ii.	**John**.
	iii.	**Ira**, b. 15 Aug. 1794, d. 8 July 1796.
	iv.	**Paul**, b. 28 Sept. 1796, d. 12 Aug. 1875, unm. He and brother **Daniel** kept the **Cooke Tavern**, succeeding their father.
	v.	**Thomas**, b. 2 Oct. 1798; m. **Catherine Chawgo**.
7	vi.	**Abner**.
	vii.	**Daniel**, b. 22 March 1802, d. 21 March 1877; unm. His death is recorded in Springfield Presbyterian Church records.
	viii.	**Daughter**, b. & d. 14 Nov. 1803.

JOHN COOK[7] b. 9 Oct. 1791; m. 1st **Mary Ann Riley** who d. c. 1823 and left six children. **John** m. 2nd c. 1825 **Clara Genter**. He d. c. 1841. **Clara** m. 2nd c. 1844 **David Stocker**. "C. 1846 the children became separated and scattered, seeking labor and homes elsewhere." Children:

i.	**David**.
ii.	**Mary Ann**.
iii.	**Amanda**.
iv.	**Susan**.
v.	**Isaiah**, b. 1839; m. 4 July 1860 **Lovina Brown** of Albany, NY and had one son, **John**. **Isaiah** took up farm labor, c. 1857 began work as a carpenter/joiner.

ABNER COOK JR.[7] was a prominent and influential citizen of Cooperstown, was elected clerk of the county in 1829. He later moved to

New York (1837-1840) and entered the practice of law; later still removed to TX and was chosen chief justice of the state. He m. at Cooperstown 21 Sept. 1830 **Catherine Hamilton Nichols**, d/o **William** and **Catherine Hamilton (Wood) Nichols**, who was b. 1812 at Cooperstown and d. 28 Oct. 1848 at Houston, TX in the same yellow fever epidemic which killed her husband; he d. 12 April 1849 at Houston. Children:

    i.   **William Nichols**, b. 7 Sept. 1831 at Cooperstown, d. 20 March 1885, Galveston, TX.
    ii.   **Catherine Cornelia**, b. 17 Jan. 1834; m. **Col. Thomas Wentworth Pierce**.
    iii.   **Augustus Paul**, b. 10 Feb. 1836; m. 1st **Frances Rebecca Bryam**, m. 2nd **Maria Kemp**.
    iv.   **Henry**, b. March 1838 at Cooperstown; d. 5 March 1840 NY City.
    v.   **James Hamilton**, b. 7 June 1841; m. **Sarah M. Branch**.
    vi.   **Anna**, b. June 1843; m. **James M. Thompson**.
    vii.   **Martha Frances**, b. Jan. 1848 at Houston, TX; d. 1860 Danbury, CT.

[SPR:8, 18, 193; *Thomas Cooke of Rhode Island, Vol. 1*, Jane Fletcher Fiske, 1987; A:332; GBM]

COPE, JOHN[1] came from England c. 1800 and with his wife and two children settled in New Lisbon, Otsego Co., in the Butternut Creek Valley. He lost his property in the financial reverses which followed the War of 1812. Children:

    i.   **John**, b. in England. Res. Unadilla and later removed to Mailpit House, Parish of Abbot Bromley, Co. Stratford, England. Made his will 17 July 1811; proved 11 Oct. 1813. It it he named his wife **Judith** of Unadilla and his brothers **Edward** and **Richard Cope**, both of England.
    ii.   **Mary**, b. in England.
    iii.   **Thomas**, first child b. in America.
    iv.   **Richard**.
2   v.   **Edward**.
    vi.   **Sophia**.
    vii.   **Elizabeth**.
    viii.   **Benjamin**.

EDWARD COPE[2] b. in New Lisbon 25 May 1806, was thrown upon his own resources at a young age due to his father's financial reverses. At age 16 he entered employ of firm of **H. & E. Phinney**, book publishers of Cooperstown as a salesman. He attended the Presbyterian Church and entered the study of the ministry in Gilbertsville, making his home with his sister (**Mrs. Zenas Washbon**) in Maple Grove. He later traveled to KY & TN furthering his studies. He was ordained at Clinton and m. 29 Sept. 1836 in Marshall, Oneida Co., NY to **Emily Kilbourne**, and soon sailed with his wife from Boston to Madras, India. **Emily** was the oldest dau. of **Thomas** and **Mary (Ballard) Kilbourne**. She was b. in 1808, and still living in 1893. They remained in India till 1849, when they returned to set up a home near Gilbertsville, NY. **Edward** d. there 10 May 1884. He preached for a time at the Presbyterian Church at North Guiford, Chenango Co., NY and other local churches. Their only child:

3   i.   **Thomas Kilbourne.**

THOMAS K. COPE^3, b. Burma, Asia [Madura, Southern India] 3 Sept. 1837; m. 25 May 1865 **Helen Eliza Botsford**, who was b. Butternuts 2 July 1837. [See Botsford family entry.] She d. 6 April 1878, aged 41 & left four children. **Thomas** was a nurseryman, a successful grower of small fruits, probably the first person in the town of Butternuts to raise strawberries. Children, b. Gilbertsville, all res. there in 1892:

   i.   **Emma Ballard**, b. 11 Jan. 1867.
   ii.   **E. Chalmers Botsford**, b. 28 June 1868.
   iii.   **Allen Wood**, b. 8 April 1873.
   iv.   **Walter Russell Rockwell**, b. 26 March 1878.

19 Dec. 1878 **Thomas K.** m. 2nd **Anne M. Quincy**, who d. 5 May 1888, aged 38. His 3rd wife was **Belle Morgan** of Elmira, where they were mar. 18 Nov. 1891.

[*A Genealogy of the Families of John Rockwell, of Stamford, Conn. 1641* ... by James Boughton, 1903; BR:424-3; GH:58; GBW]

CRANDALL, HENRY FRANCIS^5 (*Joseph*^{4} *of RI, Joseph*^{3} *of RI, Eber*^{2} *of RI, John*^{1} *of England & RI*) b. c. 1774 in Westerly or Hopkinton, RI, d. West Edmeston, NY 19 April 1859, s/o **Joseph Crandall** and his first wife **Esther Hall**. Henry m. **Polly Dennison** c. 1795. She was b. in Stonington, CT 1778, d. West Edmeston 17 March 1884. She was the d/o **George** and **Bethiah (Crandall) Dennison**. **Henry** came to Brookfield, NY in 1798 or 1799. Children, all b. Brookfield except **Polly Maria**, b. CT:

   i.   **Polly Maria**, b. 11 Oct. 1795.
6 ii.   **Henry Denison.**
   iii.   **Daniel Stanton**, b. 31 Aug. 1801; res. Clearmont, IA & d. in Pleasant Valley, IA, suicide by hanging. He m. **Polly Webb** who was b. in Villanova, NY 30 May 1801, d. 9 June 1896. They had several children, all b. IA.
   iv.   **Lurana Bethiah**, b. 17 May, 1804; d. 21 July 1884. She m. in 1827 **Marquis Alvah Welch** who was b. in Brookfield, NY 31 Oct. 1801; d. 30 Dec. 1890 s/o **Charles** and **Betsey (Butters) Welch**. Their children all b. in W. Edmeston. [See Welch family entry.]
6 v.   **Joseph Hiram.**
6 vi.   **William Riley.**
   vii.   **Esther S.**, b. 1 Nov. 1808; d. 14 Oct. 1859, unm.; bur. Edmeston.
6 viii. **George Van Renssalaer**, b. 15 Feb. 1812.
6 xi.   **Avery Clinton**, b. 1815.
   xii.   **Francis E.**, b. 25 June 1816.

HENRY DENISON CRANDALL^6 [P], b. Brookfield 17 April 1800, 1822 to Chautauqua Co., NY; 1823 back to Madison Co.; farmer. 9 Sept. 1824 he m. as his first wife **Prudence Clark** of Brookfield, b. 1796, d/o **Luke Clark**; d. 25 Nov. 1833. They had two children; both d. in infancy. He

m. 2nd **Phebe Dye** [P] of Brookfield 7 Dec. 1865; she b. 1796, d. 1865. They had five children, one living in 1878. The family experienced a brutal robbery; **Phebe** was killed and **Henry** left for dead after being shot two times. His 3rd wife was **Marian Elnora Manning** [P], m. 4 March 1867 in Utica; she b. 1841, d. 3 June 1925. Res. at Leonardsville 1867-1874, then to Edmeston, Otsego Co. Members of the Seventh-Day Baptist church at West Edmeston. **Henry** d. 14 June 1884. Children, 1st mar.:

   i.   **Louisa Prudence**, b. West Edmeston 24 July 1825; d. 28 Feb. 1861. She m. there 21 Feb. 1846 to **Russell C. Chase**, b. Pittsfield, NY 12 Feb. 1827; d. 12 April 1877, s/o **Buffum and Jemima (Chase) Chase**. [See Chase family entry.]

   ii.   **Henry Clark**, b. 19 May 1827; d. 22 Sept. 1828.

7   iii.   **Truman**.

   iv.   **Freeman**, b. 19 April 1831; d. 31 Dec. 1833.

   v.   **Nancy Maria**, b. 1833; d. 21 Nov. 1833, aged 8 mos.

Children of 2nd mar.:

   vi.   **Henry Denison Jr.**, b. 19 Oct. 1868. His dau. **Sarita Crandall** res. in MT.

   vii.   **Marian Elnora**, b. 26 Nov. 1869; m. 5 Sept. 1889 **George W. Maxson**, b. 1861 s/o **Daniel and Louisa (Tellvie) Maxson**. [See Maxson family entry.]

   viii. **Louisa Jane**, twin to **Marian E.**, b. 26 Nov. 1869; d. 18 May 1893.

   ix.   **Byron Manning**, 23 Aug. 1871; d. Norwich, NY 13 Oct. 1943. He m. 16 Oct. 1890 **Hattie Chapman**, b. Fly Creek 8 Jan. 1878. Children all b. Norwich.

   x.   **Carrie [Clara] Phebe**, b. West Edmeston 23 June 1876; m. at Utica 2 Jan. 1896 **Jay W. Jenkins**; res. Illion, NY and had two children, **Jay Stewart** and **Allen Carroll Jenkins**.

TRUMAN CRANDALL[7], b. Edmeston 4 March 1828; m. Plainfield, NY 31 March 1850 **Mary Dye**, b. Brookfield 14 Sept. 1832, d/o **Samuel and Eliza (Prosser) Dye**. Children:

   i.   **Henry T.**, b. 16 Nov. 1853; d. 18 July 1865.

   ii.   **William B.**, b. 5 June 1856; d. 30 July 1865.

   iii.   **Samuel D.**, b. 20 Nov. 1857; d. 24 July 1865.

   iv.   **Lewis J.**, b. June 1859; d. 5 Aug. 1865.

   v.   **Eliza M.**, b. 16 April 1867; m. 15 June 1885 at New Lisbon, **Almeron Page** b. 25 July 1860, s/o **Stephen Page**; no issue.

[NOTE: This source does not explain the deaths of so many children in 1865.]

JOSEPH HIRAM CRANDALL[6], twin to **Lurana**. He m. **Melinda Clark** d/o **Jonathan**, and had children, all b. Brookfield:

   i.   **Almira**, m. **James Saunders** and had a son, **Dell**.

   ii.   **Joseph (Rosy Top)**.

   iii.   **Polly Marie**, m. **Charles Lye**, res. Leonardsville, NY.

   iv.   **Esther**.

   v.   **Charles W.**

vi. William.

WILLIAM RILEY CRANDALL[6] b. in Brookfield, NY 1806; d. in Eaton, NY in 1836; res. Edmeston. He m. **Maria Clark** who d. in Walworth, WI. Child:
i. William Henry, b. Edmeston [Leonardsville] 16 March 1834; d. Kalworth, WI 5 Jan. 1910; m. 21 Oct. 1858 **Martha L. Green**, b. Mexico, NY 25 July 1842; d. Walworth 12 Aug. 1900, d/o **Horace D. and Lois (Johnson) Green**. Had several children.

GEORGE VAN RENSSELAER CRANDALL[6] b. Brookfield 15 Feb. 1812; d. W. Edmeston 29 Dec. 1894. He m. 1st 10 Jan. 1835 **Sarah Burdick** who was b. in Leonardsville, NY 27 May 1812; d. 26 Dec. 1853 also in Leonardsville, d/o **Jacob** and **Sarah (West) Burdick**. George m. 2nd Mrs. **Mary Caroline Burdick** 15 May 1872 at W. Edmeston, she was b. 26 March 1848, d. 16 Nov. 1928. Children of 1st mar., all b. West Edmeston:
i. Francis O.
ii. George VanRensselaer Jr., b. 23 Feb. 1836; d. 25 May 1837.
iii. Dolly Ann, b. 17 April 1838; d. 21 Jan. 1842.
iv. Loren Burdick.
v. Henry Duane.
Child of 2nd mar.:
vi. Jennie May, b. June 1879; m. **Fred Lynn Coman**, res. Leonardsville. No issue.

AVERY CLINTON CRANDALL[6] b. Brookfield 1815; d. West Edmeston 2 March 1894; m. **Mercy Rogers** who was b. 1809 and d. in East Edmeston 9 Oct. 1892. Children:
i. Eliza, b. 1847; m. **Samuel M. Miller** 1878; he was s/o **Chester and Adelia Miller**. They had **Alice, Chester** and **Eliza C. Miller**.
ii. Charles L., b. 1850; d. 1 Jan. 1906, unm. Res. Plainville, NY.
iii. Flora L., b. 7 June 1856; d. 10 Nov. 1904; m. **Levi C. Cutler** in 1876, b. 7 Jan. 1853, s/o **Levi** and **Nancy (Miller) Cutler**. They had **Leslie, Llewellyn** and **Leo Cutler**.

[*Denison Genealogy, Ancestors & Descendants of Captain George Denison*, E. Glenn Denison (Baltimore: Gateway Press, Inc., 1982); A:144a; *Elder John Crandall of Rhode Island and His Descendants* by John C. Crandall, 1949; *Genealogical & Family History of Western NY* by William R. Cutter, 1912 follows other branches of this family descended from the immigrant ancestor.]

CRANSTON, JOHN[6] (*Samuel*[5] *RI & NY, Peleg*[4] *MA & RI, Thomas*[3] *RI & MA, Gov. Samuel*[2] *RI, Gov. John*[1] *SCOTLAND & RI*) b. Foster, RI 5 Feb. 1783, d. at Unadilla, NY 1 June 1848. He m. at Cranston, RI 10 June 1804 **Hannah Clemmons**, b. at Cranston 8 July 1784, d. at Unadilla. She was d/o **John Clemmons**. The family removed to Unadilla prior to 1811 and John made his will there 15 May 1848, probated the same year. In it he named his wife and living children. Children, all b. Unadilla:
i. Phoebe Ann, b. 7 July 1804; d. Unadilla 11 Feb. 1831; m. 27 Aug. 1829 **Samuel Ward**.

7	ii.	**Barzillai K.**, b. 18 June 1806.
	iii.	**Elizabeth**, b. 4 Sept. 1845; m. 1st 29 May 1831 **Uriel Sisson**; m. 2nd 4 Sept. 1845 **Henry Wilsey**.
7	iv.	**George Clemmons**, b. 25 Jan. 1810.
	v.	**Peleg**, b. 27 Jan. 1812; d. unm. 26 Aug. 1831.
7	vi.	**John Clemmons**, b. 14 July 1814.
	vii.	**Hannah Thedasia**, b. 17 May 1816; m. 27 Aug. 1844 **George W. Thomas**.
	viii.	**Sarah A.**, b. 10 July 1818; d. unm. 17 Oct. 1849.
	ix.	**Zilpha Maria**, b. 20 Nov. 1820; m. 10 June 1839 **Enoch Thomas**.
	x.	**Julia Lambert**, b. 5 Dec. 1822; m. 12 May 1839 **Daniel Thomas**.
7	xi.	**William**, b. 24 April 1825.
7	xii.	**Samuel J.**, b. 27 Feb. 1827.
	xiii.	**Isah**, b. 19 Dec. 1830; d. same day.

BARZILLAI K. CRANSTON[7] was a traveling salesman, b. at Unadilla, d. Painesville, OH 21 July 1868. He m. at Geneva, OH 10 April 1831 **Eliza Maltby**, b. Norfolk, CT 25 May 1811, d. at Painesville in 1890. She was d/o **Jacob Maltby**. They had one child, **George Maltby Cranston**, b. Lockport, PA 14 Oct. 1850.

GEORGE CLEMMONS CRANSTON[7] d. at South Bend, IN 5 Aug. 1874. He m. at Unionville, OH 5 Feb. 1835 **Almira Maltby**, b. Unionville 13 Aug. 1809, d. at Painesville 6 Sept. 1855. Sister of his bro. **Barzillai's** wife. Farmer and dealer in nursery stock. The family res. Sheridan and Unadilla, NY, Painesville, OH and Lockport, PA. Several children.

JOHN CLEMMONS CRANSTON[7] of Sheridan, NY was a farmer who d. at that place 10 Oct. 1876. He m. there to **Melissa Newell** on 13 Feb. 1839. He removed to that town in early life and served as town supervisor and justice of the peace. Several children.

WILLIAM CRANSTON[7] m. 6 July 1849 **Sally Davis** who was b. 8 June 1832, d. 13 July 1897. Children:
	i.	**Betsey**, b. 6 Aug. 1851; d. 10 April 1923; m. 3 July 1873 **Winfield Pierce**.
	ii.	**Helen**, b. 18 May 1853; d. 1 Aug. 1882; m. May 1873 **Howard Merrill** and had one child, **Myron**, b. 1876.
	iii.	**Myron**, b. 1855; d. 20 Aug. 1883, unm.
	iv.	**William**, b. 1857; d. 4 Aug. 1907; m. 1893 **Florence Small**. Several children.
	v.	**Janet**, b. 1861, d. 13 Feb. 1873.
	vi.	**Mary**, b. 12 May 1867; m. 1 Oct. 1892 **Ameail M. Cross**; res. Oneonta.
	vii.	**George**, b. 15 Nov. 1869; m. 25 Nov. 1894 **Mary Quigley**. Res. Schenectady; one son, [not named here] b. 1897, d. 1917.

SAMUEL J. CRANSTON[7] d. at Fredonia, NY after 22 Aug. 1897. He m. 1st at Tompkins, NY 16 Nov. 1847 **Sarah Avery**, b. in Tioga Co., PA in

1837, d. near Jamestown, NY in 1884, d/o **Samuel** and **Clusey Avery**. He m. 2nd in Boston, MA 26 Sept. 1885, **Sarah E. Gardner**, b. in Boston in 1840, d/o **Robert R.** and **Sarah Gardner**. He was a paint salesman and in later life a farmer. He res. in various places in NY state. Children:

i.	**Elizabeth R.**, b. Chautauqua Co., NY 26 Jan. 1850.
ii.	**Jeremiah M.**, b. Unadilla, NY 2 July 1851; m. **Eva M. Wheeler**.
iii.	**John C.**, b. Unadilla 27 Sept. 1853; d. at Fredonia, NY 10 March 1881; m. **Eva Ellis**.
iv.	**Hannah Jane**, b. Delaware Co., NY 15 Feb. 1855.
v.	**Albert D.**, b. Deposit, Broome Co., NY 2 Dec. 1856.
vi.	**Mary L.**, b. 3 Nov. 1858 in Delaware Co., as were her later born siblings.
vii.	**Anne C.**, b. 17 April 1862.
viii.	**Mayo A.**, b. 13 Nov. 1864.
xi.	**Sarah M.**, b. 20 March 1867.

["Descendants of Gov. John Cranston of Rhode Island" in NEGHR Vols. 79-80, 1925; GBW]

CRUTTENDEN [CRITTENDEN], JEREMIAH[7] *(Hopestill*[6]*, Hopestill*[5]*, Daniel*[4] *CT, Abraham*[3] *CT, Abraham*[2] *CT, Abraham*[1] *England/CT)* b. in New Haven, CT 19 Aug. 1767, a s/o **Hopestill Cruttendon** who was b. 11 Sept. 1741 & d. in 1775; a physician at New Haven and at his death left four small children [**Jeremiah, Sally, Hopestill** and **Abigail**]. Jeremiah m. **Mary Brooks** 24 Dec. 1787 and they traveled to Otsego Co. on horseback. Opened a hotel in the then new village of Morris. He was a blacksmith by trade, "and a jolly, stirring business man." He d. in the village of Morris on 2 Dec. 1859. **Mary** was b. 20 Sept. 1768 and d. 22 Sept. 1836. They are both bur. at Morris. She was d/o **Benjamin** and **Thankful (Hickox) Brooks**. They had eight children; 2nd two children bapt. at Cooperstown 14 May 1797:

	i.	**Harvey**.
	ii.	**Mary**.
8	iii.	**Lyman**, b. 15 July 1793; m. at Louisville, Butternuts on 19 March 1821 to **Harriet Noble** of New Lisbon.
	iv.	**Julia**, b. 3 Sept. 1796.
	v.	**William Hubbard**, b. 4 Feb. 1801, bapt. 19 July 1802.
	vi.	**[Sarah] Sally Maria**, b. 22 May 1805, bapt. 14 July 1805.
	vii.	**Hannah**, b. 25 Jan. 1809, bapt. 20 Aug. 1809.
8	viii.	**Hopestill**, b. 20 May and bapt. 24 May 1812.

LYMAN CRUTTENDEN[8] removed to the Bowley District of Steuben Co., NY and the history of that area gives his birthdate as 13 Aug. 1793. He was a blacksmith and m. **Harriet Noble** in Bath, NY. She was b. in Nov. 1798. Lyman d. 5 Dec. 1872, aged 79; **Harriet** d. 28 July 1874, aged 75 y, 8 m. Children:

i. **Alexis H.**, b. in Morris, Otsego Co. 22 Feb. 1822; to Bath, NY in 1856; physician. He d. there c. 1897. In early life he m. **Julia M. Stephenson**, they had four children. He had attended high school in Albany and later grad. at a medical college in NY City. While in Bath he held the office of coroner, was a pension examiner for

	c. 25 years, and a member of the Pension Board from its organization. His parents res. with him until their deaths.
ii.	**Mary**, m. --- **Himrod** from Senaca Co. Went west and settled in Oakland, CA, where she d.
iii.	**Agnes**, m. --- **Clapp**; went west.
iv.	**Edward**, studied for the Episcopal ministry at Unadilla, NY; while thus engaged he was taken ill & died.
v.	**Sarah**, res. at Lake Salubria (at home) and cared for her parents.
vi.	**Lyman, Jr.**, clerked at a store on Broadway in NY City; later to FL to invest in an orange grove where he contracted yellow fever and d. there. Unm.

HOPESTILL CRUTTENDEN[8] was b. in the Town of Butternuts (now Morris) 20 May 1810. He m. 22 Oct. 1835 to **Casandana Noble** who was b. 3 Dec. 1821 at New Lisbon (Noblesville). **Hopestill** d. on his homestead in 1875. In 1876 **Casandana** removed to Chippewa Falls, WI. She was a d/o **Martin Noble** and **Abigail Lane** [See Noble family entry.] **Hopestill** and his wife had nine children:

	i.	**Annotte**.
	ii.	**Ellen**.
	iii.	**Albert**.
	iv.	**Evoline**.
	v.	**Mary**, dec'd. by 1893.
9	vi.	**Lee B**.
	vii.	**Edway N.**, dec'd. by 1893.
	viii.	**Mary G**.
	ix.	**Henry L**.

LEE B. CRUTTENDEN[9] was b. in town of Morris 14 Jan. 1848. At age 18 he clerked in a general store at Hammondsport, after five years he removed to Wellsboro, PA & clerked two months, after which he started for WI where he was in charge of the dry goods dept. of a large department store. In Jan. 1873 he returned to Morris, NY to take charge of his brother-in-law's hardware store at that plce. After one year he removed to Cooperstown and took position in the County Clerk office until 1881. He was mar. 2 Sept. 1827 to **Elle Bowne** who was b. in Morris, a d/o **Charles A.** and **Mary C. Bowne**. Members of the Episcopal Church. Children:

i.	**Harry Lee**.
ii.	**Mary C**.
iii.	**Lizzie K**.

[NASH1; GBM; GH1:56; BR:231-2; *Family of Ancestors of New Haven, CT* by Jacobus, p. 464; *Early Families of Guilford, CT* by A. Talcott; *A History of the Bowlby District* [Steuben Co., NY] by Idah M. W. VanHousen, 1949]

CUMMINGS, MOSES[1], b. NH, farmer in humble circumstances, who d. early in life, leaving one child, **Elias**[2]. Moses' widow [not named in BR, but the IGI gives her name as "Patty"] m. as her 2nd husband **Solomon Davis**, by whom she had several children. They came to Otsego Co. when **Elias**[2] was a small boy.

M. D. Cummings   Harriet Cummings

RESIDENCE OF M.D.CUMMINGS, GARRATTSVILLE, OTSEGO COUNTY, N.Y.

ELIAS CUMMINGS² b. 26 Dec. 1780 in NH [Newport Twp., Sullivan Co.], d. 31 March 1858 in New Lisbon, NY; farmer. On 4 Dec. 1803 he m. **Lucinda Church**, b. 4 Dec. 1803 [13 Aug. 1784] at NH; d. 13 July 1857. Elias served as Justice of the Peace & held other offices. Universalist church goers. Their surviving children who res. in Otsego Co.:
    i.   **Leman [Lemon]** of New Lisbon (in 1893 aged 89).
    ii.   **Harris** of Plainfield.
3 iii. **Moses D.**

MOSES D. CUMMINGS³ b. Garratsville [New Lisbon] 8 July 1807, res. in the Village of New Lisbon, retired merchant and farmer in 1878. At age 24 he was engaged in the dry goods business. At some point he was injured and his health remained poor. 30 Sept. 1835 he m. **Harriet** d/o **Austin Smith**; "an example of high moral worth and true womanhood to all who knew her, she was obliged to leave her husband in his declining years," she d. 29 Aug. 1877. **Austin Smith** was a blacksmith in the same town. Her brothers were **Collins G. Smith** of Norwich, now (1893) aged 76; **Reuben M. Smith**, proprietor of the St. James House in Utica, now aged 60. **Harriet** d. 29 Aug. 1877, aged 69 and she was bur. in Butternuts Valley Cemetery. They were Universalists. Children:
    i.   **Moses Vanness**, b. 19 Nov. 1844; d. 25 May 1845.
    ii.   **Theresa**, b. 21 Aug. 1848; d. 20 June 1853.
[A:220, 223; GH1:58; BR:663-64]

DE FOREST, GIDEON⁶ (*Joseph⁵, Samuel⁴, David³ of NY & CT, Isaac² of Holland & New Amsterdam, Jesse¹ of Holland & New Amsterdam*), b. 14 Sept. 1765, s/o **Joseph DeForest** and **Susanna Mills** his wife. Gideon m. c. 1794 **Hannah Birdseye [Birdsey]**, and c. 1795 settled in Otsego Co. He and three of his brothers, **Samuel, Abel** and **Mills**, served in the Revolutionary War. **Gideon** was counted in the 1840 census in Edmeston, aged 75 at that time; he d. 9 Dec. 1840. Children:
    i.   **Abel Birdseye**, b. 30 Dec. 1795.
    ii.   **Lee**, b. 7 Aug. 1798.
    iii. **Sally**, b. 9 March 1800; m. **Alonzo S. Campbell** of Columbus, OH.
    iv. **Cyrus Hawley**, b. 30 March 1804; d. 7 March 1888. Res. in Buffalo.
    v.   **Maria**, b. 20 July 1806; m. **Rev. Henry Snyder**.
    vi. **Charles Augustus**, b. 25 Oct. 1808; res. in Albany.
    vii. **Tracy Robinson**, b. 2 Feb. 1811, of Cleveland, OH.
    viii. **Harriet**, b. 28 July 1813; m. **Thomas A. Fuller**.
[CUT1:VI:421 This source also gives the lineage of **Thomas A. Fuller**, husband of **Harriet DeForest**. **Thomas** was a res. of Columbus, Chenango Co., b. 6 Sept. 1812; d. at Sherburne, NY in 1875. He was s/o **Elijah Fuller** and **Ruth Robinson** his wife. *Genealogical Notes of New York & New England Families* by S. V. Talcott, 1883, p. 429 gives the bible record of the family of **Jesse DeForest** (b. 1692) and wife **Nelletje Quackenbush**.

For early DeForest family see *DeForests of Avesnes and of New Netherland 1900; Lockwood deForest and His Forebears*, 1914, 2 vols.]

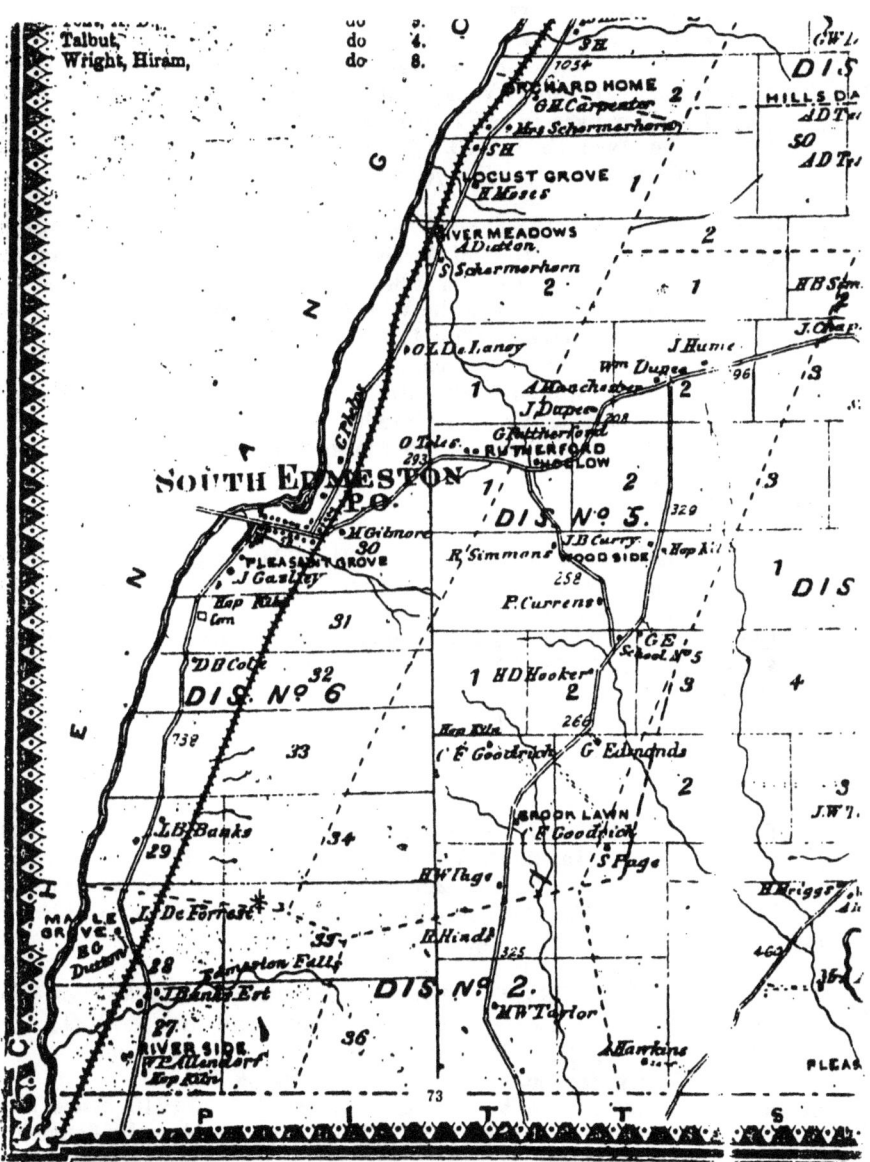

DE FOREST, ABEL[6], brother of **Gideon** above, settled in town of Unadilla. Abel m. **Betsy Rodgers**, whose family came to NY from CT at the same time as the **DeForests**. **Abel** and wife began life in a bark hut and for some time lived in a most primitive style. He lived past the age of 70, and his wife also lived to a great age. Their son:

LYMAN DE FOREST[7] after the death of his father became owner of the homestead farm, where he lived until his death at age 54. He m. **Mary Nutter**, a native of Cherry Valley. They were members of the Presbyterian Church. **Mary** lived to be 77 years old. [A **Mrs. Mary DeForest** d. at Edmeston 4 April 1831, aged 67.] They had eleven children and all resided in Otsego Co., two died young. The only one named in this source was son:

J. N.[8] m. **Lottie Curtis**, who was b. in Unadilla, a d/o **Lysander** and **Anna (Lull) Curtis**, both b. Town of Morris and Town of Unadilla. **Mr. Curtis** was a gunsmith in what is known as Rogers' Hollow and died there in 1890, aged 99. He was a veteran of the War of 1812. **Mrs. Curtis** d. aged 78. Members of the Universalist Church. **Lottie Curtis** was one of 11 children. **J. N.** and **Lottie** had two children:

    i.   **Effie**, m. **Mahlon York**, operator of five cheese factories in Otsego and Chenango Cos.; res. Unadilla.

    ii.   **Anna**, m. **Heman Quimby**, farmer of Otsego Co. One child, **Tracy**.

[BR:212; OB]

DE FOREST, MASON was an early settler of Unadilla, NY and purchased 500 acres of land at twenty shillings per acre. He lived on his farm until his death, when he was "very old." His son:

GEORGE DE FOREST[2] was b. in Town of Unadilla; farmer. He m. **Eunice Sweet**, b. Delaware Co., NY and a sister of **Dr. Joseph Sweet** of Unadilla. Children:

    i.   **Homer**, m. **Cora Slade**, res. on family farm.

    ii.   **Ida**, res. at home.

4   iii. **Clark E.**

CLARK E. DE FOREST[4] b. c. 1866, Town of Unadilla; farmer of District No. 11. He m. 1st **Ida Burdick** who d. without issue aged 29. She was d/o **Thomas Burdick**. **Clark** m. 2nd **Ellen Beach**, b. in East Masonville, Delware Co., NY. Members of Baptist church. No children mentioned.

[BR:604-5]

DIXSON, CHARLES HENRY, b. 1 March 1857; m. **Mary Amelia Monroe**, s/o **Edward N. Monroe** and 1st wife **Jane Weatherhead**. She was b. 9 Aug. 1857 at Schuyler Lake. [See entry on Monroe family.] Children:

    i.   **Emert Monroe**, b. 1 Nov. 1878, Mt. Vision, NY.

    ii.   **Grace Lillian**, b. 24 Feb. 1880; m. 1 Oct. 1910 **Bruce M. Robinson**. Res. Mt. Vision in 1912. Had son **Malcolm Bruce** b. 27 Aug. 1906.

    iii. **Leon Edward**, b. 10 July 1881; m. 1 Jan. 1912 **Lena D. Bailey**. Res. Mt. Vision.

[*Genealogy of Josiah Munroe, Revolutionary Soldier, Who Died in the Service of the Continental Army at Valley Forge* ... by G. S. Northrup, 1912]

DUNHAM, OBADIAH[5] (*Jabez*[4] *of CT, Nathaniel*[3] *of MA, Joseph*[2] *MA, John*[1] *England & MA*) physician, b. 13 March 1730 in Hebron, CT, d. Cooperstown, NY, 17 February 1813, s/o **Jabez Dunham** who was b. in 1704 in Wrentham and **Abigail Neland (Kneeland)** his wife. **Jabez** and **Abigail** m. 17 Dec. 1725 at Colchester/Hebron, CT. [NOTE: *Compendium* gives his wife as Mrs. **Salome Barrows Tiffany**, perhaps a second wife?] **Obadiah** came from Pownal, VT in 1755 and settled below Bowerstown, Otsego County. He was a physician and m. 22 November 1754, **Lucy Gillett**, b. 18 February 1740, d. 18 February 1830, d/o **Joel Gillett & Mary Kelsey**. **Obadiah**[5] was of Hebron on 3 November 1759, when he bought land in Colchester; acknowledged his conveyence 12 June 1761 in Dutchess County, NY. He and wife **Lucy** had one child baptized in 1760 while residing in Colchester [not named in this source.] He was designated '**Obadiah Jr.**' when he purchased land while still living at Hebron, to distinguish him from his uncle **Obadiah**. **Lucy's** family were residents of Windsor, CT and later of Amenia, Dutchess County, NY, although this source [TAG] states that there is no definite proof that **Lucy** is the daughter of **Joel** and **Mary Gillett**. **Obadiah** served in the Revolutionary War in Capt. **Eli Noble's** company, Col. **Ebenezer Wallbridge's** regiment, VT [Dorset] militia. Issue.

6   i.   **Obediah**, b. 17 Nov. 1761 [1760], CT.
6   ii.   **Abner**, b. 1773, Town of Middlefield, Otsego, NY.

OBEDIAH DUNHAM[6], d. 12 Oct. 1833 in VT; served in the American Revolultion as a private from VT and was granted a pension; m. **Lois Hendricks [Hendryx]**. Issue.
   i.   **Eber**, b. 1803, d. 1891, m. **Lucy Jewett**.
Another **Obediah Dunham** d. in Middlefield, NY 17 Feb. 1813, aged 83.

ABNER DUNHAM[6] occupied the farm upon which he was born all of his life. In 1795 he was a subscriber to the forming of an academy in Cooperstown in 1795. He m. at Middlefield 29 October 1815, **Gratis Griffin**; Rev. Mr. **Smith** performing the ceremony. DAR Lineage 122912 gives his wife as **Candice Irons**, b. 1779-1814. **Abner** d. 16 Feb. 1822, leaving a family of four sons and five daughters. His daughters reside in the vicinity. Children named:
   i.   **Amy**, b. 1801, m. --- **Campbell**; living at Middlefield Centre (1878).
   ii.   **Joanna**, b. 1804, m. --- **Mackey**; living near Bowerstown (1878).
   iii.   **Ferdinand**, b. 1814, d. 1910; m. 1840 **Angeline McCollum**, b. 1814, d. 1892; left at least one child, **Abner**, b. 1841, d. 1910; m. 1869 **Sophronia Boynton**, b. 1845.

[*Wrentham Massachusetts Vital Records*; *The American Genealogist*, V. 29, p. 22-23; *American Compendium*, V. 3; A:186, GBM. The early lineage of this line is featured in the *Compendium*, but this is disputed in *TAG*, Vol. 29, p. 22; DAR Lineages 122912, 124845 & 142488; OB; COP1:39.]

DUPEE, JAMES[1] b. 1 Feb. 1797, to the farm in Edmeston, NY aged 13, where he spent the rest of his life, dying 16 April 1875, aged 78 y, 2 m, 16 d. **James** was s/o **James Dupee** of Frank extraction who was b. in 1766 and m. twice; 1st **Hannah Williams** by whom he had three daughters and on1 son; his 2nd wife was **Huldah Carr**. **James Sr**. d. in 1830, aged 64. **James Jr**.[1] was a farmer; m. **Nancy Turner** 5 Dec. 1822. She was from Cherry Valley. Her parents d. when she was young and she lived with an elder sister. She d. 4 Dec. 1862, aged 66 y, 1 m, 27 d. Children:
    i.   **Evaline**, m. **Roswell Simmons**.
2 ii.   **William J**.
   iii.   **Charles**, res. on old homestead.

WILLIAM J. DUPEE[2], b. 15 June 1828, was brought up on the farm and rec'd. a limited education. He learned the cooper's trade, but eventually turned to farming. He m. 9 March 1854 to **E. Elvira Sewell** who was b. in Edmeston 2 Aug. 1826, d/o **Eliakim Sewell**. **Elvira** was one of three children, her siblings being **Almon** and **Lucinda**. After their mar. **William** bought a farm close by his old home, where he lived until his death on 5 March 1890. **Elvira** lives on the old farm with her daus. Children:
   i.   **Lucius James**; m. 27 Dec. 1876 to **Elsie M. Greene**; has one child, **William James Dupee**. **Lucius** is a dairy farmer on the old farm.
   ii. **Imogene**.
   iii. **Grace Greenwood**.
[BR:470]

EDSON, BENJAMIN[5] (*Seth*[4], *Benjamin*[3], *Joseph*[2], *Samuel*[1] *England & MA*) was a distant cousin of **Obed**[4] below. **Benjamin** was s/o **Seth** and **Irene (Howard) Edson**, and was b. in Stafford, Hartford Co., CT, 26 Jan. 1758; m. 1st in that place 13 Nov. 1783, **Dinah Washburn**. She d. in Stafford on 23 April 1784 and he m. there 2nd 23 Feb. 1786, **Anna Johnson**. In 1805 **Benjamin** sold his property in Stafford and moved to Tyringham, Berkshire Co., MA and in 1808 to Great Barrington, MA; in 1810 to Huntsville [in 1830 the town of Otego], where he d. 1 July 1843 and she d. at the same place 7 Feb. 1860, aged 95 years, 11 m, 7 d. **Benjamin** was a Revolutionary Pensioner; served in 2nd CT Line Regiment. Children, 1st by 1st wife; all b. Stafford, CT:
   i.   **Dinah**, b. 16 April 1784.
   ii.   **Edna**, b. 29 March 1787; m. **James Hewlett**.
   iii. **Elam**, b. 23 May 1789, res. Jamestown, NY.
   iv. **Irene**, b. 26 Sept. 1791; m. **Joseph Sheldon**.
   v.   **Martin**, b. 11 March 1794.
   vi. **Dorcas**, b. 20 June 1796' m. 1st **B. Saxbury** and 2nd **Joseph Howe**.
   vii. **Julia**, b. 24 June 1797.
   viii. **Caroline**, b. 18 April 1802; m. --- **Hill**.
6 ix. **Freeman Willard**, b. 17 Aug. 1804.

FREEMAN WILLARD EDSON⁶ b. Stafford, CT m. in Otego, NY 31 Dec. 1829 **Sarah Sheldon,** d/o **Henry** and **Joanna (Peckham) Sheldon,** b. there 24 June 1808; she d. in Otego 5 March 1895, and he also there on 30 March 1896. Children, all b. Otego:
- i. **Benjamin,** b. 26 May 1831.
- ii. **Henry Sheldon,** b. 9 APril 1835.
- iii. **Martin Austin,** b. 5 Aug. 1846; m. at Otego 15 April 1869 **Nancy,** d/o **Elkanah** and **Atilda (Hathaway) Mead,** b. in Otego.
- iv. **Joanna,** b. 2 July 1855; m. at Butternuts, NY 20 Sept. 1880, **Silas,** s/o **Aaron** and **Rachel (Foster) Rider,** b. in Poughkeepsie, Dutchess Co., NY. His 1st wife was **Helen Clark** and she d. in Jan. 1880.

[*Edsons in England & America* . . . by Jarvis Bonesteel Edson, NY 1903]

EDSON, OBED⁴ (*Samuel³ MA, Samuel² MA, Samuel¹ England & MA*) was the fourth s/o **Samuel** and **Mary (Dean) Edson** and was b. 31 [3] Dec. 1720 in Bridgewater, MA and d. in Richfield, NY, 8 Sept. 1804. He was a sergeant in the French & Indian War. He probably went to Richfield in his old age to join his son and namesale. He m. 1st 11 Nov. 1741 **Keturah,** d/o **Jonathan** and **Abigail (Stoughton) Willis** of Bridgewater, b. 11 April 1722, d. in Bridgewater 4 June 1750. He m. 2nd in Town of Middleborough, Plymouth Co., 2 May 1751 to **Martha Thomas** who d. Town of Richfield, NY 6 Dec. 1795. **Obed** d. there also on 8 Sept. 1804. Children of 1st mar., b. Bridgewater:
- i. **Obed,** b. 17 Sept. 1742, d. 10 Dec. 1742.
- ii. **Jesse,** b. 24 May 1744, res. MA.
- iii. **Dau.,** b. 12 Dec. 1745, d. 13 Dec. 1745.
- 5 iv. **Obed,** b. 2 May 1747.
- v. **Lewis,** b. 22 Jan. 1748.

Children of 2nd mar., also b. Bridgewater:
- vi. **Keturah,** b. 23 Feb. 1752.
- 5 vii. **Thomas,** b. 3 June 1753.
- viii. **Lydia,** b. 13 Oct. 1754.
- ix. **Silence,** 14 Sept 1756; m. in Town of Taunton, Bristol Co., MA, 18 Oct. 1782 **James Trupwell.**
- x. **Isaac,** 2 Feb. 1758. He is probably the **Isaac Edson** who res. on "The Otsdawa" in Otego and in 1814 sold his property to **Capt. Peter Bundy** and removed to Laurens. "Over in the Otsdawa ravine he owned a grist and saw mill, a distillary and carding-machine, the first of which was run by **William Niles.**" He d. 28 March 1800.

EDSON, OBED⁵, b. 2 May 1747 in Bridgewater and d. in Richfield 9 May 1840. He served in the French & Indian War. For some years he res. at Lanesboro, MA, where he was connected with a foundry. Between 1790 and 1793 he settled in what is now Richfield, then a part of the town of German Flats, Montgomery Co., NY; farmer and hotel keeper in a locality now known as Monticello. A deed was made 3 Jan. 1798 between **Levi Beardsley** and **Sarah** his wife of Richfield Springs, NY and **Obed Edson**

of Lanesborough, MA whereby **Obed** purchased for $1500 113 acres plus of land, Lot 37, in Schuyler's Patent, County of Otsego. On 20 May 1799, at a vestry meeting held at the house of **Wyllys Howe**, father of his first wife **Prudence**, **Obed Edson** was elected second vestryman of St. Luke's Episcopal Church in Town of Richfield. He was a close friend of **Rev. Daniel Nash**. **Obed** had great musical talent. He was for many years the owner of a slave named **Ike** whom he finally emancipated. On 22 April 1769 at Bridgewater, MA, **Obed** m. **Prudence**, d/o **Wyllys Howe [Fiske]**; she of Welch descent and was b. 4 Sept. 1745; d. Town of Lanesborough, MA and he m. 2nd c. 1794 **Sarah** ---. She d. Town of Richfield 7 Oct. 1724. **Obed** d. there also on 9 May 1840 aged 93. Children:

    i.   **Prudence**, b. "probably" in Town of Ashfield, MA 4 March 1771.
6 ii.   **Obed**, b. "probably" Town of Ashfield 6 May 1772.
   iii. **Keturah**, b. Lanesborough, MA 19 June 1774; m. **Willis Howe**, silversmith. She d. 1 Oct. 1853.
   iv. **Stephen Fiske**, b. Lanesborough, 9 July 1776; m. 2 Feb. 1802 **Abigail Smith**; he d. 29 Sept. 1855.
   v.   **Olive**, b. Lanesborough 14 June 1778; m. **Seth Tiffany** of Cherry Valley, NY. She d. 20 Sept. 1807.
   vi. **Hannah**, b. Lanesborough, 12 Aug. 1780; m. **Pomeroy Noble**. She d. 20 June 1803.
   vii. **Wyllys**, b. Lanesborough, 22 April 1783.
   viii. **Lucy**, b. Lanesborough, 25 July 1785; m. **Elam Willis**; she d. 14 June 1859.

OBED EDSON[6], b. 16 Aug. 1772 in Lanesbobo [Ashfield], MA, res. for a time at Cooperstown, NY, later at Richfield, whence he removed to Eaton, Madison Co., NY where he d. 6 Aug. 1804. Clothier; Episcopalian; Jeffersonian Republican, as was his father. The 19 May 1796 issue of the *Otsego Herald* carried his advertisement for employment in his clothing business. He m. 1st, before 1793, **Aurora Higgins**; she d. of smallpox in Cooperstown. He m. 2nd **Fanny Bigelow** 16 July 1794 at Cooperstown. **Fanny** was b. in Colchester, CT 7 April 1777, d/o **Elisha Bigelow**, a captain in the American army in the Revolutionary War, and wife **Thankfull Beebe**. [See Bigelow family entry.] **Obed** was well educated for his time--a student, and a reader of good literature. After his death, **Fanny** m. in Hamilton (later Eaton), NY 14 March 1805, Major **Samuel Sinclear**, s/o Col. **Richard** and **Polly (Cilley) Sinkler** [sic], b. in Nottingham, NH. **Samuel** d. in Sinclairville, Town of Charlotte, Chautauqua Co., NY in 1827 and she at the same place 12 Jan. 1852. Children:

7 i.   **Obed**, b. 11 Sept. and bapt. 8 Oct. 1796.
   ii.   **John Milton**, b. 30 July 1801, bapt. 1803. Two sources say he was b. at Eaton [Hamilton], Madison Co., NY, but his bapt. is recorded at Cooperstown. Judge; m. 1831 he m. **Hannah** d/o **Jonathan** and **Ursula (Church) Alverson**, b. Halifax, VT 3 June 1804, who came to Gerry, Chautauqua Co. with her mother in 1821. She d. 22 Nov. 1878. Children: **Obed** and **Fanny Ursula**.
   iii. **Fanny Aurora**, b. 27 Oct. 1802 [Hamilton, NY], bapt. 1803; m. **Horace Potter** and res. at her death at Kankakee, IL.

OBED EDSON[7], b. in Town of Richfield, Otsego Co.
  Obed and Prudence Edson bapt. entry: "Prudence, dau. of their son-in-law, **Mr. Noble**, b. 14 July 1801, bapt. 76 Aug. 1803." Also a **Prudence Edson**, b. 4 Sept. 1745, bapt. 14 April 1805. Also a **Fanny Edson**, bapt. 1820 at Cooperstown.

THOMAS EDSON[5] b. Bridgewater, MA 3 June 1753, m. in Lanesborough, MA 15 June 1780 **Mary d/o William** and **Mary (Wright) Jarvis**, [See Jarvis family entry] b. 12 May 1762. She d. at Fly Creek, Otsego Co. in Feb. 1835; he also d. there in 1836. He served from MA during the Revolutionary War. Children, first seven b. Lanesboro, last two at Fly Creek:
  i.   Mary [Polly], b. 29 March 1781; m. **I. C. Marvin**.
  ii. William [Billy], b. 12 July 1783, d. Lanesborough 23 March 1785.
  iii. William Jarvis, b. 23 Feb. 1786; m. **Polly Fairchild**.
  iv. Asahel, b. 7 Aug. 1788; m. **F. Stetson**.
  v.   Dau., b. 13 Feb. 1791; d. at birth.
  vi. Oramel [Orenell], b. 9 Sept. 1791; m. **Lydia Wells**.
  vii. Sarah (Sally), b. 4 Jan. 1795; d. 4 Jan. 1803.
  viii. Theodatus [Theodorus], b. 7 July 1798; lawyer, d. intestate in Otsego Co. and on 7 Feb. 1835 letter of administration on his property was granted to **Eliza Rice**.
  ix. Elizabeth, b. 15 Sept. 1801; m. **J. Price**.
[NASH1; CUT1:2:838-43; *Vital Records of Bridgewater, Massachusetts to the Year 1850*, 1916; F:78. Data on early Edson family can be found in the *History of Bridgewater* by Bradford Kingman, 1866 and in William Cutter's *New England Families, Volume 1*, 1914; *The Jarvis Family: The Descendants: The First Settlers of the Name in Massachusetts & Long Island* by George A. Jarvis et al, 1879.]

ELY, ALANSON[8] (*Samuel*[7] *MA & NY, Simeon*[5] *MA & NY, Samuel*[4] *MA, Samuel*[3] *MA, Samuel*[1] *MA, Nathaniel*[1] *England & MA*), s/o **Samuel**, was b. in Warren, Herkimer Co., NY 8 Sept. 1804 and d. in Belleville, Wayne Co., MI 9 July 1871. He m. in Richfield, Otsego Co., NY 1 Sept. 1827 **Lucia Smith** who was b. in Richfield 25 March 1801 and d. 24 Jan. 1879 in Belleville. Children:
  i.   Marian Hortense, b. 22 Aug. 1828 in Warren, NY; d. 1 Sept. 1868 in Belleville, MI.
  ii.   Daniel Dana, b. 19 Feb. 1830, Warren, NY.
  iii. Menso White, b. 25 Aug. 1832 in Richfield, NY [as are the remainder of his siblings below]; d. 24 Oct. 1834 at Warren.
  iv.   Frances Amanda, b. 2 July 1834.
  v.   Susan Sophia, b. 27 March 1838; d. 18 Sept. 1853 at Richfield.
  vi.   Lorenzo Smith, b. 23 Dec. 1840; d. 5 Nov. 1881 at Richfield, unm.
  vii. James Edward b. 26 Dec. 1842.
  viii. Maria Louisa, b. 25 May 1846.

SAMUEL ELY⁸, another s/o **Samuel⁷** was b. in Warren, Herkimer Co., NY 29 Nov. 1807, where he now (1885) res. He m. 5 May 1831 **Mary Ann Snyder**, d/o George and Betsey Snyder, b. in Springfield, NY 8 Sept. 1808, d. in Warren, NY 17 May 1880. Samuel is a farmer and has been a class leader in the Methodist Episcopal Church for many years. They have seven children, all b. Middleport, NY.
[Records of the Descendants of Nathaniel Ely, The Emigrant, Who Settled First in Newtown, now Cambridge, Mass. . . . by Heman Ely, 1885]

ELY, NOAH, wife **Elizabeth** who was b. 24 Nov. 1790, was bapt. 21 Nov. 1819 along with their children (below). Witnesses: **Charles Knap, John** and **Mrs. L. Hubby** and **Mrs. Rose**. Children:
  i.   **Lydia Amanda**, b. 28 April 1813.
  ii   **Elizabeth**, b. 3 Feb. 1818.
  iii. **Eunice Smith**, b. 31 Aug. 1806.
[NASH1]

ELY, SUMNER (DR.)⁶ (*Adriel⁵ CT, Richard⁴ CT, William³ CT, Richard² CT, Richard¹ England, MA & CT*), b. 22 May 1787, s/o **Adriel Ely** and wife **Sarah Stowe** who m. in 1780. Sumner located in Clarksville, NY [Middlefield Post Office] 11 June 1810. Sumner d. 3 Feb. 1857 and bur. at Clarksville, aged 69. He served as an officer in the 112th Regiment of Infantry, **Joseph Clyde**, Commander (Sept. 1812); was State Senator from the 5th District of Otsego Co. from 1840 to 1843. In 1816 he m. **Hannah King [Knapp] Gilbert**, b. 9 Dec. 1791; d. 17 March 1868 at Gerard, d/o **Benjamin Gilbert** and **Mary Cornwall**. Children:
  i.   **Adriel Gilbert**, b. 3 Sept. 1817, physician, res. Girard, PA, d. 27 March 1887, unm.
  ii.   **Theodore Dwight**, b. 10 Sept. 1820, d. 4 Oct. 1869, unm.
  iii. **Sumner Stow**, b. 12 April 1823; attorney, res. NY City, unm.
  iv.   **Benjamin Cornwall**, physician of Girard, Erie Co., PA. He m. 12 Feb. 1855, **Elizabeth Crippen Caryl** d/o **Leonard Caryl** and **Mary Crippen**, b. 1830 at Worcester, NY. She was living in 1917. Children: **Mary Lola, Theodore Julius, Benjamin Caryl, Gertrude Elizabeth, William Frederick, Ella Louise** and **Jennie Carlotta**. [See Caryl family entry.]
7 v.   **William Horace**.

WILLIAM HORACE ELY⁷ b. 2 Oct. 1829 in East Worcester, NY; d. 22 March 1908; merchant of East Worcester, where he and wife are bur. In 1855 he m. **Ellen Caryl**, b. 12 Feb. 1834 and d. 21 Aug. 1917, d/o **Leonard Caryl** and wife **Mary Crippen**. Children:
  i.   **William Caryl**, b. 1858, d. 1913; lawyer, State Senator, Capitalist and President of the International Railway Co., Buffalo, NY. He res. many years at Niagara Falls. He m. 1886 **Grace Courter**, d/o **Stanton Courter** of Cobleskill, NY.
  ii.   **Adriel S.**, M.D., b. 5 June 1859, d. 18 Dec. 1920 [1926/28]; bur. Worcester Cemetery. Physician of NY City; m. **Edith H. Chalmers** of NY City who was b. 10 Oct. 1862 and d. 18 Dec. 1926.

[A:186; GBC1; *The Caryl Family in England and America* . . . by Arthur S. Caryl, 1937; *The Ely Ancestry* . . . by Sumner A. Ely, Esq., 1902]

ELY, WARREN, desc. of **Nathaniel Ely** who emigrated from Tenterden, England to MA in 1634 and settled at Norwich, CT in 1626 and afterwards removed to West Springfield, CT, where the family lands are still (1935) retained under the old Indian grant. **Warren** m. 28 March, 1828, **Caroline**, d/o **Dr. Anson** and **Abigail (Havens) Tennant**, and settled in Springfield, Otsego Co., on what has since been known as the Ely farm, early in the 19th century. They were m. at the Presbyterian Church by Rev. **James Cole Howe**, pastor. Seven of their nine children named here; all settled in Springfield with the exception of **Lydia** and **Fitz-James**:

i. **Margaret**, m. **Daniel Smith**.
ii. **Eliza**, m. **Jacob Basinger**.
iii. **Harriet**, m. **Augustus Doolittle**.
iv. **Lydia**, m. **Daniel Basinger, Jr.**
v. **Addie**, m. **R. Perry Bennett**.
vi. **Smith**, m. **Martha Wikoff**, later came into possession of the home farm.
vii. **Fitz-James**.

A **Samuel Ely** kept the first post office in Springfield Center in his residence. He is not placed in the above family, but as a resident of Springfield it is likely he is related. Another **Ely, Richard**, was also an inhabitant of Springfield, and also is not placed in the above family.
[SPR:152, 174-5, 229]

EMMONS, ASA (MAJOR)[1] mechanic at Harpersfield, Delaware Co., NY, originally from VT; 1800-1815 to Oneonta, farmer, lumberman and businessman, he owned a carding and fulling mill; d. 25 July 1820. He served in the state militia. Before he came to Oneonta with **Dr. Lindsay**, German was the only language spoken in the settlement. Mar. **Eunice Prentice**, b. Harpersfield, d. 1839. She m. 2nd **William Fairchild** on 20 March 1825 at Davenport, Delaware Co., NY. **Asa** had seven children; those identified so far.

i. **Roxey Ann**, d. 22 Oct. 1821, aged 19.
2 ii. **Carlton**. [third child]

CARLTON EMMONS[2] b. Otsego Co. 26 Feb. 1804; farmer, keeper of public house in East Oneonta that was on the Charlotte Pike, the road taken by cattle drivers from the west. It was not an unusual sight to see several droves of cattle, a thousand or more in a drove, from Ohio and Indiana, as also large flocks of sheep, pass through the town in one day during the summer season. A favorate stopping place for the drovers with their herds was at Emmons, where a well-managed hotel was kept for many years by **Carlton**. He res. at Emmons in Town of Oneonta, town supervisor several terms. 3 Feb. 1828 he m. **Maria** d/o **William Fairchild** of Cooperstown. In their marriage notice in the local newspaper he is given as "of Davenport, NY." She d. 1 Aug. 1871. Children:

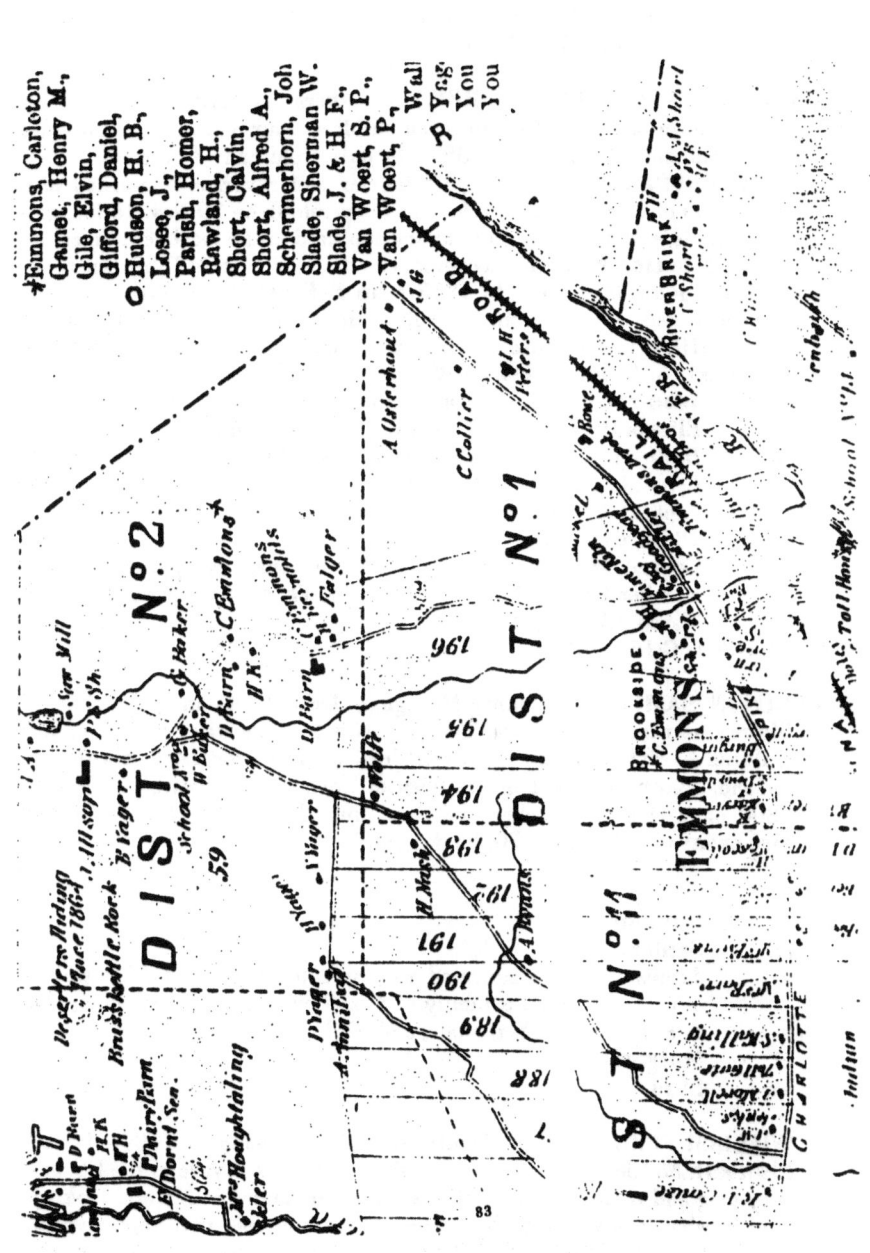

    i.   **Delos W.**, m. **Mary Stoddard** of Oneonta, res. Huntington, WV (1878).
    ii.   **Roxy A.**, widow of the late **Julius T. Aldin** of Little Falls, NY.
[ONE:34, 36, 89; A:223-5, 237-8; OB; GBM]

ERNST, JOHN FREDERICK (REV.)[1], Luthern clergyman, located in Cooperstown in 1799. He had seven children, four daus. and 3 sons. He d. at Manheim, PA 24 Oct. 1805. The only child named here:
JOHN FREDERICK ERNEST JR.[2] jeweler and silversmith; warden and vestryman of Christ Church. He d. at Cooperstown on 29 Nov. 1830, aged 52 [51]; his wife d. 1856. An obituary appeared in the local newspaper for **Mrs. Catherine Ernst** in Cooperstown; she d. 2 March 1855, aged 72, probably **John Jr.'s** wife. In 1813 **John F. Ernst** of Cooperstown rec'd. license to sell by retail, merchandise other than wines and spirits, by paying $10, as was the custom, which was countersigned by **Jedidiah Peck**. Documents in hands of **George W.**, his son. Children:
    i.   **John Frederick**, Episcopal minister, res. Buffalo (1878).
    ii.   **Elizabeth**, m. **Abel H. Clark**; d. Cooperstown.
    iii.   **Henry**, con't. his father's business until 1837; d. NY. **Florence A. Ernst**, b. 11 June 1856, child of **Henry B.** and **Louisa Ernst**, was bapt. at Cooperstown 30 June 1872. **Henry** was bur. 15 Sept. 1868, aged 59.
    iv.   **George W.**, res. Cooperstown, businessman and public servant; member Christ Church. **Mrs. G. W. Ernst** of Cooperstown d. 15 March 1882, aged 68.
[A:260; GBC1; G:165; OB]

FERGUSON, SAMUEL[1], b. County Monaghan, Ireland. As an agent of **Lord Blaney** he came to America, bringing with him his wife, and all of his children except **William**, who remained as agent for **Lord Blaney** in Ireland. **Samuel** settled in the town of Kortright, Delaware Co., NY in 1800 on a fine farm, where he lived until his death. He m. **Jennie McGowan** who d. aged c. 70; he d. aged 80.
    i.   **Thomas.**
    ii.   **John.**
2 iii.   **William.**
    iv.   **Sanford I.**
    v.   **James.** A highly educated man, an able lawyer, and a fine pulpit orator. He gave his family of 8 or 9 children a liberal education & d. at Delhi, NY at the age of 97.
    vi.   **Margaret.**
    vii.   **Eliza.**

WILLIAM FERGUSON[2] b. County Monaghan, Ireland in 1809. He m. **Elizabeth McClellan** of the same Irish county. His voyage to the US was very long and tedious, with teriffic storms. He landed at NY and took up land in what is now Otsego Co. After 18 years he sold that improvement and removed to the town of Burlington, where he lived 4 years. He sold that farm and bought another in the town of New Libson, near the old

Friends Church, which he sold 3 years later and returned to the town of Edmeston, the present (1893) home of his son **James**. This was c. 1841 and he d. upon this latter farm. **William** made his will 22 March 1843; proved in 1850. His wife d. in 1839, aged 49. Children (all dec'd. except for **James** [1893]):

    i.   **John.**
    ii.   **Joseph.**
    iii. **Fannie**, m. --- **Gross.**
    iv. **William.**
3   v.   **James.**
    vi. **Isabella**, m. --- **Matteson.**
    vii. **Robert**, never mar.
    viii. **Eliza.**

JAMES FERGUSON[3] m. 1st **Hannah Howe** of CT; she d. in 1839. Children:
    i.   **Dau.**, d. aged 3.
4   ii. **James G.**, now occupies and works the home farm.
    JAMES[3] m. 2nd [no name given], she d. Dec. 1892, aged 68.

JAMES G. FERGUSON[4] was b. 1839, his mother dying at his birth. He was raised until the age of 18 by an aunt, **Fanny Gross**. After the death of his aunt (she aged c. 50) he went to his father's home and has lived there ever since; farmer. **James G.** m. 3 July 1872 to **Elizabeth Davis** of the Town of Morris, a d/o **William J. Davis**. They have one dau., **Mary E.**, now (1893) aged 19, living at home.
[GBW; BR:400-01]

FIELD, NATHAN[1] b. RI 23 Jan. 1768, s/o **Charles Field**, of Welch ancestry who spent his entire life in RI. His son:
JAMES FIELD[2] b. RI, in 1788 came to Otsego Co. accompanied by his family and located in what is now the Town of Hartwick (now School District No. 8). He d. on his homestead 9 March 1852. He m. **Mary Pearce**, also b. RI, 5 June 1770. Members of the Universalist Church. Children:
3   i.   **James.**
    ii. **Hannah.**
    iii. **Stephen.**
    iv. **Nancy.**
    v.   **Mary A.**

JAMES FIELD[3] inherited a part of the old homestead in Hartwick and bought the rest. He spent his entire life here, d. 20 July 1856. He m. 16 Oct. 1817 to **Betsey Eddy** who was b. at Hartwick 23 Feb. 1792. She was d/o **Noah Eddy**, b. in RI 16 June 1760 and came to Otsego Co. before 1800. Noah's wife was **Mary Bowen**, also b. RI 5 Nov. 1765, d. 10 April 1839. Betsey d. 13 Jan. 1873. Children:
    i.   **George.**
    ii. **Marcus.**

iii. **Silas.**
iv. **Mary**, b. 19 Oct. 1826; m. **Chester Babbitt**. [See Babbitt family entry.]
[BR:229-30]

FIELD, WILLIAM and **Nathan** [above], s/o **Charles Field**, of Welch ancestry. The brothers were pioneers of Hartwick, emigrated from RI in 1787 and settled on lands c. one mile northeast of Hartwick Village. After selecting their land they returned to RI and married, and removed to Otsego Co. They erected rude cabins. **William** had seven children, three sons and four daus. He made his will 19 Dec. 1842 and in it named his wife **Mary** and children:
i. **Elisha**, aged 78 in 1878.
ii. **William S.**, aged 67 in 1878.
iii. **Henry**. He made his will 9 Sept. 1849 and in it named his wife **Hannah** and sons **Lewis** and **Stephen**.
iv. **Martha**, m. --- **Murdock**, res. Cooperstown.
v. **Esther**, m. --- **Lippett**.
vi. **Huldah**, m. --- **Metcalf**.
vii. **Susan**, m. --- **Livingston**.
[A:159; GBW; BR:220]

FINCH, DAVID early settler of Unadilla, was b. in 1782, s/o **Daniel Finch**, an Englishman who settled in Litchfield, CT before the Revolution. **David** m. **Ruth Mallery** of Cornwall, CT, whose father, like his own, had come from England before the war. After their marriage they lived for a time in Oxford, CT, where he engaged in the manufacture of woolen cloth and where four children were born. His business declined after the War of 1812 and in 1814 he removed to Unadilla, where he engaged in building. He made his will 24 July 1841 and in it named wife **Ruth A.** and children (below). He is bur. at St. Matthew's Episcopal Churchyard, Unadilla.
i. **David**, res. WI.
ii. **Marcus A.**
iii. **Daniel A.**
iv. **William T.**, res. DesMoines, IA with brother only identified as "D.O. Finch." He d. in Chicago.
v. **Sarah Ann.**
vi. **Elizabeth**, m. **Rufus G. Mead.**
vii. **Maria T.**, m. 2 June 1833 at Unadilla, **Dr. Harmon Gray** of New Berlin & WI.
viii. **Mary A.**
[GBW; UNA:83; A:334; GBM]

FLEMING, GEORGE m. 15 June 1828 at Butternuts **Julia Rockwell** d/o **Jabez** and 3rd wife **Elizabeth Andrus**. The family res. in Guilford, NY, but all their children were b. in Butternuts. [See Rockwell family entry.] [He is possibly the **George Fleming** b. c. 1803, of Guilford, Chenango Co., NY, listed in the LDS IGI.] Children:

	i.	Andrew M., b. 8 Nov. 1829; m. **Catharine Russell**, res. Oxford, Ny in 1892. Their children were all b. in Oxford: **Bishop A., George W., Millard A.**
	ii.	**Darius S.**, b. 6 Oct. 1830; m. **Carrie Benedict**. He d. at Oxford, NY 18 Nov. 1889. Children all b. Oxford: **Seymour, Willie, May, Lottie** and **Alice**.
	iii.	**John F.**, b. 6 Dec. 1833; not mar.; res. Preston, NY 1903.
	iv.	**Elizabeth A.**, b. 12 Feb. 1837; m. **Harvey Wells**; res. Milwaukee, WI in 1892.
	v.	**Fanny C.**; m. **George Thomas** and d. at Wells Bridge, NY 14 Oct. 1875.
	vi.	**Caroline L.**, b. 17 May 1842; m. **Rufus C. Smith** and res. Guilford, NY; no children.
	vii.	**Harriet A.**, b. 1845; m. **Albert R. Brown**.

[*A Genealogy of the Families of John Rockwell of Stamford, Conn. 1643* ... by James Boughton, 1903; GBM; IGI.]

FOOTE, OBED[4] (*Moses*[3] *CT, Nathaniel*[2] *CT, Robert*[2] *CT, Nathaniel*[1] *England/CT*) "first of that part of Waterbury, now Plymouth, afterwards of Gill, (Mass.)," b. 25 Nov. 1741; m. 3 Dec. 1761 **Mary Todd**, d/o **Rev. Samuel Todd** of Northfield [Waterbury], CT, who was b. 11 Sept. 1742. She m. 2nd 2 [26] March 1798 **Rev. Jonathan Leavitt** of Heath, MA as his 3rd wife. She d. 16 May 1815 of palsey in Bernardstown, aged 73, and was bur. in the ancient burial yard about one mile from the Meeting House in Gill. **Obed** d. 21 Sept. 1797. In May 1780 he removed with his mother and his young family to Rowe, MA and in 1784 to Gill, MA where he d. 21 Sept. 1797, mortally wounded rasing ahouse in Gill, eleven days before his death. Children:

5	i.	**Asenath**, b. 19 Sept. 1762; m. 20 June 1791 **Eliphaz** s/o **Simeon Alexander**; d. 18 Nov. 1713. [See Alexander family entry.]
	ii.	**Mary Dorothea**, b. 11 June 1764; m. dec. 1783 **Rev. Amasa Cook** of Bardstown [Bernardstown, MA]; d. 17 April 1835 of pleurisy in Persia, Erie Co., NY.
5	iii.	**Bernice**. (son)
	iv.	**Sedate**, b. 5 March 1768; m. 11 June 1809 **Josiah Jones** of Brockville, Upper Canada [originally of Williamstown, MA]; she d. 8 Dec. 1837 of dropsy in Hammond, St. Lawrence Co., NY. He appears in the 1872/3 *Gazetteer of Otsego Co.* in Town of Morris, farmer, aged 84.
	v.	**Samuel** (Deacon), b. 7 April 1770; m. 1st 8 Aug. 1794, **Sibbil Doolittle** [d/o **Capt. Oliver Doolittle** of Hinsdale, NH] and 2nd in 1833 to --- **Parker**, widow. Res. Gill, MA & Sherburne, NY and later Plymouth, NY. **Samuel** d. at the home of his youngest son, **Obed**, at Grand Rapids, MI 25 Jan. 1848.
	vi.	**Chloe**, b. 21 March 1772; m. **Issac Pierce** of Preston, CT at Burlington; she d. 1829 in Constantia, NY of a fever.
	vii.	**Lydia**, b. 15 May 1774; m. April 1794 Judge **Job Goodale**, s/o **Nathan** of Marlborough, MA. He founded Goodale Academy in Barnardstown and d. there in 1833.

viii.	**Erastus**, b. 19 Sept. 1777; m. 1st **Susan Carlton** and 2nd **Eliza Carlton** [sisters and d/o **Col. Moses Carlton**]. Res. Wiscasset, ME.
ix.	**Philena**, b. 22 Sept. 1779, m. 1st **Israel Jones Jr.** of North Adams, MA who d. in Williamsburg (Upper Canada) in 1811; she m. 2nd **Rev. William Smart** of Brockville (Upper Canada), b. in Edinburg, Scotland.
x.	**Rhoda Ann**, b. 1 Jan. 1781, m. **Nathaniel Martin** of Camden, ME 7 July 1806. She d. of a fever in NY City 14 Jan. 1837; Nathaniel d. in Wilkesbarre, PA March 1841, aged 66.
xi.	**Obed**, b. 27 April 1787, res. in Indianapolis, IN; m. 1st **Ann G. Walpole** in 1823 and 2nd **Mary Davis**, widow of **Francis Davis**, in 1831. Obed d. of "Scar. Malignus," 24 Sept. 1833.

BERNICE FOOTE[5] [Deacon] b. 5 June 1766 in Northfield, MA [b. in that part of Waterbury, now Plymouth], m. **Melinda Field** of Northfield, MA who was b. 20 July 1770; he d. of apoplexy 23 Jan. 1831; res. Northfield, MA & Burlington, NY. "Deacon Foote felt great comfort, and was mcuh engaged in promoting the social intercourse of Christians, in prayermeetings and conference. He had a pleasant gift in prayer, and was attractive and instructive at these assemblies." After one such meeting, he returned home, solemn, yet cheerful, --seated himself in a chair,-- and, in an instant, expired, aged 65. Children:

i.	**Harriet**, b. 20 July 1792; m. 29 May 1821 **Rev. Alexander B. Corning**, of Manchester, MI, at Burlington, NY. They had five children: **Erastus** b. 22 Oct. 1822; d. aged 5 mo.; **Alexander Foote** b. 3 June 1824; **Erastus B.** b. 3 March 1825, d. in infancy; **Benjamin T.** b. 23 July 1829 and **Harriet W.** b. 10 Oct. 1834.
ii.	**Horatio**, b. Northfield, MA 10 Feb. 1796; m. **Abigail Kirkland** of Bridgewater, NY on 15 Feb. 1826; a graduate of Union College and Pastor of the Presbyterian Church in Quincy, IL (1849).
iii.	**Lucius**, b. Northfield 3 Aug. 1798; m. 18 March 1824 **Electa W. Harwood** d/o **Nathan Harwood** of Winfield, NY. Pastor of the Congregational Church of Orangeville, IL. A **Lucius Foote** of Morris, farmer, aged 26, appears in the 1873/4 *Gazetteer of Otsego Co.*
iv.	**Hiram**, b. Burlington, NY 15 Dec. 1802; d. 13 July 1803. He is bur. at Burlington along with his father.
v.	**Feronia**, b. Burlington 16 Dec. 1804.
vi.	**Hiram**, b. Burlington 21 Aug. 1808; m. **Elizabeth Church** [Becker]. Served as pastor of the Congregational Church in Rock Prairie, WI.
vii.	**Horace**, b. Burlington 27 Dec. 1811; m. **Harriet N. Batchelder** 2 Feb. 1843; res. Rockford, IL.

[*Foote Family, Comprising the Genealogy & History of Nathaniel Foote of Wethersfield, CT and His Descendants* by Abram W. Foote, 1907; BUC6:358; *The Foote Family, the Descendants of Nathaniel Foote . . .* by Nathaniel Goodwin.]

FOOTE, DANIEL[1] of CT, d. in Town of Butternuts 1 Jan. 1840, aged 71. He m. **Violetta Mayham** of CT and soon after his mar. came to Otsego Co., c. 1805. He was a farmer of moderate circumstances; bought a farm of 75 acres on Chipmunk Hill, near Jockey Hollow, where he d. Violetta survived him by some 25 years, d. aged 92. Children:
    i.   **Diana**, m. 1st a Mr. **Brown** and 2nd **Loren Goff**; she d. 1882 in Buffalo.
2 ii.   **Augustus**.
    iii.   **Terressa**, m. **Lewis Hewlett** and d. in Buffalo when "past middle life."
    iv.   **Daniel**, now (1893) res. Auburn, aged nearly 80. He has two sons and one dau.
    v.   **William**, d. on his farm in New Lisbon in 1888 leaving three children.
    vi.   **Amelia**, widow (in 1893) of a Mr. **Goodrich** who d. in the army in 1863.

AUGUSTUS FOOTE[2] b. in the old red tavern in Lewisville, now Morris Village in Dec. 1808; d. at the home of his son, **Sedate** 5 March 1868, aged 61. His wife, not named in this source, b. Dec. 1803, d. 29 Aug. 1876. Both bur. in Morris Cemetery. Children:
    i.   **Cynthia**, m. **Amasa Winton** and d. in 1861 aged 20, leaving an infant son.
    ii.   **Mary Ann**, m. **Erastus Withey** and d. 7 Oct. 1859, left one child.
    iii.   **Zephaniah**, d. in the army at the age of 30.
    iv.   **Louisa**, d. 3 April 1874, aged 29.
    v.   **Moses**, d. 27 May 1890, aged 57; left a dau.
    vi.   **Reuben**, farmer aged c. 60 (1893).
    vii.   **Lucius** of Elm Grove, aged 62 (1893).
    viii.   **Delilah**, m. **Ransom Cox** of Milwaukee, WI.
    ix.   **Daniel**, farmer of New Berlin.
3 x.   **Sedate**.
    xi.   **Albert**, farmer on his brother **Daniel's** farm, adjoins the farm of **Sedate**.

SEDATE FOOTE[3] b. Morris, NY in 1836, farmer. In 1862 enlisted as a private in Company C., 121st NY Volunteer Infantry and served until the close of the war. He was one of 500 prisoners on their way to Guinea Station when he escaped with 16 comrades. In 1864 at Cold Harbor he was wounded, and now (1893) draws a pension for his services to his country. He m. 8 Jan. 1868 to **Elizabeth Taylor**, d/o **Stephen Taylor**, who was b. in Albany Co. in 1842. She d. 3 April 1878, leaving two sons:
    i.   **Stephen Augustus**, farmer two miles distant from the homestead.
    ii.   **Henry D.**, unm. and res. at home.
[BR:791-92]

FRANCHOT, ---[1] to America intending to settle his sons on the Ohio River, where there was a considerable French settlement. On their arrival in America they were encouraged by **Count De la Foret** to settle at Hillington.

April 1790 they were in Albany, removed to Schenectady, to Canajoharie, to Cooperstown to settle in the wilderness of Otsego County. **Mr. Franchot** returned to France; his children:
- i. **Louis [Lewis]**, d. 1800. He made his will as a res. of Butternuts on 31 May 1799 and in it he named only his wife **Julia Agnes**.
- 2 ii. **Paschal**.
- iii. **Auguste**.

JUDGE PASCAL FRANCHOT.

PASCHAL FRANCHOT[2] [P] b. 30 March 1774 in the Department de la Haute Marne, Canton de Sainte Dezier, Commune de Chamonilly. He m. 1st 28 Aug. 1806 **Catharine Hansen** of Greenbush, NY, m. 2nd 4 Nov. 1820 at Schenectady **Deborah Hansen**, both d/o **Derrick Hansen**. Paschal d. at Morris 30 Aug. 1855 aged 82; **Deborah** d. 12 Jan. 1862 aged 75. Children:
- i. **Julia A.**, res. village of Morris (1878).
- ii. **Helen Louisa**, b. 17 Sept. 1808, bapt 7 Jan. 1809; m. 2 June 1834 at Louisville, NY, **Volkertde Peyster Douw [Doun]** of Albany.
- iii. **Joanna**, m. **Henry R. VanRensselaer** of Morris.
- iv. **Francis G.**, m. **A. C. Powell** of Syracuse, NY.
- v. **Meeta**, m. **Robert Wells** of Riverton, NJ.
- vi. **Antoinette**, res. Syracuse.

vii.	**Charles F.**, res. Syracuse.
viii.	**Louis [Lewis]**, b. 8 Sept. 1811 and bapt. 8 Dec. the same year, dec'd. by 1878 & his widow res. Village of Morris.
xi.	**Marie Augusta**, res. Canadaguia.
xii.	**Richard**, b. 1816 Morris; preesident of Albany & Susquahanna Railroad; established cotton & woolen factories, Morris Town Supervisor; 1860 elected to Congress. He served as Colonel in the 121st Regt. NY State Volunteers. He res. in Schnectady and his widow res. there (1878). He d. 23 Nov. 1875.

[A:201-02, 216; NASH1; GBW; GBM; OB]

FRANKLIN, MOSES[5] (*Aaron*[4] *of MA & VT, Philip*[3] *of RI & VT, James*[2] *MA, James*[1] *of MA*), s/o **Aaron** and **Margaret (Luther?) Franklin**, was b. 24 Oct. 1763 at Scituate, RI. **Moses'** name appears on a tablet on a marker in the Presbyterian Churchyard in East Springfield as a Revolutionary soldier. He enlisted in the war in VT in 1776 and was pensioned 2 Oct. 1833, residing in Otsego Co. at time of application. 4 June 1789 **Moses** m. 1st **Amelia Walrath**, b. 29 Sept. 1767, d. 19 Nov. 1819; he m. 2d 24 June 1821, **Hannah Basinger [Baringer]**, b. 9 Nov. 1785, d. 3 June 1872, aged 86. **Hannah** was the first person to be bur. in the new cemetery at Springfield Center. **Moses** was a member of the Baptist church and a deacon and res. of Springfield. 4 May 1820 the records read: "**Deacon Moses Franklin** proposed to go on a journey to Vermont. Letter of recommendation given." He d. 4 Feb. 1854. Children mentioned here:

	i.	**Daniel**, b. 1822, d. 1906; res. Springfield, Town Supervisor 1863-64; sheriff in 1870 to 1873. He m. 1845 **Ann Kelly**, b. 1823, d. 1906. Their son, **Benjamin Franklin**, b. 1846, m. 2nd in 1885 to **Euphemia McGar** who was b. 1853 and they had **Anna** who m. **Leon W. Branch**.
	ii.	**Henry**, res. Springfield.
2	iii.	**Benjamin**.

BENJAMIN FRANKLIN's[2] children, b. Springfield:
i.	**Anna**.
ii.	**Jessie**.

[SPR:199, 212, 238; *The Boston Transcript* #182, #1919; *Swansea, MA Vital Records*, pp. 36-37; *Vital Records of Rehoboth*, p. 638, 140; *Salisbury/Amesbury, MA* by Hoyt, p. 267.; A:321; DARPI; OB; DAR Lineage #94066]

FRANKLIN, JABEZ[5] was a son of **Aaron**[4] above, and brother to **Moses**[5] and was b. 1750, d. 1828; m. **Sarah Starr**, d/o Capt. **Comfort Starr**.
[*Boston Transcript*, 23 Oct. 1920 #6; *The Abridged Compendium of American Genealogy*, Virkus, v. 3, p. 17]

GANO, JOHN was b. in France and settled in NJ in the US shortly before the Revolutionary War. He removed his family to Town of Richfield in 1791, with **James Williamson** (grandfather of **Cyrus Williamson** of Town of Warren) and purchased 600 acres in Schuyler's patent, Lot No. 8. He was of Richfield when he made his will 13 Nov. 1815; probated in 1818. In it

he named his wife **Caty** and three of his children. He had three sons and three daus. [those named in these sources]:
- i. **Garratt**.
- ii. **Isaac**.
- iii. **Caty**.
- iv. **James**, left two sons **James H.** and **Benjamin**.

[GBW; RS:112]

GILBERT, ABIJAH[1] from near Tamworth, Warwickshire, England where he was b. in 1747 [O.S.], to America c. 1787; accepted agency of the Morris patent; 1796 [1786] retired to England and emigrated with his family to America; farmer. He was s/o **John Gilbert** and wife **Mary Hill**. **Abijah** was one of five children, b. 2 Dec. 1747 (O.S.). His father d. of smallpox in 1761 and left **Abijah** as head of the family. His mother mar. again to **William Markham** of Middleton. When he was aged 29 he m. **Mary Yates**, and thereafter, until his departure to America, he lived near Attleborough, parish of Nuneaton. Five of his children were b. there. On his arrival in America [leaving his family behind in England], **Abijah** res. in NJ with relatives of his mother's named Hill. He met with **Lewis and Richard Morris** [see Morris family entry] and purchased, sight unseen, a tract of 1,000 acres in Montgomery Co., sight unseen (now Otsego Co.). After five years in America he returned in 1791 to England and brought his family to this country, landing in Philadelphia. They res. in Schenectady, inn owners, and in 1799 removed to Gilbertsville. He d. 17 July 1811; she d. 14 Jan. 1826. Children:
- i. **Elizabeth**, m. **Lewis Lee Morris**. [Given as youngest child in Gilbertsville history.]
- ii. **Lucy**, m. **Samuel Cotton**.
- iii. **Mary**, b. 1777, 2nd wife of **Samuel Cotton**. [Given as oldest child in Gilbertsville history.]
- iv. **Harriet Catherine**, m. **John Bryant**.
- v. **John T.**, b. 1779, m. **Lydia Smith**.
- 2 vi. **Joseph T.**, b. 1783; m. 1st **Hannah Thorp** and had 15 children; m. 2d 25 May 1831 at Norwich, NY to **Caroline Chapman** of Durham, NY.

Ref. BR states that **Lucy** was the 2nd wife of **Samuel Cotton**, not **Mary**.

JOSEPH T. GILBERT[2] associated himself with his brother-in-law, **Samuel Cotton** in business. They had sawmills, gristmills, a hat factory, a tannery, a steam distillery, a store, a mill for making linseed oil, blacksmith shops &c. They owned farms and were extensive traders. Of his busy life of 85 years, 68 were passed in Gilbertsville. He was a man of great physical strength, a magistrate whose decisions were never reversed. In 1803 he m. **Hannah Thorp**, d/o **John Thorp**, an early settler, and after her death 3 May 1830 [at Butternuts aged 45], he m. **Caroline Chapman** d/o **William Chapman** of Saybrook, CT. Of the first union were b. 15 children, and of the 2nd, three. In 1808 he joined the Presbyterian Church. He d. 13 July 1867. They had 18 children, those named here:

3 i. **Samuel C.**
3 ii. **John H.**
3 iii. **James L.**

SAMUEL C. GILBERT³, 2nd s/o **Joseph T.**, b. in Gilbertsville 6 Nov. 1807. Joined his father in business, and on his own has acquired landed property in many states of the union. He was Supervisor of the town when young, and was justice of the peace for 20 years. 25 Jan. 1832 he m. **Elizabeth A. Davis**, d/o **Benjah Davis** of Morris, NY and **Martha** his wife. Children:
i. **Julia Agnes**, d. age 10.
ii. **Elizabeth**, widow of (1893) **Judge James Colt** of Pittsfield, MA who has 2 sons and 3 daus.
iii. **Catharine Winter**, m. **Thomas Riggs** of Washington, DC; has one son, **Francis Rotch**, by her former husband and one son and one dau. by her present husband.
iv. **Martha D.**, m. **Charles A. Butler** of Utica, NY; has one son and one dau.

JOHN H. GILBERT³, b. Gilbertsville, 14 Jan. 1817. Began business in Norwich, NY in partnership with **N. C. Chapman**. After five years he returned to Gilbertsville and later m. **Ann Elizabeth Lathrop**, d/o **Dr. William Lathrop**. His business insterest are largly identified with other localities, and are scattered in various parts of the country. Children:
i. **Mrs. James Ecob** of Albany, NY.
ii. **Mrs. Arthur B. Denny**, Chestnut Hill, MA.
iii. **Mrs. Fitch Gilbert**, Eau Claire, WI.
iv. **Mrs. Keno Francke**, Cambridge, MA.
v. **Henry L.**, grad. Harvard University in 1888; banker.

JAMES L. GILBERT (MAJOR)³ b. 26 May 1822, has been a lifelong res. of Gilbertsville. He is the 11th of 18 children; 8th of 12 sons. At age 29 he m. **Jane Blackman**, d/o **James Blackman**, of CT ancestry, and an early settler in town of Butternuts. **Jane** d. in 1858, bur. Brookside Cemetery. Children:
i. **Dr. James B.**, after grad. NY Medical College, traveled in Europe and returned to NY where he has (1893) a large and lucrative practice.
ii. **Robert W.**, grad. Williams College, studied law in NY. He was handsome and courtley. He d. suddenly of a fall on 23 July 1892. His wife d. before 1861.

[A:109; BR:502-05; *Reminiscences of Early Days [Gilbertsville, NY]* ... by Helen Gilbert Ecob, 1927]

GILBERT, BUTLER¹ mar. a "New England lady" [who d. suddenly in middle life] and removed from Bowman's Creek, Schoharie Co., NY to Town of Laurens in 1791. They reared a family of eight sons and one dau. Children named:
2 i. **William**, remained in Otsego Co.
ii. **Morris**, remained in Otsego Co., Gilbert's Lake is named after him. [Youngest son.]

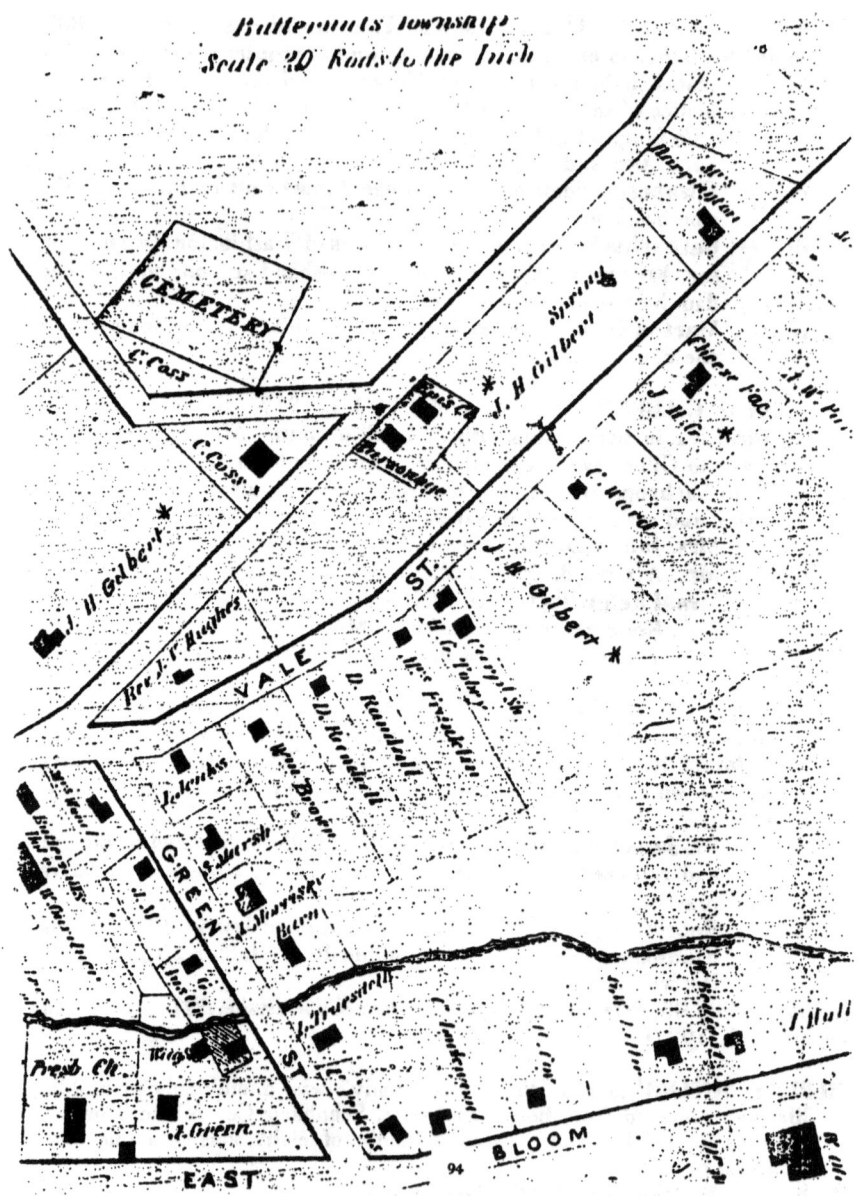

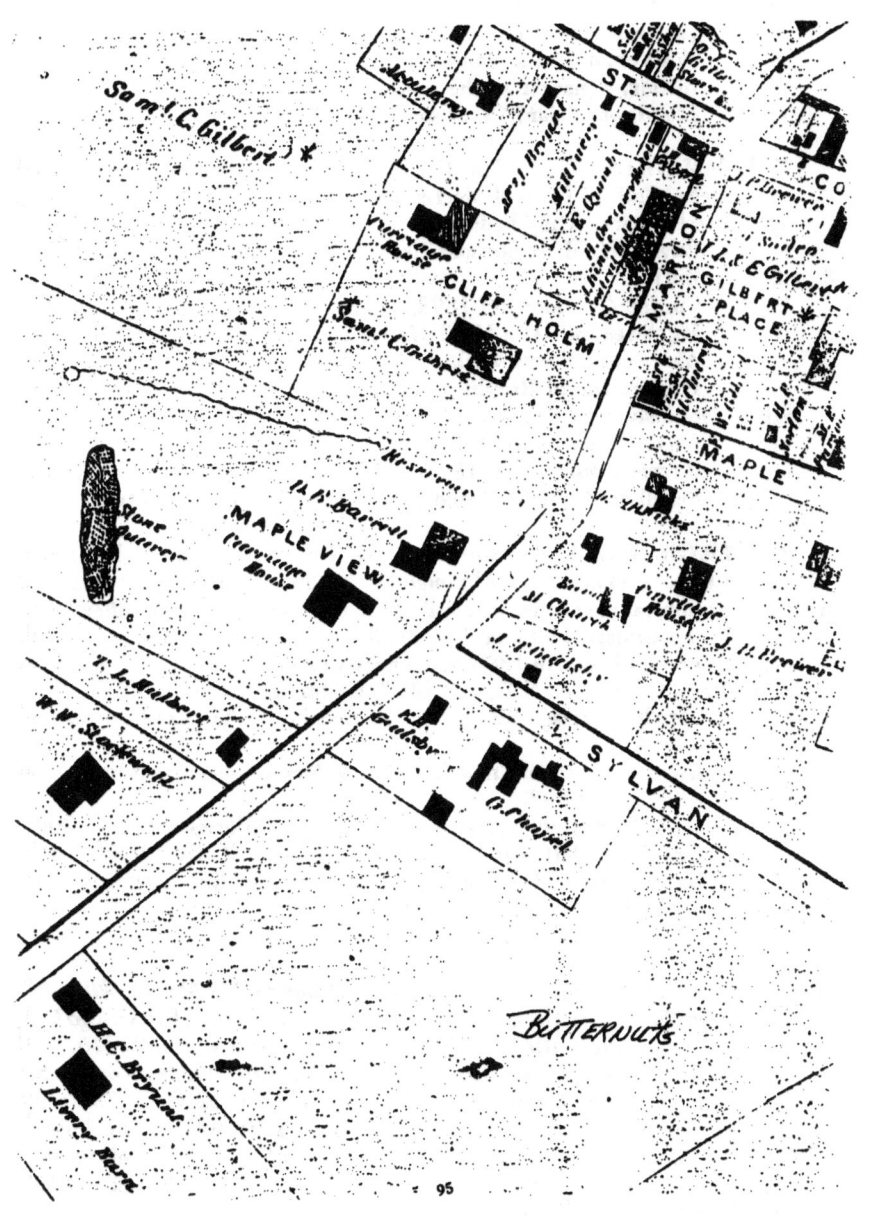

- iii. **Sylvester**, went to Ogdensburg & m. the sister of Gov. **Seymour**. Left a son, **William** who lived in China for many engaging in testing tea.
- iv. **Levi**, went "north."
- v. **Jay**, went "north."
- vi. **Walker**, owned a plantation near Baton Rouge, LA.
- vii. **Butler**, a planter in the south.
- viii. **Lloyd**, physician, "went south."

WILLIAM GILBERT[2] b. 4 Jan. 1779; m. **Martha Green** of New England at Laurens. Both d. Town of Morris, he c. 1852 aged 73 and she in 1864, aged 80. Farmers. They had:
- i. **Edwin W.**, d. at Stetsonville, where his widow now res. (1893).
3
- ii. **Butler**.
- iii. **Eunice A.**, widow (in 1893) of **Palmer Pride**, res. New Lisbon.
- iv. **Marietta**, m. 1st a Mr. **Tiffany**; 2nd **Thomas Wright**.
- v. **Abigail**, m. **Perry Lull**.
- vi. **Lois**, m. **David Hurlbutt**.
- vii. **Louisa**, twin to **Lois**, m. **Alexid Lull**.
- viii. **Asenath**, m. **Elisha Robinson**.
- ix. **Harriet**, widow (in 1893) of **Samuel Fenton**, soldier of the Rebellion [Civil War] who d. in the service of his country.

BUTLER GILBERT[3] b. near Gilbert's Lake, Town of Laurens; m. 1850 and res. on the old home farm. Although the widow of **Butler** is the focus of the biographical review in source BR, she is never referred to other than "Mrs. Butler Gilbert, widow of Butler Gilbert, who d. on the old homestead, near her present home, in 1885, when nearly seventy-four years of age, was b. in Otego, Otsego Co., N.Y., in 1822." Children:
- i. **Sarah**, d. at age 29 on the day that her father was bur.; school teacher.
- ii. **Evah Martha**, m. **Amos G. Carrick**; Mrs. Gilbert makes her home with them (1893).
- iii. **William Butler**, farmer res. near village of Morris, renting a 200-acre farm left by his father. He m. 13 Jan. 1885 **Kate Harrington** of New Lisbon. Have one son, **Roy Butler**, b. 19 Sept. 1891.

[BR:356-57]

GOODRICH, CALVIN[6] (*David*[5] *CT, David*[4] *CT, William*[3] *CT & MA, Lt. William*[2] *CT, Ensign William*[1] *England & CT*) pioneer from Sharon, CT to Otsego Co. at an early day and settled in Town of Hartwick. He was b. 27 [26, 29] April 1770, the s/o **David Goodrich Jr.** and **Anna Strong**, who m. at Sharon 5 Jan. 1769. **David** was b. 16 July 1749; d. 12 Oct. 1781 and served in the Revolution. **Anna** was the d/o **Caleb Strong** and wife **Abiah Clark** of Colchester and Sharon, CT and she was b. c. 1750. **Calvin** had four sons and five daughters and he d. in 1836. He m. 25 Dec. 1793, **Lovinia Fuller**. Children:

	i.	**Almira,** b. 15 Nov. 1794; m. --- **Weaver.**
7	ii.	**David.**
	iii.	**Lucinda,** b. 15 Dec. 1798, m. --- **Stone.**
	iv.	**Calvin Ripley.**
	v.	**Chauncey,** b. 1806, prominent res. of Milford where he has lived 30 years (1878). He has held office of postmaster for 17 years and justice of the peace for two terms.
	vi.	**Ezra.**
	vii.	**Parthena;** m. --- **Weeks.**
	viii.	**Ruanna;** m. --- **Price.**
	ix.	**Polly.**

DAVID GOODRICH[7] b. 2 April 1796; m. 1st 28 Jan. 1816, **Martha Young** who d. 26 March 1857; he m. 2nd **Matilda Young.** Children:

	i.	**Reuben A.,** b. 31 March 1817; m. 1st 9 June 1840, **Cornelia Winslow,** 2nd **Margaret Chessbro** on 13 Jan. 1846. He d. 31 Oct. 1863; res. Albany, NY.
	ii.	**Lydia C.,** b. 8 Oct. 1824, d. 1877; m. **Moses A. Westcote.**
	iii.	**Josiah H.,** b. 22 July 1829; m. **Harriet S. Norwood** 10 Feb. 1856; res. Chicago, IL.

[A:160-1; *Births, Marriages & Deaths, Sharon, CT* by L. Van Alstyne; *Dwight's History of the Strong Family,* B. W. Dwight; *Genealogies and Biographies of Ancient Wethersfield, CT* by Stiles; DARPI; Barbour Collection; *The Goodrich Family in America* ... by Lafayette W. Case, 1889; DARPI]

GRAVES, ABNER[6] (*Aaron*[5] *CT, John*[4] *MA, Benjamin*[2] *MA, John England & MA*[1]) b. 1766, d. 1855; m. **Mary Graves** in 1788. She was b. 1765 & d. 1848. To Middlefield, Otsego Co. from VT with his wife and family in 1794 and one year later they removed to Cooperstown where he d. aged 90, 4 April 1855 at the home of his son **Nelson.** Abner was a butcher in Cooperstown in 1804. They had five sons & one dau. Those so far identified:

7	i.	**Calvin.**
	ii.	**Nelson.**

CALVIN GRAVES[7] [P] was b. in Walpole, NH on 11 Sept. 1794; Presbyterian; merchant. Worked with his father at age 15 & during the War of 1812 they had charge of the commissariat and furnished troops with rations. Served as president at the organization of the Otsego Bank; also served in the same capacity at First National Bank. He handled real estate transactions in NY and IA. He d. 3 [2] June 1882, aged 76. In 1820 he m. **Fanny Carlisle,** b. Walpole, NH Dec. 1795 and d. 17 Oct. 1880. Children:

	i.	**Harriette M. [L.],** m. --- **Wilson,** res. Cooperstown and had two sons, **Frank B. Wilson** a merchant of Detroit and **George B.**
	ii.	**Frances R.,** m. 21 Feb. 1855, **Hon. George Green,** res. Cedar Rapids, IA and had: **Calvin G., George, William, Elizabeth, Robert, Francis** and **Woodward Green.**
8	iii.	**John C.**
	iv.	**George C.**

JOHN C. GRAVES[8] was b. in Cooperstown 25 Feb. 1828; merchant. In 1855 went to Cedar Rapids, IA & manufactured agricultural implements and furniture. Returned to Cooperstown, where he since res. He m. **Mary L. Keyes** on 6 [4] Sept. 1849. She was b. at Springfield, NY d/o **Webster C. Keyes** b. the same town. [See Keyes family entry.] Children:

    i.   **Fanny G.**, m. 1st **Dr. Lionel Cooke** who d. in 1886; she m. 2nd **Howard de W. Cooke**, a brother to ther first husband. They were sons of **Rev. Samuel Cooke**, many years rector of St. Bartholomew's Church in NY City, now (1893) res. in Stafford, CT. She is a member of Christ Episcopal Church. By her first husband she had two children: **Emma Waldron** and **Samuel W.** One source gives her res. as Cleveland, OH.

[A:261, 279-80; GBC1; BR:254-5; *First Families in America*, Compendium by Virkus]

GRAY, ALFRED[1] b. Canaan, Columbia Co., NY 29 July 1778; m. **Sarah Hudson** b. Cherry Valley, NY. He was a merchant and engaged in business at Sherburne and Earlville. He d. in 1820 in Montreal, Canada while there on business. At the time of his death he was a res. of Victor, Ontario Co., NY. Sarah was his 1st wife and by her he had:

2   i.   **John Hudson**.
    ii.   **Sarah [Sally] Ann**, b. 15 Feb. 1805, d. 5 June 1820.

After the death of **Sarah** at Cherry Valley, **Alfred** removed to Sherburne, where in 1806 he m. **Mary Olmstead** who was from Ridgefield, CT. Children:

    iii.   **Charles M.**, d. at his res. in Chicago 17 Oct. 1885, aged 78.
    iv.   **George M.**, b. 25 July 1818, now (1893) res. Chicago where he has been associated with the Pullman Sleeping Car Co. since 1866.

JOHN HUDSON GRAY[2] physician, b. Cherry Valley 1 Oct. 1802; m. **Lucinda Felton** who was b. in Oakham, MA 24 Feb. 1809; d. 26 March 1881. She was d/o Major **Skelton Felton** and wife **Tryphosia Ballard** who were m. in 1808. **Major Felton** was b. 15 June 1785 and d. at Oakham 31 July 1835; his wife d. 16 Aug. 1827. He studied medicine under Dr. **Delos White**. **John** grad. 1 Jan. 1826 from the Medical Society of Herkimer Co., NY and from the Medical Society of the College of Physicians & Surgeons of the Western District of NY in 1826. He practiced medicine in Schuyler's Lake until his death in 1847. Children:

3   i.   **John Felton**.
    ii.   **Sarah Ann**, b. 19 Nov. 1833; m. **Robert M. Durry** 4 Oct. 1854 and d. 31 Jan. 1878. **Robert** was a cabinet maker and hotel keeper; he d. 12 Jan. 1862. They had one child, **Robey**, who d. 15 Nov. 1859.

JOHN FELTON GRAY[3], res. Schuyler's Lake, was b. 7 Dec. 1830 at that place. He remained at home until his father's death and at age 17 worked as a clerk in the store of **Levi N. Caswell** of Schuyler's Lake for two years. He next worked for Brooks Bros., for two years and then went to Cooperstown and worked for **George W. Ernst**. He later returned to

Schuyler's Lake and still later removed to Ilion, Herkimer Co., NY for 1 1/2 years and worked for **Charles Bronson**. He then formed a partnership with **Don F. Lidell** and this firm bought out Brooks Bros. (general store). In 1853 he sold out and in 1855 wngaged in business with **Alonzo W. Henderson** and in 1858 bought him out, continuing alone until 1863. He finally closed his store and engaged in speculation until 1878. His later years have been given to looking after his farms in towns of Exeter and Otsego. He m. 19 March 1888 to **Eliza J. Pratt** who was b. in Town of Burlington 6 Dec. 1849, a d/o **Daniel** and **Eliza Pratt**, both b. Burlington. [See Pratt family entry.] **John** served as justice of the peace for 12 years and Supervisor of Schuyler's Lake for five terms; he was postmaster under Buchanan. **Eliza** is an active member of the Baptist Church. [No mention of children.]

[BR:743-44; NASH1]

GRIGGS, ICHABOD^5 (*Ensign Ichabod^4 CT & NY, Ichabod^3 MA & CT, Joseph^2 England & MA, Thomas^1 England & MA*) b. in Tolland, CT 14 [15] Oct. 1771; d. Springfield, NY 25 Feb. 1852; cord winder by trade. He was s/o **Ichabod Jr.** [a Revolutionary War veteran, as was his father, **Ichabod**^{3}] who was b. 7 June 1744 in CT and d. 30 Sept. 1776 in NY, and wife **Mercy Hatch**. **Ichabod**^{5} for a time res. in Shaftsbury, VT; m. c. 1790 **Jerusha Gurley**, b. Mansfield, CT 18 [5] Nov. 1772, d/o **Jonathan Gurley, Jr.**, a soldier of the Revolution. **Jerusha** d. 5 Jan. 1845, aged 73. **Ichabod**^{5} purchased property in Shaftsbury, VT and sold in in 1793, purchasing 50 acres in Springfield, Otsego Co., NY in 1797, where he established his home. In 1815 he purchased another 50 acres. **Ichabod** and **Jerusha** had 13 children. Last four b. Springfield; three married and lived in Springfield:

	i.	**Jerusha**, b. 15 Aug. 1792, d. 8 Jan. 1793.
6	ii.	**Ichabod**, b. 17 Nov. 1793, East Aurora, NY.
	iii.	**Jonathan G.**, b. 4 Sept. 1795, d. 18 Jan. 1796.
6	iv.	**David G.**, physician, b. Tolland 1 April 1797.
	v.	**Electa G.**, b. 15 March 1799, d. 22 [12] Dec. 1800.
	vi.	**Ann Amanda**, b. 11 Feb. 1801, d. 5 May 1864; m. **Samuel Abbott**, b. Albany, NY, 28 Sept. 1799, d. 15 Oct. 1860, s/o **Caleb Abbott** and **Hannah Wheet**. They had two children: **Albert** and **Harriet**.
	vii.	**Esther Gurley**, b. 18 Dec. 1802, d. 17 Aug. 1804.
	viii.	**Harriet**, b. 29 Jan. 1806, d. Strykerville, NY 26 May 1884; m. 1st **John Mack** of Londonderry, VT; m. 2nd **Melancthon Abbott**, b. Albany 6 Sept. 1807, d. 9 June 1889, brother of **Samuel Abbott** who m. her sister **Ann Amanda**.
	xi.	**Levantia [Leontia]**, b. 19 Aug. 1807, d. East Aurora, NY 14 Dec. 1892, m. **James Murray** of Glenwood, NY 30 Dec. 1829 at Springfield. Children: **Henry, Ann, Joseph, James** and **Ella Murray**.
	x.	**Olive Miranda**, b. 5 March 1810, d. 6 Aug. 1867; m. **Melancthon Abbott**, who m. 1st her sister **Harriet**. They had one child, **Leverette**.

xi.	**Marilla Duerer**, b. 24 Dec. 1811, d. 15 June 1895; m. **John A. Rathbun**. Children: **George A.** and **Jane Rathbun**.
xii.	**Albert Gurley**, b. 17 April 1814, d. 14 April 1884; m. **Drucilla Eaton**, granddaughter of General **William Eaton**, and continued on the Griggs' homestead.
xiii.	**Caroline**, b. 24 March 1816, d. 15 May 1880; m. **George Rathbun**.

ICHABOD GRIGGS[6], b. East Aurora, NY 17 Nov. 1793; m. **Sally [Sarah] Abbott** of Albany, NY; they m. at that place 3 Feb. 1823. The newspaper notice of their marriage states he was of Springfield, NY and she of Bethlehem. In 1832 removed to Colden, Erie Co., NY. Thirteen children [sic], seven b. in Springfield, NY, six b. at Colden. All of their children lived to be more than 60 years of age, some passed the four-score mark. Children:

i.	**Julia Ann**, b. 2 March 1825.
ii.	**Alonzo Melancthon**, b. 14 June 1826; m. **Phoebe J. Bosh**.
iii.	**Jerusha**, b. 17 Oct. 1827; m. **John F. Sibley** c. 1849. [sic]
iv.	**Sylvester**, b. 2 March 1829; m. **Rhoda P. Smith**, res. Java Village NY. Three children, first b. 1857.
v.	**Marilla Mary**, b. 1 Jan. 1831.
vi.	**Martha Miranda**, b. 10 July 1832, d. Lancaster, NY, 30 April 1920; m. 1st **Samuel Wheat**, b. NY City, d. Mapleton, Cayuga Co., NY 8 Feb. 1879; m. 2nd **Ezra Hoxie**, b. NY 1 Aug. 1818, d. Adrian, MI 4 Oct. 1914, s/o **John Hoxie** and --- **Slade**.
vii.	**John Allen**, b. 9 May 1834.
viii.	**Adeline**, b. 15 Oct. 1835.
ix.	**Ichabod Newton**, b. 22 Feb. 1837 in Colden; m. **Delia Tidd Griffin** 22 Dec. 1868. He d. 4 Nov. 1900, res. Holland, NY. Four children.
x.	**Esther**.
xi.	**Albert**, b. 10 June 1840, d. Comstock, OR 6 Jan. 1903; unm.
xii.	**Harriet Drusilla**, b. 6 March 1843.

Not in the Woodstock book:

xiii.	**John Albert**, b. 10 April 1848; m. **Dora Goodman** 26 Nov. 1879; she d. 12 Sept. 1912. Children **Bertha** and **Mattie Louise**, b. 1882 & 1884. [**Albert** above?]
xiv.	**Sarah**.
xv.	**David**, b. 1842, d. 2 Dec. 1921; m. **Miss Smith**. Three children. [Woodstock book shows a **David** b. 18 Nov. 1823.]

DR. DAVID GRIGGS[6] b. Cherry Valley b. 1 Apri 1797, d. 31 May 1855; m. Oct. 1835 **Martha Ann Staples** of Louisville, KY, b. Petersbury, VA 10 Feb. 1809, d. 24 Dec. 1859, d/o **Samuel Staples** and **Ruth Newboro**, widow of **John W. Atkinson** (b. Petersburg 24 Jan. 1801, d. 11 June 1834). **Dr. David** went on horseback to Fredonia, IN, and later to Concordia, KY. Their eight children were b. in Concordia.

[SPR:173; GBM; *Genealogies of Woodstock [CT] Families, Vol. 6*, Bowen; *Genealogy of The Griggs Family* by Walter S. Griggs, Pompton Lakes, NJ, 1926.

There are discrepancies in data from these two sources. DAR 54640; DARPI; Barbour Collection; OB. For early family information see *The Early History of Tolland: An Address, Delivered Before the Tolland Co. Historical Society ... on the 22nd day of August and 27th of September 1861* by Loren P. Waldo, 1861.]

HALE, JOHN[5] *(James*[4] *CT, James*[3] *MA/CT, John*[2] *MA, Robert*[1] *MA)* b. Ashford, CT 12 Oct. 1747; m. at Ashford 14 April 1772 **Mehitable Knowlton**, b. 1750, d. New Lisbon, Otsego Co., NY 1823. She was d/o **Daniel** and **Zerviah (Watkins) Knowlton**. John d. at Burlington, NY in 1810. The family removed to Otsego County c. 1807. **John** d. 7 Jan. 1811; he was a Revolutionary War veteran. Children, first 3 b. Ashford, remainder at Monson, Hampshire Co., MA:

	i.	**Daniel**, b. 10 Jan. 1773.
	ii.	**James**, b. 10 March 1774; Lt. Otsego Co. 1810 and Capt. 1812.
	iii.	**Mehitable**, b. 20 March 1775; m. 30 March 1797 **Shubael Reed** of Tolland, CT who was b. 1771 and d. 1844. She d. 1834.
	iv.	**John**, b. 13 Sept. 1776.
	v.	**Nehemiah**, b. 8 June 1778.
	vi.	**Stephen**, b. 6 Feb. 1780; res (1806) Ashford and in 1811 was res. in New Lisbon, Otsego Co. and in 1836 in Burlington, NY. He m. **Esther Blake Jones** and had a son, **Elias E.** who d. 1912; m. 1854 **Harriet French**, b. 1809, d. 1901.
	vii.	**Persis**, b. 29 Oct. 1781; m. --- **Carleton**.
	viii.	**Elam**, b. c. 1783; in 1805 res. Ashford and in 1806 in Monson, MA. He d. at Brimfield, MA 20 July 1811; m. **Phila** ---, who m. 2nd at Brimfield in 1813 to **Oliver Ferry**.
	ix.	**Joan**; m. --- **Knowlton**.
6	x.	**Frederick**, b. c. 1786; d. 1855.
	xi.	**Laura**, b. 16 May 1788; d. at Garrettsville, Otsego Co., NY 16 Dec. 1825; m. **Zachariah Warner**, b. Ashford 3 Dec. 1778, d. at Garrettsville 26 Feb. 1848. He was s/o **Eleazer** and **Joanna (Hale) Warner**.
	xii.	**Samuel**, b. 10 June 1790; d. 20 June 1790.
	xiii.	**Orrin**, b. 8 July 1791.

FREDERICK HALE[6] b. in CT c. 1786/9, d. Norwich, Chenango Co., NY in 1855. To state of NY between 1808 and 1812 and lived for a time in New Lisbon, NY, where all his children were born. He res. in Pharsalia and removed to Norwich in 1851 on his retirement. He m. in Otsego Co. in 1807, **Abigail Warner**, b. 1789[1787], d. 1854. She was d/o **Eleazer** and **Joanna (Hale) Warner**. Children:

i.	**Warner E.**, b. 1809; m. 1831 **Louisa Bradley**, b. North Haven, CT in 1812, she d.at Worcester MA 23 June 1876, bur. New Haven, CT She was d/o **Titus** and **Mary (Munson) Bradley**. Warner res. New Haven, where their four children were born.
ii.	**Henry**, b. 23 April 1813; m. 1st at North Haven [CT?] 19 Nov. 1840 **Ellen Amanda Barnes** and m. 2nd 31 Oct. 1870 **Elizabeth A. (Hemingway) Barnes**. Henry d. at New Haven, CT 4 June 1892 leaving three living children.

iii. **Elam W.**, m. at North Haven 6 Jan. 1842 **Mary Angeline (Sanford) Munson**, b. North Haven 1818, d. Boston, MA in 1898. She was d/o **Perit Merriman** and **Syvil (Dorman) Sanford** and widow of **George Gilvert Munson**. **Elam** had one child, **Katherine**, b. 4 Jan. 1843; d. 4 Jan. 1858.

iv. **Hiram**, b. 27 Sept. 1817; d. in Norwich, NY 1899. He m. 1844 **Abigail M. Newton**, who was b. at Preston NY 17 July 1817, d. Norwich, NY 28 May 1907. She was d/o **Jeduthan** and **Martha Maria (Smith) Newton**. **Hiram** was a farmer at Pharsalia, NY until 1851, when he removed to Norwich. Left several children.

v. **Eliza**, in 1884 res. Norwich, NY; m. **John Slater**.

vi. **Samuel**, res. in 1884 in Placerville, CA; m. at North Haven, CT 29 Jan. 1851 **Grace Angeline Todd**, who was /do **Orrin** and **Aurelia (Clinton) Todd**.

vii. **William H.**, b. 5 March 1824; m. 6 Jan. 1884 **Emma Robinson**, b. in Ireland c. 1859. Administration in **William's** estate was granted 14 Jan. 1884 to **Henry Hale**.

[CUT1:405; *Hale, House & Related Families, Mainly of the CT River Valley* by Donald Lines Jacobus & Edgar Francis Waterman, Genealogical Publishing Co., 1978; DARPI; Barbour Collection. Early New England Hale line found in *Descendants of Major Samuel Hale* by Elizabeth Hale Smith, 1902.]

HALL, EDWARD b. Scotland c. 1793, d. Burlington, NY in 1840 of the cholera. He m. in Scotland to **Dorothy Turnbull**; came to the US c. 1735 with four children; the last two b. in America. Children:

i. **John T.**, farmer of the Town of Burlington; at his death left two sons, **Edward** and **Andy**.

ii. **Ann**, now (1893) widow of Mr. **Ballcom** of Fly Creek; two children, **Isabele**, widow of **William Elliott** of Pittsfield, and **Elizabeth**, m. **Samuel Bishop** of Burlington and has three sons and one dau.

iii. **Jeannette**, m. **George Edwards**; d. in Norwich.

2 iv. **George**, b. Burlington, NY 1742; res. Oneonta.

GEORGE HALL[2] m. **Celia Barrett**, d/o **James** and **Lucinda (Fancher) Barrett**; **James** of "French origin," and settled in Otsego Co. with his family "many years ago." **Celia** d. in Oneonta 11 March 1892. They had one child:

WILLIAM W. HALL, M.D.[3], physician of the village of Morris, NY, was b. there 7 April 1863. He studied medicine at Albany, NY and Iowa City, IA and grad. from Buffalo Medical Univ. in 1885. On 15 May 1889 m. to **Elizabeth Ann Elliott**, d/o **John Elliott**. She is a member of Zion's Episcopal Church. [No mention of children.]

[BR:583]

HARDY, WILLIAM[1], b. RI and married there, later removed to Renssealer Co., and after several years, came to Otsego Co. & settled in Town of Milford, and after some years here he removed to Broome Co., until 1821 when he returned to Milford. He d. in Milford and is bur. at Milford Centre; soldier of the Revolution, he served under **George Washington** seven years, and was a pensioner. He m. **Mary Pembleton**, b. in RI & d. in Broome Co. Their son:

WILLIAM HARDY² b. Stephentown, Rensselaer Co. He m. in Town of Burlington & settled in Unadilla for a short time & then removed to Broome Co., rented land, & lived there a number of years. He then moved to Chemung Co., until the death of his 2nd wife, when he went to Chicago & lived there with his dau. until his death. His first wife was **Esther Dowd**, b. in Town of Otsego Co., d. in Broome Co., 1814. Only child so far found:

WILLIAM R. HARDY³ born 13 Jan. 1809 in Unadilla, in 1821 to Town of Milford, Otsego Co.; 25 Feb. 1835 m. **Margaret** d/o **John** and **Abigail (Hopkins) Low**, b. 15 April 1807, Town of Milford. **William** served in several county and town offices; farmer. He farmed on the east side of the Susquehanna River, two miles north of Portlandville and later on Dutch Hill, and after that the farm he now (1893) res. on. **Margaret** d. 7 Jan. 1890. Children, first four yet living (1893):

i.	**Albert**, b. 2 Feb. 1836.	
ii.	**Oscar**, b. Sept. 1839.	
iii.	**George W.**, b. 14 March 1845.	
iv.	**Elbridge G.**, b. 2 Jan. 1850.	
v.	**Abigail**, b. 30 May 1837, m. **Edgar Aylesworth**; she d. 12 June 1862.	
vi.	**William Henry**, b. 10 Feb. 1841, d. 17 June 1876.	
vii.	**Maline**, b. 7 April 1842, d. 19 Nov. 1865.	
viii.	**Esther**, b. 28 Dec. 1846, d. aged 15 on 16 June 1861.	

A **William Hardy** of Springfield made his will 4 May 1824; probated in Jan. 1825. In his will he named his wife **Margaret** and children:

i.	**William**.
ii.	**John**.
iii.	**Charles**.
iv.	**David**.
v.	**Joshua**.
vi.	**Jeremiah**.
vii.	**James**.
viii.	**Margaret**, m. --- **Allen**.
ix.	**Mary**, m. --- **Geutier**.
x.	**Elizabeth**, m. --- **Lansing**.
xi.	**Fidelia**.

[A:200; GBW; BR:239-40]

HOKE, FREDERICK¹, of English ancestry, b. in Greenbush, Rensselaer Co., NY c. 1750, was one of the first to settle in the forest wilds surrounding Otsego Lake. Five generations of his family lived on this homestead on the west shore of the lake. His wife was **Margaret Shaver [Shaves]**. She d. aged 85; he d. 16 Feb. 1829, was a veteran of the Revolutionary War. Their son:

2   i.   **Philip**.

PHILIP HOKE[2] was young when his parents brought him to Otsego Co. He was a farmer in the town of Otsego & d. there aged 66 years. He purchased a hotel across the line in Town of Otsego & res. there until his death. His wife was **Eve Countryman**, d/o **John**. It is thought that she was b. in NY. She lived to be age 85 and reared eight children. Only children mentioned here:

3   i.   **Menzo.**
3   ii.   **Frederick.**

MENZO HOKE[3] in 1893 was one of the oldest native-born sons of Otsego Co. living within its borders. He lived with his parents until his mar. on 16 March 1848 to **Catherine Getman**. She was b. 4 Aug. 1826 in Ephratah, Fulton Co., NY, the birthplace of her father, **John Getman**, and of her grandfather, **George Getman**. The family were one of the early Dutch families in NY. **John** was a shoemaker and spent the latter part of his life in the Town of Springfield. He m. **Betsey Nellis**, b. in Ephrata and a d/o **William** and **Mary (Getman) Nellis**. Children:
   i.   **Menzo, Jr.**, m. **Ella Nellis**, who d. leaving him with one child, **Earl**.
   ii.   **Flora**, m. **Adelbert Mallory**, farmer of Otsego.

FREDERICK HOKE[3] was reared in Town of Springfield; his father gave him a part of the old farm, and he bought the interests of the other heirs, thus becoming owner of the entire place, where he lived until 1850 when he sold out and bought land in Columbia, Herkimer Co., where he d. He m. **Maria Fashouris** and she d. on the home farm in Otsego Co. Their son: **RICHARD HOKE**[4] was c. age 13 when his parents removed to Columbia. He learned the carpenter trade and engaged in farming in the Towns of Otsego, Hartwick and Laurens before removing to Columbia, where he lived eight years. He then located in Springfield, Otsego Co., until 1880 when he removed to Richfield Springs. In 1857 he m. **Mary J. Gardner** who was b. in New Lisbon, d/o **William Gardner** who was b. in New Lisbon, s/o **Jared Gardner** of New England, a pioneer settler of Town of New Lisbon. **Mary's** mother was **Harriet Hollister** who was b. in Saratoga Co., NY. Children:
   i.   **Melvin.**
   ii.   **Hattie**, m. **Henry C. Thayer**. [See Thayer family entry.]
   iii.   **Clara C.**
   iv.   **Morris.**
[BR:218-19 & 684-86; SPR:200; DARPI]

HOLT, GEORGE (DEACON)[5] (*William*[4] *CT, William*[3] *CT, Nathaniel*[2] *CT & RI, William*[1] *CT*) b. 6 April 1759 [1757], Old Lyme, CT, s/o **William Holt**, school teacher, tanner and currier and wife **Phebe Lay**, of Lyme. Holt's Tannery was started prior to 1800 and is cited as one of the earliest businesses in Town of Cherry Valley. **George** was the 5th generation of the Holt family in America. **Deacon George** served three years in Continental service, enlisting from New London CT in 1777 and was a pensioner living in NY in 1818. He moved his family to NY by ox team and brought the old family grandfather clock, the first brought to Springfield, Otsego Co. His wife was **Hannah Sarah Hall**. [the 2nd source gives her as **Hannah** d/o **Joshua Holt** of Wilbraham, MA. DARPI states he m. 1st **Hannah Holt** and 2nd **Sarah** --- and 3rd **Lovisa** ---.] George d. 19 Dec. 1839 at Springfield, aged 82. A Mrs. **Sarah Holt** d. at Springfield on 3 Feb. 1830, aged 68. Children:

 i. **Nathan**, b. Wilbraham, MA 6 July 1783; m. 24 June 1804, **Polly** d/o **Samuel Hall**; removed to Otsego, NY and subsequently to Byron, NY. Had 8 children.

 ii. **Lucy**, b. Wilbraham, MA, 15 Sept. 1784, m. **Jonathan Kinne** in 1807 and lived in Springfield, Otsego Co. and had seven children. [see entry under **Kinne**]

 iii. **Phebe**, b. 18 Sept. 1785; m. **Daniel Harris**; res. Oxford, Canada West in 1864.

 iv. **Rev. George Holt**, b. 3 May 1790; minister of Free Will Baptist church at Schroeppel and Palermo, Oswego Co., NY and first source says he served churches in Otsego Co. He d. July 1859.

 v. **Hannah**, b. 17 March 1792; m. 22 Nov. 1812 **Peter P. Elwood**. She d. in Westfield, NY 1835. Had 8 children.

6 vi. **Gen. Walter Holt**.

GENERAL WALTER HOLT[6] b. 16 [17] Dec. 1793, m. **Sarah Van Benschoten** [Van Scoten] and made his home near Allen's Lake, where they reared nine children. She is probably the **Mrs. Sarah Holt** who d. at Springfield on 25 April 1857, aged 58. Children:

 i. **Camilla**, b. 1817, m. **Hiram Hutchins** and lived for a time in Monticello, NY and then in Charleston, MA, where she died. Her husband then moved with the children to Brooklyn, where he became pastor of the Baptist Bedford Avenue Church.

 ii. **Calista**, m. **Christopher L. Flint** in 1849 at Springfield Center. They lived in Otsego Co. four years and then moved to Hazel Green, Del. Co., IA.

 iii. **Walter**, attorney of Chautauqua Co., NY.

 iv. **Lucy**, m. --- **Kennedy**, res. Springfield at age 94 in 1878.

[SPR:180-82; *A Genealogical History of the Holt Family in The United States* . . . by Daniel S. Durrie, 1864; A:321; DARPI; Barbour Collection; CH!:103]

HOPKINS, CORNELIUS m. **Jane Platt** of Butternuts, d/o **Peter** and **Keziah (Rockwell) Platt** of Butternuts. [see Platt family entry]. Hopkins family res. in Binghamton, NY. Children:

 i. **Charles J.**, b. 1 Aug. 1845; m. **Sarah Burr** 10 Oct. 1866. He d. 24 May 1884.

 ii. **J. Belle**, b. 10 Sept. 1850; m. 15 Oct. 1868 **John J. Kinne**, res. Gilbertville, NY.

 iii. **Benjamin S.**, b. 27 Feb. 1857; m. in June 1876 to **Alice Hastings**, res. Norwich, NY in 1894.

 iv. **Kate A.**, b. 10 Aug. 1860; m. in Nov. 1880 **Gustavius Millard**, res. Binghamton in 1894.

[*A Genealogy of the Familes of John Rockwell of Stamford, CT 1641* . . . by James Boughton, 1903.]

HOUGHTON, JOTHAM[5] (*Israel[4] MA, Jacob[3] MA, John[2] England & MA, John[1] England & MA*) was the s/o **Israel Houghton** and **Martha Wheelock**. He settled in Town of Maryland, NY, near what is now Chaseville in 1793. He m. **Eunice Wilder** and had:

    i.   **Lydia.**
6 ii. **Jerehamel.**
   iii. **Daniel,** served as Captain in the War of 1812. A Mrs. **Daniel Houghton** of Chaseville d. 19 Sept. 1868, aged 95 years who could be his wife. His children: **Daniel E.**, physician of village of Schenevus and **Eliphalet E.**
   iv. **Tomason.**
   v.   **Rhoda.**
   vi. **Abigail.**

JEREHAMEL HOUGHTON[6] b. 8 Nov. 1776, m. **Anna Spencer** and settled in Chaseville and built an ashery and manufactured potash among other activities; served as colonel in the militia and in 1814 removed to OH. [Houghton family book says he settled in what is now Chanville, Oswego Co., NY and gives his children, but there is no indication from this source where the children were born or resided.]

   i.   **Alva,** b. 30 Sept. 1804.
   ii. **Milton W.,** b. 29 March 1807.
7 iii. **Madison.**
   iv. **Anna H.,** b. 20 May 1811.
   v.   **Angeline,** b. 2 July 1813; m. a Mr. **Walker** and had one son, **John**, of Louisville, KY.
   vi. **William H.,** b. 20 Jan. 1816.
   vii. **Lydia D.,** b. 3 May 1818.

MADISON HOUGHTON[7] b. 11 Jan. 1809; d. 9 July 1870; m. 21 March 1833 **Sarah King** who was b. 7 Nov. 1814. He was a portrait painter, designer, engraver, and wood carver. Children:

   i.   **William A.,** b. 22 Jan. 1834; d. 15 April 1892. Res. Almeda, CA and had one child, **Mildred.**
   ii. **Anna S.,** b. 19 Oct. 1837; d. young.
   iii. **Julia A.,** b. 21 Dec. 1842; m. Mt. Vernon, OH, to **Reuben C. Chase** on 30 Sept. 1862. He was b. 1 Feb. 1835 and served two years in the Civil War. Went from Otsego Co. to Hiawatha, KS.
   iv. **Josephine E.,** b. 12 June 1849, mar. and res. in Hiawatha, KS.
   v.   **Lester,** b. 6 March 1853, res. St. Louis, MO.

[A:175-6; OB; *The Houghton Genealogy: The Descendants of Ralph and John Houghton of Lancaster, MA* . . . by John W. Houghton, A.M., M.D., NY]

HUBBARD, EBENEZER[5] (*John[4] CT, John[3] CT, John[2] [MA?] & CT, George[1] CT*) b. 20 Feb. 1752 in Pomfret, CT, s/o **John** and **Bridget Hubbard.** They were res. of that part of Pomfret incorporated in 1786 as Brooklyn. **Ebenezer** m. at Brooklyn on 12 Oct. 1780 **Molly Simons**. Before 1797 they removed to Otsego, Otsego Co., NY. In 1804 they res. in Hardwick. Children, all b. Brooklyn:

i.	**Reuben**, b. 10 Dec. 1784. Probably the **Reuben** who m. M. **Lester** and had their son **John Lester Hubbard**, b. 10 Feb. 1811, bapt. 2 June the same year.
ii.	**Lydia**, b. 26 June 1786.
iii.	**Ebenezer Jr.**, b. 5 July 1789.
iv.	**William**, b. 4 June 1791.
v.	**Polly**, b. 30 Aug. 1793.

[TAG:23:221-23; *Woodstock, CT Families*, Bowen; CCD; *The American Genealogist*, Vol. 27]

HUBBARD, ELIJAH, d. 20 Oct. 1815, aged 46 years; **Phebe** his wife d. 2 Jan. 1873, aged 101. Bur. Burlington Flats. He was a res. of Burlington when he made his will 30 June 1815 and in it named **Phebe** his wife and children (below). **Samuel, Julia** and **Asena Hubbard** witnessed his will. Children:

i.	**Levi**.
ii.	**Eri**.
iii.	**Jarard**; m. **Abigail** ---.
iv.	**Serena**, m. --- **Johnson**.
v.	**Levina**, m. --- **Day**.
vi.	**Selinda**.
vii.	**Beulah**.
viii.	**Drusilla**.

[GBW; NER101:233]

HUDSON, SAMUEL[1] b. 14 Dec. 1765 in RI and mar. there to **Sally Windsor**, also of RI, b. 5 April 1772. They remained there until their children were grown, later removed to Chenango Co., NY where they both died; she in middle life and he at a great age. Only children named here:

	i.	**George**.
2	ii.	**Cyrus**.

CYRUS HUDSON[2] removed to New Berlin, Chenango Co. from RI in 1816; 1818 to Laurens with his brother **George**. They had tried to enlist in the War of 1812, but failed because the quota of RI had been filled. Their intent in moving to NY was to enlist. When they were unable to enlist in NY, they decided to settle there. **George** settled in Chenango Co. They both won their titles in the local state militia, **George** as Colonel and **Cyrus** as Captain. In later life **Cyrus** was a shoemaker and served as a Justice of the Peace. He was widely known for his extended reading and scholarly qualifications. He m. at Laurens, **Eliza Toby**, who was b. in town of Morris, Otsego Co. 10 Aug. 1800 and d. at Laurens 1 March 1880, aged 79. Her parents were early settlers of that part of the county. Her father was accidentally killed in the prime of life by a falling tree. Tanner, res. with dau. at age 82 (1878); d. 26 April 1882 [aged 86 years, 5 months]. They had twelve children [five living in 1893]. Those named here:

i.	**Stephen T.**, hardware merchant in Laurens.

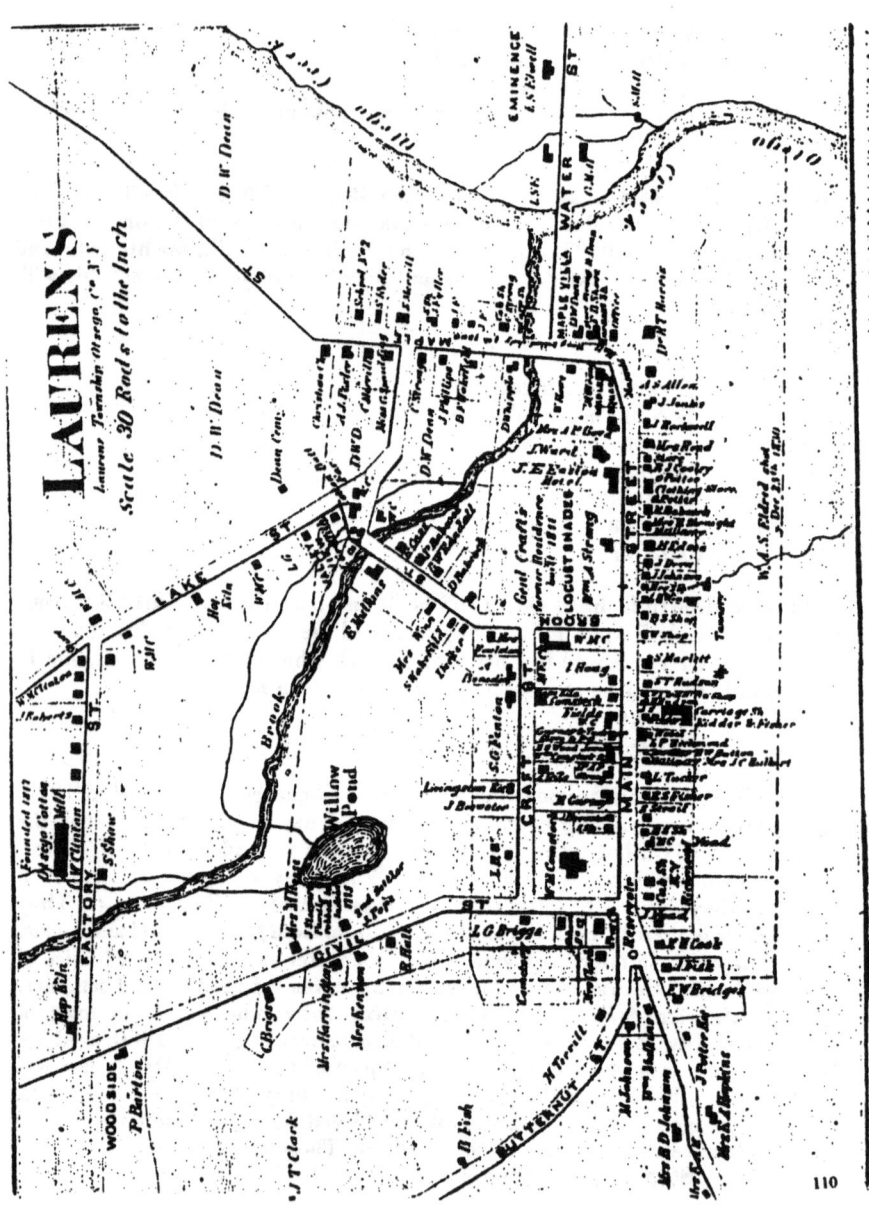

ii.	**Horace**, hardware merchant in Laurens. Served in the 3rd NY Cavalry early in the Civil War and later was 2nd Lt. and Acting 1st Lt. of a colored regiment raised in the south.
iii.	**Henry**, res. New Lisbon.
iv.	**Cyril [Sarel]**, res. Oneonta.
v.	**William**, 1st Sgt. of Co. G, 3rd NY Cavalry in the Civil War. He was never wounded, but left the service in poor health and d. about 22 Feb. 1867 at Oneonta at age of 26. He left a widow, but no children.
v.	**Caroline**, m. --- **Curtis**, res. Laurens.
vi.	Dau. res. Chenango Co.
vii.	Dau. res. Monroe.

CYRIL/SAREL HUDSON[2] was b. in town of Laurens, NY 9 April 1825. He m. at that place to **Mary Clark**, b. in the same town, 21 Oct. 1827, a d/o **William** and **Anna (Whitcomb) Clark**, natives of Otsego Co. **William Clark** was a farmer and d. aged 49; his wife d. aged 69. Members of the Baptist Church. They had four children, but only **Mary** was living in 1893. **Cyril** was in partnership with his brother **Horace** in the hardware firm of Hudson Brothers. Children:

	i.	**M. Lavantia**, d. aged 30 years, unm.
	ii.	**Ann E.**, m. **J. C. Sanford** of Margaretville, Delaware Co., NY, a machinist in the Albany & Susquehanna Railroad shops at Onetona. They had one child, **Gertrude**, who d. aged 15 months.

[A:170; BR:689-90; OB.]

HUNTINGTON, SAMUEL[5] (*Samuel*[4] *CT, Simon*[2] *MA, Simon*[1] *England*) b. Canterbury, CT 4 June 1764, was s/o **Samuel** of Lebanon who d. 1797. **Samuel**[5] removed to Middlefield, NY 1803, where he d. 8 Oct. 1826. [There is an obituary of a **Samuel Huntington** of Otsego who d. 6 Feb. 1836.] Children:

6	i.	**Samuel**.
6	ii.	**Mason Coggswell**.
	iii.	**Royal**, b. 18 March 1792, d. unm. at Sackett's Harbor, NY, July 1820.
	iv.	Son, d. in infancy.
	v.	Dau., d. in infancy.
	vi.	**Edwin Wells**, b. 16 Jan. 1803; m. **Dimis Abbott**. Res. Minetto, Oswego Co., NY; he a farmer.
	vii.	**Delia**, b. 19 May 1804; res. with bro. **Edwin**.

SAMUEL HUNTINGTON[6] was b. at East Haddam, CT 26 Jan. 1789; m. 3 Nov. 1814 to **Jenett Mosley**, d/o **Josiah** and **Esther (Gates) Mosley** [Esther (Smith) Gates]. **Samuel** removed with his father to Otsego Co. where his wife d. 5 Dec. 1848 and he m. 2nd 31 March 1852 **Mrs. Eliza Stilliman**. He served as first lieutenant in the volunteer corps formed in Cooperstown in 1798. He d. Sept. 1871; children:

i.	**Martha Adeline**, b. East Haddom, CT 23 Oct. 1815, d. unm. in Middlefield, NY 12 Dec. 1812.

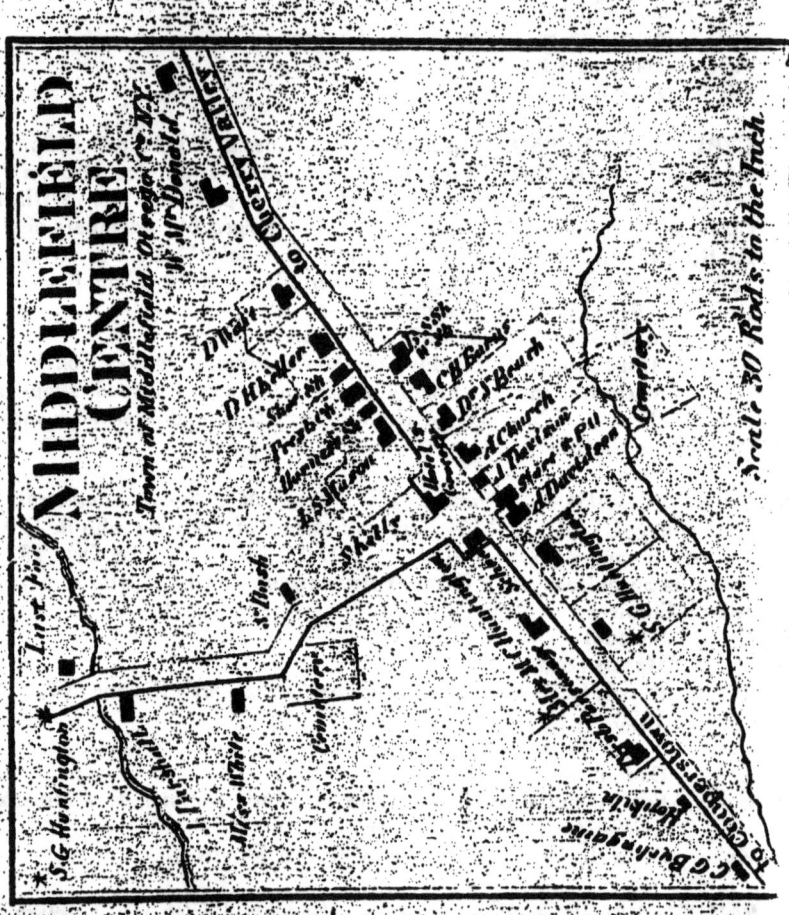

RESIDENCE OF S.G. HUNTINGTON, MIDDLEFIELD CENTRE, OTSEGO CO., N.Y.

 ii. **Mary Amelia**, b. Middlefield, NY 14 May 1818; m. 1 May 1814 **Waldo Skinner**, who was b. in Woodstock, CT. He is a merchant & manufacturer and res. Madison, WI. They have five children.
 iii. **Samuel**, twin with **Mary A.**; he d. 17 May 1818.
7 iv. **Samuel Gates**, b. Middlefield, NY 28 May 1820; m. 21 Sept. 1848 **Jane Hannah Church** who d. in that same place 5 June 1851. He m. 2nd 20 July 1852 **Adeline Julia Parmale**, res. at Middlefield Centre, NY. She was d/o **Rev. Alvin** and **Viletto Parmale**.
 v. **Dorothy Jennett**, b. in Middlefield 28 May 1820; m. **Dr. Aborn T. Bigelow** of Worcester, NY 8 Jan. 1850 and had: **Polly**

	Josephine b. in Worcester 6 Feb. 1851; **Uriah Huntington** b. 1 Aug. 1852 and **Martha Irene**, b. Sept. 1854.
vi.	**William Silliman**, b. Middlefield 22 Sept. 1822; m. 1 Aug. 1850 **Mary Ann Walker**, d/o **Dea. William** and **Sarah (Ingalls) Walker**. Res. Middlefield; he is a manufacturer.
vii.	**Laura Almira**, b. 14 Aug. 1826; m. **William Orrin Brainard**, s/o **William** and **Lucy (Day) Brainard** of East Haddam, CT on 9 Oct. 1851. They res. in East Haddam and have one dau., **Mary Almira**, b. there 17 Jan. 1853.
viii.	**Esther Elvira**, b. 4 Aug. 1826 in Middlefield, where she d. 17 Jan. 1827.

SAMUEL GATES HUNTINGTON[7] b. Middlefield 28 May 1820; m. **Jane H. Church** 21 Sept. 1848. She d. 5 June 1841 and he m. 2nd **Adaline Julia**, d/o **Rev. Alvin** and **Violetta Parmalee** 20 July 1852. Children, all b. Middletown:

i.	**Helen Wilson**, b. 27 Nov. 1849.
ii.	**Agnes Church**, b. 4 Jan. 1851.
iii.	**George Mason**, b. 2 Aug. 1853.
iv.	**Alice Parmalee**, b. 25 June 1857.

MASON COGGSWELL HUNTINGTON[6], b. 19 Oct. 1790; m. 14 May 1818 **Harriet Gates**, sister of his brother **Samuel's** 1st wife, she b. in East Haddam 31 Jan. 1800. He removed to Middlefield, NY, where he d. 21 Nov. 1857. Children, all b. Middlefield:

i.	**Jonas Gates**, b. 2 March 1819, d. 17 Jan. 1820.
ii.	**Royal**, b. 19 March 1821, d. 4 March 1849.
iii.	**Harriet**, b. 20 May 1824; m. 3 Feb. 1846 **George Clyde Allen** of Albany, NY, where they res. Have two children: **Lorena** b. 20 Jan. 1850 & **Ella**, b. 25 May 1857.

[A:191-2; OB; *Genealogical Memoir of the Huntington Family* ... by Rev. E. B. Huntington, Stamford, CT, 1863.]

HUNTINGTON, SOLON was b. in Harwinton, Litchfield Co., CT 15 Jan. 1812. At an early age he entered the employ of Curtis, Candy & Styles, silverware manufacturers in CT. He later left the employ of the firm, establishing himself in the same business. His trade soon extended over severl states, and by age 28 he had accumulated enough to retire. 2 June 1840 he m. **Harriet Saunders**, d/o **Henry**, physician of Ballston, Saratoga Co., NY and took up res. in Oneonta, where he lived until his death 11 Aug. 1890. There he built the "Mendel stone store," and purchased several hundred acres of land. For c. 15 years he engaged in the general merchandise business, at first with his brother **C. P. Huntington** as a parter, and afterward with **Jacob Dietz**. Solon also engaged in the carriage manufacturing business, which he continued until the close of the Civil War, when he became extensively engaged in real estate in Otsego and Delaware Counties. He was survived by his wife and four of his children. Children:

    i.   **Mrs. B. W. Foster** of Huntington, WV.
    ii.   **H. E.** of San Francisco, CA, identified with the Southern Pacific Railroad system, assistant to **C. P. Huntington**, president of the company, with headquarters in San Francisco.
    iii.   **W. V.** of San Francisco, CA, deals in real estate.
    iv.   **Caroline D.**, res. Oneonta.
[BR:590-91]

HUNTLEY, JAMES⁴ *(Daniel³ CT, Aaron² MA & CT, John¹ MA & CT)* b. in Lyme, CT 16 [17] Aug. 1725, d. at the home of his son **Marvin** in East Lyme, aged 94 years on 25 Feb. 1816, and is buried in the "Old Stone Yard" in Lyme. He m. in Lyme 21 Aug. 1750, **Lucretia Smith**, d/o **Samuel** and **Mary (Marvin) Smith**. James received a gift of land from his father and lived there most of his life. In his later years he lived with his son in West Exeter, Otsego Co., NY. He commanded a company of Militia in 1776 in **Experience Storr**'s regiment. [Cutter reference gives **James** as s/o **Ezekiel Huntley** and wife **Mary Wallbridge** of MA & NY; b. near Norwich, CT c. 1750.] He removed to the town of Exeter, NY where he made his will 7 Feb. 1809. He was a man of considerable property and divided it among his children before his death, and each was given a nominal sum. Children:

2   i.   **Phineas**, b. 14 Jan. 1754.
    ii.   **Re[y]nold**. b. 30 March 1756; m. 1st in Lyme in 1780 **Jerusha Mack** and 2nd in 1787 **Mrs. Esther McKnight**. Res. New London, CT & Manlius Center, NY.
    iii.   **Enoch**, b. 1 Oct. 1758; d. 1 June 1786.
    iv.   **Irene [Reny]**, b. 9 March 1761; m. 1st 21 Dec. 1780 **James Ryan** of New London, CT; m. 2nd **William Moor** of Waterford, CT. She had by her 1st husband **Polly, Joseph** and **Lucretia Ryan**.
    v.   **Ira**, b. 3 June 1764; m. 1786 **Polly Lee**, b. 1763 & d. 1839. Res. Manlius, NY where **Ira** d. 1814.
    v.   **Marvin**, b. 11 Nov. 1766; m. 1st 1789 to **Caroline Lord** who d. in 1807 and he m. 2nd 1808 **Mary Douglas** of New London. Res. Lyme.
    vi.   **Anna**, b. 2 Jan. 1769; m. --- **Lewis** & res. in PA They had a son, **Charles**.
2   vii.   **James**, b. 17 May 1771.
    viii.   **Seth**, b. 8 July 1773; d. 9 Sept. 1787.
    ix.   **Elknah**, b. 19 Sept. 1775.
    ix.   **Silas**, b. 3 Aug. 1777.
    x.   **Lucretia**, b. 18 Aug. 1781; m. **Silas Beebe**.

PHINEAS HUNTLEY² of Exeter made his will 17 March 1830 and in it named his wife **Hannah** and children and grandchildren:
    i.   **Albert Phineas**, b. 20 Nov. 1810.
    ii.   **Calvin**, b. 15 Jan. 1818, d. 1 April 1834 at Plainfield.
    iii.   **Betsey**, m. **Ely T. Marsh** of West Winfield, NY. Had children **Elisha, Jacob** and **Ira Marsh**.
    iv.   **Ruhamah**, m. --- **Peck**; had son **Calvin**.

v. **Lucretia**, m. --- **Matheson** of West Winfield, NY; had son **Abner**. Res. in Sergeant's Bluff, IA.

Lydia and **Jack Huntley** were witnesses & brother **James** was executor with son **Calvin**.

JAMES HUNTLEY² farmer of West Exeter, Otsego Co. where he d. and is bur. with his father in the Huntley burying ground. He was a deacon of the Baptist Church. He m. **Lydia Calkins** in 1795; she d. 14 Aug. 1865, aged 89. He enlisted in the War of 1812, but never saw service. The family removed to West Exeter, NY and then to West Winfield. **James** made his will on 30 Dec. 1847 [d. in West Winfield, NY 26 Aug. 1849] and named his wife and children (all b. West Exeter):

3
- i. **Eunice**, b. 1796; d. 11 April 1796.
- ii. **James Calkins**, b. 10 April 1797.
- iii. **Experience**, b. 19 Jan. 1799; m. 16 March 1819 **Benjamin Prescott** who d. 28 July 1847. She d. 31 March 1883.
- iv. **Eliza**, b. 1 April 1800; m. 4 Nov. 1817 **Daniel Josslyn** who d. 14 June 1873. She d. 16 July 1856.
- v. **Isaac**, b. 22 Jan. 1802.
- vi. **Lydia**, b. 12 Aug. 1803; m. 14 Feb. 1827 **Phineas Hall**. She d. 10 July 1963.
- vii. **Eunice**, b. 19 March 1805; m. 6 Feb. 1828 **Charles Barstow** who d. Nov. 1887, aged 89 years. She d. 24 Aug. 1841.
- viii. **Charles**, b. 5 July 1807.
- ix. **Lyman**, b. 3 Feb. 1809.
- x. **Lester**, b. 17 Dec. 1810.
- xi. **Roxy Ann**, b. 27 June 1812; m. 24 June 1840 **Myron Eldred**. She d. 12 June 1911, aged 99 years.
- xii. **Elisha**, b. 13 Nov. 1813.
- xiii. **Loring**, b. 26 July 1815.
- xiv. **Porter Calkins**, b. 26 March 1818.
- xv. **Washington**, b. 28 Dec. 1819; d. aged 1 day.
- xvi. **Florus**, b. 19 May 1822; d. aged 2 years, 1 month.
- vii. **Isaac**.
- ix. **Lydia**, m. --- **Hall**.
- x. **Roxana**, m. --- **Eldred**.

The family were remarkable for longevity and their large stature. Also named in **James'** will, with no relationship given, were **Lyman, Elisha, Loring** and **Porter Huntley**.

JAMES CALKINS HUNTLEY³ b. West Exeter in 1796, d. at West Winfield, Herkimer Co., NY in 1879. He was bur. in the Huntley burying ground in Exeter, but was later removed to West Winfield by his grandson, **Charles Russell Huntley**, of Buffalo. James was a prominent farmer, major of a militia regiment, Baptist and strongly opposed to slavery. He m. **Laura Wood** and had:
- i. **Russell**, d. Ilioin, NY 28 Dec. 1900; m. **Clorinda**, d/o **John** and **Almira (Adams) Talbot**
- ii. **Alonzo**, d. CA leaving issue.

iii.	**George**, d. Madison, WI.
iv.	**Porter**, d. Hartford, Oneida Co., NY.
v.	**Carlos**, d. San Luis Obispo, CA.
vi.	**James Floras**, M.D., grad. Albany Medical College; d. at Oneida, Madison Co., NY.
vii.	**Olive**, d. West Exeter; m. **Calvin Huntley**.
viii.	**Lydia**, d. Sweetwater, MI; m. **James Tanner**.
ix.	**Julia**, d. Newark, NJ; m. **E. O. Hovey**.
x.	**Laura**, d. Otsego Co., NY; m. **H. H. Babcock**.

[CUT1:2:561; GBW; *Genealogies of CT Families From the New England Historical & Genealogical Register, Vol. II*, Genealogical Publishing Co., 1983; DARPI; OB.]
LEAVE ROOM 1 MAP

HURLBUTT, JOHN¹, m. 10 Nov. 1831 **Caroline Rockwell**, d/o Ezra [see Rockwell family entry]. Children:

	i.	**Henry R.**, b. Butternuts 22 July 1834; m. 5 Aug. 1863 **Mary A. Hurd**, res. at Scranton, PA 1892.
2	ii.	**Gould L.**
	iii.	**Charles A.**, b. 6 May 1838; d. 24 April 1892.
	iv.	**Ezra B.**, b. 3 Aug. 1847; res. Gilbertsville 1892.

GOULD L. HURLBUTT² b. Butternuts 25 April 1836; m. 1 Sept. 1864 **Adelia Donaldson**, b. 20 Feb. 1838. He d. 5 June 1872; she res. Gilbertsville in 1892. Children, b. Gilbertsville:

i.	**Frank L.**, b. 14 Aug. 1866; res. Galesburg, IL in 1891.
ii.	**Francis D.**, res. Gilbertsville 1891.
iii.	**Lizzie B.**, b. 23 Oct. 1868; m. 25 Dec. 1890 **Solon Benedict**, res. Gilbertsville in 1891.

[*A Genealogy of the Families of John Rockwell, of Stamford, Conn. 1641 . . .* by James Boughton, 1903]

HYDE, GUSTAVUS⁵ (*Matthew⁴ CT, John³ CT, Samuel² CT, William¹ England & CT*), brother to **Ira⁵** below, was b. at Norwich, West Farm, (now 1864) Franklin, CT, 18 June 1777, the eldest s/o **Capt. Matthew** and 2nd wife **Hannah Pember**. Gustavus m. 1 Oct. 1801, **Mary Cole** of Richfield, NY. They settled at Richfield, where he d. 27 Nov. 1824. She survived him and d. in Nov. 1849 at that place. Children, all b. Richfield:

i.	**Parley**, b. in March 1804; m. 1st **Julia Harris** and 2nd the widow **Adeline Amanda Lewis**.
ii.	**Adolphus**, b. May 1807; m. 1833 **Keziah Coon** of Otsego Co., and d. 1 March 1851. Two children: **Louisa** b. 1835 and **George W.** b. 1843.
iii.	**James**, b. 1820; m. **Marinda Risley**.
iv.	**Isaac**, b. 1822; m. c. 1839, **Hannah Shoots** of Otsego. No children in 1857.
v.	**Maria**, b. 28 Feb. 1803; m. c. 1845 **Horace Scott** of Geneva, Walworth Co., WI and was res. there in 1857; no children.
vi.	**Hannah**, b. 5 March 1806; m. c. 1831 **David Garnet** of Richfield;

| | vii. | Delina, b. 28 June 1809; m. 1831 **David J. Parks** of Albany, NY. Res. Binghamton and res. at Fond Du Lac, WI in 1857. Eight children. |

res. in IA in 1857; three children.

- vii. **Delina**, b. 28 June 1809; m. 1831 **David J. Parks** of Albany, NY. Res. Binghamton and res. at Fond Du Lac, WI in 1857. Eight children.
- viii. **Elizabeth**, b. July 1811; m. 1839 **Timothy Filkins** of Richfield who d. 1848. Three children: **Andrew, Clarence** and **Alexander Filkins**.
- ix. **Sarah**, b. July 1815; m. **Abner Pier**.
- x. **Delia**, b. 1817; m. 1832; m. 1832 **John Filkins** of Richfield. Res. Fort Ontarion, NY in 1857 with children: **Orson, George** and **Mary**.

[*Hyde Genealogy . . . from William Hyde of Norwich* by Reuben H. Walworth, 1864, Vol. I]

HYDE, IRA[5] (*Matthew*[4] *CT, John*[3] *CT, Samuel*[2] *CT, William*[1] *England & CT*) is uncle to **James Hyde**[6] in the above entry. He was b. at Norwich West Farms, (now [1864] Franklin] CT 26 March 1779, 2nd s/o **Capt. Matthew Hyde**[5] and 2nd wife, **Hannah Pember**. Ira m. 10 March 1802, **Susannah Torrey**, b. Franklin, CT, d/o **Michael Torrey** and **Lucy** his wife. The Hydes settled at Otsego, NY, where they were living in 1857. Children, all b. Otsego:

- i. **Ira**, b. 23 Sept. 1813; m. **Mary Shumway**.
- ii. **Ambrose**, b. 7 Oct. 1819, d. 27 Oct. 1842, unm.
- iii. **Abel**, b. 3 June 1821; m. 1st **Almira Singleton** and 2nd **Sarah Dairy**.
- iv. **Eli**, b. 5 Oct. 1824, d. 1 Aug. 1826.
- v. **Eli**, b. 7 Dec. 1827, unm. in 1856.
- vi. **Lucinda**, b. 15 Oct. 1803; m. **John Southerland**.
- vii. **Wealthy**, b. 12 Dec. 1811; m. **Stephen Hull**.
- viii. **Susan**, b. 8 Aug. 1815; m. 9 Feb. 1844, **Harvey Layton** of Richfield, NY; res. there in 1850 with no children.

[*Hyde Genealogy . . . from William Hyde of Norwich* by Reuben H. Walworth, 1864, Vol. I]

HYDE, JAMES[6] (*James*[5] *CT, Matthew*[4] *CT, John*[3] *CT, Samuel*[2] *CT, William*[1] *England & CT*) b. Norwich, CT 19 April [17 May] 1772, eldest s/o **Capt. James Hyde** (1741-1785) and **Eunice Backus** of Norwich. He m. 18 Feb. 1796 **Elizabeth [Betsey] Starr** of Franklin. He was a farmer and they settled at Franklin and in 1800 removed to Richfield, NY. He held various offices and twice represented the county in the state legislature. He d. 26 March 1826; she d. 10 Nov. 1833, both at Richfield. Children, later ones b. Richfield:

6
- i. **James**.
- ii. **Roswell**, b. 31 Dec. 1798 at Franklin; m. 3 Feb. 1824 [1823] **Eunice Grey** of Springfield, NY, where he d. 10 Dec. 1825. They had one child who d. in infancy.
- iii. **Charles Backus**, b. 4 Dec. 1801; m. Nov. 1828 **Laura Williams** of Richfield. They removed to Hamburgh, NY where she d. in 1842 and he d. 10 March 1846. They had three children, all b.

iv.	Hamburgh. **Nathaniel S.**, b. 12 Nov. 1804; m. 1839 **Martha Jamison** of Hamburgh, NY, where he d. 1844. No issue.
v.	**Alonzo**, b. 11 June 1809, where he d. 11 Jan. 1832, unm. (Richfield) His obituary says "late of Jamestown, NY."
vi.	**Robert T.**, b. 13 Dec. 1812; m. 18 Sept. 1840 at Geneva, NY, **Anne Bennet Keith**, d/o his third cousin, **Eliza Tracy** by her 2nd husband, **Israel Keith** of GA. They settled in GA and in 1856 were living in Marshall Co., TX. Five children.
vii.	**Elizabeth**, b. 6 Dec. 1806; m. 13 Oct. 1833 **Judah Swift** and d. 1 Aug. 1834 at Jamestown, NY. No issue.

JAMES HYDE[6] [P] b. 26 May 1797 at Franklin. He m. 3 Jan. 1822, **Fanny Beardsley** of Richfield, d/o **Obadiah** and sister of Judges **Levi** and **Samuel Beardsley** of Utica. She was still living in 1874, the only surviving member of her father's family. **James** was a lawyer and judge; res. Richfield Springs; Presbyterian. In early life he res. in Buffalo and engaged as a merchants' clerk. In 1818 he returned to Richfield. **James** was a Mason and master of the lodge at Richfield Springs for many years. He was the first postmaster of Richfield Springs, then known as East Richfield. Served as captain and lt.-col. of artillery in the State militia and served as judge of the county from 1847 to 1852, as well as justice of the peace for more than 30 years. He d. 1 May 1862 and is bur. in the village churchyard. Children:

i.	**Jay**, b. 12 Oct. 1822; lawyer, res. Syracuse, NY 1863, unm.
ii.	**Olive Beardsley**, b. 11 July 1824; m. 16 July 1846, **Augustus R. Elwood** of Richfield, where they were living in 1860. Had one child, **Arthur Hyde Elwood**, b. 1 May 1847.
iii.	**Eugene**, b. 22 July 1828; d. 19 Jan. 1832 at Richfield.
iv.	**Mary Frances**, b. 13 Oct. 1832; m. 10 Dec. 1857, **Demas S. Barnes**, merchant of NY City, where they were living in 1862.
v.	**Laura Emily**, b. 25 Dec. 1836; m. 5 March 1861 **James F. Smith, Esq.** of New York.

[*Hyde Genealogy; of the Descendants... From William Hyde of Norwich... by* Reuben H. Walworth, 1864; RS:103-08; GBM; Barbour Collection; DARPI; OB; Franklin Church Records]

JARVIS, WILLIAM[3] (*Thomas Jr.*[2], *Thomas Sr.*[1] *Long Island, NY*) b. 20 March 1727 at Brainard's Bridge, Columbia Co., NY, d. 15 June 1772. He was an officer in the French War; by trade a weaver. He m. **Mary Wright** who was b. 11 March 1730, d. 22 Dec. 1804 at Fly Creek, NY. Children:

	i.	**Joseph**, b. 14 May 1752, d. 17 Oct. 1806. He m. 12 Jan. 1783 **Abigail Church** who was b. 25 Jan. 1763. They had 14 children, none of which are recorded as having res. Otsego Co. **Joseph** studied medicine at Lanesboro, MA; served in the Revolution as a surgeon. Nov. 1805 he removed to New Baltimore on the banks of the Hudson River, where he died.
4	ii.	**Bill**.
	iii.	**Elijah**, d. aged 18.

	iv.	Kent; officer in the Continental Army, massacred near Saratoga by Indians in the Revolution.
	v.	**Elizabeth**, b. 10 Nov. 1760, m. 29 Jan. 1783 to **Malatiah Hatch**, b. 22 June 1764, d. 28 July 1812. Eight children.
	vi.	**Mary**, b. 12 May 1762, d. Feb. 1835; **Thomas Edson** 15 June 1780. [See Edson family entry.]
	vii.	**Chloe**, d. young.
	viii.	**Asahel**, d. young.
4	ix.	**Asahel 2nd**, b. 15 Feb. 1768, d. 10 Sept. 1823.
	x.	**Chloe 2nd**, b. 15 Aug. 1770, d. c. 1846. She m. 19 Feb. 1790, **John Miles**.
	xi.	**Sally**, b. 19 Aug. 1772, d. 16 Dec. 1831. She m. 14 Feb. 1793, **Elnathan Osborn** who was b. 12 June 1769. Seven children.

DR. BILL JARVIS⁴, b. 30 Dec. 1753, d. 14 Feb. 1830; m. 30 Aug. 1780 **Mary White** who was b. 25 Dec. 1761 & d. 6 July 1820. He came into Otsego Co. with Judge **William Cooper** in 1790. He was a physician, surgeon and land surveyor. Children:

	i.	**Alfred**, b. 15 Sept. 1781, d. 20 Aug. 1798.
	ii.	**Polly**, b. 17 March 1784, d. 12 June 1792.
5	iii.	**William Cooper**.
	iv.	**James White**, b. 25 Jan. 1790, d. 30 July 1853; m. **Clarissa Clark** on 13 Sept. 1812. She was b. 15 Dec. 1794. They had eleven children.
	v.	**Griethene**, b. 27 Nov. 1792.
	vi.	**Rev. Asahel Hatch**, b. 30 May 1793, d. 16 Dec. 1877. He m. **Mary Cooley** on 25 Dec. 1821. She d. 16 Oct. 1852 at Ovid (later Mt. Hope), Rochester, NY. Four children.
	vii.	**Polly 2nd**, b. 28 May 1797; m. 23 March 1817, **Capt. William Williams** who was b. 13 June 1793. They had five children.

WILLIAM COOPER JARVIS⁴ was the first white child born on what was known as Cooper's Patent on 25 Aug. 1787. This patent was secured by Judge **William Cooper**, the father of the celebrated **James Fenimore Cooper**. Judge Cooper made the child a present of an eighty-acre [100] tract of land in recognition of the compliment paid him in naming the child after himself. **William Cooper Jarvis** m. 25 Feb. 1813, **Daphany Taylor**, d/o **Erastus Taylor** who was b. in Bennington, VT. Children:

5	i.	**Loren [Lorenzo] Taylor**, b. 22 March 1815.
	ii.	**Erastus**, b. 4 Sept. 1826, d. 14 Feb. 1827.

LORENZO TAYLOR JARVIS⁵ was a farmer. Before his mar. he bought a tract of land in what is now (1893) School District No. 11, Town of Otsego, where he spent the rest of his life, dying 19 Nov. 1883. He m. 3 Oct. 1841 to **Abigail Preston** [P - BR:623], who survived him, res. with her son **Rufus**. She was b. in Schuyler, Herkimer Co., 22 Dec. 1818. Her father was **Rufus Preston** and he was b. in a pioneer home in the Town of Otsego, a s/o **Daniel Preston**, a native of CT; her mother was **Esther Cummings**. Children:

	i.	**Emma E.**
	ii.	**Mary White.**
6	iii.	**Rufus P.**

RUFUS P. JARVIS[6] was b. 6 Nov. 1842 in Otsego Co. He always res. with his parents, and they with him; farmer. He m. **Annie Rice** on 1 Nov. 1883. She was b. in West Winfield, Herkimer Co., d/o **Michael Rice** who was b. in Germany and came to America when a young man and located in Herkimer Co. where he m. **Mary Webster**, a native of that county and a d/o **John** and **Nancy Webster**. Children:

  i. **Eloise.**
  ii. **Marietta Taylor.**

ASAHEL JARVIS[4] was b. in Lanesboro, MA 15 Feb. 1768 [1760]; he learned the trade of wheelwright; in 1793 removed to Fly Creek, NY where in 1813 erected the first foundry and machine shop at Fly Creek. He m. 18 March 1790, **Abigail Griswold**, who was b. 2 June 1770, d. 26 Sept. 1862 at Morris, aged 92. He d. 10 Sept. 1823. Children:

5	i.	**Chester**, b. 9 Dec. 1792, d. 10 Aug. 1870.
	ii.	**Dwight**, b. 27 May 1797; bapt. 30 July 1797; m. **Frances Upham** b. Dec. 1812, d. 7 July 1866. They m. 27 Jan. 1837.
	iii.	**Alma**, b. 3 April 1799, d. 26 June 1803.
	iv.	**Kent**, b. 14 [13] June, bapt. 26 July 1801, at Fly Creek; he d. Massillon, OH 15 Jan. 1877. He m. 17 May 1821 **Euretta M. Williams**, d/o **Elpihalet**. The located in Lowville, NY in 1828 and later at Massillon. Several children.
	v.	**Edwin**, b. 4 May, bapt. 29 June 1803; m. at Fly Creek 19 Feb. 1829 to **Lydia E. Grace**. He was of Lowville, NY.
	vi.	**Mary Ann**, b. 11 March 1805, d. 14 Feb. 1832.
	vii.	**Jerta Maria**, b. 30 May 1806.
	viii.	**Joseph Sidney**, b. 23 Oct. 1807, d. 15 Sept. 1855.
	ix.	**Horace Benjamin**, b. 11 Sept. 1809.
	x.	**Harriet**, b. 8 March 1812, d. 30 Sept. 1878 at Massillon, OH.

CHESTER JARVIS[5] b. 9 Dec. 1792 ["born 30 May and bapt. 2 July 1806"] in town of Lanesboro; was an infant [young boy] when brought to Otsego Co. He learned the trade of machinist from his father. On attaining his majority he went into business for himself and continued his residence at Fly Creek, where he was post master and justice of the peace. He went to Cooperstown, and later to Morris, and still later to Cheshire, MA. He returned to NY, settled at Kinderhook and d. there 10 April 1870. Notice of his mar. in the local newspaper cites him as Colonel. His 1st wife is given as **Aurelia Content Morris**, b. in Otsego 3 July 1797 and d. 27 May 1830. She was d/o **Samuel Morris**, who was b. in RI 8 Aug. 1767, and wife **Betsey Bradford**, b. Woodstock, CT. Children of **Chester** and **Aurelia**:

	i.	**Fran. Griswold**, b. 19 June 1819, d. 19 Sept. 1828.
6	ii.	**Frederick Tiffany**, b. 22 Sept. 1822.
6	iii.	**Henry Kent**, b. 7 Sept. 1824.

iv. **Aurel Content**, b. 7 July 1827.
Chester[5] m. 2nd **Maria Bowne** [Mrs. **Maria Brown** nee **Perry**] who was b. 1 July 1799, d. 17 Dec. 1848; they m. 9 Dec. 1830 and had one child:

6 v. **Asahel Amos**, b. 29 March 1834 in Cooperstown.
Chester[5] m. 3rd **Ann Brown** who was b. 30 April 1801.

FREDERICK TIFFANY JARVIS[6], res. Hartwick, farmer. He was b. in Otsego 22 Sept. 1822. At age 17 he was a school teacher in the winter terms. When young he went to CA and tried his luck in the mines, was gone from home 14 months. He wrote an account of his adventures which appeared in *The Otsego Republican*, a newspaper of Cooperstown, published in 1889 in a series of 13 articles entitled "Leaves from My Diary, and Reminiscences of a Trip to California and the Gold Mines and Return." He farmed in NY until he enlisted in Company I, 152nd NY Infantry in 1862. He served for five months when he was discharged on account of disability. As soon as he was able he returned to farming. He m. 16 Nov. 1843 **Minerva J. Steere** who was b. in Hartwick 7 Oct. 1826, d/o **Ira Steere** who was b. in RI in 1793 and his father was **Nicholas Steere** b. in 1764. Members of Universalist Church; he a Prohibitionist. Children:
i. **Frank G.**
ii. **Chester B.**
iii. **Ira S.**
iv. **J. Wilson.**

HENRY KENT JARVIS[6] [P] b. 7 Sept. 1824, Town of Otsego; m. 13 Feb. 1846 and settled on a farm he had purchased in Town of Hartwick, where he res. three years. He then sold that farm and bought a larger one in Town of Otsego, where he res. until 1873, when he bought his present home in Town of Otsego. Was a general insurance agent many years, still (1893) agent of the New York Equitable Mortgage Co. He also has a half interest in a large drug store in Cooperstown. Active member of the county Agricultural Society. Universalist. His children [wife not named in this source] have all died, but they have living with them an adopted dau.:
i. **Lena E.**, b. 22 Sept. 1884.

ASHEL AMOS JARVIS[6] b. in Cooperstown, remained at home and attended school till age of 14, when he shipped as a passenger on the brig *Ann Eliza* bound for Key West, FL to meet a brother, for whom he was to act as clerk. After a year he returned home to Otsego county. During his absence his mother had died, and the next summer he spent in travel thorugh the west, returning in the fall to Key West. After three winters in FL, he again came north on account of the yellow fever, and engaged with his uncle, **H. M. Perry**, in a general store. Later, in company with **W. K.Bingham**, he opened a drug store, which he ran until 1862 when he was burned out [later rebuilt]. **Asahel** later removed to Towanda, PA, where he was engaged in the hardware business for 16 years. He has also been involved in cattle ranching, banking and railroads. He m. in Cooperstown 19 Nov. 1863 to Miss **J. Ella Hannay** [when she was aged 21], who is desc. from one of the earliest settlers of the county, and who was b. 21 July 1844. Her father, Dr. **John Hannay**, was b. in Germany and brought to American as a child by his parents. They settled in Canajoharie, NY; he a pharmacist, physician and surgeon. **Ella's** mother was **Julia Babcock**, b. in NY and she d. when **Ella** was aged five. **Ella** then being raised by her maternal grandparents in Cooperstown. Children:

   i.   **Emma Bowne**, m. Lt. **Walter McLean**, grad. of the Naval Academy at Annapolis, now (1893) of the US Navy.
   ii.   **G. L. Bowne**, physician, grad. class of 1891 of College of Physicians & Surgeons, NY City.
   iii. **William Hamilton**, aged 21 (1893), engaged with Dye & Breese of Towanda, PA, hardware merchants.

[BR:53-55; 577-78; NASH 1; OB; A:247; *Edsons in England & America and Genealogy of the Edsons* by Jarvis Bonesteel Edson, 1903; BR:53-54, 491 & 577-78; NASH1; OB; A:247]

JARVIS, MELANCTHON BRYANT b. Norwalk, CT 1775, s/o **Bryant Jervis**; removed to Unadilla. He was a friend to other Unadilla settlers, **Curtis Noble, Isaac Hayes** and **Josiah Thatcher**. He settled on the **Timothy Beach** farm near the mouth of the Ouleout, but later moved to the village and occupied part of the house **Sheldon Griswold** long lived in. Melanchton m. **Polly Smith** 24th Sept. 1797; he d. in 1856. Children:

   i.   **Hannah**, b. 9 Oct. 1798; m. --- **Knapp** of Norwalk.
   ii.   **Sally**, b. 25th Feb. 1800; m. **Elias Foote**.

Melanchton m. 2nd to **Clarissa Jennings** and had:

   iii. **Eliza**, b. 1805; m. **A. S. Ames**.
   iv. **George**, b. 1809; m. **Cath. Williams**.

[UNA:73; *Historical Records of Norwalk, CT* by Edwin Hall, p. 257; *The Jarvis Family; or The Descendants of the First Settlers of the Name in Massachusetts and Long Island . . .* by George A. Jarvis et al, 1879.]

JEWELL, JOHN M.[4] (*Nathaniel*[3] *MA, Joseph*[3] *MA, Joseph*[2] *MA, Thomas*[1] *England/MA*) m. **Sarah Pratt** and had:

   i.   **William**.
   ii.   **John**, b. 1772, res. MI.
   iii. **Susan**, m. **Joseph Upham**, res. Steuben Co., NY. Two of their children res. in Hartwick, Otsego Co.: **Clarissa** who m. **Arthur Luther; Mary Ann** who m. **William Bottsford**.
5 iv. **Whitney**, b. MA. [BR:400-01 gives his father as **Edward Jewell** of MA who res. in the state of his birth his entire life. He is identified further as a Revolutionary War soldier.]
   v.   **Adonijah**, d. in New Orleans, LA c. 1808.
   vi. **Sally**, m. **David Burrell** in 1797; res. Middlefield, NY. [See Burrell family entry.]
5 vii. **Jared**, b. 8 March 1780; d. 26 Dec. 1820.
   viii. **Betsey**, b. 12 Sept. 1782; m. **Reuben Beal**, res. Milford, NY. [See entry under Beal family.]
   xi. **Charlotte**, b. 21 July 1791; m. **William Morse**; d. Waterford, ME 16 Oct. 1833. Several children.

x.   Ezra, b. 21 March 1794; d. Waterford, ME, 2 July 1836.

WHITNEY JEWELL[5] to Otsego Co. as a young man. He m. **Abigail Salisbury** 20 Dec. 1797. She was b. in Central NY, probably Otsego Co., her parents having come from New England at an early day. she lived to age 92 at the home of one of her daus. **Whitney** was of Westford [Westville], NY when he made his will 1 Feb. 1845 [he d. aged 70, 18 Jan. 1846] at Westville] and in it named his wife **Abigail**, granddau. **Mrs. Abigail Grover** and children:

i.   **Harvey C.**, b. 26 Nov. 1798, res. Milford, NY.
ii. **Abigail C.** [M.?], b. 27 Nov. 1801; m. **Aaron B. Cornish** 12 Jan. 1819, res. Middlefield, NY. They had **Aaron B. Cornish** and **Sylvania** who m. **Myron Joslyn** & res. in Middlefield.
iii. **Sally T.**, m. **Elisha Cornish**, res. in Maryland, NY & had **Thompson, Elvira, Rhoda Jane, Ann E., Sylvester** and **Angeline**.
vi. **Paschal A.**, d. in infancy.
v. & vi. **Whitney**, d. in infancy (two Whitneys).
vii. **Betsey C.**, b. 7 June 1809; m. **Thomas J. Bates**. [See Bates family entry.]
viii. **Paschal A.**, res. Middlefield.
ix. **Relief**, b. 30 Nov. 1816; m. **Stephen Burton**. [See Burton family entry.]
x.   **Jared**, b. 8 March 1780; d. 26 Dec. 1820.
xi. **Betsey**, b. 12 Sept. 1782; m. **Reuben Beal**, res. Milford, NY.

JARED JEWELL[5] m. **Esther Durrell** and had:
i.   **James**, b. 19 March 1802; res. New Albion, NY.
ii. **Relief**, b. 1803; d. 28 Oct. 1816.
iii. **Jonathan**, b. 1 Feb. 1806; res. New Albion, NY.
iv. **Mary Ann**, b. 13 March 1808; m. **Orrin Sibley** 6 Oct. 1831. [See Sibley family entry.]
v.   **Osborn**, b. 25 Feb. 1810; m. **Electra Russell** 24 Sept. 1849 at Mlford. Is supposed to have been murdered at Buffalo, NY in 1855-6.
vi. **Esther**, b. 19 Feb. 1812; m. **James Worden** 2 Feb. 1837; res. Franklinville, NY; several children.

There were other **Jewell** family members in this area early. A **Lemuel Jewell** was a subscriber to Cooperstown's academy in 1795.
[GBW; *The Jewell Register* ... by Thomas Jewell of Braintree, 1860; BR460-61; OB; COP1:39.]

JEWELL, MYRON[2], s/o **Oliver Jewell**[1] who removed to Vernon, Oneida Co., NY in 1806. His 4th son, **Myron** was b. in CT and aged 12 when the family removed to NY; he learned the harness-maker's trade and established his own business. In 1844 he removed to Syracuse and later to Rochester. After some yers **Myron** returned to Madison Co., d. at Oneida. **Myron** m. **Sophia Taylor** who was originally from Pittsfield, MA. She d. in 1888, aged 90. Children:

	i.	Mary Frances, m. **William Brown**; she d. 1844. He now res. Philadelphia.
3	ii.	**Norman D.**
	iii.	**Susan Beyoux.**
	iv.	**Josephine**, m. **Horace Tuller**; she d. 1853. He d. 1893 in NY City.
3	v.	**Niles Demoresse.**
	vi.	**Emerald F.**, in crockery buisness in Oneida.
	vii.	**Edward Vernon**, of Cleveland, OH; m. **Fannie Hone**.

NORMAN D. JEWELL[3] of Oneida Co., carriage trimmer, b. 1824; m. **Harriet M. Foote** of Clinton, Oneida Co., NY. She was d/o **Orange** and **Marilla (Ives) Foote**. Children:

	i.	**Edward B.** of Homer, Courtland Co., NY.
4	ii.	**Myron D.**
	iii.	**E. M.** of Cleveland, OH.
	iv. & v.	Daus., d. in infancy.

MYRON D. JEWELL, D.D.S.[4] [P] b. in Chenango Co., 29 Jan. 1852. Early in life he worked as a prescription clerk at a drug store until he was 22. In 1877 he began studying with **Dr. Bailey** of Richfield Springs and later attended the Philadelphia Dental College, grad. in 1885, since that time engaged at Richfield Springs. During the summer months he gives his undivided attention to the "Davenport," of which he is proprietor, a popular resort for summer tourists "of the better class," who visit this famous place to avail themselves of its medicinal waters. He m. 18 Oct. 1876 to **Helen M. Davenport**, only d/o **James S.** and **Harriet (Tuller) Davenport**.

NILES DEMORESSE JEWELL[3] b. at Vernon, NY 12 Dec. 1827; remained at home until 1845. He spent two years in Canada and on returning to NY worked at trade of carriage trimmer in Binghamton and other places, going to Oneida in 1858. In 1859 he m. **Caroline B. Tuller**, who was b. in Richfield Springs, Otsego Co., d/o **Henry Tuller** who was b. there 14 March 1799. Henry d. in 1874, his wife, formerly **Maria Shipman**, had d. some years before. They removed to Richfield Springs in 1867. Episcopalian. They had one child:

i. **Niles Harry**, d. aged 9.

[BR:556-57 & 675-76; DAR Lineage #94063]

JOHNSON, CALEB[5] (*James*[4] *of CT, John*[3] *of CT, John*[2] *of England & CT, Robert*[1] *of England & CT*), s/o **James** and **Anna Johnson** of New Haven, Lebanon and Chatham, CT. Caleb res. in Chatham and in old age lived in Burlington, Otsego Co., where he and his wife were buried. He served in Gen. Spencer's 2nd regiment during the siege of Boston; enlisted 5 May 1775, discharged 19 Dec. 1775. He m. 19 Sept. 1745, **Mary Cook**, children:

i. **Joseph**. He could be the **Joseph Johnson** who m. 18 Feb. 1830 at Otsego to **Abigail Tefft**.

ii. **Elisha.** Bur. at Burlington Flats with **Ira's** family below is **Phila,** wife of **Elisha Johnson,** who d. 22 July 1877, aged 66 and their son, **Alonzo G.,** who d. 9 Sept. 1852, aged 1 y, 3 m, 3 d.
iii. **Ira.** He is probably the **Ira Johnson** who d. 20 Feb. 1859, aged 93; bur. Burlington Flats along with his wife **Mary,** who d. 17 Jan. 1842, aged 73. An **Ira Johnson** m. --- **Gardner** on 11 Oct. 1821, both of Burlington. [NYB&G:61:41]
iv. **Harris,** d. 30 Jan. 1818, aged 48. He is bur. Burlington Flats with **Martha** his wife, who d. 10 Sept. 1856, aged 78.
v. **John.**
vi. **Mary.**

JOHN JOHNSON[6], b. c. 1758 in Chatham, d. 28 June 1842 there. He served in the Lexington alarm. He m. 1st 31 Oct. 1771, **Lois Brainerd,** b. 15 Sept. 1753 in Chatham; d. 29 June 1833, 2nd d/o **Othniel** and **Lucy (Swaddle) Brainard.** John m. 2nd 26 June 1836 Mrs. **Mary Bailey,** widow of **Solomon Bailey** and d/o **Marcus** and **Phebe (Scoville) Cole,** b. 1761, d. 23 March 1857. Children:
i. **Phebe Brainerd.**
ii. **Lois.**
iii. **Lucy.**
iv. **Nancy.**
v. **Liva.**
vi. **Jared,** d. 21 Oct. 1839, aged 52. Bur. Burlington Flats along with **Serena,** his wife, who d. in Albion, OH 28 Jan. 1867, aged 77 and their dau. **Julia** who d. 2 Aug. 1819, aged 2.
7 vii. **Enos.**

ENOS JOHNSON[7], b. 21 March 1786 in East Hampton. He was a farmer of Burlington, NY, later in North Pitcher and South Otselic. Universalist. He m. 23 Sept. 1810, **Anna Parmelee,** b. 25 June 1785, d. at South Otselie, NY, 24 Sept. 1858, d/o **John Parmelee,** b. 17 May 1761 and m. at Chatham, CT, 28 March 1782, **Lucy Annable,** b. 29 Nov. 1763. **John Parmelee's** family background in CT is covered in the first source. Children:
i. **Lucy Ann.**
8 ii. **John Jewett.**
iii. **Lois Louisa.**
iv. **Enos.**

JOHN JEWETT JOHNSON[8], b. 12 Oct. 1814 in Easthampton Parish, Chatham, CT. Removed to Burlington, Otsego Co. in early manhood and later settled in North Pitcher, Chenango Co., NY; farmer. He d. 21 Jan. 1878. He m. 28 Jan. 1841 at North Smithfield, Bradford Co., PA, **Jane L. Pierce,** b. 19 July 1818 in that town; d. 9 Feb. 1883 in Norwich, NY, d/o **Abram Pierce** and wife **Sarah Satterlee.**
[CUT1:3:1531-32; NER101:234; GBM]

KELLEY, STEPHEN[4] (*Joseph*[3], *Jeremiah*[2] *of MA, David*[1] *of MA*), s/o **Joseph Kelly** and **Tabitha Baker** his wife, b. c. 1730; settled first in Otsego Co. and later in Cortland Co., NY. He served in the First Regiment of minutemen, Suffolk Co. Militia, **Col. Josiah Smith** and enlisted from Otsego Co. He m. **Hannah** d/o **Gideon Wells**, whose family were early settlers of the Wyoming Valley, PA, and all lost their lives in the Wyoming massacre, **Gideon** only escaping. Children:

 i. **John.**
 ii. **Phoebe** m. **Robert Sloat.**
 iii. **Stephen.**
 iv. **Amy** m. **Earl Pierce.**
 v. **Edie**, b. 16 Oct. 1796, m. in Cortland Co. **Betsey Parker.**
 vi. **Polly** m. **Simeon Evens.**
 vii. **Ezekiel.**

[CWNY:370-71]

KELSEY, DANIEL[5] (*James*[4] *CT & NY, John*[3] *CT, Stephen*[2] *CT, William*[1] *Emgland & CT*) 2nd son and 3rd child of **James** and wife **Eunice (Andrews) Kelsey**, b. c. 1741 at Farmington; res. at Sheffield, MA; Crum Elbow, Dutchess Co. and Easton, Washington Co., NY; d. after 1 Sept. 1822. He m. 1st c. 1766 **Ann** --- and after her death he m. 2nd c. 1804 **Patience** ---, who was living in Sept. 1822. **Daniel** and his 1st wife joined the Quakers in Washington Co., NY in 1794. The records show that he was disowned by the church in 1804 for being asleep during meeting and for marrying a woman not of the Quaker faith. He had removed from Sheffield, MA to Crum Elbow, Dutchess Co., NY with his parents sometime before he became of age. Children, all by 1st wife:

6 i. **Solomon**, b. 10 Sept. 1767; d. 16 June 1814.
 ii. **Anna**, b. c. 1769; d. 13 Dec. 1857 at New Lisbon, NY. She m. **Crowell Gross**, b. c. 1766;, d. 2 Jan. 1847, s/o **Jebez** and **Dorothy Gross**.
 iii. **Benedict**, b. 31 Jan. 1772; d. 30 Sept. 1822.
 iv. **Susanna Mary**, b. 15 May 1774.
 v. **James**, b. 4 Aug. 1776, d. 2 Jan. 1869.
 vi. **John**, b. c. 1779
 vii. **Joseph**, b. c. 1782.
 viii. **Daniel**, b. c. 1785; living unm. in 1822.
 ix. **Polly**, b. c. 1787; m. **John Penny**.

SOLOMON KELSEY[6] m. before 1789 in Washington Co., NY and removed to [first Burlington and in 1800 to Edmeston?] Edmeston, Otsego Co., 1789, where he d. 16 June 1815 [1814]. He m. 17 Sept. 1789, **Anna Brown**, also b. Washington Co.; she d. three weeks after **Solomon** [7 July 1814], both of typhus fever and were bur. in the old Quaker Cemetery at Edmeston. She was d/o **Asa** and **Sarah Brown** and sister to Gen. **Brown** of the War of 1812. Family were Quakers. They had twelve children; two living in 1878. Some of their children were assigned guardians by the court:

 i. **Mary**, b. 20 Sept. 1790; d. 1 March 1853.
 ii. **Phebe**, b. 15 Feb. 1792; d. 17 March 1864.

	iii.	Robert, b. Nov. of Dec. 1793; d. 21 Feb. 1846. He m. **Abigail Bennett**, b. 1797, d. 1856, in Delaware Co., NY, d/o **Prince Bennett** and **Phebe Moisier**.
	iv.	Asa, b. 1 Oct. 1795; d. 3 Oct. 1814; unm.
7	v.	**Roswell**.
7	vi.	**Daniel**.
	vii.	Silas, b. 18 June 1801; d. 22 or 26 Nov. 1870.
	viii.	Calvin, b. 7 April 1803; on 7 April 1815 **John Cuer** of Town of Butternuts appointed his guardian. He m. **Rebecca** ---; went to Pelham, Canada and later to Augusta, Washtenaw Co., MI. Several children.
	ix.	Solomon D., b. 15 Nov. 1805; d. 1 Oct. or Nov. 1873.
	x.	William, b. 17 Dec. 1808; aged 7 on 7 Dec. 1815 when **Ira Cone** of New Lisbon declared his guardian. **William** d. 24 April 1861.
	xi.	Julia Ann, b. 20 June 1811; aged 4 on 20 June 1815 when **Caleb Hoag** of Town of Burlington appointed guardian of **Solomon** and **Julia Ann**. She m. **Alfred Pierce**.
	xii.	Joseph, b. 26 Sept. 1813, aged 2 on 26 Sept. 1815 when **Thomas Clark** of Butternuts declared his guardian. **Joseph** m. and had a son, **Fred**, and three daus. **Mrs. Livingston**, **Mrs. Wesley** and **Mrs. Fred. Lay**.

ROSWELL KELSEY[7] [P] b. Edmeston 13 July 1797, 1820 he and brother **Silas** purchased the homestead of their father, where **Roswell** res. until 1840 when he sold his share and removed to Burlington. **Roswell** m. 30 March 1820 at Brookfield, NY, **Rhoda Dye** [Quaker], b. Madison Co., NY 7 Dec. 1803 and d. 27 May 1870, bur. Burlington. He d. 15 Oct. 1880 at Burlington, NY. **Rhoda** was d/o **Daniel Dye** and wife **Rhoda Taft**. Children, b. at Edmeston or Burlington, NY:

	i.	Henry H., b. 19 April 1821; d. 11 May 1821.
	ii.	Sarah, b. 6 Nov. 1822; m. **Julius Lines** who was b. Susquehanna Co., PA 17 Nov. 1847 and d. 4 Feb. 1874. They had at least one child, **Laura**. **Sarah** d. 2 March 1913, and she and **Julius** are bur. in Otsego Co. along with **Laura M. Lines** (1842-1922), the wife of **Edgar Bootman**.
	iii.	Solomon, b. 28 Jan. 1825; d. 16 Oct. 1905 or 06 at Libertyville, IL. He m. 1st at Edmeston 16 Jan. 1861 **Helen Arlina Monroe** who d. 29 Dec. 1865 at Avon, IL. He m. 2nd **Lucy Thayer**.
	iv.	Rachel, b. 12 Nov. 1827; d. 26 Feb. 1898 at Pittsfield, NY. She m. 7 Feb. 1855, at Cooperstown, **Levi Thayer**, b. 6 March 1827 at Pittsfield and d. the same place, date unknown, s/o **Lemuel Thayer** and **Hannah Siver**. No children. Both bur. at St. Andrew's Cemetery, New Berlin, NY.
	v.	Jerusha, b. 23 Nov. 1830; d. 27 Feb. 1871 at Pittsfield, NY. She m. **Delos A. Bates** who was b. 3 Jan. 1835 at West Burlington, NY and d. there on 19 Aug. 1901, s/o **LeRoy Bates** and **Betsey Southworth**. Both b. at Edmeston, NY; no children.
8	vi.	Daniel Dye, b. 3 July 1834; d. 8 Dec. 1924.

ROSWELL KELSEY.   MRS. ROSWELL KELSEY.

	vii.	**Mary Elizabeth**, b. 20 Nov. 1837; d. 9 May 1917 at West Burlington. She m. 10 July 1862, at Burlington, **William Lines**, b. 27 Nov. 1839, West Burlington; d. there on 26 July 1919, s/o **Rufus Lines** and wife **Louisa Tubbs**. No children. Both bur. at West Burlington, where they res.
8	viii.	**William Henry**, b. 14 Dec. 1840; d. 6 Nov. 1930.
	ix.	**Celia Aurelia**, b. 1 May 1844; d. 29 Sept. 1925. She m. **Henry Brown Hopkins**, b. at Edmeston, NY 6 Dec. 1846; d. at South Edmeston, 13 Dec. 1906, but bur. at Columbus, NY.
	x.	**Martha Augusta**, b/ 7 July 1847; d. 17 March 1872. Could be the **Martha Jane Johnson** who d. 22 Sept. 1822, aged 14 months and bur. Cherry Valley Presbyterian Church Cemetery.

DANIEL DYE KELSEY[8] b. at Edmeston and d. there. He m. 1st 13 Dec. 1857 at Burlington, NY, **Mary Pope**, b. 23 March 1836 at Burlington, d.

21 Feb. 1872 at Edmeston. She was d/o **Marcus Pope** and **Meribah Nichols**. Daniel m. 2nd 15 June 1872 at Edmeston, NY Mrs. **Jane (Toles) Hastings** who was b. 3 Aug. 1838 at Ambler Settlement, NY, d. 31 Jan. 1918 at Edmeston. She was d/o **Myron Toles** and **Amy Aylesworth**. All three bur. Edmeston. Children:
    i.   **May**, b. 15 Nov. 1869; m. 7 Feb. 1894 at Edmeston, **Vesta** or **Verta Vern Johnson**, b. 29 May 1871 at Exeter, NY; s/o **Marquis D. Johnson** and **Rosamond Porter**.

WILLIAM HENRY KELSEY[6] b. Burlington, d. at Syracuse, NY. He m. 1 June 1862 at Warren, IL, **Ellen Whitmore**, b. 31 Jan. 1840 at Perrysburg, OH; d. 26 Sept. 1912 at Kalispel, MT and bur. there. She was d/o **Alfred D. Whitmore** and **Marion Lyons**. They had two daus.

DANIEL KELSEY[7] was b. 11 Jan. 1799 at Burlington; d. at Lockport, IL. He m. **Susan White**, b. in England, d/o **John Edward White** a member of Ontario, Canada Parliament. Several children, probably b. Erie, PA.

EPHRAIM KELSEY[5], s/o **James**[4] and brother to **Daniel**[5] above, was the 3rd son and 4th child of **James Kelsey** and **Eunice Andrews** his wife. **Ephraim** was b. 25 Feb. 1742/43 at Farmington; res. at Sheffield, MA, Crum Elbow, and Saratoga, NY, and still later in Otsego Co.. He d. after 1813. There is no record of his wife. Children, presumed all b. at Sheffield, MA:
    i.   **William** b. c. 1770.
    ii.   **Elias**, b. c. 1773.
    iii.   **Martin**, b. c. 1776.
    iv.   **Dimmis**, b. c. 1778; m. **Francis Drake**.
    v.   **John**, b. c. 1781.
    vi.   **Erastus**, b. c. 1784.

[SCR; A:107a, MOHAWK; *A Genealogy of the Descendants of William Kelsey Who Settled at Cambridge, MA in 1632* ... by Edward A. Claypool & Azalea Clizbee & Earl L. Kelsey, 1928.]

KEYES, JOHN[1] from England to Middletown CT and served in the Revolutionary War; farmer. He m. a "lady in Middletown, and moved to Montgomery Co., NY, and settled on a farm." His son:
THOMPSON KEYES[2] m. in 1797 **Mary Lane** of Montgomery Co., NY, a d/o of **Cornelius Lane** of German desc. [German birth]. **Cornelius** served in the Revolutionary War and m. **Elizabeth** ---, also of German desc., and removed to then Mongtomery Co., NY. In 1805 **Thompson** moved his family to Otego (now Laurens), NY [then Montgomery Co.] and settled on a farm in the valley of the Otego Creek. He d. near Mount Vision when nearly 80; his wife d. at the home of her dau., Mrs. **Mary Mosher**, in Oneonta, aged 86. Children, first three b. Montgomery Co., NY; remaining b. in Otego:
    i.   **Josiah**, b. 30 Dec. 1799, Methodist minister, d. at Cazenovia, NY in middle life leaving four daus.

	ii.	**Betsey**, b. 11 Jan. 1801; m. **Owen Wilcox** and d. as his widow at age of 75, having reared seven children; three daus. living in 1878.
3	iii.	**Hervey [Harvey]**.
	iv.	**Diantha**, b. 3 April 1807.
	v.	**Maria**, b. 10 April 1809.
	vi.	**Emily**, b. 25 Aug. 1813.
	vii.	**John T.**, b. 21 Sept. 1816, res. (1872) Winchester, KY. He was a wealthy man before the war, but in that conflict lost nearly all his earthly possessions, his property being in salves.

HERVEY [HARVEY] KEYES[5] **[P]** b. 30 Oct. 1803, worked on the farm with his father until he was 22; m. **Margaret Marlett[e] [P]** d/o **Peter** and **Elizabeth (Pattengille) Marlett[e]**, and settled in the town of Laurens. Because of ill health after years of working on the farm, the family removed to Jacksonville and **Hervey** turned merchant, a profession which he followed 12 years and was in that time also postmaster, justice of the peace and various political offices. He served in the local military units. **Hervey** and his sons **Omar** and **Josiah** are named as "old residents" of Mount Vision along with **Harvey Kenyon** [A:169] **Margaret** d. 9 April 1885, nearly 80; **Hervey** d. 1 June 1887. He filled a number of local offices in his town such as justice of the peace. Rec'd. a commission as captain of a company of cavalry in the 11th NY Reg't. from Lt. Gov. **Nathaniel Pitcher** on 20 Dec. 1827. On 15 May 1830 commissioned major of cavalry by **Enos T. Throop**. Children:

	i.	**Irvin**, d. at age 3.
	ii.	**Hiram**, d. at age 12.
	iii.	**Washington T.**, b. 7 June 1827; merchant at Jacksonville [Schenevus]. Had been merchant of Mt. Vision over 30 years; is mar. but has no children.
	iv.	**Mary**, B. 15 Aug. 1828; m. **Henry Shove** 1 Jan. 1860, and had 3 sons: **Melville, Hiram** and **Henry Jr.** [She widowed by 1878.]
	v.	**Omar**, b. 20 Sept. 1830; m. **Mary Cheny**, d/o **William**, and they have one son: **Franklin C. Omar** d. 19 Feb. 1890.
4	iv.	**Josiah D.**
	vi.	**James H.**, b. 10 July 1836; m. 1st **Adeliza Lane** 7 Aug. 1862 and had: **Harvey, James** and **Anna [Annie K.]**. **James** m. 2nd **Jennie Monfort** at St. Paul, MN, 28 Dec. 1874. **James** a lawyer of Oneonta.
	vii.	**Marquis [Marcus] L.**, b. 24 Oct. 1841; m. **Helena Pruine** 1 Jan. 1878 and has one dau., **Eva** and a son **DeForest**. He cashier of the First National Bank at Oneonta.
	vii.	**Melville**, b. 16 Jan. 1845; m. **Emma Bassett**, children: **Ralph, Washington B.** and **Thomas B.**; the first two dec'd. by 1878. **Melville** a lawyer of Oneonta. [BR gives four children: **Thomas, Victor, Marvin** and **Margaret**.]
	viii.	**Irvin [Irving]**, b. 1 Jan. 1847, d. 15 Feb. 1850.

MRS. MARGARET KEYES.

JOSIAH D. KEYES[4] was b. Town of Laurens on his father's farm 18 Jan. 1833; farmer, clerked in a store for a time. He m. **Margaret Lane** on 28 Dec. 1853, she d/o **Cornelius** and **Rebecca (Hardenburg) Lane**. Members of the Methodist Episcopal Church. Children:

    i..   A son, d. in infancy.
5   ii.   **Irvin J.**
    iii.   **Laverne**, res. at Otego; m. **Emily V. Day** of that place. Laverne was formerly a merchant, but is now (1893) a farmer.

IRVIN J. KEYES[5] b. in Laurens in 1855; res. Mt. Vision. He m. in Jan. 1879 to **Maggie A. Wellman** of Milford, NY, d/o **Alfred** and **Sarah (Pattengille) Wellman**. He is a farmer, specializing in raising hops and dairying. His farm is known as "Maple Shade Stock Farm." [No mention of children.]

[A:170a; BR:272-3; BR:752-54]

KLUMPH, GUSTAVUS[1], the first of his family to the America; settled immediately in Springfield, NY. He is mentioned in the journal of **Richard Smith**, a traveler in the Otsego region in 1769. In 1777 the Klumph family and others were driven from their farms by Indians. His great-great grandson, **Arch C. Klumph** of Cleveland, states that **Gustavus** had several sons, but he has knowledge of only **Thomas** below.

THOMAS KLUMPH[2], b. 1779 at Springfield, d. 24 Oct. 1850 [DARPI gives his death date as Jan. 1818 and is the only source of his wife's name, below] and bur. in a little cemetery on the bank of Lake Erie, immediately north of Kingville, OH. He and his wife [**Margaret (Peggy) Davis**] were members of the First Presbyterian Church of Springfield. **Thomas** had seven sons, those named here.

3   i.   **Lester R.** of Maryland, NY m. at Springfield 11 Nov. 1832 to **Laura Adelia Slayton**.
    ii.   **John**.
    iii.   **Fayette**.
    iv.   **Alexis**.
    v.   **Cornelius**.
    iv.   **Dr. Almond**.

LESTER R. KLUMPH[3], blacksmith at Springfield Center. His initials are on a stone in the foundation of the present shop today (late 1800's). Family moved to Conneantville, PA c. 1850. His children, all b. Springfield:

    i.   **Morton**, b. 1841.
    ii.   **Ida**, b. 1845.
    iii.   **Dorr** (son), b. 1847.

From records at the county clerk's office at Cooperstown, Book B., page 484: "**Augustine Klumph** and wife, **Sally**, **Jeremiah Klumph**, **Jacob Klumph** and wife, **Catharine**, **Mary Klumph**, **Thomas Klumph** and wife **Pattie**, **Margaret Klumph**, **Leonard Vibbard** and **Elizabeth** his wife and **Perry Hall** and **Lany**, his wife, heirs of **Thomas Klumph**, deceased, of the first part and **Garret Wikoff** of the second part for $2,000.00... land in

lot No. 8 in Prevost purchase, in Croghan Ptent, containing 100 acres..."
All so far unplaced in this work.
[SPR:156-7; GBM; DARPI.]

KNAPP, WILLIAM², s/o **William¹** and **Patty [Martha] (Liscom/Liscum) Knapp** of Taunton (now Raynham), MA was b. there 29 Nov. 1764/4. William Sr. was a soldier of the Revolution and collected a pension. He enlisted in Dec. 1780, giving his age as 18, when he was 16. At the time of his enlistment he was a res. of Poultney, VT. **William Jr.** d. 6 Aug. 1846 at Athens Twp., PA at the home of his son, and is bur. at East Wavery, NY. **William Jr.** m. Jan. 1788, **Fanny Temple**, of a CT family, a d/o **William** and **Jemima Temple**. She was b. 6 Nov. 1767 at Winchester, NH Children, all b. at Springfield, NY:

3   i.   **William.**
     ii.   **Sylvester**, doctor; m. **Lucy Fitch.**
     iii.   **Isaac**, m. **Isabelle Taylor.**
     iv.   **David**, m. **Sarah Sayre.**
     v.   **Fannie**, m. **Jeremiah Walling.**
     vi.   **Hiram**, doctor, m. **Haley Eastbrook.**
     vii.   **Martha**, m. **Nathan Eldbree.**
     viii.   **Jemima**, m. --- **Beals.**
     ix.   **Eleanor**, m. **Amos Canfield.**

WILLIAM KNAPP³, b. 28 Oct. 1788 in Otsego Co., near Springfield; d. 3 Feb. 1874, on his farm in Athens, PA. He studied medicine as a young man and practiced many years at Factoryville (now East Waverly), NY. In later life he retired and farmed. He m. 14 June 1812, **Armenia Gates**, b. 19 Jan. 1792, d. 29 Nov. 1850, d/o **Azel** and **Margaret (Holbrook) Gates**. She was a niece of "Light-Horse Harry" Lee and other military personalities. Children:

     i.   **William**, b. in Bainbridge, Chenango Co., NY, 16 Nov. 1813; d. Waverly, NY 8 April 1895. He m. 18 Feb. 1843, **Mary Ann Shackleton.**
     ii.   **Augusta**, b. 20 Feb. 1816.; d. 26 June 1848; m. 2 April 1838 **B. F. Snyder.**
     iii.   **Emily Margaret**, b. 14 April 1818; m. 22 Sept. 1843, **Thomas Yates.**
     iv.   **Mary Gates**, b. 22 April 1820; d. 4 May 1858.
     v.   **Jerome B.**, b. 17 Aug. 1822; d. 22 Jan. 1853, physician; m. 12 Jan. 1851, **Maria Armstrong** and has a son **Frederick Jerome.**
     vi.   **Lucia**, b. 7 May 1825; m. 31 March 1850 **Rev. A. B. Stowell**, Baptist clergyman.
     vii.   **Arnebua**, b. 27 March 1828; d. Feb. 1809; m. 20 Oct. 1856, **John Cheney.**
     viii.   **Azel**, b. 29 Sept. 1834; m. 14 Jan. 1860, **Hattie Babcock.**

[CUT1:V.3:1230-32; *Boston Transcript* #5458, Dec. 1932 & 3 Jan. 1933; DARPI.]

LUCE, NATHAN⁴ (*Nathaniel³ CT, Josiah² MA & CT, Henry¹ MA & England*) was b. 15 or 16 Oct. 1736 at Windham, CT, s/o **Nathaniel** and **Mary (Prentice/Prentiss) Luce**; d. 11 Dec. 1816, at Otsego. He m. 18 or 19 Nov. 1756 at Windham to **Elizabeth Lasell/LaSalle** who was b. 3 May 1739 at Hingham, CT. She d. 21 Aug. 1819. **Nathan** made his will 16 July 1816 and in it named his wife and children, most b. in Windham, CT:

5   i.   **Nathan [Nathaniel]**.
       ii.   **Othniel**, b. 11 Nov. 1758; d. 22 Aug. 1759.
       iii.   **Hannah**, b. 14 March 1760 in Windham; m. **Joseph Baldwin** 12 April 1795 at Brooklyn, CT. **Hannah** d. 1833 at "Peth, Hartwick Co., NY." Had one child, **Aschsah** who m. **Nathaniel Pierce**.
5   iv.   **Othniel**.
5   v.   **Uriah**, b. 18 Aug. 1763; d. at Otsego 9 Dec. 1841.
5   vi.   **Rufus**, b. 17 July 1765 CT, d. 10 Jan. 1806, Paris Furnace, Oneida Co., NY.
       vii.   **Elthea**, b. 10 Nov. 1766; d. 20 Dec. 1768.
       viii.   **Elizabeth [Patty]**, b. 17 Jan. 1768; d. 1839; m. **Joseph Baldwin**.
       xi.   **Irene**, b. 2 April 1769; m. Deacon **John Gott**.
5   x.   **John LaSalle/Lassell**.
       xi.   **Mary [Polly]**, b. 22 March 1772; m. **Antepus [Andesus] Utley**.
       xii.   **Patty**, b. 2 Jan. 1774; m. **Joseph Holt**.
       xiii.   **Lois**, b. 18 Feb. 1776; d. 8 Aug. 1777.
       xiv.   **Nathan Jr.**, b. 30 Sept. 1777.
       xv.   **Lois**, b. 23 Dec. 1779.
       xvi.   **Asa**, b. 25 Jan. 1782 Windham Co., CT; d. Manchester, MI at the home of his son **George**. Other child was **Eloisa**. Neither had children.
       xvii.   **James**, b. 24 Jan. 1785; d. 31 Jan. 1785.

[There are two sons of **Nathan⁴** named **Nathan/Nathaniel**; one b. 15 July 1757, the other b. 30 Sept. 1777. The Luce genealogy states that they are unable to distinguish between them and to determine which m. **Hannah Boies**. The **Nathan** below could be either.]

NATHAN LUCE JR.⁵ b. 30 Sept. 1777 in Canterbury, CT; d. 6 Aug. 1837 in Cooperstown, NY. He m. 20 Sept. 1809 Blandford, Hampshire Co., MA to **Hannah A. Boies**, she b. 18 Jan. 1787, d. 14 Jan. 1864 in Cooperstown. **Nathan** was a mail carrier and merchant. Children:
    i.   **Catherine E.**, b. 1810 at Homer, Cortland Co., NY; m. **Frederick Pratt**, no children.
    ii.   **Alonzo Boiles**, b. 7 Nov. 1815; d. 13 July 1879. He m. **Penthesiler Lawrence**. One son d. aged 18.
    iii.   **Charlotte M.**, d. 12 Nov. 1854, unm.
    iv.   **Samuel Dickson**, b. 22 April 1822; d. 4 May 1907; was an attorney and separated from his wife in 1891 [Mrs. **Harriet Lucretia Boies**]. No children.

OTHNIEL LUCE⁵ b. 17 Jan. 1762 in Windham Co., CT. Served in the Revolutionary War from CT; d. 17 [19] March 1818. Res. MIddlefield, NY

and m. 16 Feb. 1786 in Norwich, CT to **Joanna Kimball**; she d. 2 Aug. 1829, aged 72. [He is not named in his father's will.] Children:
i. **James**, left dau. **Caroline** b. Oswigathie, NY.
ii. **Ira**; m. **Jane Lammon** and had: **Zadoc, Asa** and **Martha**.
iii. **Lydia**, m. **David Fling**.
iv. **Eunice**, m. **William Ray**.

URIAH LUCE[5] b. 18 Aug. 1763 at Windham, CT; served in the American Revolution in the CT Line; farmer. He d. 9 Dec. 1841 at Cooperstown; m. 24 Aug. 1792 to **Dille Lyon**; she d. at Otsego 22 June 1838, aged 70. Children, all b. Windham Co., CT:
i. **Clarissa**, b. 19 May 1793; d. 1876; m. 1st 1813 to **Whitney Sweeting**; m. 2nd **Thomas Blanchard**, a farmer and Justice of the Peace; res. Fayettsville & Syracuse, NY.
ii. **Sophia**, b. c. 1795.
iii. **Artimassa/Artimessa**, b. c. 1797.
iv. **Nancy May**, b. c. 1799.
v. **Charles**, b. c. 1800, d. 15 May 1882 at Utica, NY. "Indolent." He was mar. but wife's name "unknown."
vi. **Morgan**, b. c. 1804.

[Note: Source "A" states that **Uriah**[5] had a son, **Uriah Jr.**[6]. This person does not show up in the Luce Genealogy, and the **John Luce** [s/o **Uriah**[6]] in the Luce Genealogy is given as **John Lasell Luce**[5], s/o **Nathan**[4]. Both versions are printed below.]

URIAH LUCE JR.[6] served as sheriff of Otsego in 1798 and had:
JOHN LUCE[7] who m. **Sally Ingalls** and had: [See note above and entry for **John Lassell Luce**[5] below.]
i. **Rufus P.**, town superintendent and merchant.
ii. **Henry J.**, res. Exeter.
iii. **Torrey J.**, b. Cooperstown [Middlefield] 1798; res. Exeter in 1837, merchant & Justice of the Peace. He d. 24 Aug. 1872 in Hartwick. Merchant and Universalist; he m. 14 March 1825 at Hartwick to **Huldah Eliza Peters** who was b. 3 April 1807 at Hartwick, d/o **Amasa Peters** and **Sarah Swift**. She d. 1 April 1885

RUFUS LUCE[5] m. **Lovina Benton**, b. c. 1778 in Norwich, VT, d/o **Medad Benton** who went to Norwich, VT from Tolland, CT. **Rufus** served in the War of 1812; he d. 10 Jan. 1806 at Paris Furnace, Oneida Co., NY. **Lovina** m. as a widow **Eliphalet Sweeting** of Paris Hill and had several more children. Children, most b. in Middlefield, NY:
i. **Zabad**; had **Frederick** and **George**.
ii. **Zabine** (twin to **Zabad**).
iii. **Nancy**, m. **Mr. Sage**, res. Ann Arbor, MI in 1893.
iv. **Patty**, m. **Thomas Butler**, res. New Hartford, NY; their dau. m. **Mr. Price**.
v. **Horace**.
vi. **Willard**, in Washington, DC in 1893.
vii. **Winifred** (twin to **Willard**).

JOHN LASELL LUCE⁵ b. 10 Oct. 1770 in Windham Co., CT; farmer of Otsego, NY; served in the War of 1812. He came to the county with his parents and d. 1 Aug. 1844/5 in Gilbertsville; Baptist. He m. c. 1797 at Middlefield, NY to **Sally Ingalls** who was b. 15 Oct. 1778 in RI or Rehoboth, MA, d/o **Stephen Ingalls** of RI. She d. 14 April 1863 at Hartwick. [BR gives the father of **Torry James Luce⁶** as **John H. Luce⁵**, b. at Martha's Vineyard, MA; blacksmith. They say he res. in Middlefield many years and then removed to Butternuts.] Children:

6   i.   **Torry James**, b. 5/6 April 1798.
6   ii.   **Lovell Bernard**, b. 15 Nov. 1799.
6   iii.   **Stephen Ingalls**, b. 5 Oct. 1802.
    iv.   **Jacob M.**, b. 14 July 1806 at Middlefield, NY; d. 21 April 1861 at Hartwick. He m. 18 Jan. 1827 **Sally Walker**.
6   v.   **John Lassell Jr.**, b. 6 April 1811.
    vi.   **Richard O.**
    vii.   **Dr. Chauncy P.**, b. 24 April 1817 in NY; m. **Sarah Lee** and res. at Arcadia, NY. One child, **Catherine Ella** b. 2 Nov. 1853, res. Munroe, MI.

TORRY JAMES LUCE⁶ b. Middlefield, NY 5 April 1798; d. 24 [25] Aug. 1872 in Hartwick, aged 74. He res. in Butternuts and removed to Hartwick in 1837. Merchant, Universalist; he m. 14 March 1825 at Hartwick **Huldah Eliza Peters** who was b. 3 April 1807 at Hartwick. She d. 1 April 1885 and was the d/o **Amasa Peters** [b. CT] and **Sarah Swift** (d/o Gen. Swift in the Revolution). Children:

7   i.   **Rufus Peters**, b. 12 May 1826.
    ii.   **Caroline** b. at Gilbertsville; m. **Alonzo H. Slayton** and had **Caroline, Charles, Ruth, Torry** and **Grace Slayton**.
7   iii.   **Dolphus [Adolphis] Skinner**, b. c. 1832.
    iv.   **Henry James**, d. 1890, unm.
    v.   **Cynthia P.**

RUFUS PETERS LUCE⁷ b. in Middlefield Center, NY; m. in 1855 at Hartwick **Cornelia Lewis** who was b. 25 Jan. 1728 at Brookfield, Madison Co., NY; she d. 19 Jan. 1900, was d/o **Jeremiah Lewis** [b. in Petersburg, Rensselaer Co., NY 26 Feb. 1792; d. Ellisburg, Jefferson Co., NY] and wife **Mary Procter** [b. Bradford, MA 11 Jan. 1797, d. Ellisburg, NY]. **Rufus** began teaching at the age of 16 for five years; at age 21 he engaged in the manufacture of linseed oil, the mill being located one mile south of the village of Hartwick. He continued this business for eight years, and then, with his brother **Dolphus**, engaged in the mercantile business. Children:
    i.   **George Torry**; m. **Julia May Briggs**, res. Hartwick, NY. He is in business with his father.
    ii.   **Robert Lee**, b. 19 Sept. 1862 at Hartwick; attorney, grad. Yale College class of 1889, now (1893) in office of Platt & Bower of NY City.

DOLPHUS (ADOLPHUS) SKINNER LUCE⁷ of Hartwick m. 2 Jan. 1860 at Hartwick **Emma Wentworth** who was b. 17 April 1841, d/o **Elisha**

Wentworth and Lucy Brockway. **Dolphus** d. 5 Oct. 1876. Children:
- i. **Daniel (Dr.)**, b. 20 Dec. 1863 at Plymouth, Richland Co., OH. He m. **Emily Grace Shumway**.
- ii. **John Wentworth**, b. 29 March 1865 at Spartayarmouth, Ontario Canada [?].
- iii. **Levi**, d. aged 18.
- iv. **Infant**, nothing further.

LOVELL BERNARD LUCE[6] b. 1799 in Chenango Co., NY, d. 11 Dec. 1854 in Gilbertsville, NY. He m. 18 June 1830 at Gilbertsville to **Mary Lillie**, d/o **Jared Lillie** and **Susan Tuckerman** of CT. She was b. c. 1802 in CT and d. 20 Dec. 1870 at Gilbertsville [Butternuts]. Children:
- i. **Marie Antoinette**, b. 6 April 1832 at Cincinnatus, Cortland Co., NY; m. 12 Oct. 1869 **Richard Hollis**.
- ii. **E. Byram**, b. 5 Dec. 1837; m. 1881 **Kate Richardson**.
- iii. **Frances Ellen**, b. 6 Aug. 1839; m. 31 Dec. 1867 **Ferdinand Shaw** who was b. 25 July 1835 at Butternuts Twp., near Gilbertsville. He d. 10 May 1892, was s/o **Col. David Shaw** and **Sephe Chapin**. Children: **Francis Lillie** b. 15 Sept. 1870; **Mary Lillie** b. 15 Sept. 1870, d. 23 April 1872 and **Roger Ferdinand** b. 10 Aug. 1881.
- iv. **George Henry**, d. aged 17 [15 April 1854, aged 18 according to his obituary, in Butternuts].

STEPHEN INGALLS LUCE[6] b. in Cooperstown (or Chenango Co., NY), d. 24 March 1887 in West Burlington. Farmer, Universalist; he m. 5 April 1827 to **Elizabeth (Betsey) Pierce** who was b. 20 July 1798 at Cooperstown; she d. 3 [2] Oct. 1845 in Otsego Co. [Burlington Flats according to her obituary], was d/o **Milo Pierce**. Children:

7
- i. **VanRensalear Williamson**.
- ii. **Stephen M.**, b. 29 Nov. 1830 in NY; d. 1909. He m. **Mary Campfield**. In 1891 he res. W. Burlington, NY and had a dau., **Dora** who m. **Mr. Shaw** and they lived in KS in 1891.
- iii. **Harry P.**, b. 5 May 1832; d. 20 June 1867.
- iv. **Harriet E.**, b. 17 Oct. 1834 in Warren, NY; m. 18 Jan. 1851 **Leonard H. Price**.
- v. **Mary**, b. 13 Jan. 1839 in Richfield Springs; m. 1863 **Andrew Eldred**.
- vi. **Sarah P.**, b. 28 May 1840; d. 27 March 1871.
- vii. **Torry James**, b. 3 Jan. 1843; m. 1 Sept. 1868 **Tresa Shoemaker**, res. Scranton, PA in 1902.
- viii. **Anna**, m. **George C. Courtwright** of Chicago, IL.

VANRENSALEAR WILLIAMSON LUCE[7] b. May 1828, d. 7 Sept. 1898 in Scranton, PA; insurance agent, Presbyterian. He m. **Adelia Tedrick**, d/o **John** and **Amy (Armstrong) Tedrick**. Children:
- i. **Anna**, m. **Mr. Cortwright**.
- ii. **John Stephen**, b. 10 July 1859.
- iii. **Henry Winters (Harry)**, b. 24 Sept. 1868.

iv. **Carrie**, d. young.

JOHN LASSELL LUCE JR.[e] shoemaker, Methodist-Episcopalian, b. 6 April 1811 in Cooperstown. He d. 1 Aug. 1855 in Exeter, NY; m. 4 Nov. 1832 in Cincinnatus, Cortland Co., NY to **Perlina Fish** who was b. 10 June 1814 in Cortland Co., d/o **Reuben Fish** (b. Easton, NY, d. Cortland Co.) and wife **Betsey Cleveland**. Family res. in Exeter, Spooner's Corner and to Parma MI in 1880. Children:
- i. **Cynthia**, d. aged 14 mo. 11 Aug. 1831, Gilbertsville.
- ii. **Lucinda**.
- iii. **Marilla**, in 1897 res. Pasadena, CA; m. **Mr. Robbins**.
- iv. **Lavinia**.
- v. **Horace**.
- vi. **Ira**, dealer in Hops, d. 18 May 1889 in Oneida, NY; m. **Nancy A. Robinson** of Richfield Springs. They had one child, **Alfred John**, b. 14 Jan. 1847 at Richfield Springs who m. **Julia L. Hudson**.
- vii. **Orrin C.**, b. 7 June 1825 Seneca, NY.
- viii. **Harriet**; m. **R. H. Dunbar**.
- ix. **Kate**; m. **J. E. Weeks**.
- x. **Mary Etta**.
- xi. **Theron J.**
- xii. **Martha**; m. **Eugene Conklin** and in 1890 res. Hartwick, NY.

[GBW; OB; A:160; G:1789; *The American Descendants of Henry Luce of Martha's Vineyard 1640 to 1985* by Martha F. McCourt and Thomas R. Luce, 1985; *Boston Transcript*, 23 Aug. 1909 #709; BR: 177-78]

LULL, BENJAMIN[1] to Town of Morris with five of his sons and their families. Along with them came **Ebenezer Knapp, Increase and Moses Thurston** families. They came from New-Town-Martin, of Tryon, late county of Albany, together with **Hugh M. Irish, Benjamin Stone, William Pierce, Esquire Brooks, Jack Johnson** and **Robert Garrett**, all English, and settled with their families in Hillington and Wells' patent [Butternuts] in 1773 or before. All these people were harrassed and driven off by the Indians under **Col. Brant** during the Revolutionary War. He m. **Elizabeth**, d/o **Ebenezer Knapp**. **Benjamin's** children named here:
- i. **Benjamin Jr.**, b. c. 1760.
- 2 ii. **Joseph**.
- iii. **Caleb**. His son **Ezra** res. Morris aged 88 in 1878.
- iv. **Nathan**. Could be the **Nathan Lull** d. at Butternuts 27 Sept. 1842, aged 85.
- v. **William**.

DEACON JOSEPH LULL[2] [P] (d. 1840, Butternuts) was aged 17 when he came with his father, **Benjamin**[1] above, to Otsego Co. He m. **Martha Knapp**, theirs' the first marriage celebrated in the new town of Butternuts. She was the d/o **Ebenezer and Mary Knapp**, b. 1762 in Nine Partners, NY. **Martha** d. 6 June 1851 in Louisville, NY. In 1773 **Martha** removed with her parents from the place of her birth into a dreary wilderness, uninhabited except by savages and wild beasts. On several occasions she had her nerve tested by being attacked by wild beasts and savages. At the onset of the Revolution, her husband, father and brother were all arrested on the charge of being Tories and conveyed to Albany for trial. Her brother and husband were released, having been found innocent. In 1778 **Joseph** and **Martha** were obliged, in consequence of the war, to leave their home. **Martha** carried two children in her lap, on horseback, to Dutchess Co., over 160 miles, where they resided five and one-half years, during which time **Deacon Joseph** experienced religion. After his return to Otsego Co. he was instrumental in helping found the first church of Butternuts in 1793, where he served as deacon for 42 years. At the time of her death **Martha** res. with her son **Jacob** in Louisville. She retained her faculties until the last and died surrounded by her kindred. They had 16 children; 15 lived to adult age and married. Twelve of them have made a profession of Christian religion; nine united with the church. At the time of his death at age of 84 **Joseph** left 11 children and 99 grandchildren. His will was dated 6 May 1837; probated in 1840. Children:

3   i.   **Nathaniel W.**
    ii.   **William.**
    iii.   **Joseph.**
    iv.   **Jacob K.**, res. of village of Morris, aged 83 years (1878).
    v.   **Ebenezer.**
    vi.   **Cyrus**, m. **Lydia Ann Kaner** in 1829 in New Lisbon; now res. Jordans, Onondaga Co., NY (1878). A notice of their marriage appeared in the local Otsego newspaper issue of 12 Oct. 1829.
    vii.   **Rachel.**
    viii.   **Martha.**
    ix.   **Clarissa.**
    x.   **Laura.**
    xi.   **Sarah.**
    xii.   **Lucy.**
    xiii.   **Mary.**

NATHANIEL W. LULL[3] of Butternuts is named as "Nathan" in his father-in-law's will and in his own will, which he made out 2 March 1839; probated 20 June 1843. He d. 27 Sept. 1842, aged 85. He does not name his wife in this document, but he does name his children and a granddau. **Orphson Lull**. One source states that **Nathan** is a res. of Jefferson Co., NY and names **Mrs. Turner Davis** as a granddau. of his, a resident of Morris Village. **Nathan** m. **Ruth Moore**, d/o **Jonathan** and **Anna Moore Jr.** **Ruth** was b. 3 Oct. 1764 in Salisbury, CT. Children:

    i.   **Luther.**
    ii.   **Oliver F.**
    iii.   **Nathan.**
    iv.   **Paschal F.**
    v.   **Jonathan M.**
    vi.   **Lorena**, m. **Samuel Drew.**
    vii.   **Charlotte**, m. **Sheffield Bennett.**
    viii.   **Anna W.**, m. **Lysander Curtis.**

MRS. J. K. LULL.

DEACON JOSEPH LULL.

MRS. MARTHA LULL.

WILLIAM LULL³, m. **Charlotte Moore**, sister of the wife of his brother **Nathaniel**. He was a res. of Laurens when he made his will 13 Nov. 1834; probated Nov. 1829. Children:
    i.   **Rodwick**.
    ii.   **Caleb**. He left at least sone child, **Ezra**, b. c. 1798; a res. of Town of Morris in 1878.
4   iii. **Joel**.
    iv.   **Ginnett** (dau.), m. --- **Johnson**.
    v.   **Ruth**, m. --- **Green**.

DR. JOEL LULL⁴, m. **Caroline Harrington** on 29 Sept. 1831 in Laurens. He d. 13 Nov. 1845, aged 45; will was dated 3 Nov. 1845. In it he named his wife, nephew **Latia Johnson**, nieces **Sarah Ann** wife of **Lafayette Mills**, **Miranda Mickle** and **Eliza** and **Charlotte Johnson**.
[A:201-5, 218; GBW, GBM; OB; *Salisbury, Connecticut, Volume One: Vital Records 1730-1800, Gravestone Inscriptions*, Catoctin Press, Middletown, MD, n.d.]

MC CLINTOCK, CHARLES² (*Joseph¹ of Ireland*) was b. in Ireland, his wife **Jane** --- b. in Scotland. Both were quite young when the came to the US. **Charles** was one of six children and five came to the US. **Charles** and **Jane** m. in Harpersfield, NY and settled in Delaware Co. and after five years removed to Town of Worcester, Otsego Co. **Charles** d. on his farm, now occupied by his son **John**, at the age of 86. **Jane** d. there aged 56. Members of the Presbyterian Church. Children:
3   i.   **John**.
    ii.   **Alexander**.
    iii. **Margaret Ann**.
    iv.   **James**.
    v.   **Charles**.
    vi.   **William**.
    vii. **David**, d. aged 45, leaving wife and two children.

JOHN MC CLINTOCK³ was b. in Delaware Co., was five when his parents removed to Otsego Co. He is a general farmer of Town of Worcester and keeps a dairy of c. 25 cows. His sister, **Margaret Ann**, lives with him.
[BR:609-10]

MERCHANT, LEMUEL³ (*Gurdon² CT, John¹ CT*) bapt. 7 March 1771, was s/o **Gurdon** and **Sarah (Gilbert) Merchant** [Marchant]. He m. at Danbury, CT, 27 March 1795, **Betsey** [Elizabeth] **Rockwell**, d/o **Jabez** and **Phebe (Bedient) Rockwell**. She was b. at Danbury 20 Feb. 1774. [See Rockwell family entry.] Res. Butternuts and had children:
    i.   **Niram Rockwell**, b. Danbury, CT 1 March 1800; m. **Maria Dibble**, b. 22 July 1801; d. at Guilford [Chenango Co.], NY. They had four children, all b. Guilford: **Andrew Percival, Jane Elizabeth, Helen Maria** and **Mary Eveline**.
    ii.   **Orrin Gilbert**, b. Danbury 18 June 1803; m. **Sally L. Smith**, b. 8 Oct. 1809 and res. Guilford. She d. 16 Aug. 1855; he d. 6 March 1880.

iii. **Eliza Ann**, b. Danbury 10 May 1806; m. **Harvey Olmstead Nash**, b. 1 June 1804; res. Butternuts, NY. [See Nash family entry.]
iv. **Eleanor**, b. Butternuts 16 July 1809; m. **Lewis H. Nash**, b. 11 June 1811; res. Guilford, NY.
v. **Paschal**, b. Butternuts 6 Nov. 1811; m. 1st **Susan Smith**, b. 31 Dec. 1813; d. 31 Dec. 1847; m. 2nd **Emma Harris**. Res. Guilford. She d. 28 June 1880.
vi. **Olive**, b. Butternuts 23 Sept. 1816; d. at Guilford, NY 1 March 1846.

[*A Genealogy of the Families of John Rockwell of Stamford Conn., 1641, and Ralph Keeler of Hartford, Conn.* by James Boughton, 1903; *The Families of Old Fairfield [CT]* by Jacobus; *Stratford, CT Genealogies* by Orcutt.]

MERRIMAN, SAMUEL[6] (*Samuel*[5], *Theopolis*[4] *CT & MA, Samuel*[3] *CT, Nathaniel*[2] *CT, George*[1] *England*) s/o **Samuel Merriman** and 1st wife **Mary Hawks**, was b. 11 Sept. 1749 in Northfield, MA. He was of Unadilla, NY when he made his will there 24 May 1822; proved 22 Oct. 1824. He is listed as a settler of the Sand Hill-Hampshire Hollow region of Town of Unadilla before 1800. In his will he names his wife **Thankful** and children (below). One source says he m. **Eunice Severy** in 1768 [11 June 1772 in Worcester, MA]. Children:
i. **Samuel**.
ii. **Sarah**, b. 16 Nov. 1769, not named in her father's will in 1822.
iii. **Theophilus**, b. 16 July 1773; m. **Phoebe Childs**, b. 30 July 1780.
iv. **Sylvanus**.
v. **Mary**.
vi. **Zelpha**, m. **Eli Buckley**.
vii. **Phebe**, m. --- **Cowles**.

[GBW; UNA:99, 101; *History of Northfield, MA* by Temple & Sheldon; *At Rest in Unadilla* by Shirley B. Goerlick, 1988; *Hartford Times, 10 Jan. 1942, #175*; IGI; UNA:101; *Families of Ancient New Haven* by Jacobus.]

MERRITT, DANIEL W.[3] (*Martin*[2] *NY, Caleb*[1] *NY & OH*) b. Marbletown, Ulster Co., NY 3 Sept. 1838. He is the proprietor of four farms in Otsego Co. His grandfather **Caleb** migrated to OH and left behind son **Martin** to be reared by an aunt in Ulster Co. **Martin** by early manhood acquired two farms in Ulster Co. and in 1859 he sold his property and took up res. in Sullivan Co. in Fallsburg, where he died. His wife was **Maria Fitch**, also b. Ulster Co., a d/o **William Fitch** (originally of CT) and wife --- **VanHouser**, also of CT. **Daniel** purchased 45 acres of land in District No. 15, Otsego and other land from time to time. He m. **Melissa Pierce** on 13 Sept. 1865, d/o **Hiram** and **Emeline (Woodward) Pierce**, both of Otsego. They have one son living (1893):
HIRAM MERRITT[4] m. **Ella Reed** and have children:
i. **Daniel W.** Has lived with his grandparents since he was four weeks old, is of the 6th generation to dwell on the old farm.
ii. **Nathan**.
iii. **Hiram**.
[BR:573-74]

MILLER, CLEMENT of Hartwick, formerly of Barbadoes, West Indies, made his will 3 March 1824 and it was probated 15 Dec. 1830. His obituary names him as **Capt. Clement Miller**, d. 26 Oct. 1830. In his will he names his wife **Margaret** and children (below). He named his son **Joseph Richard** and his son-in-law **Joseph D. Husbands** executors along with **Rev. Thomas H. Orderson** of Barbadoes. **Margaret** d. 21 Oct. 1829, at Hartwick, aged 71.

    i.   **Joseph Richard**, was of Hartwick when he m. **Mrs. Harriet P. Roach** of Barbados in New York City on 1 Oct. 1829. A **Mrs. J. R. M. Miller** d. at Hartwick on 28 June 1828, and perhaps Harriet was not his first wife..

    ii.   **Anna Maria Blackman**, m. **Joseph D. Husbands**. Joseph d. 17 Dec. 1832 in Hartwick.

    iii.   **Katherine Martha.**

    iv.   **Mary Margaret.**

    v.   **Elizabeth.**

    vi.   **Francis [sic] Ford**, m. **Richard H. Farmer**. **Mrs. Frances M. F. Farmer**, formerly of Hartwick, d. Oxford, NY 23 Sept. 1831.

[GBW; GBM; OB]

MILLER, JOHN, s/o **Edward Miller** who lived & d. in Co. Suffolk, England, a small farmer and shoemaker who d. at age 72, and his wife **Fannie Felkins**, who d. about the same age. Members of the Church of England. **John** is one of six children. His bro. **George Miller**, the only other member of the family who came to America, d. at Norwich, Chenango Co., NY c. 1885. **John** was aged 28 when in 1832, a single man, he took passage, alone, to America. For a time he res. in Poughkeepsie, NY. He m. 12 Nov. 1833 to **Susanna Holl**, also b. in England and educated in London. She came to America with her parents **Edward** and **Betsy Holl** in 1832; the family settled near Poughkeepsie. **Betsy** d. of cholera and **Edward** removed to Chenango Co., where d. aged 91; farmer. **Susanna** d. at her home in Oneonta 18 Aug. 1892, nearly aged 84. Presbyterian. They had seven children, first two living in 1893, the others dec'd.:

    i.   **Fannie M.**, m. **Dr. Ozias W. Peck** of Oneonta.

    ii.   **Mary**, m. **James Forbes**, res. N.J.

    iii.   **John Jr.**, "ex-soldier."

    iv.   **Anna.**

    v.   **Adeline.**

    vi.   **Elizabeth.**

    vii.   **Susanna.**

[BR:610-11]

MIRICK, JAMES 4th, b. at Princeton, Worcester Co., MA 19 Nov. 1771; d. at his farm in Gilbertsville, Otsego Co. 8 May 1853. He was a s/o **James Mirick (3rd)** who was b. 6 Jan. 1773, "it is believed" also at Princeton. **James Mirick (2d or Jr.)** is recorded as settled at Newbury, MA where he was m. and where the first of his six daus. was born 6 Feb. 1657. A **John Mirick** was also one of the early settlers at Charlestown, MA. **James 3rd** was a patriot soldier of the French & Indian Wars, also of the Revolution;

Capt. of Company 12, Shirley's Regiment, and was at the taking of Oswego.
James 4th m. **Esther Coye** 24 Dec. 1795 at her father's farm in Gilbertsville. They had 17 children; three d. in infancy and early childhood: Those named here:
i. **Willard**, d. at age 21.
ii. **Lucy**, m. **Almon Rockwell** 27 March 1834, at age 25. [See Rockwell family entry.]
   Esther d. 27 Feb. 1827 and **James** m. 2nd Mrs. **Abbie Lewis**, nee **Beardsley** on 17 Feb. 1833. She reared a son and dau. by her first husband.
[BR:530-31]

MORRIS, JACOB (GENERAL)[1], b. 1755 Old Morrisania; d. 10 Jan. 1844 Butternuts. Morrisania was the estate of **Lewis Morris**, signer of the Declaration of Independence, which was destroyed by the British. **Lewis** and his brother **Richard** were given a patent [Morris Patent in then Montgomery, now Otsego, Co.] of 35,000 acres as an indemnity for the loss of the property. Although the brothers had the patent surveyed and sold lots, neither ever visited their possessions in the Western Wildnerness. **Richard** was the first to emigrate to American, was an officer in **Cromwell's** army, and on the restoration of Charles II he emigrated to the West Indies and from there to New Netherlands (now New York). In 1650 he purchased from the Indians for himself and brother **Lewis** a tract of 500 acres on the Harlem. By the time of the Revolution three generations of Morris' had lived on the estate. During the Revolution **Jacob**[1], s/o **Lewis**, served on the staff of **Maj. Gen. Charles Lee**, settled near the site of "Morris Memorial Chapel." He was land agent for his father and uncle. He m. 1st **Mary Cox** (1759-1827) of Philadelphia, 2nd **Sophia Pringle** of Richfield on 1 March 1830, at which time **Jacob** was a res. of Butternuts. He was also a res. there when he made his will on 6 June 1833 (proved in 1844). In his will he named his wife, his children, several grandchildren, his brother **Capt. Lewis Morris**, his father-in-law (1st mar.) **Capt. Stowe** of the British Army, his father-in-law (2nd mar.) **John Pringle** of Richfield. He also mentioned in his will **William Augustus Pringle**. Children:

2 i. **Lewis Lee**.
 ii. **John Cox**, b. 1781 Philadelphia, attorney in NY & later to Morris; judge. He made his will at Butternuts on 4 May 1847 (proved 1849), and in it named his brothers and sisters and other family members. **James** and **John Cope** of Butternuts, witnesses.
 iii. **Richard**, b. 1782 Philadelphia, to Morris with parents; m. --- **Upton** and settled at "Upton Park." He d. 1 Feb. 1865 at Butternuts.
 iv. **Mary Ann**, b. 1784, m. **Isaac Cooper** of Cooperstown 24 Dec. 1804. Had at least one son, **Jacob Morris Cooper**.
 v. **George**, d. infant.
 vi. **Sarah Sabina**, b. 1788; m. 1st **Peter Kean**, 2nd **Looe** [Loos?] **Baker**; now (1878) res. NY with a dau., **Mrs. Hamilton Fish**. They also had at least one son, **John**.
 vii. **Jacob Walton**, b. 1792 Butternuts; m. 11 Sept. 1823 at Butternuts to **Serena Burgess**. Left a son **Charles** who occupies

	homestead (1878) and another son **John Cox Morris**. A **Harriet E. Brown**, wife of **Charles Morris**, is bur. at Edmeston, she was b. 16 Sept. 1826, d. 6 June 1892.
viii.	**Catherine Cox**, b. 1794 Butternuts, she was bapt. at age 2 y 6 m on 15 May 1797; m. **John Prentiss** of Cooperstown. Had at least two children: **Mary M.** and **Catherine L. Prentiss.**
ix.	**William Augustus**, b. 1796, bapt. at age 7 months at Cooperstown on 15 May 1797; accidentally killed c. 1818.
x.	**James Elliott**, d. infant, b. 2 Aug. 1800, bapt. 14 Sept. 1800.
xi.	**Charles Valentine**, b. 4 May 1802, bapt. 10 Feb. 1802; navy midshipman at age 14; career navy, now (1878) retired & res. Sacket's Harbor.
xii.	**Mary Cox**, b. 10 Feb. 1811, bapt. July 21 same year.
xiii.	**William Pringle**, b. 1832, atty. at Madison, WI.

LEWIS LEE MORRIS[2] (1778-1853) to Butternuts c. aged 16. He m. 1st --- **Gilbert**; 2nd **Hannah Winter** (1788-1866) of Butternuts 11 Sept. 1815, by Rev. **Russell Wheeler**. Children:

i.	**Lewis**, res. Binghamton (1878). He could be the **Lt. Lewis Morris** "of U.S.A." who m. at Albany, NY 7 Oct. 1822 to **Catherine Ford** of Albany. Notice of their marriage appeared in the local Otsego newspaper.
ii.	**William**, res. NY.
iii.	**John Cox**, res. Friendville, PA.
iv.	**Charles Lee**, res. Australia.
v.	**Mrs. John A. Collier**, res. Rochester.
vi.	**Mrs. John A. Davis**, res. NY.
vii.	**James R.**, res. on father's homestead.
viii.	**Robert Hunter**, b. 1826, d. 1865; m. 1853 **Martha E. Wright** (1832-1919).

[A:204; GBM; GBW; DCI:171; DAR 142437, v. 143; NASH1]

MULTER, CHRISTIAN[1] was b. on the Atlantic Ocean; his wife **Mary Multer** was b. in Schoharie Co., NY. **Christian** was s/o **Philip Multer** who was b. in Germany, as was his wife **Catharine**. They came to America in the late 1700's and settled in Albany Co., NY, where **Philip** erected the first glass factory in the country. He also was a physician. He moved his family to Otsego Co., among the first to settle in the Town of Worcester where he bought 400 acres of land. He d. on his farm at the aged of 80; his wife d. aged 75. Members of the Presbyterian Church. **Christian** was a farmer and served two terms as Justice of the Peace; he and his wife are members of the Methodist Episcopal Church. They raised nine children; the only one named here:

JOHN D. MULTER[2], general farmer and stock raiser, b. 25 March 1816 in Town of Worcester, NY. At the age of 21 he m. **Polly Mitchell** who was b. in Town of Summit, Schoharie Co., NY, d/o **Harmon** and **Patta Mitchell**, early settlers of that town. The Mitchells were Baptists. After his mar., **John** moved to his own farm of 200 acres. Both still living in 1893. They are described as very pleasant and social people; members of

the Methodist Episcopal Church. Children:
i.   **Martha A.**, m. **H. I. Fox**, res. Binghamton, NY.
ii.   **Mary A.**, m. **Wallace Crapsher**, res. Schoharie Co.
iii.   **Alice**, m. **Thomas Spangler**, res. Town of Worcester.
iv.   **Libbie B.**, m. **Merrill Bulson**, res. Town of Worcester.
v.   **Rose H.**, at home.
[BR:581-82]

MYRICK, FRANK H., b. Butternuts 1826, m. 17 Sept. 1850 to **Helen Tryphena Rockwell**, b. Butternuts 30 July 1829. [See Rockwell family entry.] Family later res. Norden, NE. Children:
i.   **George A.**, b. Gilbertsville, NY March 1853; d. there 2 July 1854.
ii.   **Kate Evelyn**, b. Gilbertsville, NY March 1856; m. **Lewis C. Porter** and res. Norden, NE in 1892.
iii.   **Charles Rockwell**, b. Norris, NY 28 Sept. 1859; m. April 1889 **Emma Storey**.

[*A Genealogy of the Families of John Rockwell, of Stamford Conn. 1641* ... by James Boughton, 1903]

NASH, ABRAHAM² (*Abraham¹ CT*) was b. c. 1775 and settled in Troy, NY, proprietor of a brewery. He m., at Norwalk, CT, **Sarah Benedict** of West Lane District, Ridgefield, CT. Children:
i.   **Jared**.
ii.   **Samuel**.
iii.   **Sally**, m. **Silas St. John**.
iv.   **Abiah**, m. **Thaddeus Seymour**.
3   v.   **Lewis F.**

LEWIS F. NASH³, b. 24 July 1800, "doubtless" in Cooperstown, NY. He d. in Norwich, NY 5 July 1871. He m. 2 April 1822, **Sophia Shipman**, b. 16 May 1800, d. 7 Aug. 1878. Children:
4   i.   **Alphonso DeMortimer**.
ii.   **Silas A.**, b. 21 July 1824, d. 3 July 1865. Was a barber in Cooperstown in 1847 listing.
iii.   **Aaron S.**, b. 17 Oct. 1825, drowned 17 July 1832.
iv.   **Sophia S.**, b. 9 Oct. 1837, d. 25 Jan. 1903.

ALPHONSO DE MORTIMER NASH⁴ b. in Toddtown, Otsego Co., NY 2 Nov. 1822; d. 16 July 1878. He learned the trade of piano making, which he followed all of his life, and he was foreman of a large piano manufacturing plant in NY City for some time. He m. 28 Dec. 1842 **Emily E. Crandall**, b. in Cooperstown, d/o **Edward** and **Mary (Todd) Crandall**. Children:
i.   **Henry C.**, b. 3 Jan. 1846, d. 6 March 1893.
ii.   **Mary E.**, b. 7 June 1848; m. **Albert Clayton** of Ilion, NY.
iii.   **Edward Lewis**, b. Forrestville, Chautauqua Co., NY 20 July 1853 and removed to Norwich, NY with his family.
iv.   **Alphonso Nelson**, b. 12 June 1856; res. St. Joe, MO.
[CUT1:3:1460-61; COP1:92]

NASH, DANIEL[6] (*Abraham*[5] *of CT, Abraham*[4] *of CT, John*[3] *CT, John*[2] *of CT, Edward*[1] *of England*) s/o **Abraham Nash** and **Sarah Olmstead** his wife, was b. in Ridgefield, CT and d. in Butternuts on 5 Oct. 1844, aged 81. **Abraham** was a Revolutionary War veteran, b. 17 Nov. 1740, d. Nov. 1821. **Daniel** removed to Butternuts c. 1805. He m. 30 April 1783, **Olive**, b. 5 April, 1766, d. 24 Oct. 1840, d/o **Eliakim Nash**. [An Olive Nash, b. 24 Jan. 1772, was bapt. at Cooperstown 18 July 1797. A Mrs. Olive Nash d. at Exeter 27 May 1838 aged 46.] **Daniel Nash** served in the Revolution; d. at Butternuts 5 Oct. 1844, aged 81. Children:

    i.   **David**, b. 10 Nov. 1783, d. 22 March 1860. Served in the War of 1812.
    ii.   **Dorcas**, b. 22 Feb. 1787, m. **Nathan Gray**.
    iii. **Sarah**, b. 3 May 1709, d. 10 Aug. 1801.
7 iv. **Harvey Olmstead**.

HARVEY OLMSTEAD NASH[7], b. Ridgefield 1 Jan. 1804, d. 11 Jan. 1875 at Harpersville, Broome Co., NY. To NY state with his parents when a young child. He was a miller and a farmer; lived many years at Butternuts, where all of his children were born; later removed to Guilford, NY and then to Harpersville. He m. 1839, **Eliza A.**, d/o **Lemuel Merchant**; she b. 21 May 1806 in Danbury, CT and d. 16 July 1886 in Guilford. [See Merchant family entry.] Children:

    i.   **Elizabeth Olive**, b. 25 July 1840 at Butternuts; m. 1st **Joseph Thurston**, m. 2nd **William S. Usher** of Kingston, Ontario. Res. Toronto, Canada in 1892. Children: **Edwin Thurston**, b. Butternuts 6 Dec. 1865 and removed soon after with parents to Toronto, where he res. in 1892. He is a portrait painter. **Gould Thurston**, b. Toronto 1872.
    ii.   **William Olmstead**, b. 9 March 1842 Butternuts; 17 Oct. 1867 m. **Marcia Irene Winsor**, b. 24 Aug. 1846; lived in Guilford, NY. Son **Willis Winsor Nash** b. 6 Nov. 1867.
8 iii. **Martin Marion**.
    iv. **Ellen Maria**, b. 31 May 1845 Butternuts; m. **William B. Harvey** [Hovey] of Guilford who was b. 19 June 1845; res. Guilford in 1892. Children: **Flora Belle, Robert Henry** and **Eva May**.
    v.   **Gould Merchant**, b. 23 Feb. 1847 Butternuts, merchant, lives Eagle River, WI. Mar. 1st **Nellie Cook** and 2d **Bina Thompson** b. Burnham, ME in 1859. Res. Tomahawk, WI in 1892. Children b. WI: **Eva, Lena** and **Grace** [first wife]; **Olive**, b. Eagle River.
    vi. **Phebe Ann**, b. 30 Aug. 1848 at Butternuts; m. **Oliver C. Bentley**, res. Gilbertville, NY in 1892.

MARTIN MARION NASH[8] b. 9 Oct. 1842 at Butternuts; m. **Lucinda R. Beatty**, d/o **Charles H.** and **Hannah (Main) Bentley**. Family res. at Guilford in 1892; d. in Kingston, NY 27 April 1905. Served in the Civil War in Co. F, 89th Regt. NY Volunteer Militia. Member of the Methodist Episcopal Church. Children, b. Guilford, NY:

    i.   **Charles Gould**, b. 7 Feb. 1869; res. Norwich in 1894, unm.
    ii.   **Mary Elizabeth**, b. 3 May 1870, d. 9 April 1875.

[CUT1:321; CUT1:3:1460-61; OB; NASH 1; *A Genealogy of the Families of John Rockwell of Stamford Conn., 1641, and Ralph Keeler of Hartford, Conn.* by James Boughton, 1903; DARPI]

Another **DANIEL NASH (REV.)**, this one of Burlington, made his will 25 May 1836 (d. 5 June 1836 at Exeter, aged 74) and in it named children (below). He was the first pastor of the Episcopal church at Schuyler's Lake Village in 1797 [Leroy, Richfield Springs]. A **Mary Nash**, b. 22 Feb. 1767, bapt. 24 June 1809 at Cooperstown could have been his wife. Witnesses to the bapt.: **Martin Noble, Abigail Noble** and **Hannah Noble**. Rev. Nash d. at Exeter on 5 June 1836, aged 74. Children:
- i. **Daniel**.
- ii. **William C.** of Exeter, m. in Richfield 21 Jan. 1827 to **Barbara Weber**.
- iii. **John Frederick**. [His baptismal record shows him to be the s/o Daniel and Olive Nash, b. 21 Feb. 1804; bapt. at Cooperstown 8 April 1804.] Mrs. **John F. Nash** of Butternuts, late of Exeter, d. 29 April 1839, aged 26.
- iv. **Olive L.**, m. --- **Munro**.
- v. **Hannah M.**, m. --- **Hisbis** [sic].
- vi. **Elizabeth**, m. --- **Norton**.
- vii. **Edward**, d. 19 Aug. 1819, aged 4 years.

[GBW; OB; NASH1; GBM; RS:82]

NILES, NATHANIEL[1] in 1797 purchased part of the farm of **Abner Mack**. The family were famous for their apple orchard. Nathaniel's will was made in Otsego 1 May 1813 and proved 20 Feb. 1816.; he d. 2 Feb. 1816, was b. 25 Feb. 1728. His wife [**Martha Joslyn**, b. in Feb. 1729, d. 21 Dec. 1820] is not named in the will but he does name his children:
2
- i. **Nathaniel**.
- ii. **Henry**.
- iii. **Abigail**, m. --- **Martin**.
- iv. **Jane**, m. --- **Carey**.
- v. **Elizabeth**, m. --- **Stanton**.
- vi. **Freelove**, m. --- **Crandall**.

NATHANIEL NILES[2] b. in Dutchess Co., NY 16 Aug. 1765, d. 27 Aug. 1850. He m. **Martha Buckston** who was b. in RI 4 Feb. 1763, d. 22 March 1841. Res. on the family homestead. They had 11 children, those so far identified:
- i. **William**, b. 21 June 1791, d. 26 Oct. 1864 at his home in West Oneonta. He reared a family of five children two living (1893): **Nathaniel** and **Asenath**, res. West Oneonta. Dau. **Catharine** m. **William Cooley** and d. 7 June 1793.
3
- ii. **Hanson**.
- iii. **Jane**, m. **Ephraim Sleeper**.
- iv. **Julian**, named in her grandfather's will in 1816.
- v. Dau., widow (1892) of **Jacob Heaton** of Ulster Co., NY.
- vi. **Hannah**, b. 27 Dec. 1789, d. 5 May 1870, unm.

vii. **Alpha**, b. 16 April 1799, d. 15 Aug. 1885, unm.
viii. **Mary**, b. 30 Aug. 1803, d. 10 Jan. 1888, unm.

HANSON NILES[3] b. West Oneonta 21 April 1801, d. 8 Jan. 1881; farmer. He m. **Amy Hoag** who was b. in Otsego Co. in 1802 and d. May 1842 at her home in West Oneonta. The family were Quakers. Children:
i. **Elizabeth**, b. 8 April 1842.
ii. **Deborah**, b. 29 Oct. 1831. The sisters res. together on the home farm. (1893)
[GBW; GBM; ONE:110; BR:652-3]

NOBLE, ELNATHAN[5] (*Thomas CT*[4], *John Jr.*[3] *CT, John*[2] *CT & MA, Thomas*[1] *England & MA*) s/o **Thomas** and **Mary Noble**; m. **Jehannah [Johannah] Bostwick** d/o **Nathaniel** on 10 Feb. 1774. They lived in Brookfield and Elnathan was a prominent citizen. They moved to Butternut Creek, Otsego Co., NY in 1793. Their residence was a log house ten feet by twelve, covered with elm bark, with a chimney made of sticks and clay, and containing two rooms. He was for many years a magistrate of the town and d. of apoplexy 11 Jan. 1824, aged 74. **Elnathan** was of New Lisbon when he made his will on 18 May 1814; proved in 1824. He d. 11 Jan. 1824, aged 72. In his will he named his wife and children:

6 i. **Curtis** b. 19 Nov. 1774 [1776], New Milford, CT.
ii. **Cyrenus**, b. 27 Sept. 1776.
iii. **Elnathan**, b. 15 July 1779.
iv. **Thomas**, b. 18 July 1781; d. young.
v. **Sally**, b. 12 April 1783, m. **Willis Edson**.
6 vi. **Sylvanus**, b. April 17, 1785.
vii. **Bostwick**, b. 30 Dec. 1788.
viii. **Guaradus**, b. 5 July 1795 m. **Sophia Utley** of Butternuts 26 March 1821.
xi. **Harriet**, b. 26 Nov. 1798; bapt. 3 March 1799 at Cooperstown.
Children of **Elnathan** and **Mary Noble**, both bapt. at Cooperstown 8 Sept. 1805:
xii. **William**, b. 9 May 1803.
xiii. **George Weston**, b. 15 June 1805.
xiv. **Nathaniel**. [?]

NOBLE, CURTIS[6], early res. of Unadilla, merchant; wife **Anna Hayes**, sister of his business partner **Isaac**. their children, all bapt. Cooperstown 7 March 1808, except the last bapt. 23 Sept. 1810. **Curtis** d. aged 60 on 21 Feb. 1835.

7 i. **Col. George Hayes**, b. 15 Dec. 1803.
ii. **Charles Curtis**, b. 10 Jan. 1805.
iii. **Mary Ann**, b. 17 Jan. 1808; m. **Peter J. Betts** and is bur. at Marshall, MI (1808-1893). Peter was of Bainbridge NY and they m. 23 Sept. 1829 at Unadilla.
iv. **Henry Carrington**, b. 6 Aug. 1810.
v. **Julia Sophia**, d. at Unadilla 11 March 1831, aged 7.

GEORGE NOBLE[7] of Unadilla made his will 11 Oct. 1842; proved 1847; he d. 27 July 1847. In it he named his wife **Elizabeth B.** --- and his father **Curtis.** His brother **Charles C.** of Unadilla was executor.

SYLVANUS NOBLE[6], wife **Sally** ---, children:
i.   **Lewis Leonard,** b. 26 Sept. 1811, bapt. Cooperstown 26 April 1812.
ii.   **Sally Jennette,** b. 28 May, bapt. 5 Dec. 1813.

[NASH1; *History of the Towns of New Milford and Bridgewater, Connecticut 1703-1882* by Samuel Orcutt, 1882; GBM; GBW; *At Rest in Unadilla* by Shirley B. Goerlick, 1988; OB.]

NOBLE, LAY, s/o **Martin,** was b. in New Lisbon 17 Sept. 1800; d. 12 April 1879. **Martin** was b. in Litchfield Co., CT 18 June 1774 and m. **Abagail Lane,** b. 29 July 1782. C. 1795 **Martin Noble, Sr.** removed to Otsego Co., where he worked as a carpenter and joiner and later purchased a farm in New Lisbon, where he d. 23 Feb. 1828. **Abigail** then came to Bath and res. with her son **Lay** until her death, 21 Aug. 1857. **Lay** was the 2nd of six children. At age 18 he was apprenticed to learn cabinet making in Geneva, NY. He removed to Bath in 1824; was Paymaster of the 96th Regt. of Infantry, NY State Militia from 1827 and served as Major of the 96th Regt. of State Militiamen from Sept. 1831. 22 Oct. 1826 he m. **Lucinda Brooks,** d/o **Lemuel** and **Amelia (Blakslee) Brooks** of Butternuts, and in 1832 he purchased in Bath the present (1940) farm owned by his grandson, **Henry M. Noble,** called the Jersey Home Farm. They had several children and after the death of his first wife, **Lay** m. 2nd 24 Oct. 1868, **Mrs. Fanny Beger,** sister to his first wife. He d. 1879 at Bath. Members of the Episcopal Church. Children:
i.   **Martin William,** b. Otsego Co., 1828; farmer of Steuben Co. He m. **Lucinda Hunter,** b. 1830, a d/o **Peter** and **Lucinda (Dimmick) Hunter,** natives of Bath and Orange Co., NY respectively. **Martin** and **Lucinda** had three children.
ii.   **Adelia,** m. Dr. **J. C. Velie** of Rock Island, IL.
iii.   **Edward,** m. **Louesa Fairchild** 12 Aug. 1858. She was b. in New Lisbon, Otsego Co. 3 July 1838, the only d/o **Charles Stone Fairchild** and wife **Lucy Ann Starkey.** Res. Bath, NY. They had three children.

[*A History of the Bowlby District* [Steuben Co., NY] by Idah M. W. VanHousen, 1940; *A History of Steuben Co., NY* . . . by Irvin W. Near, Vol. II, p. 631, pub. 1911]

NORTH, STEPHEN[6] (*Jedediah[5] CT, Isaac[4] CT, Thomas[3] CT, Thomas[2] MA, John[1] England & MA*) b. Berlin [Middletown], CT on 26 Jan. 1757 and d. at Fly Creek 11 Jan. 1842. **Stephen** was the 5th s/o **Jedediah** and first wife **Sarah (Wilcox) North.** He served as corporal in the Revolutionary War in the CT Line. settled in Otsego Co.; farmer, mechanic, merchant and one of the founders and elders of the local Presbyterian Church. He m. 1st 7 Jan. 1788. **Susanna[h]** (1765-1836), d/o **Elisha Savage,** a Revolutionary soldier of CT, and his wife **Thankful Johnson.** She was b. 14 April 1765

151

and d. 11 Nov. 1833. **Stephen** m. 2nd in 1834 to **Matilda Cheney**. His children, all b. Fly Creek, Otsego Co. (sons were founders of the Presbyterian Church):

7
- i. **Albert.**
- ii. **Emily**, b. 1791, d. 1817; m. Feb. 1811 **William Higby.** Two children.
- iii. **Linus (Rev.)**, b. 2 Nov. 1794; d. 24 Jan. 1846 at Palmyra, NY. He m. at Cooperstown 26 Oct. 1819 **Justa Maria Fitch** who was b. 31 March 1800 and d. at Ann Arbor, MI 3 June 1883. Nine children, all b. Palmyra, NY.
- iv. **Almira**, b. 1795, d. 1878; m. 1st 1813, **Benjamin Todd**, 2nd in 1819 **Rev. J. R. St. John**; 3rd **Daniel Carr**; 4th --- **Rogers.**
- v. **Mercy**, b. Jan. 1798, d. 14 Jan. 1872; m. 14 Sept. 1826, **Deacon Hart** of Seymour who d. 18 Aug. 1868.
- vi. **Stephen Jr.**, b. 7 Nov. 1799 Fly Creek; d. 18 Oct. 1842 in MI. He m. 13 Jan. 1823 **Patience Spalding** who was b. 24 May 1798 & d. 22 June 1863, d/o Rev. **Jacob** and **Sarah (North) Spalding** and granddau. of **Jedediah North**[5]. **Stephen Jr.** was a tin and iron merchant at Jonesville, MI and an elder in the Presbyterian Church. Four children.
- vii. **Hepzibah**, b. 4 Nov. 1802, d. 1850; m. **Deacon Horace Galpin.** Children: **William, Abigail** (1822-1873) and **Judson Galpin.**
- viii. **Susan**, b. 13 May 1804, d. 16 Aug. 1850; m. 28 [29] Sept. 1825 at Fly Creek, **Joseph William Lawrence** who was b. 27 Jan. 1803, s/o **Joseph William** and **Sybil (Heath) Lawrence** of Quincy, MI [Genesso]. They had ten children.

Children of 2nd wife, **Matilda Cheney**:
- ix. **Ann H.**, b. 1835; d. 1835.
- x. **Sarah**, b. 1836; m. 1st **Harry Lyman**; 2nd **James Parsons.**
- xi. **Mary**, b. 1836 (twin to **Sarah**); m. **Augustus Parsons.**

ALBERT NORTH[7], b. 18 July 1789 at Fly Creek & d. there 18 Dec. 1849. He m. there 28 Feb. 1811 **Irena [Irene] Taylor.** [See Taylor family entry.] **Albert** was a farmer, mechanic, merchant and elder in the Presbyterian church, as was his father. He was a resident of Fly Creek when he made his will 26 May 1849 and d. 19 Dec. 1849, aged 60. **Albert** educated at his own expense two heathen youths who bore his name; one a Cherokee and the other a Hindu from Ceylon, a member of the mission church. Children:

8
- i. **Ceylon** [son], b. 9 Dec. 1811; d. 6 Sept. 1879.
- ii. **Ceylina N.**, b. 18 Aug. 1813; d. 19 June 1845; m. 31 Aug. 1835, **Rufus C. Swift.** They res. at Palatine Bridge NY and had children: **Charles** and **Henrietta** who m. **Augustus Frey.**
- iii. **Emily**, b. 24 April 1817; d. 21 June 1878; m. 23 Oct. 1834, **Cheney Ames** of Oswego, NY and had children: **Helen, Albert, Coman Cheney, Arabella** and **Ceylon D.** and **Emily.**
- iv. Son, b. and d. 5 May 1821.
- v. Daughter, b. nd d. 5 May 1821.

	vi.	**Albert,** b. 5 Feb. 1823; d. at Calumetsville, WI 18 April 1892; unm. He was for years a merchant at Schuyler's Lake, NY.
	vii.	**Susan,** b. 19 Dec. 1826, d. Nov. 1879; m. 16 Sept. 1844, **William C. Harp,** merchant of Hoboken, NJ. They had children **Albert** and **Susie.**
	viii.	**Edwin,** b. 31 March 1829; d. 4 March 1830.

CEYLON NORTH[8] b. 9 Dec. 1811; d. 6 Sept. 1879, bur. Ripon, WI; merchant at Fly Creek. He m. 17 July 1833 **Dolly Ann Frances Lyman,** b. Cortland, NY 26 Oct. 1810. After **Ceylon's** death she removed to Beloit, WI. Children:

	i.	**Charles Gilbert,** b. 9 Aug. 1835; d. 31 Dec. 1908.
	ii.	**Frances A.,** b. 28 July 1837; d. Oswego, NY 14 Jan. 1870, unm.
	iii.	**Ceylon Henry,** b. 18 Oct. 1842.
	iv.	**Asahel,** b. & d. 15 Feb. 1845.
	v.	**Albert,** b. & d. 15 Feb. 1845 (twin).
	vi.	**George Lyman,** b. 23 Dec. 1846.

[*John North of Farmington CT & His Descendants,* Dexter North, Washington DC, 1921; DAR 105001; A:249; GBW; *John North of Farmington CT & His Descendants,* Dexter North, 1921; *The New England Ancestry of Albert Wilcox Savage Jr., Volume I,* Albert Wilcox Savage, Jr., 1988]

NORTON, CAPT. ELIJAH[6] (*Capt. Elijah*[5], *Jabez*[4], *Nicholas*[3], *Benjamin*[2] of England & MA, *Nicholas*[1] of England & MA), b. 9 May 1782, d. 2 April 1839, s/o **Capt. Elijah**[5] who was mar. twice; 1st **Freelove Burroughs** and 2nd **Hannah West** in Nov. 1776 at Dartmouth, MA. **Elijah**[6] was a son of the 2nd mar. and was bapt. at Cooperstown as an adult on 13 May 1804. Served as captain in the War of 1812, commander of a company from Richfield, Otsego Co., stationed at Sacketts Harbor. He was a carpenter by trade and after the war removed to Batavia, Genesee Co., NY, but later to Otsego Co. In late life he removed to Ellington, Chautauqua Co., NY, where he died. He m. 23 Dec. 1804, **Mary [Polly] Moon Beardsley,** b. 9 March 1788, d. at Cherry Valley 15 May 1837. She was the d/o **Obadiah Beardsley** and **Eunice Moore.** Children:

	i.	**Merritt Milton,** b. 1 Dec. 1805, d. 17 Oct. 1846; m. **Mary Jane Cleveland.**
7	ii.	**Morris.**
	iii.	**Sullivan Sedgwick,** b. 5 Feb. 1809, d. 31 Aug. 1811.
	iv.	**Eunice Beardsley** [name given as **Lucy Beardsley** in bapt. record NASH1], b. 23 April 1811, d. April 1830.
	v.	**Frances Malvina,** b. 20 April 1813; m. **Dr. Potter** of Cape Vincent, NY.
	vi.	**Mary Moore,** b. 31 Jan. 1815; now (1911) living; m. **Robert J. Merrill.**
	vii.	**Samuel Herman,** b. 6 July 1817; d. 7 May 1864; m. **Mary Howard.**
	viii.	**Levi Warren,** b. 17 Oct. 1819; d. 1900; m. **Elizabeth Leonard.**

MORRIS NORTON[7], b. 9 June 1807, Richfield; d. at Jamestown, NY 23 Oct. 1878. Learned the cabinet makers' trade in Buffalo, then studied and practiced law. He was a frequent contributor to the magazines and periodicals of his day, his articles dealing mainly with political subjects. A search of the files of the *Jamestown Journal* reveals his columns. He was a well-known local poet. Served 37 years as justice of the peace of Ashville, NY and many years as superintendent of the poor. He m. 8 Sept. 1833 in Buffalo, **Olivia Kent**, b. Rome, Oneida Co., NY, 25 Dec. 1810; d. 11 Aug. 1880 at Cambridge Springs, PA. She was d/o **Warren Kent** who came to Foxboro, MA to Sacketts Harbor and Rome, NY, later settling at Grand Island, Erie Co., NY, where he died. Her mother was Mr. Kent's 2nd wife, **Lois Dorrill**. Mr. Kent's forebears are documented in this source. Their children, all b. in Ashville, Chautauqua Co.:

  i. **Helen Olivia**, b. 25 July 1834; d. 7 March 1874; m. **Dr. William P. Bemus**.
 ii. **Mary Jane Elizabeth**, b. 25 April 1836, m. 3 Oct. 1855 **Major Enoch Arnold Curtis**.
iii. **Theressa M.**, b. 21 Dec. 1839; d. 7 Feb. 1894; m. 1862, **William W. Partridge**.
 iv. **Eunice Gertrude**, b. 10 Jan. 1842; m. in Ashville **Charles Thomas Douglass**, b. in Busti.

[Cutter's *Western NY*:210-12. This source gives details of English progenitors of this family; NASH1; DARPI.]

O'CONNOR, FRANCIS[4] (*Francis*[3] *NY, Francis*[2] *NY, Edward*[1] *Ireland & Albany, NY*) s/o **Francis**[3] **O'Connor** who was b. at Helderburg, near Albany, and m. **Fannie Caulder**, who was b. at Catskill. **Fannie's** parents were b. in Scotland. **Francis**[3] and family were among the earliest settlers of Bloomville, NY, and later one of the first settlers of Bovina, moving to that place in 1803. **Francis**[4] was b. in Bloomville 18 Sept. 1801. He obtained some knowledge of general law and served as Justice of the Peace, but he was mainly a farmer. He m. **Prudence Faulkner** of a CT Yankee family of Scotch descent in Dec. 1825. They res. in Town of Andes, Delaware Co., NY, where he d. 10 June 1880. **Prudence** was b. 6 Nov. 1800 & d. 21 Dec. 1892. Children:

   i. **Fannie**, m. **Noah Vermilyea**; she dec'd. by 1893.
  ii. **Francis**, res. Middletown, NY.
 iii. **Milo**, dec'd. by 1893.
  iv. **Mary**, m. **Hermon Bronson** of Croton, Delaware Co., NY.
   v. **James**, b. 26 Jan. 1835, res. Griffin's Corners, Delaware Co., NY. Known as the "Deaf Poet," his works are "of a high order." Studied law at Union College and grad. 1857, but because of hearing failing he went to City of Oswego and learned the art of printing, which he followed until 15 Oct. 1863 when he m. **Mary Dickson** of Lumberville, Delaware Co., NY. Soon afterward he bought a farm, which he sold to publish a book of his poems.
  vi. **Harriet N.**, m. **James Harkness** of Kortright, NY.
 vii. **Julanna H.**, m. **William H. Dickson** of Delaware Co.
5 viii. **Edward**.

EDWARD O'CONNOR[5] b. at Andes, Delaware Co., NY 12 Feb. 1844, was a teacher at age 17 to 25. Studied at the law offices of **W. H. Gardineir** of Oswego and was admitted to the bar at Syracuse in Nov. 1870. He worked in the law office of **Frank Shevlin** and then went to Davenport, where, on 1 April 1871, he began the active practice of law. In 1889 **Edward** removed to Oneonta, Otsego Co., continuing to practice law. He m. 4 June 1873 to **Annie H. Taylor**, b. in NC. Children:
- i. **Charley**.
- ii. **Harvey**, twin to **Charley**; dec'd. by 1893.
- iii. **Lindsay**, at home.

[BR:553-54]

PARKER, ELISHA[1], b. 6 Aug. 1746 in RI. He served as a Captain in the Revolutionary War; m. **Maria [Mariah] Ellsworth**, b. near Plymouth, MA. They had 11 children, all b. in New England states. Some time after 1800 he removed his family to Burlington, NJ, where they both died; **Mrs. Parker** 24 Sept, 1828 and the **Captain** on 19 March 1813. [BR states he removed to Otsego Co. in 1800.] One child:

PARKER, ALEXANDER[2] b. 8 Jan. 1768 RI, d. 27 Feb. 1845 at Burlington, Otsego Co. When a small boy he served in the Revolutionary Way as a servant to Gen. **Washington**. While still a boy he worked out by the month to aid his father in the support of his large family. At age 22 he began to save money for himself. In Jan. 1791 he m. **Sarah Gardner** of Pownal, VT, a d/o **Abram Gardner**. Alexander made his will 20 March 1844 and d. 17 Feb. 1845. **Sarah**, his 1st wife, d. 27 May 1792. She was sister of **Joanna** his 2nd wife, who d. 4 June 1792 [27 May 1792?], aged 19. His second wife **Joanna Gardner** was b. 28 Aug. 1777 at Pownell, VT and d. 28 June 1860; they m. Feb. 1793. In his will **Alexander** named his wife **Joanna**, their children and a grandson, **Willis D. Parker**. They are bur. in West Burlington along with dau. **Polly**. Alexander was a farmer and member of the Baptist Church. Child by first wife:
- i. **David**, d. in infancy.

By 2nd wife:
- ii. **Ira**.
- iii. **Betsey**, now (1893) res. town of Edmeston, aged 85.
- 3 iv. **Abraham**, b. c. 1796.
- v. **Elisha**.
- vi. **Alexander Jr.** Res. Cleveland, OH (1893), aged 80.
- 3 vii. **David G.**
- viii. **Mehitible**, res. with nephew **Isaac**, aged 83. (1893)
- ix. **Sarah**.
- x. **Polly**, d. 24 April 1830, aged 32.

ABRAHAM PARKER[3] d. 4 Feb. 1868, aged 72 y, 8 m, 14 d; and his wife **Patience** d. 15 July 1861, 65 y, 11 m, 29 d. They are bur. in West Burlington along with their children:
- i. **John** d. 30 March 1826, 5 m, 15 d.
- ii. **Sally** d. 29 May 1827, 4 m.
- iii. **Charles** d. 26 Nov. 1822, 1 d.

    iv.   **Norman** d. 4 Feb. 1822, 1 d.
    v.   **Joanna** d. 10 May 1850, 17 y, 1 m, 6 d.

DAVID G. PARKER[3] [P], farmer, born on farm at West Burlington 29 Nov. 1822, lived with parents until their death; m. **Susannah Bolton** 27 May 1852, d/o **Lemuel** and **Ruth** from Pownell, VT. **Susannah** was b. Burlington 14 July 1817. Children, all living at home (1878):
    i.   **Ella M.**, b. 16 Sept. 1853, d. 15 June 1859. Died of a broken neck.
4 ii.   **Isaac B.**
    iii. **Dexter A.**
    iv.   **Otis M.**
    v.   **Ruth H. J.**

ISAAC B. PARKER[4] has spent most of his life on the family farm. After his schooling was complete, he accepted a position as bookkeeper in a large wholesale house in NY City, but returned to Otsego Co. after five months because of his father's failing health.
[NER104:47; A:108-09; GBW; OB; BR:784-85; DARPI]

PECK, JEDEDIAH[5] (*Elijah*[4] *CT, Samuel*[3] *CT, Joseph*[2] *CT, William*[1] *England & CT*), b. Lyme, CT 28 Jan. 1748, s/o **Elijah Peck** and **Hepsibah** his wife. [Lyme, CT Vital Records gives "**Jedediah Peck** son of **Elijah** and **Mehipsabah Peck** was born January 28th Day AD 1747/48."] He served in the Revolutionary War and in the War of 1812. Removed to Otsego County (then Montgomery) in 1790, settling in what is now the Town of Burlington. He had early m. a sister of **Dr. Sumner Ely**, who later settled in Middlefield. **Jedediah** is described as a man of little education but great natural ability, strong intellectual powers, coarse and uncultivated, yet shrewd and tactful. He had not great gifts as an orator, but was a preacher of local notoriety. He circulated petitions against the Alien and Sedition Act in 1798 and was arrested and taken in irons to New York City for trial, but was never tried and upon repeal of the act was discharged. He became the leader of the Republican (Jeffersonian) party of the county and served as member of Assembly from 1798 to 1804, State Senator and Member of the Council of Appointment, 1804-08. He is known as the founder of the State Common School System of NY. He enlisted to serve in the War of 1812 when nearly 70 years of age under **Col. Stranahan**, was under fire at the battle of Queenstown. **Jedediah** m. **Tabitha Ely** 5 Nov. 1772 in Lyme, CT. He is noted as of Burlington when he made his will 28 June 1821, and d. aged 74 on 27 [15] Aug. 1821. In his will he named his wife, children (below) and his brother **Elisha** and grandson. All children but the last b. in Lyme CT.
    i.   **Hepzibah**, b. 24 Jan. 1774; m. **Abel Sill** 9 March 1796. Had at least one child, **Jedediah Peck Sill**. **Hepzibah** d. at Burlington on 19 Jan. 1860, aged 86; **Jedediah P. Sill** of Cooperstown, d. 27 Sept. 1875, aged 68 years.
    ii.   **Polly**, b. 6 Nov. 1776 [1775 according to Lyme Vital Records]; m. **David Willard** on 7 Jan. 1802 & d. in Otisco, NY 22 June 1856.

	iii.	**Elijah**, b. 29 Aug. 1780; d. 20 Sept. 1780 in Lyme, CT.
6	iv.	**Elijah**, b. 1 Oct. 1781.
6	v.	**Peter**.
	vi.	**Anna**, b. 27 May 1786, d. unm. in Burlington, NY 8 Aug. 1815.
	vii.	**Jedediah**, b. 19 May 1788; m. **Sarah Peck**, widow of his bro. **Peter**. **Jedediah** d. in Frederick, OH 8 March 1844. He left only one child, **Tabitha E.**, b. Fredericktown, OH 13 June 1829.
	viii.	**Abel**.

ELIJAH PECK⁶ m. **Clarissa Bates** 22 Jan. 1897. He d. 7 June 1840 in Sheffield, OH. Children:

i.	**Richard E.**, b. in Burlington, NY 8 Feb. 1808; m. 1st **Mary Taft** 14 Feb. 1833; m. 2nd **Almira Taft** on 10 Sept. 1840 and m. 3rd **Olive A. Griggs** 10 Dec. 1857. In 1867 res. Monroe, OH. All of **Richard's** children were b. in OH.
ii.	**Erastus**, b. in Burlington, NY 20 Aug. 1809; m. **Candace Fox** on 1 July 1832 and in 1867 res. Kingsville, OH. All their children b. in OH.
iii.	**Jedediah**, b. Burlington, NY 15 Dec. 1811 and d. unm. in Sheffield, OH 29 Feb. 1832.
iv.	**Elisha**, b. Monroe, OH 7 Sept. 1816; m. **Amanda Richmond** 26 Nov. 1843. In 1867 res. Elkhart, IN.
v.	**Elijah**, b. Monroe, OH 9 Dec. 1818; m. **Adaline Colby** 7 June 1844. In 1867 res. Sheffield, OH.
vi.	**Clarissa**, b. Monroe, OH 14 Oct. 1820; d. unm. in Sheffield, OH 7 Sept. 1839.
vii.	**David W.**, b. Monroe 22 July 1823; m. **Julia A. Smith** 22 Feb. 1856. In 1867 res. Denmark, OH.
viii.	**Emeline**, b. in Monore 22 Sept. 1826; m. **William O. Lillie** 23 Sept. 1853 and in 1867 res. Sheffield, OH.

PETER PECK⁶ b. 12 Nov. 1783; m. **Sarah Colgrove** 5 March 1809; he d. in Monroe, OH 8 April 1826. Children (1st three b. in Burlington, NY & last three b. in Monroe, OH):

i.	**Elijah**, b. 2 Jan. 1810 & d. in Burlington, NY 21 Aug. 1811.
ii.	**Polly**, b. 21 April 1811; m. **Daniel Campbell**, 25 March 1838, and, in 1868 res. Columbus Grove, OH.
iii.	**Esther**, b. 9 Sept. 1813; m. **John Kitchell** 29 March 1833 and in 1868 was res. Palmyra, IA.
iv.	**Peter**, b. 25 Jan. 1818; m. 1st **Mary Maxwell** 26 Sept. 1836 and m. 2nd **Sarah Tyler** 20 June 1848 and in 1868 res. Millburgh, MI. All of his children were b. in OH.
v.	**Sarah**, b. 18 June 1819 & d. in Monroe, OH 19 April 1821.
vi.	**Sarah Ann**, b. 15 June 1823; m. 1st **Joseph Jenkins** 4 July 1844 and 2nd **Lewis Wells** 25 Jan. 1846; in 1868 res. Indianola, IA.

[GBW; CENT:72; OB; *Births, Marriages and Deaths in Lyme, Conn.*; *Genealogical Account of the Descendndants in the Male Line of William Peck, One of the Founders in 1838 of the Colony of New Haven, Connecticut*, Darius Peck, 1877; DARPI]

PECK, ELISHA[5] (*Elijah*[4] *CT, Samuel*[3] *CT, Joseph*[2] *CT, William*[1] *England & CT*), b. Lyme, CT 3 April 1762, brother to **Jedediah**[5] above. He m. **Olive Emmons** of East Haddam, CT; settled in Burlington, NY in 1800 and d. in Victor, NY 15 July 1829. His wife d. in Ypsilanti, MI 29 April 1847. Children:

6   i.   **William E.**
    ii.   **Luther P.**, b. East Haddam 19 June 1788; d. unm. in Ypsilanti, MI 19 Feb. 1851.
6   iii.   **Joseph H.**
    iv.   **Anna G.**, b. East Haddam 15 Sept. 1792; m. **Amos Graham** in 1812 and d. in Tully, NY 23 July 1827.
    v.   **Elizabeth [Betsey L.]**, b. East Haddam 9 March 1795, d. unm. in Burlington, NY 15 [14] March 1813.
    vi.   **Olive L.**, b. East Haddam 7 July 1797; m. **Ephraim Huntington** in 1828 and d. in Burlington, WI 17 Jan. 1861.
    vii.   **Elisha**, b. Canaan, CT 3 Oct. 1800; m. **Olive Bailey** 6 Nov. 1826 and in 1869 res. Victor, NY. All of their children b. in Victor.
    viii.   **Benjamin**, b. Canaan, NY [sic] 28 Feb. 1803; m. **Mary Alby** in 1826 & in 1865 res. Delaware, OH.
    ix.   **Lois**, b. Burlington, NY 21 May 1805; m. **Isaac N. Green** in Oct. 1832; in 1861 res. London, MI.
    x.   **Asa** b. Burlington, NY 8 Feb. 1808, d. unm. in Ypsilanti, MI 17 Jan. 1842.
    xi.   **Silas**, b. Burlington, NY 10 June 1811; m. **Mary Rappler** 29 Dec. 1833; d. in Burlington, WI 23 April 1865. [Another **Silas Peck**, s/o **Dan Peck** and wife **Lovinia**, was b. in Lyme, CT and a relative of this **Silas**. The 2nd Silas was b. 8 May 1789; m. **Abby Cutting** 28 Oct. 1810, who d. 10 March 1865. Silas settled in Pittsfield, NY and d. there 7 Sept. 1864.]

WILLIAM E. PECK[6] b. in East Haddam, CT 5 Sept. 1786; m. **Ruamah Huntley** 22 Feb. 1809 and in 1865 res. Spring Prairie, WI. Children, all b. Burlington, NY:

    i.   **Ruama H.**, b. 6 Jan. 1811; m. 1st **Clark Burdick** and 2nd **Nelson Bromley**; in 1866 res. York Center, WI.
    ii.   **Betsey Ann**, b. 31 Aug. 1813; m. **Austin Holdridge**; in 1866 res. Holley, MI.
    iii.   **Calvin H.**, b. 15 April 1814; m. **Lydia Briggs**, in 1866 res. Ives Grove, WI.
    iv.   **Lucretia**, b. 29 April 1816; m. **Alexander Dewey**; in 1866 res. Winfield, NY.
    v.   **Deborah T.**, b. 20 June 1819; m. **Welcome Manchester**; in 1866 res. Prairie, WI.
    vi.   **Jedediah W.**, b. 25 July 1821; m. **Adaline Randall**; in 1866 res. Elkhorn, WI.
    vii.   **Caroline H.**, b. 26 July 1823; m. --- **Hicks**; in 1866 res. Spring Prairie, WI.

viii. **Charaldine**, b. 11 May 1826; m. **William McLellan**; d. in El Paso, IL 24 June 1865.
ix. **Albert E.**, b. 10 July 1834; m. **Alvira Huntington**; in 1866 res. Pleasant Valley, MI.

JOSEPH H. PECK[6] b. East Haddam 5 Aug. 1790; m. **Sophara Churchill** in 1821; d. in Ypsilanti, MI 15 Feb. 1849. Children, all b. in Burlington, NY:
i. **Elisha Erwin**, b. 11 Nov. 1831, d. in Ypsilanti, MI 23 Jan. 1839.
ii. **Elizabeth L.**, res. unm. in Rockford, IL in 1865.
[*Genealogical Account of the Descendants in the Male Line from William Peck* . . . by Darius Peck, 1877; OB]

PLATT, DANIEL[1], b. CT of New England ancestry. After his m. in CT removed to Columbia Co., NY. In the winter of 1800 (a few years later) he removed with his wife and three children, on a covered sled drawn by two yokes of oxen, to Town of Maryland, Otsego Co. where he settled on a farm in what has ever since been known as Platt Hollow. He d. here, aged past 70. His wife was **Jerusha Dibble**, who d. at the old home aged 80. The family were Baptists. They had six children, all lived to be old people, one of them recently dying in SD aged 86 (1893). The only one of their children named here:
STEPHEN PLATT[2] was aged 3 when his parents moved to Otsego Co. Also a Baptist, he d. at age of 69; farmer. He m. in the Town of Maryland **Nancy Burnside** who was b. in Albany Co., NY and came with her parents, **Gloud T.** and **Margaret (Wilson) Burnside** at an early day to Milford, NY. Nancy was b. in 1799 and d. aged 75. They had eight children, **Andrew H.** below being the eldest. All lived to marry and four are yet living (1893). The only child mentioned here:
ANDREW H. PLATT[3] b. Town of Maryland on the family farm 22 Nov. 1820; m. 1st in Town of Milford, NY to **Hannah Coon** who was b., reared and educated in that town. She d. in 1853 aged 33 and was the mother of:
i. **Merlin J.**, farmer in town of Milford, m. **Catherine Ray**.
ii. **Viola**, m. **J. S. Newton**, a commercial traveler, living in Oneonta (1893).
iii. **George**, m. **Clara Gurney** who was b. and reared also in Milford.
iv. & v. **Martha** and **Mary**, twins. **Martha** m. **Charles Armstrong**, lumberman and saw mill owner; **Mary** m. Prof. **James Pitcher**, has been for some years at the head of the Hartwick Seminary.
Andrew n. 2nd **Melissa Dunham** and after her death he m. 3rd **Ann Dunham** b. Town of Maryland, NY.
[BR:805-06]

PLATT, PETER m. **Keziah Rockwell** [see Rockwell family entry] of Butternuts, NY and had, all b. Butternuts:
i. **Rufus H.**, b. 19 Jan. 1805; m. **Clarissa Cook** and d. 11 Aug. 1861 at Oswego, NY.
ii. **Nelson H.**, b. 4 Feb. 1807; m. 3 May 1828 **Miranda Hitchcock**. He d. at Utica, NY 12 Feb. 1844. They had 3 children: Amelia

	res. Norwich, NY in 1894 (Mrs. **Henry L. Marsh**); **Melvia** (Mrs. **Daniel Allen**) res. Syracuse, NY 1894; and **Horatio N.**, Civil War veteran, m. **Mary A. Gibson**, res. at McDonough.
iii.	**Nathan E.**, b. 4 Feb. 1807; m. **Rachel Moss**. He d. Kirkland, NY 4 March 1875. They had one child, **William**, who never mar.
iv.	**L. Paschal**, b. 7 Feb. 1809; m. **Sophrona State**. They d. in MA: he 10 Jan. 1883; she in 1886. Their children were b. in Gill, MA.
v.	**E. Ophelia**, b. 1 Oct. 1811; m. **Cutler Parlin**; she d. Jan. 1841. They had two children, **Marcus** and a dau. who d. young.
vi.	**Delia A.**, b. 20 Aug. 1813; m. 1st **Waterman Davis**, 2nd **Alvin Chamberlain**; res. Washington [Wissington], Dak., 1894. Their children, **Addie**, **Louise** and **Permillia**, res. in the west.
vii.	**Leroy R.**, b. 8 Mary 1816; m. **Abigail Smith**, 25 Dec. 1838, d. Butternuts 4 Jan. 1843.
viii.	**Benjamin S.**, b. 20 March 181-; m. 4 Sept. 1843 **Elizabeth Thomas**; res. Clinton, NY in 1894. Had one child, **Belle**, b. 1844; m. Nov. 1865 **Henry R. Osborn**, res. Clinton.
xi.	**Slawson M.**, b. 1 July 1820; m. **Caroline Tyler** and d. Oswego, NY 20 Nov. 1865. Their children b. Oswego: **Minnie, Julia, Grace**.
x.	**L. Jane**, b. 9 Aug. 1822; m. **Cornelius Hopkins** 19 Oct. 1843; res. Binghamton, NY in 1894. [See Hopkins family entry.]
xi.	**L. Juliette**, b. 20 Jan. 1827; m. **John A. Prentice** 23 June 1864. She d. South Hampton, MA 12 May 1888. No children.

[*A Genealogy of the Families of John Rockwell, of Stamford, Conn. 1641* . . . by James Boughton, 1903]

POMEROY, GEORGE[6] (*Quartus*[5] *MA, Seth*[4] *MA, Ebenezer*[3] *MA, Medad*[2] *MA, Eltweed*[1] *England/MA*) b. Northampton, MA 8 Aug. 1779, s/o **Quartus Pomeroy** a smith, gunmaker, farmer and Revolutionary soldier [served as a private from PA in DARPI] and his 2nd wife **Rachel Pomeroy** (his cousin), d/o Lt. **Daniel Pomeroy** and **Rachel Moseley**, brother to **Seth Pomeroy**[4]. His first wife was **Phoebe Sheldon**. George is grandson of this Seth Pomeroy, who fought at Bunker Hill. George m. 26 [16?] May 1803, **Ann** only d/o **William Cooper** and **Elizabeth Fenimore** (formerly of Burlington, NJ). Bride and groom were both of Cooperstown m. by **Rev. Isaac Lewis**. Mr. **Cooper** built them a home in Cooperstown in 1804 which came to be known as Pomeroy Place, still standing in 1888, was a wedding gift to the couple. **George Pomeroy** was called "the doctor;" served many years as Town Clerk. He d. 24 Dec. 1870. **Ann** "until her final brief illness was a model of industry. Some of the wonderfully knitted zephyr shawls which she knit are still extant." She d. 7 April 1870, aged 87. Pomeroy Place is said to be the American representative of Berry-Pomeroy Castle, Devonshire, England, built in 1066 by **Sir Ralph de Pomeroy** who came over with **William the Conqueror**, and from whom the Pomeroys in this country are direct descendants. Children, all b. Cooperstown:

i.	**William**, b. 15 Nov. 1804; d. 1805.

	ii.	**Georgianna**, b. 8 Dec. 1806, Cooperstown. Attended Troy Seminary 1823-1824; m. in 1827, **Theodore Keese** of NY City. Had one son, **George Pomeroy Keese** of Cooperstown. She d. in Cooperstown in 1865.
7	iii.	**Hannah**, b. 15 Nov. 1808; m. **Charles Jarvis Woolson**. Their dau. **Constance Fenimore Woolson** was a famed novelist.
	iv.	**William Cooper**, b. 23 Feb. 1811, d. 29 July 1811.
7	v.	**George Quartus**, b. 11 Feb. 1815.
	vi.	**Elizabeth**, b. 10 Nov. 1817, d. young.
	vii.	**Ellen Cooper**, b. 4 Nov. 1818, d. 8 Sept. 1819.
7	viii.	**Fenimore Cooper**, twin of **Ellen**, b. 4 Nov. 1818.
	ix.	**Edgar Cooper**, b. 3 July 1820, d. 10 Aug. 1820.
	x.	**Laura Cornelia**, b. 3 Sept. 1823.

HANNAH COOPER POMEROY[7] b. Cooperstown. Attended Troy Seminary 1823-1824; m. 1830 **Charles Jarvis Woolson** of Keene, NH. Res. for a time in Cleveland, OH. Hannah d. 1879 at Green Cove Springs, FL. Children (only Mrs. **Clara Woolson Benedict** is still living and is a res. of Cleveland, but spends much of her time with her only dau. in Southern Europe and in NY City):

i.	**Georgiana Pomeroy**, m. **S. L. Mather** of Cleveland.
ii.	**Emma Clark**, m. **Rev. L. Carter**, Cleveland.
iii.	**Annie**.
iv.	**Gertrude**.
v.	**Julia**.
vi.	**Alida**.
vii.	**Constance Fenimore**, noted authoress, d. suddenly in Venice in 1893.
viii.	**Clara**, m. **George S. Benedict** of Cleveland.
ix.	**Charles Jarvis Woolson**.

GEORGE QUARTUS POMEROY[7] b. 11 Feb. 1815; m. 20 Sept. 1837 **Phebe Hart** who was b. 13 Feb. 1813 at Claverack, NY and d. 26 Nov. 1878. She was d/o **Jacob Hart** ahd **Anna Mena Moore**. Children, all b. Troy, NY except the last:

i.	**Isaac Hart**, b. 7 July 1838; d. 9 Aug. 1838.
ii.	**Helen**, b. 16 Sept. 1840.
iii.	**Theodore Keese**, b. 7 May 1842; d. Jan. 1845.
iv.	**Phebe Hart**, b. 5 Aug. 1844; d. 1848.
v.	**Anna**, b. 26 Aug. 1846.

FENIMORE COOPER POMEROY[7], named for his mother's brother, **James Fenimore Cooper**, attended Dartmouth College; m. in Nov. 1840 **Stella Woolson**; he d. 25 Aug. 1870. At age 21 he went to Green Lake, WI to take possession of a family tract of land; later to Milwaukee, WI where he became principal of a school and later superintendent of public instruction, a position he held until his death. His children were all b. at Green Lake and Milwaukee: **William, Francis, Walter, Mary, Catherine** and **Georgianna**.

[CENT:170; G:160, 173, 175; WILL:92; *Boston Transcript* 1 Sept. 1845; A-5070; NEGHR43:40-43; *History & Genealogy of the Pomeroy Family* . . . by Albert A. Pomeroy, 1912; *Hartford Times* 5070-Sept. 1, 1945; DARPI; OB.]

PRATT, DANIEL, b. Town of Burlington, as was his 2nd wife **Eliza**. He d. on his farm in Town of Burlington 8 Aug. 1854, aged 46. **Eliza** d. in Town of Exeter at the home of her son **George**, 27 Jan. 1881, aged 76. Children:
- i. **Henry**, farmer of town of Otsego.
- ii. **Caroline**, res. Schuyler's Lake (1893).
- iii. **George**, farmer of Town of Exeter.
- iv. **Eliza J.**, b. Town of Burlington 6 Dec. 1849; m. **John Felton Gray** of Shuyler's Lake. [See Gray family entry.]
- v. **Mary**, res. Schuyler's Lake.

[BR:743-44]

PRENTISS:

This family is traced in England back to **Thomas Prentiss** in 1318; and to **Valentine Prentiss**, American progenitor, who came to this country with the "Apostle" **Elliott** in 1631.

COL. JOHN HOLMES PRENTISS [P], third s/o **Col. Samuel Prentiss (Prentice)** Revolutionary soldier of CT and wife **Lucretia Holmes**, b. Worcester, MA in 1785 [17 April 1784], apprenticed to a printer. (**Mrs. Lucretia Prentiss** d. aged 88 (?) [sic] at Montpelier, VT on 20 Sept. 1841. Notice of her death appeared in the Otsego newspaper. Another notice that appeared in the local paper was the announcement of the death of **George H. Prentiss**, s/o **Samuel Prentiss** [brother to **Col. John**], who d. Montpelier, VT on 3 Sept. 1833.) **John** removed to Cooperstown in Oct. 1808 and established weekly newspaper, *Freeman's Journal;* sold out in 1849 & retired. He served two terms in Congress and after his retirement from his newspaper career he served as president of the Bank of Cooperstown until his death, 26 June 1861 at Cooperstown. He m. 1st 18 Jan. 1815 **Catherine Cox Morris** who d. 28 June 1818. She was the youngest d/o **Gen. Jacob Morris** of Butternuts, granddau. of a signer of the Declaration of Independence. **John** m. 2d to **Urilla Shankland** 3 June 1828, d/o **Thomas** of Cooperstown. **Col. John Prentiss** d. at Cooperstown on 26 June 1861, aged 78 of an illness of about three months (dropsy). He left a widow and four children: Children by 1st wife:
- i. **Mary Margaret**, dec'd. by 1878. Could be the child **Mary Martha** who was b. 5 Aug. 1816 and bapt. at Cooperstown on 16 March 1817.
- ii. **Catherine Lucretia**, m. **John C. Dodge** of Boston, MA. Could be the **Ann Lucretia** b. 23 Sept. 1817, bapt. 23 Nov. the same year at Cooperstown.

Children by 2d wife:
- iii. **Alexander S.**, dec'd. by 1878.
- iv. **John H.**, res. Chicago, IL; d. 27 May 1838, aged 25 at Little Falls (although the county history gives the impression that he was still living in 1878). Another **John H. Prentiss** d. Ellicottville, NY d.

v.   20 July 1842, aged 8.
Rachel A., dec'd. by 1878
vi.   Charlotte Derbyshire, bapt. 5 Jan. 1838; m. --- Browning, res. Cooperstown.
[G:160, 173, GBM, A:285-6; CENT:84; OB; NASH1; CPC; COP1: 168-69]

PRENTISS, DR. SAMUEL[7] (Col. Samuel[6] CT, Jonas[5] CT, Samuel[4] MA, Thomas[3] MA, Capt. Thomas[2] MA, Capt. Thomas[1] England/MA) s/o Col. Samuel Prentice/Prenciss a Revolutionary soldier of Stonington CT. Samuel[7] was b. in Stonington 1759; m. Lucretia Holmes d/o Capt. John Holmes, a farmer who d. in Northfield, MA in 1818. Samuel moved his family to Worcester, MA in 1783, c. 1786 to Keene, NH and later to Saratoga, NY. He served as his father's waiter during the Revolution. His 3rd son:
COL. JOHN H. PRENTISS[8] [P] was b. Worcester, MA 1785. In youth apprenticed to a printer. To Cooperstown Oct. 1808, owned weekly newspaper *Freeman's Journal*, which he sold in 1849 and retired at age 66. He m. 1st 18 Jan. 1815, Catherine Cox Morris who d. 28 June 1818. She was youngest d/o Gen. Jacob Morris of Butternuts. John d. 26 June 1861. His son:
HENRY PRENTISS[9] was a printer. He served apprenticeship in his father's office in Keene, NH, res. at Cooperstown and d. at Rome NY in Aug. 1875. He was once a proprietor and editor of a paper in Herkimer, NY. of Burlington made his will 1 May 1836. He d. 20 May 1836, aged 48 y, 6 m, 20 d. In his will he named his wife Phlolebe, his second wife, who d. 12 April 1858, aged 64 y, 5 m, 21 d. His first wife, Hannah, d. 5 Feb. 1819, aged 32 y, 1 m, 11 d. All are bur. in the family plot at Burlington. Henry's children:
2   i.   John H.
    ii.   George L.
    iii.   Truman, d. 8 Nov. 1847, 23 y, 4 m.
    iv.   Daniel S.
    v.   William L. P., 1830-1906.
    vi.   Henry.

JOHN H. PRENTICE[2] b. 29 Oct. 1817 and d. 27 June 1900; m. Lydia Monroe [see Monroe family entry]. They are bur. in the family plot at Edmeston, along with some of their children. Children, b. Edmeston:
i.   George William, b. 21 Sept. 1845; d. 25 Feb. 1852.
ii.   Henry Josiah, b. 8 Oct. 1850; d. 12 March 1852.
3   iii.   George Henry.

GEORGE HENRY PRENTICE[3] b. 17 Jan. 1853; m. 4 April Hattie V. Chamberlain who was b. 24 March 1861. He is pastor of the Methodist Episcopal church at Wanamie, PA in 1912. Children:
i.   Pearl Anna, b. 17 April 1886 at Mount Upton, NY. Res. Wanamie, PA 1912.
ii.   Neil Leslie, b. 30 Oct. 1889 at Gilbertsville, NY. Res. Wanamie, PA 1912.
iii.   Ruth Edna, b. 10 Oct. 1891 at New Berlin, NY.

iv. **Julia Florena**, b. 17 June 1893 at New Berlin.
v. **Blanch Lydia**, b. 4 Aug. 1895 at Waymart, PA.
vi. **Myrah Henrietta**, b. 28 May 1899 at Moscow, PA.

[GBW; BUC1:354-5; NASH1; *Genealogy of Josiah Munroe, Revolutionary Soldier, Who Died in the Service of the Continental Army at Valley Forge* ... by G. S. Northrup, 1912; *The History & Genealogy of the Prentice, or Prentiss Family of New England, etc.* by C. J. F. Binney, 1883; A:285-6]

QUACKENBUSH, ISAAC[1], of Dutch descent of a family of Albany Co., before 1819 occupied the farm in Otego formerly owned by **Ebenezer Rice**, living first in a log cabin near the river. **Isaac** was b. in Albany & settled in Delaware Co. when it was wild and covered with woods. He m. **Catherine Gardiner**. Isaac had seven sons and he was a private from NY in the Revolutionary War; he d. 1830. The farm is now (1893) owned and occupied by **Orlando Quackenbush**. Children:

2 i. **Jacob**.
   ii. **Garret**. Served as one of the overseers of highways of Town of Otego at first town meeting in 1822.
   iii. **John**.
   iv. **Nicholas**.
   v. & vi. Two daus., not named.

JACOB QUACKENBUSH[2] was b. in Albany and removed with his parents to Delaware Co. where he m. **Sarah Bovee**, who was b. in Otsego Co. He was a farmer; of Otego when he made his will 28 Aug. 1846 in which he named his wife and children (below). His brother **Garret Quackenbush** was executor.

   i. **David**, dec'd. by 1893.
3 ii. **Orlando**.
   iii. **Peter**, dec'd. by 1893.
   iv. **Jacob**, res. Oneonta.
   v. **John**, of North Franklin, Delaware Co.
   vi. **Mariah**. [Possibly the **Nancy Maria** below.]
   vii. **Caroline**, m. **Henry Wickham**, dec'd. by 1893.
   viii. **Rachel**, m. **Milton Ward** of Dutchess Co.
   ix. **Catherine**, m. --- **Bates**. [In BR she is named as the widow of **John Northrop**, res. Otego.
   x. **Betsy**, not named in her father's will; probably predeceased him.
   xi. **Nancy Maria**, also not named in her father's will.

In the *History of Otego* [p. 120] a **Jacob Quackenbush** is listed under veterans of the town from the War of 1812. "(d. 26 Aug. 1846, ae. 53; buried in the yard on the **Orlando Quackenbush** place)--was stationed at New York."

ORLANDO QUACKENBUSH[3], farmer of Town of Otego, was b. on the farm upon which he now (1893) res. He was aged 23 when his father died and the farm was willed to him and his eldest brother. After six years **Orlando** bought out his brother's interest. He took care of his mother and five of

her children until her death when she was aged 71. He m. c. age 30 to **Ann Eliza Woolf** of Oneonta, a d/o **Isaac** and **Elizabeth (Quackenbush) Woolf**. **Isaac** was of German extraction, farmer. His father was b. in Germany and came to America with two of his brothers. **Ann Eliza** was one of four children. They have one child:
    i.   **Emma**, res. at home.
[GBW; F:51, 128; DARPI; BR:525-25]

QUAIL, ROBERT[1] from Ireland to America when young and res. in Worcester, Otsego Co. He had at least one child:
    i.   **William C.**

WILLIAM C. QUAIL[2] held town offices. His sons:
    i.   **Luke.**
    ii.   **William.**
    iii.   **Atchenson.**
[A:353]

RAWLINGS, ISAAC H.[1] b. Burbage, Leicester County, England; m. **Mary Munson**, to America in 1834, settled in Town of Butternuts; farmer; Presbyertian. **Isaac** d. 8 Aug. 1870; **Mary** d. 7 Nov. 1870. Their son:
JOHN H. RAWLINGS[2] [P] was the only surviving of four children, b. 5 April 1833, Burbage, England, was one year old on his parents' immigration. 1 Jan. 1856 he m. **Ann Beale** [P], d/o **William** and **Hannah**, also natives of Leicestersire. **Ann** b. 9 March 1826; family settled in town of Butternuts in 1841. She was the eldest of nine children. Her parents removed to Chenango Co., NY.
[A:112A]

RIDER, STEPHEN[1] was b. in CT and an early settler of town of Exeter in Otsego Co. He settled in that town in 1803, in the woods, and res. on his farm until his death c. 1856, when he was nearly 81 years old. He and his wife reared eight children, all now dead (1893). **Stephen** was mar. twice, no children by his 2nd wife. Member of the Methodist Episcopal Church. Only child named:
JOHN RIDER[2] farmer, first wife was **Catherine Chapman**, who d. 6 Jan. 1834, aged 30, leaving three children. He m. 2nd **Sophia Summer [Sumner]** [see Sumner family], by whom he had two children. **John** d. 24 Aug. 1869, age 72 y, 8 m, 22 d; **Sophia** d. 14 Oct. 1875, aged 77 y, 7 m. He was a Baptist, she a Presbyterian. They are bur. at Exeter along with their first two daus. (below) Children:
    i.   **Gracie A.** d. 4 May 1876, 3 months.
    ii.   **Sophia** d. 21 Dec. 1861, aged 26.
3 iii.   **John J.**
    iv.   **Mary**, now (1893) widow of **Israel Veber**, res. in village of Schuyler's Lake.

JOHN J. RIDER[3], s/o 2nd wife **Sophia**; general farmer & stockraiser of Schuyler's Lake; also a manufacturer of cheese. He was b. in town of

Exeter 23 Feb. 1840. Bought the family farm at the time of his marriage, 17 Oct. 1866. He m. **Harriet A. Turner**, who was b. in Town of Exeter 18 June 1843, d/o **James** and **Sopheria (Adkins) Turner**, the former a farmer of that town. Baptists. Children:
    i.   **Adelbert J.**, b. 23 Aug. 1868, m. **Adda Town**; is Deputy Postmaster of Richfield Springs.
    ii.   **George L.**, b. 28 Aug. 1870, res. at home (1893).

[The LDS Ancestral file gives the father of **Stephen Rider**, b. 1805 in NY as **Nathan Rider** and wife **Polly** ---. It also says that both **Stephen** and **John** d. in Ioni Co., MI.]
[EXC:307; BR:769-70; Woodstock Book, Vol. 7; OB.]

ROBINSON, DAVID[1], farmer of England, m. **Elizabeth Garrett** who d. aged 90. Children:
    i.   **John**, a prodigy who d. at age 4.
    ii.   **William**, came to America; farmer of Richfield, NY for a time and later res. NY City and Milwaukee, WI; now (1893) dec'd. and bur. at Richfield.
    iii.   **Mary Ann**, m. **Thomas Rowland**; d. at Chatsworth, England aged over 70.
    iv.   **Matilda**, m. **John Townsend**. She d. a few years after her mar. leaving a son **James** in Kettering, England.
    v.   **Charles**, to America with bro. **Joseph**; d. at Richfield, NY aged 52. Has many descs. in Town of Richfield.
    vi.   **Ann**, dec'd. (1893)
    vii.   **George**, farmer res. at Doddington Lodge, England with wife and family.
    viii.   **William**, d. before his father.
    ix.   **John**, inherited the family estate and m. a wealthy woman named **Ann Freeman** of Pyschly Lodge. He d. at Kettering.
2   x.   **Joseph**, b. England 10 Feb. 1811.

JOSEPH ROBINSON[2] attended Kimbolton Boys School and after apprenticed to a baker. He and bros. **George** and **Charles** to America on the ship *St. Lawrence*. After a visit to an uncle in Cherry Valley, he walked to the Town of Richfield where he had a brother who was a forman and manager of a farm. **Joseph** worked 1 1/2 years for **Capt. Thomas**. 22 March 1838 he m. **Maria Brown** who was b. in Brookfield, Madison Co., NY 4 Nov. 1809, a d/o **Asa** and **Lucy (Dow) Brown**. Her mother was a cousin to the famous preacher **Lorenzo Dow**. **Asa** was b. in Sterling, CT; **Lucy** b. in Stonington. [See Brown family entry.] Children:
    i.   **David G.**, d. aged 4 mos.
    ii.   **George W.**, m. **Sarah Phillips**; merchant at Ilion, NY.
    iii.   **Charles Nelson**, d. aged 16 mos.
3   iv.   **John Garrett**.
3   v.   **Albert D.**
    vi.   **Wallace B.**, d. at 10 weeks.
    v.   **Lucy Maria**. Principal at Hendrick's School in St. Paul, MN.

JOHN GARRETT ROBINSON³ res. Warren, Herkimer Co.; farmer and businessman. He m. **Alice Schooley** and had:
i. Annie B.
ii. Carrie.
iii. Josie.
iv. Mabel.
v. Garrett.
vi. Irving.
vii. Willie.
viii. Alice A.

ALBERT D. ROBINSON³ res. Richfield; m. **Libbie Monk**. Children:
i. Christabel.
ii. Myrtle.
iii. Jennie, dec'd. by 1893.
iv. Vera.
v. Earl A., dec'd. by 1893.
vi. Claude, farmer.
[BR:599-602]

ROCKWELL, JABEZ JR.^{5} (*Jabez*^{4} *CT, Thomas*^{3} *CT, John*^{2} *CT, John*^{1} *England/CT*) b. 1 July 1740, Ridgefield, CT s/o **Jabez** and **Keziah Rockwell**. Jabez Sr. was a veteran of the Revolutionary War. He served from Danbury in 7th Co., 6th Regiment; discharged 13 Nov. 1775. He was at Valley Forge with Washington's troops in the winter of 1777/78. **Jabez Sr.** d. before Aug. 1757 when his will was probated at Danbury and his wife was appointed administratrix of his estate. **Jabez Jr.** at that time chose **Jonah Foster** as his guardian. Soon after the burning of Danbury in 1777, **Jabez Jr.** removed to Butternuts, NY; many of his relatives followed and settled in the vicinity. **Jabez's** first wife was **Elizabeth Sperry** and they m. 30 June 1759 at Danbury; after her death he m. 2nd 11 Oct. 1778 at Ridgebury [Danbury] **Phebe Bedicut [Bedent]**. His 3rd wife was **Elizabeth Andrus** and after their marriage they settled in Guilford, NY. **Jabez** d. in 1839 in NY. The old family Bible was still in possession of his descendants in 1894. Children by first wife:

6 i. Benjamin.
6 ii. Levi.
   iii. Betsey, b. Danbury; m. **Lemuel Merchant** and res. Guilford, NY. [See Merchant family entry.]
6 iv. Eli, b. 26 April 1778.

Children by second wife:
   v. Theodosia, b. Danbury 26 Sept. 1779; m. **John Brewer** who was b. 9 May 1776 and d. 18 Feb. 1852. They had one child, **Ezra B. Brewer**. [See Brewer family entry.]
6 vi. Ezra Bedent, b. 12 April 1782.

Child by his third wife:
   vii. Julia, b. Guilford, NY 3 June 1805; m. **George Fleming**, res. Guilford. [See Fleming family entry.]

BENJAMIN ROCKWELL[6], b. Danbury, CT 19 [17] May 1762; m. as his 2nd wife **Tryphena Starr**, b. 19 May 1762, and removed to Butternuts c. 1797. He d. there 30 Oct. 1835, she 25 March 1851. Child by his 1st wife [name not known]:

    i.   **Benjamin S.**, b. Danbury, CT 12 Feb. 1780; m. **Phila Judd**, who was b. at Bethel 14 Jan. 1783. He d. 18 Dec. 1818; she d. in 1851.

Children by his second wife:

7	ii.	**Ard S.**
	iii.	**Kezia**, b. Danbury 3 Sept. 1785; m. 22 Feb. 1804 **Peter Platt**; he d. Butternuts. She m. 2nd 29 Feb. 1844 **N. Donaldson** and res. at Butternuts where she d. 19 March 1865. [See Platt family entry.]
7	iv.	**Ashbel R.**
7	v.	**Amos.**
	vi.	**Andrew**, b. Danbury 20 Oct. 1791; m. 14 Oct. 1819 **Alice Riley**. They moved to Stittsville, Oneida Co., NY, where he d. 2 April 1858. Two children, b. Stittsville: **Mary** and **Frances A.**
	vii.	**Asahel**, b. Danbury 12 Jan. 1794; m. 1st 1 Sept. 1822 **Ana Dally**; m. 2nd **Hannah Frazee** and settled at Violet, Ontario Co., NY where he d. Nine children, all b. Violet: **Sperry, Mary Ann, Victoria, Albert, A. Starr, Andrew, George, John** and **Eva**.
	viii.	**Rachel**, b. Butternuts 18 Aug. 1796; m. 2 April 1818 **William Stewart** and res. at Butternuts; later moved to Trenton, Oneida Co., NY, where she d. 5 July 1827. Two children: **Horatio** b. Trenton, and **Laura**, b. Louisville, NY.
	ix.	**Laura** b. Butternuts 9 July 1800; m. 19 Nov. 1840 **Asahel B. Roberts**; he d. at Franklin, NY 21 Nov. 1881. No children.
7	x.	**Anson.**
7	xi.	**Almon.**

ARD S. ROCKWELL[7] b. Danbury 5 Dec. 1783; m. 2 March 1809 **Betsey Shaw** of Butternuts, where they lived for a time before moving to Elkhorn, WI and later to Columbus, WI where he d. 5 July 1866. He served as a colonel in the war. She d. there 5 Dec. 1875. Children, all b. Butternuts:

    i.   **John S.**, b. 25 March 1810; m. 28 Oct. 1839 **Lovina Hard**. He d. 26 May 1863 at Columbia, WI; she d. 1852.

    ii.   **Legrand**, b. 21 March 1812; m. 22 Aug. 1844 **Frances A. Hickox**. Both d. at Elkhorn, WI.

    iii.   **Elizabeth**, b. 22 May 1814; m. 8 Nov. 1837 at Otego, **Edward A. Austin**. He d. March 16, 1843.

    iv.   **Lester R.**, b. 17 July 1816; m. 31 Aug. 1857, **Marie E. Page**. Both d. Columbia, WI.

    v.   **Abbyrene S.**, b. 21 Aug. 1818; m. **Delos W. Dean**, res. in Laurence, Otsego Co. She d. at Columbia, WI 12 Oct. 1886.

    vi.   **Mary**, b. 3 June 1821; m. 15 Jan. 1849 **John R. Wheeler**. They res. Buffalo, NY and she d. there 12 Oct. 1889.

    vii.   **David Henry**, b. 27 July 1823; never mar. He res. at Burlington Junction, Nodaway County, MO in 1894.

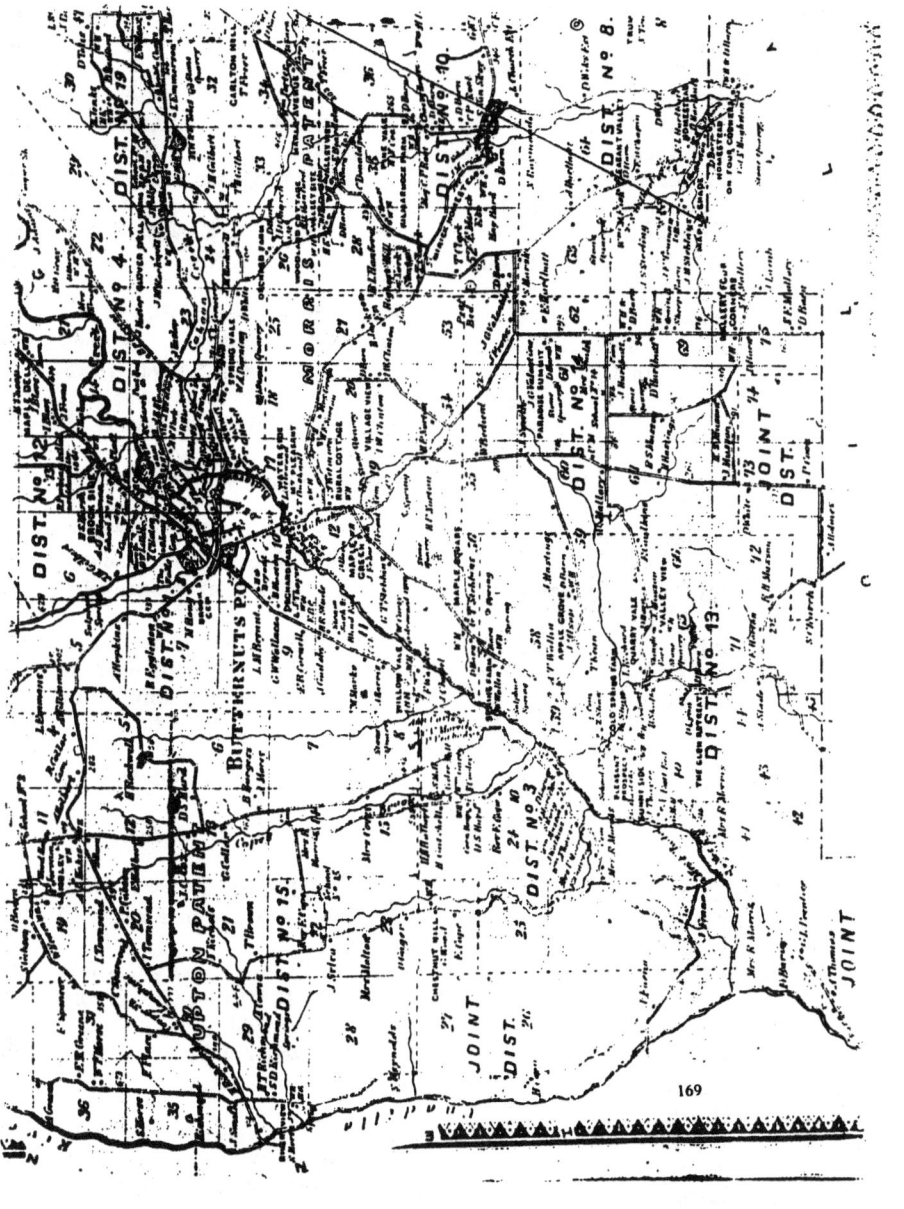

viii. Sarah J., b. 9 Sept. 1825; m. 24 Sept. 1853 **Amasa G. Cook**, lawyer and farmer, res. Columbus, WI in 1891.

ASHBEL R. ROCKWELL[7], b. Danbury 10 Sept. 1787; m. 1st 25 Jan. 1814 **Caty Shaw**, b. Palmer, MA 19 March 1793. He m. 2nd 8 April 1841 **Rebecca Hoyt** of Gilbertsville. They res. Butternuts and later in Norwich, NY. He d. 27 May 1861; **Rebecca** d. at Norwich. Children, all b. Butternuts:

i. **Catharine V.**, b. 23 Nov. 1814; m. 28 Oct. 1840, **Albert L. Comstock**. She d. Norwich 15 May 1883. They had children: **Catharine Louise**, b. NY City and **Albert Ruggles Comstock**, b. Norwich 1857, d. Buffalo 1862.

ii. **Mary Laura**, b. 19 Aug. 1817; m. 4 Sept. 1835 **E. Winchester Stebbins** b. at Butternuts 27 July 1812. He d. Norwich 7 Aug. 1891. [See Stebbins family entry.]

iii. **Cornelia Ann**, b. 18 Jan. 1820; m. at Butternuts, 4 Nov. 1841 **William Delos Babcock**, s/o **Joshua** and **Clarissa**, b. 26 April 1817. He d. 26 July 1889. She d. at Gilbertsville 14 Oct. 1855. [See Babcock family entry.]

iv. **Ashbel Ruggles Jr.**, b. 8 Sept. 1822; did not marry; d. Gilbertsville 21 Feb. 1845.

v. **David Shaw**, b. 10 Oct. 1824; went to Nevada and has not been heard from since 1855.

vi. **George Albion**, b. 17 Dec. 1826; m. 10 Feb. 1852 **Rachel M---**. She d. June 1877; he d. 27 March 1881 at Gilbertsville. Had one child, **Edward Brewer**, b. Gilbertsville 1865; d. at Minneapolis, MN 17 March 1883.

vii. **Starr A.** b. 15 Sept. 1829; m. 26 June 1855, **Susan M. Noble**, res. Cedar Falls, IA in 1891. Children: **Kate Augusta** b. Franklin, NY 1858; **William Noble**, b. Franklin 1866; **Mary Laura** b. Lansing, IA 1871 and **Florence S.** b. IA 1876.

Children by 2nd wife:

viii. **Frances Augusta**, b. 26 Feb. 1842; m. **H. W. Benson**, res. Minneapolis, MN in 1901. He d. there 18 May 1885.

xi. **Benjamin Albert** b. Norwich 20 Feb. 1844; d. Anoka, MN.

AMOS ROCKWELL[7], b. Danbury 25 July 1789; m. 2 April 1818 **Elizabeth Emmons** b. 6 Sept. 1794; settled Butternuts, where he d. 25 May 1870. Children, b. Butternuts:

i. **Elizabeth**, b. 4 Sept. 1819; m. 1st **William E. Gray** 21 July 1835; 2nd **Richard Cole**. She d. 26 Oct. 1880. [See Cole family entry.] [BR states she d. at the age of 62 in 1880.]

ii. **Alice Adelia**, b. 20 May 1821; m. **S. Valentine Shaw**. She d. Lansing, NY 14 Sept. 1858. [See Shaw family entry.]

iii. **James**.

iv. **Rachel**, b. 20 July 1825; m. 10 Sept. 1854, **George A. Rockwell** and res. Butternuts. She d. 12 July 1877. They had one child, **Edward B.**, b. Butternuts 3 July 1864; d. unm. 1893.

v. **Caroline L.**, b. 12 July 1830; m. 11 June 1850, **Ezra V. Bottsford**. She d. at Scranton, PA in Dec. 1883. No children.
vi. **Adaline M.** b. 21 Oct. 1833; m. 15 Oct. 1856 **Porter F. Buell**, res. Stittsville, NY in 1892. Children b. Stittsville: **William R., Annie E., Frederick**.

JAMES ROCKWELL[6] b. 13 Sept. 1823; m. 9 Jan. 1851 **Jane A. Shaw**; he d. Butternuts 9 Dec. 1889. Children, b. Butternuts:
i. **Lizzie S.**, b. 22 May 1853; res. Gilbertsville in 1892, unm.
ii. **Florence A.**, b. 20 May 1855; d. 14 Dec. 1867.
iii. **James S.**, b. 11 Sept. 1857; res. Hartford, CT 1892, unm.
iv. **Jennie A.**, b. 11 Feb. 1862; m. 18 Nov. 1890 **Jared S. Adams**, res. Gilbertsville in 1892.
v. **Robert M.**, b. 2 Aug. 1864; d. there unm., 5 Jan. 1887.

ANSON ROCKWELL[7], b. Butternuts 28 May 1805; m. 10 July 1828 **Hannah F. Coye**. He d. at Whitewater, WI 8 April 1885. She d. Janesville, WI 3 Dec. 1892. Children, b. Butternuts:
i. **Helen Tryphena**, b. 30 July 1829; m. 17 Sept. 1850, **Frank H. Myrick**, b. Butternuts in 1826. Res. Norden, NE. [See Myrick family entry.]
ii. **Ann Lucinda**, b. Oct. 1830; m. 1850 **Robert A. Abell**, b. 23 Oct. 1829; res. Chicago, IL. [See Abell family entry.]
iii. **Priscilla Augusta**, b. Oct. 1837; m. Prof. **Elias Dewey**, res. DesMoines, IA. Children b. Oconomowoc, WI: **Helen Augusta, Winifred Coye, Laura Mayo, Mary Rockwell** and **Isabel Starr**.
iv. **Mary Stewart**, b. 17 May 1840; m. May 1860 Judge **Henry O. Montague**. Res. for a time at Oakland, CA and he d. there in Dec. 1892. Their home was at Silverton, CO.
v. **Maria Victorine**, b. 27 April 1852; m. **Frank Filmore Lewis**, b. 1850. Res. Janesville, WI in 1891. Two children, b. Whitewater, WI: **Mabel B.** and **Edward Rockwell Lewis**.

ALMON ROCKWELL[7], b. Butternuts 22 Jan. 1807, millwright; m. 27 March 1834 **Lucy Mirick [Merrick]** [see Mirick family entry]; d. at New York Mills 3 Nov. 1860. **Almon** was lame for some 17 years, the result of a severe illness. During his long years of inactivity his wife kept a large family of boarders. Members of the Presbyterian Church. Two children:
i. **[Almon] Ferdinand** b. Butternuts 17 Oct. 1835, veteran of the Civil War and res. Philadelphia, PA. Served in the regular army for 27 years. He has a wife and two children living: **H. Donnell Rockwell**, single man, aged 30 (1893) and his dau. [not named] is wife of **Samuel Aldrich Crozer, Jr.** of Philadelphia.
ii. **Amelia Lucy**, b. New York Mills, NY in 1844. **Amelia** m. 1st Capt. **W. A. Musson** killed at Hatcher's Run, VA in 1864; 2nd **Theodore H. Musson**, brother to her first husband; res. at Gilbertsville, NY. By **Theodore** she had two children: **Winifred D. Musson**, b. Rondout, NY 9 March 1873 and **Robert Rockwell Musson**, b. Gilbertsville 2 April 1877; d. 25 Aug. 1877.

Almon is described as "the youngest member of a family of ten children, and the youngest of seven sons, all of whose names began with 'A,' and an old lady neighbor remarked that his parents ought to name him 'Amen.'"

LEVI ROCKWELL[6] b. Danbury 7 May 1769; m. **Ruth Bassett** who was b. 1772. He d. 26 Sept. 1852. Two children, b. Butternuts:
- i. **Betsey**, b. 19 Sept. 1800; never mar.
- 7 ii. **Levi Clark Rockwell.**

LEVI CLARK ROCKWELL[7] b. 1 Aug. 1809; m. **Pamelia R. Knapp**, b. 18 Nov. 1815; he d. San Pierre, IN, 7 Oct. 1890. Children, b. Butternuts:
- i. **Oscar B.**, b. 8 Sept. 1837; m. **Mary A. Cantwell**, res. at San Pierre, IN in 1892.
- ii. **Wallace H.**, b. 26 April 1840; not mar.; d. in Andersonville Prison, 5 Aug. 1864.
- iii. **Alphonzo P.**, b. 18 Oct. 1841; m. **Mattie Declems**, res. Medarysville, IN in 1892.
- iv. **Frances M.**, b. 27 Aug. 1844; m. **Thomas Robinson**, res. Medarysville, IN 1892.
- v. **Edward S.**, b. 27 Nov. 1845; not mar.; res. Medarysville, IN. He d. 8 May 1865 at Mobile, AL.
- vi. **George S.**, b. 5 July 1847; m. **Catherine Pope**, res. Valpariso, IN.
- vii. **Ida E.**, b. 31 May 1849; not mar.
- viii. **Malcom V.**, b. 3 July 1847; m. **Hattie Murray**, who was b. 27 May 1867.

ELI ROCKWELL[6] b. Danbury 26 April 1778; m. at Butternuts **Hannah George**; res. Butternuts. Children, all b. Butternuts:
- 7 i. **Seeley.**
- ii. **Amos**, b. 29 Sept. 1808; m. **Mary Briggs**; moved to IN and d. 30 Oct. 1873.
- iii. **Sperry**, b. 24 June 1816; m. 1st 28 Nov. 1838, **Mahalia Van Dusen** and settled in Rochester, NY. He m. 2nd **Charlotte A. Sage**. He d. 25 March 1852; she d. 12 March 1872.
- iv. **Ambrosia**, b. 29 March 1823; m. **Benjamin Haden**; res. Guilford, Chenango Co., NY in 1829.

SEELEY ROCKWELL[7] b. 22 Feb. 1804; m. **Susan Van Deuson** and moved to Michigan City, where he d. 3 July 1878. Children:
- i. **Emeline**, b. Guilford 1833, m. **Charles Davis** 4 June 1851 and had one child, **Eugene Davis**, who was b. Butternuts 12 June 1855; m. 12 Aug. 1879 **Inez Webster**. Eugene d. 6 Sept. 1887; shed. Baraboo, WI in 1887. No children.
- ii. **Annetta J.**, b. Guilford 4 Nov. 1838; m. 14 Feb. 1854 **Augustus Moody**. He d. Butternuts 12 Jan. 1862. Children, b. Butternuts: **Gertrude V.**, b. 1856; m. **Bassett Cadwalder** 25 April 1881; **Seeley R.**, b. 1860; m. 1890 to **Ione Gambrill**; no issue.

  iii. **Abeyrlene S.,** b. Guilford 6 June 1840; m. 20 Oct. 1858 **William Bard.** One child, **Chester M. Bard,** b. Butternuts 9 July 1860; m. in 1886 **Carrie Gosse;** res. Portage, WI.

EZRA ROCKWELL[6] b. Danbury 1780; m. **Annie Griffin** and res. Butternuts. Children:
 i. **Phebe,** b. Danbury, CT 6 May 1804; m. 19 Sept. 1827, **Daniel Botsford.** She d. at Scranton, PA 1 Feb. 1891; he d. 22 April 1882. [See Botsford family entry.]
 ii. **Caroline,** b. Danbury 2 June 1806; m. 10 Nov. 1831 **John Hurlbutt.** She d. at Gilbertsville, NY 2 Nov. 1877; he d. 13 June 1881. [See Hurlbutt family entry.]
7 iii. **John.**
7 iv. **Charles D.**
 v. **Henry B.,** b. Butternuts 20 Dec. 1818; m. **Anna Bishop** 29 Feb. 1848; she d. 9 Oct. 1883. He moved to Scranton, PA where he d. 3 Sept. 1890.

JOHN ROCKWELL[7] b. Butternuts, NY 27 Sept. 1809; m. 6 Nov. 1839 **Elizabeth Wellman.** He d. there 5 March 1867; she d. at Scranton, PA 4 May 1884. Children, b. Butternuts:
 i. **Abareen,** b. 26 Dec. 1843.
 ii. **Mary,** b. 29 May 1846; res. NY City in 1894.
 iii. **Charles D.,** b. 16 July 1849; m. 10 Nov. 1873 **Helen Garland;** res. Scranton, PA in 1892. Son **Lewis,** b. Scranton 1875, res. there in 1892.

CHARLES D. ROCKWELL[7] b. Butternuts 12 Feb. 1813; m. in NY City 31 Oct. 1853, **Jenny White.** He d. at Gilbertsville, NY 3 Sept. 1865. She res. NY City, corner 3d Avenue & 9th St. in 1891. Children, b. Gilbertsville:
 i. **John,** went West & d.; particulars unknown.
 ii. **Percy;** d. NY City 1892.

[*A Genealogy of the Families of John Rockwell, of Stamford, Conn. 1641* . . . by James Boughton, 1903; GBM; Barbour Collection; DARPI; BR:530-32]

ROGERS, SAMUEL came to Unadilla before 1795 with his wife [**Sarah Skinner** and they m. 24 Nov. 1785] and four children. He was b. at North Bolton, CT in 1764, and his wife a native of the neighboring town of East Windsor. He d. 1829; was a shoemaker. He had a great love of books and was possessed of much knowledge in several directions. He was a practical surveyor and knew enough medicine to have practised it. He had learned some law and after the age of 55 acquired a good reading knowledge of Latin. **Samuel's** son **Jabez** was a long resident of the village as was his grandson, **Perry P. Rogers,** whose later life was spent in Binghamton, where he d. in 1894. Perry was b. on the Unadilla River, but in boyhood went to Steuben Co. and thence to Buffalo, attorney. He practiced law in Unadilla from 1857 to 1871, when he went to Binghamton. He is bur. in St. Matthew's churchyard and his son **Joseph** grew up in the village and is bur. with his father. Children:

 i. **Dr. Gustavus**, d. MI and left son **Hon. Sherman S. Rogers** of Buffalo. **Gustavus'** obituary states he d. 26 Nov. 1872, aged 74, in Chicago; bur. Buffalo.
 ii. **Charles S.**, d. at Sidney Plains.
 iii. **Jabez J.**, res. Sideny Plains; stepson **Hon. David P. Loomis**, attorney of Unadilla.
 iv. **Henry W.**, attorney, formerly of Buffalo, res. Ann Arbor, MI. (1878)
 v. Dau. m. --- **Miles** and had several children who were missionaries in China.

Other daughters, not named in this source.

[A:337; UN:108; *Erie Co., NY Obituaries* . . . by Bill & Martha Reamy, Pipe Creek Pub., Inc., 1992; Barbour Collection.]

ROGERS, EDWARD b. & educated in Ireland, in early manhood, c. 1850, emigrated to the US and located at Cooperstown; tanner. He later removed to Wellsboro, PA and in 1896 settled in Corning, NY. He m. in Elmira, NY **Margaret Cullinan**, who was b. in Ireland and came with her parents to Elmira in 1855. Children:
 i. **Thomas F.**, lawyer of Corning, Steuben Co. Was b. in Wellsboro, PA 26 June 1879.
 ii. **James**, d. Corning 1906.
 iii. **Mary**, m. **Patrick McManus** of Rochester; d. in 1897 leaving two children.
 iv. **Edward R.** of NY City in employ of NY Central Railway Co.
 v. **Ella M.**, m. **Thomas J. Curtin**, res. Corning.
 vi. **Rose M.**, m. **Dr. J. L. Ronan** of Corning.
 vii. **Emma C.**, res. with parents.
 viii. **John J.** of Corning, proprietor of St. James Hotel.

[*A History of Steuben Co., NY & Its People* by Irvin W. Near, 1911, p. 723-24]

ROSEBOOM, ABRAM [ABRAHAM][1] pioneer settler (1806) of the Town of Roseboom [Richfield], b. Schenectady, NY 10 Aug. 1777, s/o **John [Jacob?] Roseboom** and wife **Susannah Veeder [Vedder]** d/o **Myndert** and wife **Elizabeth Douw**. Susannah was b. in Schenectady 18 April 1744 and was desc. from **Simon Volkertse Veeder**, b. 1624 and settled in New Amsterdam in 1652. **John/Jacob** was a soldier of the Revolution, b. 23 Oct. 1738 and d. 5 Arpil 1805 in NY. **Abram** to Roseboom [Cherry Valley] c. 1800 from Canajoharie, his previous residence. One source gives him as a member of a family prominent in mercantile circles in Fort Orange (later Albany) for 150 years previous. The homestead farm in Otsego Co. was part of the original patent granted in 1688 to **Jacob Roseboom** and others and the town was named in honor of **Abraham**. **John [Jacob?] Roseboom**, probably the father of **Abram** here, of Schenectady left at his death (1805, aged 65) 2244 acres of land in Cherry Valley. **Mrs. Ruth Roseboom**, wife of **Abraham** of Town of Roseboom, d. 2 March 1864, aged 84 and is bur. in Cherry Valley Cemetery. In 1817 **Abram** freed his slave **Bob**, who had formerly been the slave of **Capt. Peter Low**. **Bob** was judged at that time to be under the age of 45 and

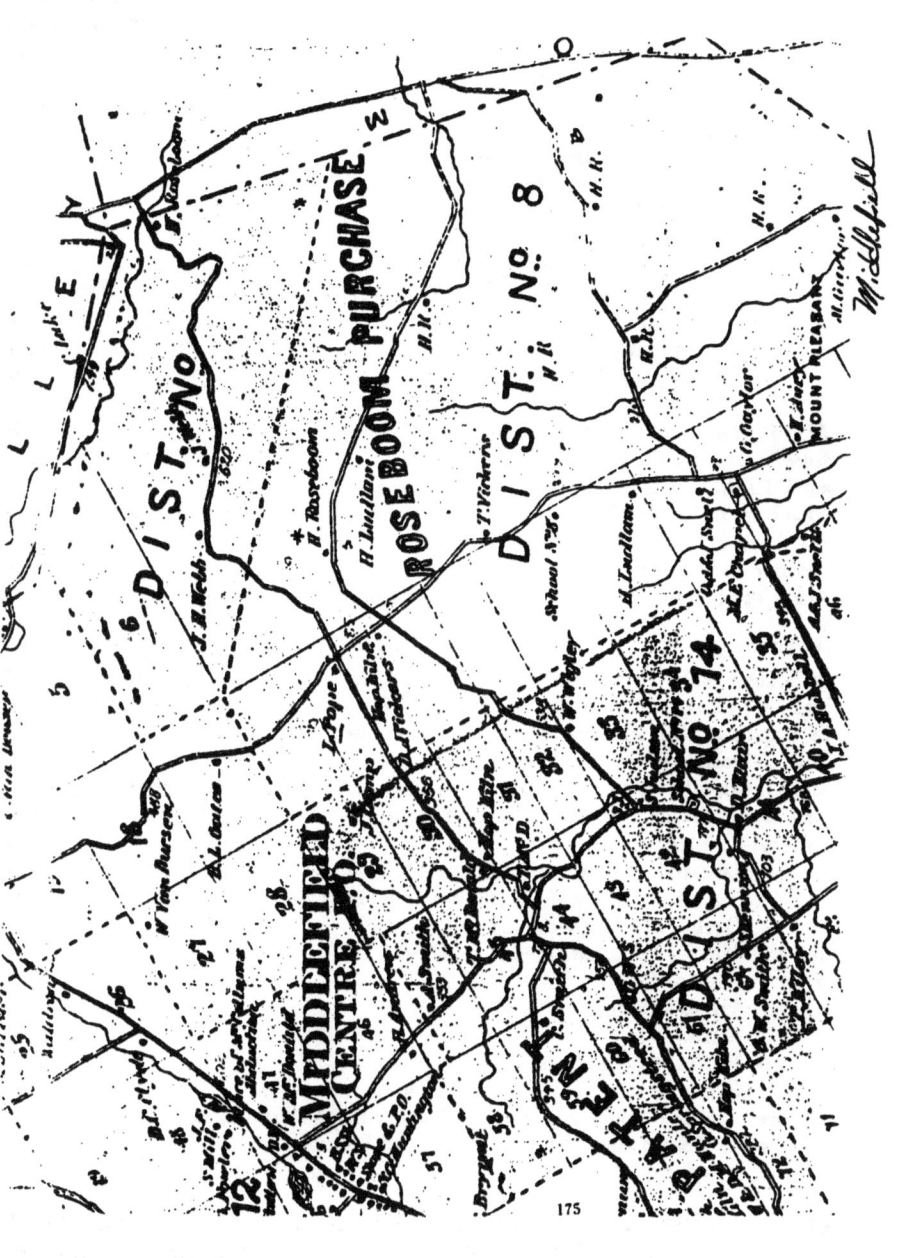

able to provide for himself. **Abram's** household was counted in Cherry Valley in 1850 at the time of the census. He was aged no at the time and his real estate was valued at $31,000. Everyone in his household was b. in NY, with the exception of the last two. His wife at that time was **Lucy** and she was aged 70 also. **Abram** d. 3 Jan. 1867, aged 89, bur. Cherry Valley Cemetery. He had nine children, those so far identified:

    i.   **Susan M.**, in 1878 widow of **Moses Belcher**, res. Cherry Valley.
2   ii.   **Henry [P]**.
    iii.   **Marietta**, m. **Dr. Joseph White** of Canajoharie.
    iv.   Dau. m. **William Hall** of Geneva, NY.
    v.   **Sarah Ely**, res. in Binghamton.
    vi.   **Catharine**, res. Cherry Valley.
    vii.   **John**, d. May 1879, aged 58 [55?], bur. Cherry Valley Cemetery. [MOHAWK says a **John** s/o **Abraham** d. 16 May 1839, aged 58 years, an obituary from a local newspaper gives **Major John Roseboom** d. at Cherry Valley 16 May 1839, aged <u>32</u>. Another obituary of a **John Roseboom** appears, he d. 16 Aug. 1870 at Cherry Valley, aged 25.]

Also in their household in 1850 were **Luch Shamon**, aged 33; **Elizabeth Roseboom**, aged 29; **Catherine Roseboom**, aged 27; **Bridget Colerton**, aged 19, b. Ireland and **Mary Meade**, aged 14, b. Ireland.

Also bur. in Cherry Valley Cemetery are **John I. [J.] Roseboom**, s/o **John** and brother of **Abraham**, d. 15 March 1828 [1829], aged 55 and another brother **Henry Hyndert [M.] Roseboom**, d. 29th of June 1824, aged 24. Also **Cornelia**, d/o **Henry** and **Cornelia Roseboom**, no dates.

HENRY ROSEBOOM[2], b. 1811, res. for a time in NY as a merchant, ret. to Roseboom in 1835. He was considered one of the men of wealth and high social standing in the town. In 1843 he m. **Cornelia Rutgers Livingston**. He was one of the first members of the Grace Episcopal Church vestry in 1846. Their household was enumerated in the 1850 census, when he was a res. of Cherry Valley. At that time he was aged 38, farmer; **Cornelia** was aged 35. Communicant of Grace Church, Cherry Valley. Children:

    i.   **Levantia [Laracha?] Livingston**, aged 6 in 1850; m. **Rev. H. U. Swinnerton**, pastor of the Presbyterian Church at Cherry Valley.
    ii.   **Catherine Augusta**, aged 4 in 1850.
    iii.   **Mary Elizabeth**, aged 2 in 1850.
    iv.   **Abram Hendrick**.
    v.   **Jacob Livingston**.
    vi.   **Ruth**.
    vii.   **William Campbell**.
    viii.   **Cornelia Livingston**, d. in infancy.

Also res. in the household in 1850 were **Eliza Woodbrom**, aged 17; **Catherine Meade**, aged 17, b. Ireland; and **Isaac Linnedoe (?)** aged 10, laborer, b. NY.

Source MOHAWK shows **Myndert Roseboom**, merchant, of the City of Albany, sold to **William Cook** of Cherry Valley, Montgomery County, in

deed dated 23 Feb. 1786, Lot #16 (64 acres) situated in Newtown Martin for 62.10.0. Witnessed by **Volkert Oothout, John Roseboom**.
[A:315; CH1:99, 118, 121, 130; *1630-1897, A Brief History of the Ancestors and Descendants of John Roseboom, 1739-1803 and of Jesse Johnson 1745-1832* by Catharine, J. Livingston Roseboom, Henry U. Swinnerton & Joseph H. White, ??; 1850 census; CVC; MOHAWK; DARPI; OB; CH1:70; BOWMAN]

RUGGLES, ELI⁴ (*Samuel³ CT, Joseph² CT, Benjamin¹ CT*) was s/o **Samuel** (1751-1795) **Ruggles** and wife **Huldah Wakelee**. **Samuel** served in Capt. **Joseph Smith's** 8th Company, Fifth Regiment from May to Nov. 1775 (Brookfield, CT); he was b. 1751 & d. 1795 in CT. **Eli⁴** was b. in 1781, d. 1847. His brother, **Samuel⁴**, b. March 1795, was a missionary to Hawaii. **Eli**, of Brookfield CT, made his will 1 Sept. 1846 and in it named his sisters **Lucinda Tomlinson, Thiray Bishop, Huldah Keeler** and **Marcia** wife of **Amos Williams**; his brothers **Isaac W., Eldred** and **Samuel**; his nephews **George, Eldred** and **William Keeler**, executors; nieces **Sarah Sanford** and **Mary Keeler** and nephew **Horace Northrop**. **Thomas S. Holman**, executor. His will appears in the will abstracts for Otsego Co., NY.
[*TAG*:34:123-25; *Families of Ancient New Haven* by D. L. Jacobus p. 1571-72; *History of New Milford, CT* by Orcutt, p. 756-57; *Annals of Brookfield, Fairfield Co., CT* by Emily C. Hawley, 1929, p. 648-49; *NEHGR*:118:61-63; DARPI.]

RUSSELL, JOHN¹ of Yorkshire, England, to America with **Mr. Tunnicliff** as an employee in 1758. **John** was a carpenter and shipbuilder, and received one acre of land for each day's work from **Mr. Tunnicliff**, working for three years. His land was on the Otego Creek in the western part of the Town of Otsego, 900 acres on which he resided until his death in 1832. He made his will 12 Sept. 1830; he d. 25 March 1832, aged 75. In his will he identifies himself as a res. of Otsego and names his wife **Mary** (nee **Johnson**, originally of Lincolnsire, England) and children (below). Mrs. **Mary Russell** d. 13 June 1850, aged 90.

2 i. **William**, d. 16 March 1859, at 72 y, 3 m, 10 d.
 ii. **Robert E.**, d. 21 Aug. 1864 at Edmeston, aged 75.
 iii. **John**. Is probably the **John Russell** of Otsego who m. in Hastings, NY 14 Feb. 1831 to **Lucy Ann Douglass**. An obituary appears for **John Russell** of Cooperstown who d. 2 Aug. 1843, aged 71.
 iv. **Thomas**, b. 12 July 1799, bapt. Cooperstown 29 Sept. 1799; d. 5 Dec. 1857, aged 58 years.
 v. **Joseph**. **Phebe** wife of **Joseph Russell**, d. 11 Nov. 1859, aged 88 y, 10 m. Bur. at West Burlington. **Joseph Russell** d. at Hartwick Seminary 17 Oct. 1855, aged 54.
 vi. **Elizabeth**, m. **Richard Garratt**; had at least two children per her father's will: **John R.** and **Richard Garratt**.
 vii. **Sarah**, m. **Daniel Marvin**.
 viii. **Mary**, b. April 1797; bapt. 9 July 1797 at Cooperstown.

WILLIAM RUSSELL² b. Albany Co., NY; d. in Otsego Co., aged 75. He m. **Sarah Garrett** who was b. in Hampshire, England and came to America with her parents, **Robert** and **Marcia Garrett**, farmers who d. in town of

New Lisbon, Otsego Co., each c. 75 years of age. Children:
  i.   **Harriet.**
2 ii. **Dorr.**
  iii. **Rensselaer.**
  iv. **Sarah.**
  v.   **Richard.**

DORR RUSSELL[3] b. 11 Oct. 1823 in Otsego Co. At the age of 13 he went to attend school at the Cooperstown Academy, grad. at the age of 17. He was clerk for **James Stowell** of Cooperstown, and after graduation he opened a general store at Burlington, backed by his employers. He was there eleven years, and served as postmaster under President VanBuren four years. He m. 7 Jan. 1850 **Lucy G. Fitch** who was b. in Richfield, NY 29 Sept. 1829, and d. 9 Oct. 1888. She was d/o **Prosper** and **Maria (Vaughn) Fitch**; he of CT and she of RI. After five years **Dorr** sold out and removed to Cooperstown where he organized the Bank of Cooperstown, was Cashier of that institution for twelve years, and at the same time dealt in hops and wool. He then removed to NY City and was Vice President of the American National Bank for three years, when organized the New York Loaners' Bank. After several years he went to CA (leaving his family in NY) and engaged in mining two years, after which he went to San Francisco. In 1888 he returned to Cooperstown on account of the death of his wife. Now retired (1893). Children:
  i.   **Arthur D.**, b. 18 Oct. 1850; now (1893) in NY City in the Auditor's office of the US Express Co.
  ii. **Lucie**, b. 20 June 1862, at home.
  iii. **Minnie**, b. 28 Aug. 1863, at home.
[SPR/RS:114; GBW; GBC1; GBM; OB; NER104:48; NASH1; BR:265-66]

SANDS, FREDERICK AUGUSTUS[5] (*Obadiah*[4], *Benjamin of NY*[3], *John*[2] *NY*, *John*[2] *RI & LI NY James*[1] *England, MA & RI*), was s/o **Judge Obadiah Sands** and **Elizabeth Teed** his wife, was b. at Sands Point on Long Island [Bainbridge, NY] 17 Feb. 1813 [19 Feb. 1812]; d. 10 March 1886; m. 1st **Maria Page** d/o **Judge Sherman Page** and she d. after two years of marriage. On 20 Jan. 1841 Frederick m. **Clarissa A.**, sister of the late **Henry R. Mygatt** of Oxford, who survived him only six months. **Clarissa** was b. in 1815, was a woman of rare qualities; members of the Episcopal Church of Unadilla. Frederick's father, **Judge Obadiah Sands**, was for many years a resident of Franklin, Delaware Co., NY, and d. in Oxford in 1858. Frederick is descended from **Capt. James Sands**, Englishman, who came to America c. 1642, landing at Plymouth. **Capt. Sands** was of Reading, England, where he was born in 1622. Frederick was a contributor to the building of a Baptist Church in Unadilla; he was a prominent banker and businessman of Otsego and Chenango Cos. He is bur. at Unadilla in St. Matthew's Episcopal Churchyard along with his father, who d. at Franklin and whose remains were removed to this place. Frederick was engaged in business with **Christopher D. Fellows** and later with **Mr. Watson**. On removal to Oxford he was in business with his brother-in-law, **James W. Clark** and an old personal friend **Henry L. Miller** and others. Children:

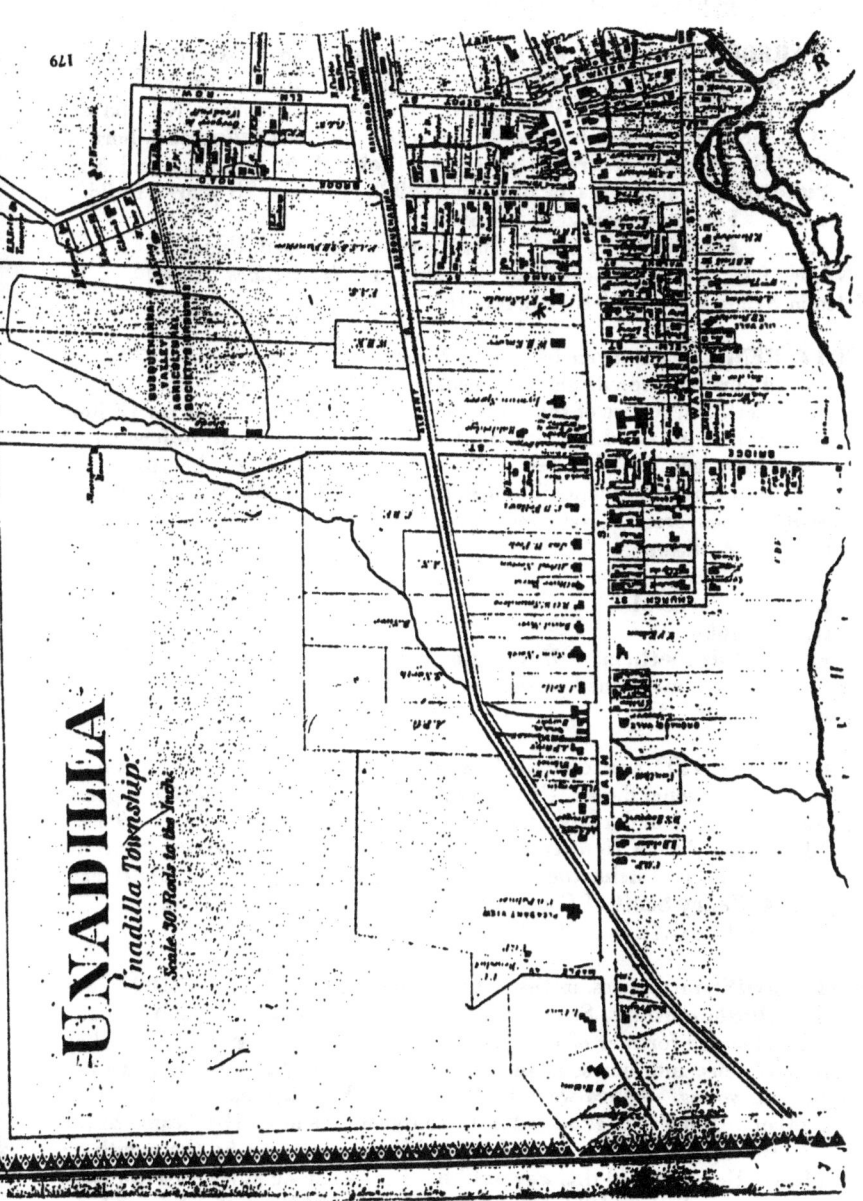

6   i.   **J. Frederick.**
     ii.   **Clara M.** m. **Hon. Frank B. Arnold** b. Ireland, res. Unadilla. She dec'd. by 1893.
     iii.   **Henry,** a publisher in Chicago; m. **Ada Wilson** of LaPorte, IN.
     iv.   **Belle,** m. **S. S. North** of Unadilla.

J. FREDERICK SANDS[6] was b. c. 1855 in the village of Oxford, Chenango Co., NY. He was less than two years of age when his parents removed to Unadilla. He m. **Clara L. Pulletreau,** who was b. in Brooklyn, NY who was of French and English origins. She was the d/o **John Puletreau,** born in the US, although of French parentage. **John** d. in Brooklyn and **Mrs. Pulletreau** is still a res. of that city (1893), now aged 75 years. Child:
     i.   **Florence,** now aged 6 (1893).
     ii.   **Frederick A.,** bur. St. Matthew's Churchyard, Unadilla.
[UNA:84, 91, 124-29; *Descendants of James Sands of Block Island* . . . by Malcolm Sands Wilson, 1940; BR:440-1]

SCOTT, HENRY[1] came from Ireland with his wife and dau. before 1796 and settled north of the village of Milford, Otsego Co. He was a farmer and 1st town clerk and justice of the peace. He made his will in Milford on 12 June 1828 and in it named his wife **Mary** and children. He d. at Milford on 11 Feb. 1829, aged 74 [75]. There must have been another dau., because in his will Henry names grandchildren **Henry S.** and **John M. McCall. Henry Scott** of Cooperstown was executor.
     i.   **William.**
2   ii.   **Henry.**
     iii.   **George M.**
     iv.   **John.**
     v.   **Elizabeth,** m. --- **Harrington** and had **Mary S.** and **Allen B.** who were mentioned in their grandfather's will.
     vi.   **Mary Ann.**

HENRY SCOTT[2] was for four decades connected with the Otsego County and First National Banks. He was a good businessman, a prudent and painstaking official and pleasant gentleman in social circles. He d. 19 Dec. 1873, aged 82. In New York City on 14 Nov. 1827 a **Henry Scott** of Cooperstown m. **Catherine M. Strong** of that place; probably this Henry. A **Mrs. Henry Scott** of Cooperstown d. 26 Sept. 1885, aged 76.
[GBW; GBM, OB; G:161, 175]

SCOTT, JOHN[1], farmer res. in District 4 of Town of Cherry Valley (1893), was b. in Roxburghshire, Scotland 4 Sept. 1828. He was s/o **John Scott,** carpenter and forester of that place, and his wife **Elizabeth Black.** They had six daus. and four sons; the sons and one sister, **Jane,** came to the US. **Jane** d. young. **Agnes** went to Australia. The other daus. remained in Scotland. **John**[1] was educated in Roxburghshire and in 1849 came to the US. He came to Otsego Co. and began life here working by the month on a farm. He continued this way until his mar., when he purchased the farm he now occupies. In 1852 he m. **Ann (Green) Whiteman,** who was b. in

England, d/o **George** and **Rebecca Green**, and widow of **Gerry Whitman** [sic]. She d. in Feb. 1891. Children:
i. **Elizabeth**, m. **Walter Furman**; dec'd. by 1893.
ii. **Agnes**, m. **William Furman**.
[BR17-18]

SEEBER, WILHELM¹, b. 1721 Germany, d. 1777 killed in the battle of Oriskany; served as major of the 1st battalion of Canajoharie, NY. He m. 1745, **Maria C. Walbrathin**, b. 1729, d. 1756. Children:

2   i.   **William**.
    ii.   **Heinrich**, listed as a son of **Wilhelm Seeber**, m. 9 May 1790, **Anna Eva Kessler**, d/o **Thomas Kessler** at Fort Plain Dutch Reformed Church.
    iii.   **Johannes**, listed as s/o **Wilhelm Seeber**, dec'd., m. **Margaretha Diel**, d/o **John Diel**, dec'd. 9 Jan. 1791, also at the Fort Plain Church.

WILLIAM SEEBER², b. 15 June 1747, d. 1828; lieutenant in the 1st regiment Tyron Co., NY Militia. An early inhabitant of Canajoharie, now Springfield. His name [or his father's] is on the list of attendees of a meeting held by the Tryon Co. Committee of Vigilance in 1777. He m. 1764, **Elizabeth Schrierrin [Schnerr]**, b. 1747, d. 1821. They had at least one son, **Adolph [Adolphus]**, b. 1773, d. 1857, m. **Sally Yates**, b. 1775, d. 1857. There is an obituary for another **Adolphus Seeber** d. Springfield 17 Oct. 1868, aged 64.

The LDS Ancestral File gives the family of **Adam Seeber**, b. 21 Aug. 1810, NY, d. 12 Feb. 1833, and wife **Eleanor Putman** who was b. 22 June 1815 in Cherry Valley. Children, b. South Valley, Otsego Co.:
i.   **David**, b. 17 Aug. 1837.
ii.   **Alvin**, b. 22 Sept. 1840; d. 5 July 1849.
iii.   **Waldo**, b. 22 May 1843.
iv.   **Caroline**, b. 4 Nov. 1846.
v.   **Martha A.**, b. 22 June 1849.
vi.   **Mary M.**, b. 11 March 1853; m. **Oliver G. Engell**, b. 18 March 1846 in NY.
[SPR:13, 113; DARPI; DAR59245, 59171 & 106687; MOHAWK; OB]

SHAUL, JOHN¹, b. 18 Feb. 1760 probably in the town of Stark, Herkimer Co., d. 18 June 1844; m. 1784 **Elizabeth B[r]onner**. **John** was a Revolutionary War veteran; captured by Indians at Cherry Valley, NY in 1788 and kept a prisoner for five years in Canada, suffering untold hardships. He made his escape, hotly pursued by the Indians, and reached the nearest fort only an hour or two in advance. Two of his brothers were captured at the same time [unnamed in this source]. He received a pension for 13 months' actual service as a private, NY Line. **John** and **Elizabeth** had at least one child: **DANIEL SHAUL²**, veteran of the War of 1812 and was stationed at Sacket's Harbor; farmer of the Town of Stark. He m. **Rachel Smith**, b. in Stark, d/o **Gersham** and **Laney (Reese) Smith**, both b. in Herkimer Co.

Children:
    i.   **Gershom Smith**, m. **Martha Malvina Gilchrist** and had at least one child, **Sylvia**, b. Springfield.

3 ii.   **John D.**

3 iii.   **Cornelius.**

The LDS IGI shows the christening of one **Johannes Schall**, s/o **Bastian** and **Lena Schall**, on 11 March 1798, St. Paul's Lutheran Church in Minden Twp., Montgomery Co., NY. Probably an early branch of this family.

JOHN D. SHAUL³ [P] from earliest youth evinced a decided taste and aptitude for military matters. At age of 18 he was appointed corporal of a company of militia. He was of Stark at the time of his marriage to **Betsey [Mary] S. Carroll [Caldwell]** [P], d/o **Davis** and **Phebe Carroll** of Springfield on 16 March 1834. In 1839 he removed to the Town of Springfield, where he has since resided. He was one of the most successful farmers of the county. In 1850 elected colonel of the 39th NY State Militia, of which he was in command at the outbreak of the Civil War eleven years later. His regiment was consolidated with the 76th NY Volunteers in Albany in January 1862 and he took the position of lieutenant-colonel. He was honorably discharged on 20 Nov. 1862 on account of physical disability, from which he never fully recovered. He supervised his farm of over 400 acres, "Soldier's Retreat" in Otsego Co. from that time. They had no children, but have reared and educated several orphans. The household of **John C. Shaul** was enumerated with his household in 1840 as res. of Cherry Valley with real estate valued at $3,300. All of his household were b. in NY. His wife is listed only as "Mrs. J. Shaul." Others in the household [their children]:

    i.   **Merzie (?) [Menzo]**, aged 20, farmer. [The LDS Ancestral File gives this as **Menzo** and lists his spouse as **Christina Eckler**, b. Jan. 1831 at Cherry Valley. Gives their children as **Henry, Adolph, Viola** who m. **Andrew Hollenbeck** and **John C. Shaul**.]

    ii.   **Norman**, aged 18 [female sic], farmer.

    iii. **Sarah**, aged 19 in 1840. [LDS Ancestral Fives her spouse as **William McFee**.]

    iv. **John A.**, aged 10.

    v.   **Henrietta**, aged 7. [Mar. --- **Woodbeck**.]

    vi. **Mary**, aged 4. [Mar. **George Tucker**.]

Also in the household is **Eleanor Mickler**, aged 40, b. NY. The LDS Ancestral File also names children **Albert** b. 1840, m. **Selina Gillett** and **Martha** b. 1852, who m. **David A. Dockstander**.

CORNELIUS SHAUL³ b. In Stark, 15 Nov. 1827. He farmed many years in Stark and in 1869 removed to Town of Richfield in Otsego Co. and owned land in several towns in that county. 7 Sept. 1857 he m. **Margaret Yule**, who was b. in Town of Warren, Herkimer Co., d/o **George** and **Catharine Yule**. Children:

    i.   **Libbie.**

    ii.   **Laura L.**

    iii. **Daniel.**

[DARPI; A:331A; DAR#57390; GBW; BR643-44]

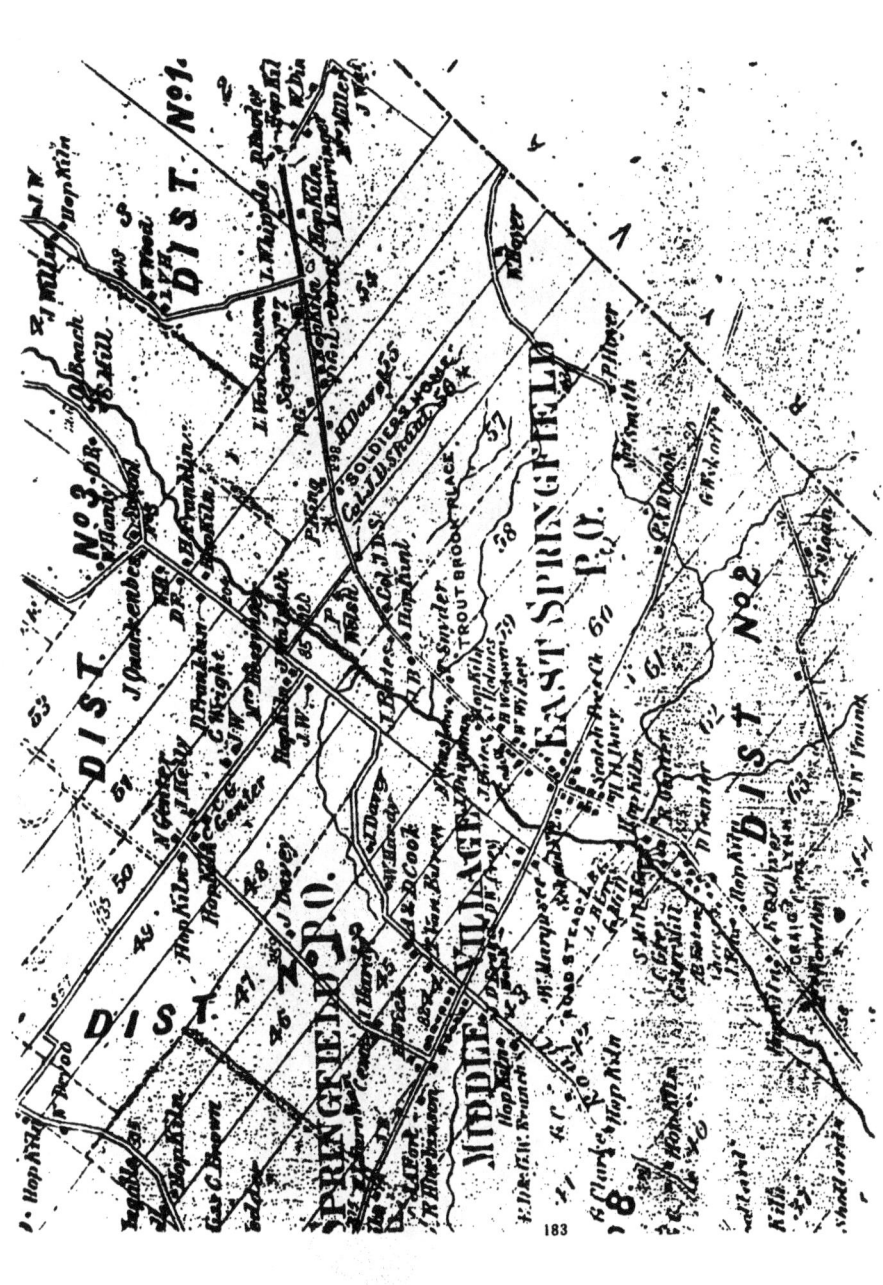

COL. JOHN D SHAUL

SHAW, S. VALENTINE m. **Alice Adelia Rockwell**, b. Butternuts 20 May 1821, d/o **Amos** and **Elizabeth (Emmons) Rockwell**. [See Rockwell family entry.] Children, all b. Butternuts:
- i. **Ella J.**, b. 25 June 1846; m. 3 Jan. 1867 **James A. Coard**. Their children, **Clara Adelia** and **Josephine Ella**, both b. Lansing, IA.
- ii. **Florence Madeline**, b. 24 Jan. 1848; m. **Herman Schierholz** and res. Lansing, IA in 1892. No children.
- iii. **James Henry**, b. 5 June 1850; m. **Mary E. Wood** 3 Feb. 1877. Two children, both b. LaCrosse, WI: **Samuel S. V.** and **James Rockwell**.
- iv. **Frances Elizabeth**, b. 6 Dec. 1852; m. 14 March 1878 **George H. Markley**. Two children: **George Herman Jr.** and **Charles Edward**.
- v. **George Valentine**, b. 25 June 1855; m. Jan. 1882 **Clara Cutting**. One child, **Allen D.**
- vi. **Samuel Charles**, b. 2 Sept. 1858 and d. in childhood.

[*A Genealogy of the Families of John Rockwell, of Stamford, Conn. 1641 . . .* by James Boughton, 1903]

SIBLEY, JOHN[1], s/o **Hezekiah** who was b. in Wales and came to American as a young man and settled in CT. **John** was b. in Ashford, CT 6 June 1797 and m. **Esther Bellamy** when he was aged 19 and she 16. He was an early settler in Otsego Co. by 1803. He d. aged 75 and **Esther** d. aged 73. Their son:

ORRIN SIBLEY[2] was b. in Willington, CT 14 April 1803; aged 10 weeks when his parents removed to Otsego Co. He was a distiller, whaler, gunsmith. He m. **Mary Ann Jewell** [see Jewell family entry] 6 Oct. 1831. She had been b. in Otsego Co., d/o **Jared** and **Esther (Barrett) Jewell** and she d. 24 July 1846 at Middlefield, aged 38, the mother of five children. Children:
- i. **Jared**, b. 24 Oct. 1832; m. **Mary J. Teachant** 2 Nov. 1853; res. Ceresco, WI.
- ii. **Aaron**, b. 23 Nov. 1833; m. **Anna Maria Hoose** 3 Sept. 1854, res. Westville, NY.
- 3 iii. **James**, b. 24 Nov. 1835; res. Westville.
- iv. **Esther M.**, b. 26 Dec. 1838; m. **William M. Bowen** 27 Dec. 1855; res. Ceresco, WI.
- v. **Laura**, b. 25 Feb. 1810; res. Westfield, NY.

JAMES SIBLEY[3] was b. Town of Middlefield, Otsego Co. 24 Nov. 1835. Farmer & logger, he went to WI at age 20 and after two years returned to Otsego and worked with his father. Later he traveled to MN and returned again to NY. He m. 8 Feb. 1862 to **Lucy J. Pratt** who was b. in Town of Middlefield 1 March 1836, d/o **Thomas** and **Louisana (Jones) Pratt**. The **Pratt** family had formerly res. in MA and removed to NY c. 1801. He was a s/o **Thomas Pratt** of MA. The **Sibleys** are Baptists. **James** and **Lucy** had one son:
- i. **Frederick O.**, b. 27 Nov. 1870.

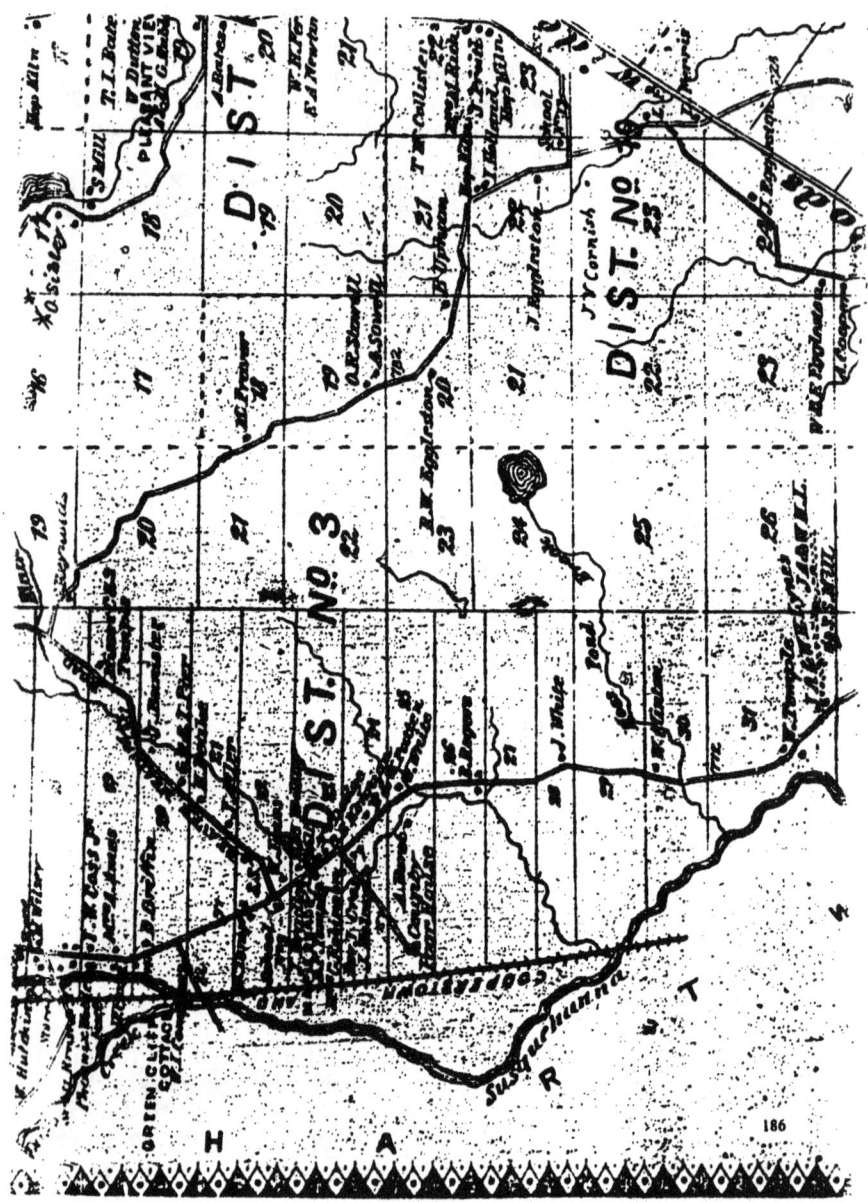

The LDS IGI shows an **Orin Sibley**, s/o **Eber Sibley** and **Caroline Rebecca Hazen**, b. 5 March 1810, Richmond, NY who could be the Orrin above. However, they show another **Orin Sibley**, s/o **John Sibley** and wife **Esther** who was b. in 1803 in Ashford, CT who could also fit.
[GBW; *The Jewell Register* . . . Hartford, CT, 1860; BR:406-07; Barbour Collection]

SISSON, GEORGE, belived to be related to the below **John Sisson** Unadilla family, but so far not proved. He was b. in Unadilla 10 May 1803 and d. in Brighton, IA 19 Dec. 1866. He m. **Mary Ann Howe**, d/o **Artemas** and **Fanny (Parker) Howe**. [See Howe family entry.] After **George's** death, **Mary Ann** went to live with a dau. in CA. Children:

i.   **Lucy Ann**, b. 24 Aug. 1830; res. CA.
ii.   **Julia E.**, b. 12 Dec. 1840; d. 1 Feb. 1841.
iii.   **Elbert N.**, b. 2 Nov. 1841; m. **Maggie Dix**.
iv.   **Julia W.**, b. 27 Dec. 1842; m. **David F. Funston**.
v.   **Melville C.**, b. 8 July 1844; d. 2 Nov. 1886.
vi.   **George W.**, b. 16 Oct. 1846; res. Wyoming.
vii.   **Mary**, b. 11 July 1848; res. CA.
viii. **Henry E.**, b. 16 Feb. 1850; m. **Mary A. Stephens**.
ix.   **Ellen T.**, b. 15 June 1852; m. **Theodore W. Rowan**.
x.   **Fanny A.**, b. 29 Dec. 1852; m. **Joseph S. Day**.
xi.   **John E.**, b. 22 April 1857; res. Los Angeles, CA.

The LDS Ancestral File shows this **George Sisson** to be s/o **Samuel** of Milford, Otsego Co.
[*Howe Genealogies* by Daniel Wait Howe, Indianapolis, IN, 1929]

SISSON, JOHN[5] (*Giles*[4] *RI, IN & NY, Thomas*[3] *RI & NY, George*[2] *MA & RI, Richard*[1] *RI & MA*), b. 10 [21] April 1749 in CT, was ancestor of all Sissions in Otsego Co., NY. He was a Revolutionary soldier. Settled his family in the Sand Hill-Hampshire Hollow area of Town of Unadilla c. 1790, first living on the river road and then removing to the area afterwards known as Sisson Hill; farmer. He m. **Alcha Crandall**, d/o **Samuel**, and they had 13 children live to adulthood. **Alcha** was b. 21 May 1755 in either VT or Dutchess Co., NY; she d. 12 Aug. 1832 in Unadilla. It is thought **John** was in the Albany area during the Revolutionary War, as he served in the Albany Co. militia. His first 3 children [**Amos, James & Sarah**] were born before the move to Unadilla. **John** d. 21 Oct. 1818 in Switzerland Co., IN [according to the LDS Ancestral File]. Children:

i.   **Amos**.
ii.   **James**.
iii.   **Sarah**.
6 iv.   **Aaron**, b. 14 Sept. 1780.
v.   **John Jr.** [appears only in LDS Ancestral File records], b. 20 June 1773 in Hoosick, Renssealer Co., NY. He m. c. 1793 to **Hannah Gardner**; both d. in Switzerland Co., IN. It lists a dau., **Lydia**, b. 9 Aug. 1797 in Unadilla who mar. 10 Jan. 1816 to **A. R. Osborn** b. in Albany Co. in 1793.

187

AARON SISSON[6] [native] early settler in Town of Unadilla in the Sand Hill-Hampshire Hollow area. He m. **Polly [Mary] Sisson**, a distant relative. Polly d. aged past age 70. Children:

7   i.   **Christopher.**
     ii.   **Samuel.**
     iii.   **Putnam**; m. **Sally Merriman** who d. young & childless. He removed with several of his brothers to Erie Co., PA.
     iv.   **Theodore.**
7   v.   **Alanson.**
     vi.   **Alvin.**
     vii.   **Ann.**
     viii.   **Sarah.**
     ix.   **Rosemund.**
     x.   **Harriett.**

CHRISTOPHER SISSON[7] m. **Mary Burras** and had:
     i.   **Sally Ann**, m. **Jonas Wyman.**
     ii.   **Jane**, m. **Charles Wilsey.**
     iii.   **Clarissa**, m. **George Foot.**
     iv.   **Henry.**
     v.   **Edwin.**

ALANSON SISSON[7] b. Sisson Hill farm c. 1817. He d. in 1890; farmer. He held numerous of the offices of his town. Baptist. His widow is still living, aged 73 (1893). She was b. in Sidney, her maiden name was **Maria Earl**. They had seven children, two are dec'd. (1893). Only child named here:

8   i.   **Francis M.**

FRANCIS M. SISSON[8] was the eldest child of the family, was b. in town of Unadilla 26 July 1843. He attended the Gilbertsville Academy and the Delaware Literary Institute, and afterward taught school for a time. On 6 Sept. 1862 he enlisted in Co. G, 152nd NY Volunteer Infantry. He was wounded at Reem's Station and was confined in the hospital at Washington and Philadelphia for six months. He is now (1893) Quartermaster of C. C. Siver Post No. 124, G.A.R. at Unadilla. He has been somewhat prominent in local politics, having served as Supervisor of his town two times, and had charge of the post office at Well's Bridge for 20 years. He m. at Town of Unadilla to **Laura Stiles** who was b. in Wayne Co., PA 20 Jan. 1846. Baptists. Children:
     i.   **William H.**, b. 9 July 1867, in business as a member of the firm of Root & Sisson, general merchandise at Wells' Bridge. He m. **Nellie Burnside** of Town of Otego. One child: **Delmar F.**
     ii.   **Benjamin F.**, a painter and res. of Wells' Bridge. He m. **Myrtle Youmans**, one child: **Leo.**

[UNA:99; *At Rest in Unadilla*, Shirley B. Goerlich, 1988; *Genealogical Dictionary of Rhode Island*, Austin; A:336-7; DARPI; BR:124-25]

SISSON, JOSHUA C.[1] of Plainfield made his will 13 Nov. 1845 and in it named his wife **Catherine** and children:
  i. **Joshua G.**
2 ii. **Luther S.**
  iii. **Fanny.**
  iv. **Harriet A.**
  v. **Tacy L.**

LUTHER SPENCER SISSON[2], b. Plainfield, NY 13 June 1824, d. 15 May 1887. He m. **Mary Eliza Loomis** b. Plainfield 27 Feb. 1827, d/o **Henry and Eliza Ann (Morris) Loomis.** [See Loomis family entry.] **Luther** and **Mary Eliza** m. at Unadilla Forks 9 March 1851. Children:
  i. **Frances A.**
  ii. **Kathryn L.**
  iii. **Mary Eliza.**
  iv. **Henry Spencer.**
  v. **Hattie Maud.**
  vi. **Ella Mae.**
  vii. **Leila Agnes.**

[GBW; *Descendants of Joseph Loomis In America And His Antecedents In the Old World*, by Elisha S. Loomis, 1908]

SLADE, JAMES[1], b. 30 May 1770 in New England of English descent; he d. at Westerloo 30 May 1840. He m. **Lois Barber**, b. CT 4 March 1775; d. Westerloo 31, Dec. 1836. Their child:
JAMES SLADE[2] b. Town of Westerloo, Albany Co., NY 19 Oct. 1791, the second son in a family of ten children. He was a teacher in his youth; in 1820 purchased timberland in Town of Meredith, Delaware Co., NY. 27 Dec. 1820 he m. **Samantha**, d/o **Sylvester Ford** and **Lydia Reed** of Westerloo; both dec'd. (1878). In 1832 the Slade family moved to Oneonta. **James** served as clerk of the meeting called to establish the First Baptist Society of Oneonta in 1833. **Samantha** d. 15 Oct. 1875. Children:
  i. **Lumon Reed.**
  ii. **Sherman Winslow.**
  iii. **Theron Ford**, d. aged 1 year.
  iv. **Lewis Sherrill.**
  v. **Elvina**, d. in infancy.
  vi. **Hamilton Ford**, m. **Lucy Michael** of Davenport, res. on old homestead.
[A:237; D:116]

SLADE, ALFRED[1] was the s/o **Aaron Slade**, a native of VT who settled in Afton, Chenango Co. **Aaron** later removed to Chemung Co., d. there "full of years." He was mar. twice and reared nine children by his first wife, who at the time of the Mormon "excitement" followed **Joseph Smith** to Nauvoo, IL. **Aaron's** wife was the d/o **Rev. Joshua** and **Hannah (Reniff) Rogers**, he of MA, she of RI. "Later Mr. Slade [presumably Aaron] became a Methodist minister, and had charge of a circuit extending over Otsego, Chenago and Madison Counties." **Alfred** was b. in VT. He m. **Eliza A.**

Rogers, b. in MA. Both b. 1802, they were m. in Afton, Chenango Co. in 1827 and removed to Butternuts, Otsego Co. in 1832. He was in the lumbering business and a farmer. Their second child and son [the only one named here]:
ORVILLE F. SLADE² was b. in Afton 21 Sept. 1830. He m. in Unadilla to **Henrietta Fisk** who was b. at that place, d/o **Charles Fisk**, early Otsego Co. settlers. **Charles** was killed fighting for the Union Army in the Civil War. Children:
    i.   **Melvin E.**, b. c. 1880.
    ii.   **Mabel A.**, b. c. 1882.
Family are members of the Methodist Episcopal Church.
[BR:575-76]

SLEEPER, JOHN¹, b. Mount Holly, NJ 14 Aug. 1731; his wife was **Hannah** [**Haines** according to the LDS Ancestral File and they mar. 26 Sept. 1754]. Quaker preacher, brought his family from Mount Holly, NJ to Otsego County in 1774. During the war they became alarmed at the inroads of the Tories and Indians, and returned to NJ until 1784, when they returned to Otsego County, where **John** d. 24 Nov. 1794. He made his will as a res. of Unadilla on 1 Nov. 1794; probated 1795. His wife was **Hannah** --- who was b. 13 March 1735. He had seven sons and five daus. Those identified:
    i.   **Nehemiah**, built a mill below Laurens on the Otego Creek, which was afterwards known as Boyd's mill.
    ii.   **Samuel**, took up several hundred acres of land; built a grist-mill and saw-mill on the Otego Creek, just below the iron bridge this side (east) of West Oneonta. Early poor master and fence viewer of Town of Otego. An active businessman and noted surveyor. Sold his property after some years to **David Smith**, and went to Stroudsburgh, PA and thence to OH. His oldest son, **Ephraim**, m. **Jane Niles**, d/o **Nathaniel Niles** and remained in the neighborhood.
2   iii.   **Joseph**.
    iv.   **John**.
    v.   **Benjamin**.
    vii.   **Phebe**, m. **Calvin Straight**.
    viii.   **Mary**, m. **Freeman Harrison** and had son **John Sleeper Harrison**.
    ix.   **Anna**, m. **John Cully**.

JOSEPH SLEEPER² b. in Burlington Co., NJ 1765. Came with his father to Otsego Co. c. 1774 and lived with his father until he was aged 21. In 1790 he m. **Irene Frisbee**, d/o **Capt. Greckson Frisbee** of Cherry Valley. **Joseph** made his will 5 Jan. 1830 & it was probated Oct. that same year. He had nine children, all dec'd. by 1878 except **Hiram, Hannah** and **Hudson**:
    i.   **Cynthia**.
    ii.   **Jonathan**.
    iii.   **Lucy**.
    iv.   **Reuben**, of Mt. Morris.

v. Lydia.
vi. Lydia (2nd).
vii. Morris, res. Laurens.
viii. Hiram.
ix. Hannah.
3 x. Hudson.

HUDSON SLEEPER[3] [P], b. on the family homestead, on which he now lives. He m. **Manda Weller** [P] d/o **Daniel**. Children:
i. Caroline Eliza, b. 9 Jan. 1833.
ii. Charlotte, b. 12 Nov. 1838.
iii. Julia, b. 14 Jan. 1840; m. **Elias Cosseler** 2 May 1863.
The LDS Ancestral File gives **John[1]**'s ancestry as *John[1], Jonathan of Kingston NH, Aaron of Hampton, NH, Thomas.*
[ONE:111-12; A:174a; GBW; F:31]

SMITH, GILBERT[6] (*Ephraim[5] MA & CT, John[4] MA, Daniel[3] MA, Daniel[2] MA, John[1] England & MA*), b. Stonington, CT 20 Jan. 1756 s/o **Ephraim** and 2d wife **Lucy Stevens** of Watertown, MA & Stonington, CT. Gilbert m. **Delilah Bundy** in 1783 and moved to Otego, Otsego Co. She was d/o **Peter Bundy** and wife **Priscilla Prentice**. Gilbert d. 13 March 1795. Their child:
CAPT. ELISHA S. SMITH[7], b. NY State 19 Oct. 1785, m. **Elizabeth Birdsall** who was b. 13 Jan. 1784. He could be the **Elijah Smith** who opened a tavern in Otego before 1796 and later removed to OH. Children:
i. Gilbert.
ii. Anteneta.
iii. Ejesta.
iv. Delia.
v. Mary.
vi. Ursula.
vii. Squier.
viii. Melania.
xi. Melvina.
xii. Archaleus.
[*History of Stonington [CT]*, Richard Wheeler; *The Compendium of American Genealogy, Vol. 6,* Virkus; DARPI; F:67]

Another SMITH family that is probably related to the above family, but no firm connection made.

SMITH, EPHRAIM[2] s/o **Ephraim Smith[1]** who was b. in CT c. 1750 and "at an early day" removed to Oneida Co., NY, where he died. **Ephraim[1]**'s wife was **Anna Baldwin**, d/o **Josiah**. Ephraim[2] was one of eight children and was b. in CT; came to NY with his father. "Early in life" m. **Sybil Stevens** and res. Camden, Oneida Co. for many years; merchant. He d. in Cleveland, OH and Sybil in Palmyra, Wayne Co. Children:
i. Abigail, m. **Robert H. Burr**.
ii. Deloss of Wadsworth, OH; now [1893] aged 84.

	iii.	**Rossiter P.**, d. in Louisville, KY in 1848.
3	iv.	**Alfred James.**

ALFRED JAMES SMITH[3] b. in Camden, Oneida Co., 28 May 1815. At 18 learned trade of harness-maker at Camden and Lee. In 1844 he went to KY, where he remained two years and returned to Camden to mar. 1st **Zabiah C. Stone** in 1846 and removed to Akron, OH. In 1850, after several losses by fire, his family returned to Camden and he went to CA for 21 months. On his return he moved his family to Cape Vincent, Jefferson Co., NY, working at harness-making until 1869 when he removed to Richfield Springs, NY. He is a member of the drug firm of A. J. Smith & Son at that place. He began the business with a nephew, **Augustus L. Stone** of Camden, a competent pharmacist. After **Zabiah** d. 19 Oct. 1868, he m. 2nd **Maria E. Freeman**. Members of the Prestyberian Church. By his 1st mar. he had four children:

i.	**Frederick N.**, dec'd. by 1893.
ii.	**Willard A.**, in partnership with his father.
iii.	**Caroline E.**, at home.
iv.	**Mary A.**, at home.

[BR:709-10]

SMITH, GEORGE C.[1] b. in England or CT 11 April 1780 and d. in West Burlington, Otsego Co., 20 Nov. 1829. He settled in Otsego Co. as a young man. His father, **Dr. George Warden Smith**, was b. in England and came to CT before the Revolution, in which he served as surgeon. He was taken prisoner and confined on a British prison ship. His wife was **Lucinda Crippen**. George[2] m. **Betsey Newman** who was b. 10 Dec. 1789, d. 26 Oct. 1868, d/o **Abraham Newman** who served in the Revolutionary War. Children:

	i.	**Abraham Newman**, b. 7 Jan. 1810.
	ii.	**Lucinda Crippen**, b. 7 April 1812; d. 12 Feb. 1885.
	iii.	**Martha Ritta**, b. 4 April 1814; d. 5 Nov. 1889.
	iv.	**Welcome W.**, b. 8 March 1816; d. 22 Feb. 1901.
	v.	**William Potter**, b. 6 Aug. 1820; d. 25 Dec. 1906.
2	vi.	**Moses Gage.**
	vii.	**Cornelia Betsey.**

MOSES GAGE SMITH[2] b. West Burlington 19 March 1823; d. in McGraw, NY 8 May 1889. At the age of nine he went to Homer, NY to live, his father having died 2 years previous. He lived there with an uncle [unnamed here], attended public schools and learned the trade of tailor. He removed to McGraw and was postmaster there from 1860 to 1872. He m. **Polly Betsey Doud** of McGrawville, NY, d/o **Reuben Griffin** and **Betsey (McGraw) Doud**. Their children were: **George Henry** and **Kittie M.**

[*Genealogical & Family History of Central New York* by William R. Cutter, Vol. 1, p. 213.]

SOUTHERN, EDWARD[1] was b. in Sheffield, England in 1792 and d. 1877. He was s/o **Richad Southern**, an innkeeper of that place. **Edward** was m. in England and bur. his wife within a year, she dying of heart disease. C. 1816 he came to America and brought with him a number of blooded, long-wooled sheep, a successful speculation. He brought some of the sheep to Otsego Co., Town of Laurens. He made three trips back to England, each time bringing with him a number of the same breed of sheep. In Otsego Co. he m. **Mary Herring**, d/o **James Herring**, of town of Laurens. **Edward** d. at the home of his son **James** in Town of Morris. "His 2nd wife was a d/o his first wife's brother, and she was brought to America by her parents when she was but two years old." Children (2nd wife):

  i. **Jane**, widow (1893) of **John Hewell**, res. Village of Morris.
2 ii. **James**.
  iii. **William**, wagon maker of Village of Morris.
  iv. **Elizabeth**, m. **Ransom Shark** of New Lisbon.
  v. **Nettie**, m. **Loren Shark** of Village of Morris.
  vi. **Sarah**, m. **Waring Davis** of Village of Gilbertsville.
  vii. **Edgar**, farmer of Norwich, Chenango Co., NY.
  viii. **Nelson**, meat dealer of Laurens.

JAMES SOUTHERN[2], farmer of Town of Morris, was b. Town of Laurens in 1838. He m. 1859 **Harriet L. Reeve**, then aged 19, a d/o **Ellis Reeve**. She d. 16 Feb. 1887, having borne five children. **James** enlisted as a private in Company C, 152nd NY Volunteer Infantry in 1862 and served 3 years, 15 days. After the way he was Commander of the **George Kidder Post No. 61, G.A.R**. He served several local political offices, keeps a dairy of 12 cows and raises young stock of horses and cattle. Member of Zion's Episcopal Church. Children:

  i. **Son**, d. in infancy.
  ii. **Adelbert**, farmer.
  iii. **James L.**, cheese manufacturer of Holmesville, Chenango Co., m. **Ernestine Conkling**, has 5 children.
  iv. **George R.**, at home running the farm; m. **Jessie Bourne**, d/o **Albert L. Bourne**.
  v. **Jennie M.**, m. **Francis Hathaway**, farmer of Town of Laurens.
[BR:584-85]

SPENCER, NATHANIEL[2] was the s/o **Gerard Spencer**[1] who was bapt. at Stotfold, Beds, England, 25 April 1614, d. at Haddam, CT in 1685. **Gerard's** first wife was **Hannah** and he m. 2nd after 1677 to **Rebecca (Porter) Clark**, who was bapt. at Felsted, County Essex England in 1630. She d. 9 Jan. 1682/3 at Saybrook. **Rebecca** was d/o **John** and **Anne (White) Porter** of Windsor and widow of **John Clark** of Saybrook. **Nathaniel**[2] was one of 13 children and b. c. 1658, d. at Haddam, CT before 1722. He m. 1st c. 1681 to **Lydia Smith**, d/o **Thomas**; **Nathaniel** m. 2nd **Hannah** ---. Children by 1st wife, b. Haddam:

  i. **Lydia**, b. 20 Aug. 1682.
3 ii. **Nathaniel**, b. 15 July 1684.
  iii. **Elizabeth**, b. 18 Jan. 1686/7.

3   iv.   **John,** b. 30 March 1688/9.
    v.   **Mary,** b. 9 June 1692; d. at Wethersfield, CT 28 Oct. 1751, aged 60. She m. 1712 **Samuel Belden,** b. 1689, d. 1771.
    vi.   **Daniel,** b. 20 Aug. 1695, d. 1770/1.
    vii.   **Susanna,** b. 8 Nov. 1696.
    viii.   **Dorothy,** b. 8 March 1699.
    ix.   **Phinehas,** b. 20 March 1701. "A cousin of **Israel** and **Eliphas,** pioneer carpenter. His step-dau. was 1st wife of **Josiah Chase,** the first death in the Town of Maryland." [A:175]

NATHANIEL SPENCER[3] b. at Haddam, CT 15 July 1684, d. (perhaps at Spencertown, NY) after 1761. He m. 1st 25 July 1708 to **Hannah** ---, who d. at Haddam in 1741/42. He m. 2nd at Haddam 27 March 1744 to **Elizabeth Lee,** d/o **Joseph** and **Lois (Plumb) Lee.** Children by 1st wife, b. Haddam:

  i.   **Hannah,** b. 9 Sept. 1709; d. 1 June or 24 July 1787; m. 12 Sept. 1738, **Josiah Brainard** who was b. 1711 and d. 1792 at Haddam Neck.
  ii.   **Nathaniel,** b. 18 July 1712, d. 14 July 1714.
  iii.   **Susanna,** b. 28 Oct. 1714, m. at Middletown 5 June 1735, **Daniel Hubbard** of that place.
  iv.   **Amos,** twin b. 4 Feb. 1716/17; d. young.
  v.   **Elizabeth** (twin), b. 4 Feb. 1716/17.
  vi.   **Lydia,** b. 26 May 1720, d. 5 Feb. 1747.
  vii.   **Nathaniel,** b. 8 April 1723; d. 19 May 1809.
  viii.   **Elisha,** b. 26 Aug. 1725, d. 25 March 1812 (?).
  ix.   **Thomas,** b. 1 June 1728. Could he be the **Thomas Spencer** [CH1:20], the Indian interpreter, res. Cherry Valley, NY?

Children by 2nd wife:

4   x.   **Jonathan,** b. 14 March 1745, d. 1821.
    xi.   **Amos,** b. 23 March 1747. Killed by falling of a tree Jan. 1760.
4   xii.   **Eleazer,** b. 17 May 1748, d. 31 Jan. 1814.
    xiii.   **Eliphaz,** b. c. 1750. He is "possibly the s/o **Nathaniel**[3]," and *The American Genealogist* article "The Four Spencer Brothers" states that he d. in Otsego Co., NY before Feb. 1834. In the 1790 census his family consisted of 3 males over 16, 5 males under 16, and 3 females. His children that have been thus far identified are sons **Henry** and **Alexander,** "and it is believed that **Lois** wife of **Elijah Smith,** and **Lucretia,** wife of **Philip Waite,** were his daughters. Other Otsego County Spencers, such as **Abner, Jesse** and **Seth J.,** who are otherwise unplaced, may belong to this group. **Lois Smith** named her three sons **Seth, Jesse** and **Ira.**"
    xiv.   **Jabez,** bapt. 1 Aug. 1756 at Haddam, CT. He d. at Cato, Cayuga Co., NY 7 June 1835; m. at Granville, Washington Co., NY 21 March 1783, by Elder **Joseph Craw,** a Baptist, **Patience Farnsworth,** b. 10 April 1765, d/o **Josiah Farnsworth** from Groton, MA. **Jabez** lived at Spencertown until age 17 when he moved to New Lebanon, Columbia Co., where he res. when he entered the Revolutionary service in 1775. He removed to

Granville, Washington Co.,NY in 1779, enlisted in a VT outfit. Other places of rs. were Crown Point, Delaware Co. NY and Cayuga Co. In the 1790 census he is found at Westfiedl (now Fort Ann), Washington Co., with 2 boys under 16 and 2 females. In 1800 he was at Whitehall, he and wife 26 to 45, with 2 boys and a girl 10-16, and 3 boys under 10.

xv. **Lois**, bapt. July 1758.
xvi. **Seth**, b. 7 Jan. 1761.

JONATHAN SPENCER[4], b. 14 [17] March 1745 [1744] at Haddam, CT; d. 1 June 1821 in Unadilla. Sisters of **Jonathan** became the wives of **Jeremiah Birch, Jonathan Stark** and **Jeremiah Thornton**. Another sister m. a **Billings** and had a son **Jalleal**. This sister's second husband was **Enos Yale**. [UNA:106-07] Jonathan came to Unadilla from the town of Spencer, CT. He was the s/o **Nathaniel Spencer** and 2nd wife **Elizabeth Lee** d/o **Joseph** and **Lois (Plumb) Lee**. He was counted in the 1790 Federal census of the Otsego Co. area: six white males over the age of 16, four white males under 16 and one white female. In his will, dated 24 March 1821, he names his wife, his sons, one daughter and a grandson. He m. 1st in Dutchess Co., NY 26 Sept. 1764, **Ruth Mudge** who d. 25 Oct. 1780, aged 33; m. 2nd, probably at Warrensburgh (Florida, NY), Tryon [Montgomery] Co. 23 July 1781, **Martha Keech**, b. c. 1765 and d. at Unadilla 11 Dec. 1843. Jonathan and <u>Orrangh</u> [Orange] Spencer are listed as serving in the Revolution in the 3rd Regt., Tryon Co. Militia. Source BR states that after leaving CT he settled in Warren Co., NY and then Otsego Co., being one of the first settlers of Unadilla. **Jonathan** d. a little past the age of 60, his wife [Aunt Patty Spencer] over 80 at the home of her son Barzilla. Children:

i. **Orange**, b. 30 July 1765; had his own household by 1790 when the first census was taken. He was alone in his household as only one white male over the age of 16 and two slaves were counted. In his pension application he stated that he was b. at Richmond, MA; that he was living at enlistment in the winter of 1778-9 in Warrensbush, "now called Florida," Montgomery Co., NY; and that he moved from there about 1784 to Unadilla. He later removed to Vernon, Oneida Co., to Monroe Co., and to Chautauqua Co., last to North East, Erie Co., PA, where he d. 10 Jan. 1843. He m. 4 Dec. 1789, **Sarah Bostwick**, b. 25 Dec. 1768, d. at North East, 24 Jan. 1845. They had eight children.
ii. **Amos**.
iii. **Jonathan Lee**, b. 25 March 1770.
iv. **Miea [Micah]**, b. 4 Dec. 1772.
v. **Nathaniel**, b. 12 Feb. 1782.
vi. **Elisha**, b. 24 May 1784.
vii. **William D.**, b. 1 July 1787.
viii. **Francis U.**, b. 5 Nov. 1789.
ix. **Barsilla**, b. 21 June 1792; d. young.
x. **Barsilla**, b. 5 May 1796.

	xi.	Marcy [Mercy], b. 9 April 1798 [?] m. --- **Allen** and had **Francis Allen**.
	xii.	**Asher**, b. 2 June 1800.
	xiii.	**Solomon**, b. 11 July 1803.

BARZILLA SPENCER[5] was b. on the home farm on the Unadilla River; farmer, a Universalist. He m. in Town of Unadilla **Lovina Todd**, who was b. near Albany and came with her parents to the town when quite young. "She d. one year and one day after her husband and was at the time of her death 87 years old." She was a member of the Baptist Church and two of her brothers were Baptist ministers. They had six children; those named in BR:

	i.	**Orange**, farmer of Unadilla.
	ii.	---, m. **Cornelius Jones** of Bainbridge, Chenango Co.
6	iii.	**Francis**.

FRANCIS SPENCER[6] has always lived in Town of Unadilla where he was b. 4 Aug. 1836. Presybterian Church member. Farmer & mechanic, he m. there **Harriet DeForest** who was b. in the same place, the d/o **Eber** and **Deborah (Barber) DeForest**. Her father was an early settler there, farmer. Children:

	i.	**Brinton**, in 1893 aged 26, single, living at home.

ELEAZER SPENCER[4] b. at Haddam, CT 17 May 1748, d. Spencertown, Columbia Co., NY 31 Jan. 1815. He m. by 1766 **Mary Johnson**, b. at Middletown, CT 9 May 1748, d. at Spencertown 31 Dec. 1822, d/o **Thomas** and **Mary (Johnson) Johnson**. Eleazer served as an officer in the Revolution. Children:

	i.	**Elizabeth** b. 23 Nov. 1766; d. 1831. "Probably" m. as his 1st wife, **John Youngs**, b. c. 1769, d. 1847, of New Baltimore, Greene Co., NY, s/o **John** and **Mehitable (Wiggins) Youngs**.
	ii.	**Mary**, b. 1 Oct. 1768; d. 30 Oct. 1846.
	iii.	**Hannah**, b. 11 Feb. 1771; d. 9 Aug. 1840.
5	iv.	**Eleazer**.
	v.	**Zeruah**, b. 24 Dec. 1775; d. 23 Jan. 1844; m. **Isaac Brainard** of Russia, Herkimer Co., NY.
	vi.	**Enos J.**, b. 17 March 1779; d. 22 March 1833; m. **Sally Rose**, d/o **Nathan** and **Sarah (Haskell) Rose**.
	vii.	**Chloe**, b. 7 Aug. 1781; d. at Austerlitz, Columbia Co., NY 7 Nov. 1844; m. 1812, **Ephraim Bemiss**, who d. 4 June 1843, aged 51. Four childer.
	viii.	**Lovina**, b. 24 Nov. 1783; d. 2 Aug. 1868; m. **William Fitz Youngs**, b. 15 Jan. 1789, d. 28 May 1812, s/o **John** and **Mehitable (Wiggins) Youngs**. Res. Coxsackie, Greene Co., NY. Had dau. **Mehitable Youngs** who m. **William Higgins** who lived in Austerlitz in 1855. **Lovina** was then living with them.
	ix.	**Seth**, b. 21 Oct. 1786; d. 29 Jan. 1794.
	x.	**Lydia**, b. 25 Sept. 1789; d. 19 May 1796.

xi. **Billa**, b. 15 Dec. 1791; d. 10 Feb. 1847, bur. St. Peter's Presbyterian Church Cemetery in Spencertown, NY, unm.

ELEAZER SPENCER[5], b. 23 July 1773, d. in Otsego Co., NY, 26 April 1846. He m. **Peggy** ---, who d. aged 63 before her husband. Settled in Maryland, NY as early as 1816. He d. on his farm aged 73; **Peggy** d. aged 63. Nine children, four now (1893) living:
- i. **Elisha H.**, res. Cattaraugus Co., NY.
- 6 ii. **William C.**
- iii. **George L.**, res. Greene Co., NY.
- iv. **Harvey H.**, res. village of Schenevus.

WILLIAM C. SPENCER[6] b. town of Maryland, NY 18 March 1818. From age 21 he worked on a farm for about three years, and at age 24 was m. to **Elizabeth Hull**, b. Westford, NY in 1821. She is d/o **Nathaniel** and **Polly Hull**, farmers of that town. After his mar. they res. in Westford until 1847 and then removed to Town of Maryland. He was trained as a carpenter and followed that trade along with farming. Member of the Episcopal Church. They had five children, three still (1893) living:
- i. **Eugene S.**, farmer on old home farm.
- ii. **Irving S.**, res. Boston, MA, manufacturer of spring beds.
- iii. **Edith**, m. **Silas Shepherd**, res. Town of Maryland.

JOHN SPENCER[3], s/o **Nathaniel**[2], was b. at Haddam, CT, 30 March 1689; d. at Spencertown, Columbia Co., NY c. 1773. He m. at Haddam 18 Feb. 1713/14 **Mary** ---, b. prob. 1694-6, d. in her 85th year. **John** was the founder of Spencertown, Columbia Co., NY, "but some of his children were already settled when he removed from Haddam, and not all of them accompanied him, though eventually most of them followed him." Children:
- i. **John**, b. 19 May 1715; d. before 1772. He m. at Haddam 26 Sept. 1745, **Martha** ---. It is not known if they res. in Spencertown, NY.
- ii. **Simeon**, b. 12 Aug. 1717, d. c. 1777; m. at Wilton (then in Norwalk), CT 22 Feb. 1743/4, **Rachel St. John**. Removed to Spencertown (now Austerlitz), NY.
- 4 iii. **Joel**, b. c. 1719, d. 25 Feb. 1806.
- iv. **Ahimaaz**, b. c. 1721; m. 1st Middletown, CT 15 Sept. 1743 **Mary Wetmore**. She d. at Spencertown in 1764 and he m. 2nd **Zipporah Brainard**, d. Spencertown in 1767 and he m. 3rd. **Susannah** ---. Several children, none res. Otsego Co.
- v. **Lucy** ("perhaps"), b. c. 1723, d. at Sharon, CT 26 Nov. 1754; m. at Sharon 1 Sept. 1741 **Micah Mudge** b. at Hebron CT in 1741. He d. at Florida, Montgomery Co., NY in 1813. **Micah** m. 2nd 10 Feb. 1755 to **Lucy Chapman**, widow of **Daniel**. They then moved from Sharon to Richmond, MA and New Canaan, Columbia Co., NY. **Ruth**, d/o **Micah** and **Lucy (Spencer) Mudge** m. **Jonathan Spencer**[4].

	vi.	**Nehemiah**, b. Haddam, CT c. 1723-31, d. after 1800; m. **Experience** ---. Res. Chatham and Kinderhook, Columbia Co., NY.
	vii.	**Mary** ("probably"), b. c. 1725; m. at Wilton, CT in April 1746 to **Ephraim Ketchum**.
4	viii.	**Ithmar**, b. c. 1733.
	ix.	**Tabitha** ("perhaps"), b. c. 1736, d. at Whitehall, Washington Co., NY, "probably" after 1817; m. 31 May 1759 **Moses Cleveland** of Windham, b. there 20 July 1736 and d. at Whitehall c. 1790. They res. in East Haddam for a time. **Ithmar** (above) named a dau. **Tabitha**, which may have been this **Tabitha**, if she is his sister.

"Probably" other daus.

JOEL SPENCER[4] b. at Haddam, CT c. 1719, d. at Maryland, NY 25 Feb. 1806. He m. 1st, before 1745, **Mary Bevins** who was b. at Middletown, CT in Nov. 1719, d/o **Thomas** and **Martha Bevins** of Glastonbury, Middletown (Portland) and Haddam. **Joel** m. 2nd **Elizabeth** ---; he m. 3rd, after 1789, **Sarah (Haskell) Rose**, b. at Hardwick, MA 8 April 1747, d/o **Zachariah** and **Keziah (Goss) Haskell**, widow of **Nathan Rose** of Green River, Columbia Co., NY. **Joel** res. at Spencertown, Green River, Rupert VT and Maryland, Otsego Co. Children:

i.	**Israel** b. c. 1743; d. at Steuben, Oneida Co., NY before 1 March 1822. He m.1st c. 1767 **Lydia** --- and m. 2nd before 20 Feb. 1815 **Anna** --- who survived him.
ii.	**Asa**, b. c. 1745, served in the Revolutionary War; of Pittstown, NY by 1782; returned to Green River in 1784/5. He m. **Asenath Graves**, bapt. at East Haddam in 1750, d/o **Jonah** and **Ruth (Crosby) Graves**. Nine children, none listed as res. in Otsego Co.
iii.	**Mary**, bapt. Haddam 12 April 1747.
iv.	**Jerusha**, m. **John Taylor**.
v.	**Desire**, d. young.
vi.	**Desire**.
vii.	**Eunice**.
viii.	**John**, b. 24 May 1758; d. at Busti, Chautauqua Co., NY 25 Aug. 1826; m. at Spencertown 14 Feb. 1782, **Rebecca Spencer** who was b. 14 April 1763, d. 1852. She was d/o **Ithmar** and **Rebecca Spencer**. **John** served as a lieutenant in the Revolution. He came from Maryland, NY to Spencertown where he studied divinity under Rev. **David Porter**, thence to Freehold, Greene Co., NY, thence to Vernon, Oneida Co. In 1807 to Pomfret (now Sheridan), Chautauqua Co. Eleven children, none noted as res. in Otsego Co.
ix.	**Dorcas**, b. 19 Aug. 1760, d. 29 May 1843; m. Nov. 1779 **Amos Spencer**, b. 26 April 1759, d. 13 July 1843.

ITHMAR SPENCER[4], Deacon, b. Haddam c. 1733, d. at Maryland, Otsego Co., NY 1 April 1825, aged 92. He m. **Rebecca** ---, b. c. 1740, d. 2 Aug. 1826 in Maryland, NY. In 1790 census he was listed at Hillsdale, Columbia Co., NY, 3 males over 16 and 6 females. In 1800 1 male and 1 female over 45, 1 female 26-45, one male and one female 16 - 26; and 1 male and 1 female 10 to 16. **Ithmar** was a Revolutionary War soldier in the 9th NY Regiment. He removed his family to Otsego Co., 1796/98 from Hillsdale, then Berkshire Co., MA, now part of Columbia Co., NY. His migration to Otsego was lead by his son **Amos**. Children:

5 i. **Amos**.
 ii. **Rebecca**, b. 14 April 1763; d. 1852; m. 14 Feb. 1782 in Spencertown, NY, **Rev. John Spencer**, s/o **Joel** and **Mary (Bevins) Spencer**. She called herself d/o **Ithmar** and **Rebecca** in her pension application.
 iii. **Louana [Lousanna]**, b. 5 Aug. 1767; res. Maryland, NY in 1844. She m. --- **Willard**, alive in 1880 and res. in **Amos Spencer** homestead.
 iv. **Rhoda**, m. c. 1800 **Gloud Burnside**, res. Potter Co., PA.
 v. **Lovina**, b. 2 March 1772, d. at Maryland, NY 17 Dec. 1853; m. 1791 **Nathaniel Rose**, b. at Chester, MA 6 April 1770, d. at Maryland 19 July 1846. He was s/o **Nathan** and **Sarah (Haskell) Rose** and he d. in Maryland, NY 17 Dec. 1853; bur. Rose-Chamberlain Cemetery near the town.
 vi. **Maryette**.
 vii. **Philip**, b. c. 1776 in Columbia Co., NY, d. at Maryland, NY 30 Nov. 1805. He m. **Lois Peck** 6 Jan. 1830; had children **Harriet** and **Naomi**. He d. in Alexandria, IL 1826.
 viii. **Joel**, b. 1776, d. 1826; m. 1805 **Lois Peck**. He was a noted singer, res. near Muncie, IN. Six children, three d., a dau. m. and went to AR, another dau. m. and went to TX. His surviving son was **Almeron**, b. 1806, d. 1854; m. in 1830 **Rebecca Delaney**, b. 1811, d. 1893.

AMOS SPENCER[5], [Capt. & Deacon] b. 26 April 1759 at Hillsdale, Berkshire Co., MA (now Columbia Co., NY); d. at Maryland, NY 13 July 1843; m. at Hillsdale Nov. 1779 while home on leave from the army, **Dorcas Spencer**, b. 19 Aug. 1760 and d. at Maryland 29 May 1843. She d/o **Joel** and **Mary (Bevins) Spencer**. [DARPI gives his wife as **Dorcas Woodcock**.] At age 16 **Amos** joined the 9th NY Regiment as a private and served throughout the war. After the war he and wife settled in Hillsdale, at least two of his cildren were bapt. at the nearby Green River Congregational Church. **Amos** is bur. on his farm in Town of Maryland, NY, next to Rt. 7 near Potato Creek, halfway between towns of Maryland and Colliers. He was a farmer and innkeeper. Children, 1st nine b. Hillsdale, others in Maryland, NY:

 i. **Simeon**, b. 11 Feb. 1781, d. 8 Aug. 1808; bur. Potato Creek Cemetery, between Maryland and Cooperstown Junction. He m. **Catherine Dean** who was b. c. 1784, d. 11 Jan. 1860. They had one son [not named]. She m. 2nd his brother, **Nathan**.
 ii. **Ithmar A.**, b. 27 Aug. 1782; d. 4 Nov. 1870; m. c. 1805 **Caroline Matilda Houghton** who predeceased him. Ten children. **Ithmar** owned Lot #9 in the Franklin Patent until 1838 when he sold it to his nephew and moved to Unadilla where he d. 4 Nov. 1876. He is bur. there at Evergreen Cemetery.

	iii.	**Deborah,** b. 20 April 1784; unm. and still living in 1855 NY Census with her brother **Uriah;** unm.
	iv.	**Amos,** b. 15 Jan. 1787; d. young.
	v.	**John,** b. 9 Feb. 1789; d. at Blodgett's Mills, Cortland Co., NY, 17 May 1870; m. c. 1811 **Polly Ketchum,** b. c. 1789, d. 2 July 1873.
	vi.	**Isaac,** b. 19 Jan . 1791; d. at Cortland, NY 29 Dec. 1869 at home of his dau. **Mrs. Isaac Edgcomb. Isaac** settled at Blodgett's Mills in 1807 and m. 1st either 1 or 7 July 1816, **Nancy Peabody** who d. c. 1846, d/o **Jireh Peabody. Isaac** m. 2nd **Rebecca** ---, b. in VT c. 1798. In 1807 to Blodgett's Mills, where he died. Ten children.
6	vii.	**Nathan,** b. 4 Jan. 1793; d. 13 Feb. 1865.
	viii.	**Enoch,** b. 6 Dec. 1794, bapt. 25 Jan. 1795 at Green River Congregational Church, Columbia Co., NY.
	ix.	**Calvin,** b. 30 April 1796; d. aged c. 8.
6	x.	**Uriah.**
	xi.	**Desire,** b. 2 Nov. 1799, living in 1878. She m. **Sandford Babcock** and removed to MN. Had children.
	xii.	**Amos P.** b. 22 March 1801, d. 5 March 1837. He m. **Sarah Babcock** who d. 11 April 1864, having m. 2nd **Daniel Wilbur.** Three children.
	xiii.	**Abram,** b. 6 Dec. "1801 or 1806."

NATHAN SPENCER[6] b. Hillsdale, Berkshire Co., MA (now Columbia Co., NY) 4 Jan. 1793; m. 1815 to **Catherine Dean,** his brother's widow. He was owner of lots in the Franklin Patent; one property was purchased from one of his brothers (**Ithmar**) and ultimately sold to his son-in-law, **Henry D. Marble.** Nathan d. in Maryland, NY 13 Feb. 1865. Farmer. Children:

	i.	**Catherine M.** [Catherine Dorcas], b. 6 Dec. 1815; m. 6 Jan. 1834 **Everett Sigsbee Burnside,** local lumberman, sawyer & farmer. She d. 6 Aug. 1911.
	ii.	**Olive R.,** b. c. 1819; m. 1847 **Henry L. Marble.** She d. c. 1906.
7	iii.	**Amos Daniel,** b. 22 Nov. 1822.
	iv.	**Caroline C.,** b. c. 1825; m. **Hiram Bonner,** farmer of Village of Schenevus, Town of Maryland. She was alive as late as 1877.
	v.	**Mary S.,** b. c. 1828; m. **John M. Talmadge,** owner of a brickyard near Schenevus; alive as late as 1877.

AMOS DANIEL SPENCER[7] b. in Maryland, NY; m. there 17 Jan. 1852 to **Mary Elvira Barnes.** He d. there 16 Nov. 1895 & bur. in Amos Spencer Cemetery. For many years he lived with his father in the latter's home on the Crumhorn Mountain side of present Rt. 7. He m. **Mary Elvira Barnes** [see Barnes family entry] and had:

8	i.	**Herbert Eugene.**
	ii.	**Helen R.,** b. 25 Dec. 1855; m. in Maryland 1 Aug. 1872, **Ezra H. Wright;** res. NY City & Oneonta.
	iii.	**Jane B.,** b. 26 June 1862; d. 7 Jan. 1849.
	iv.	**A. Lincoln,** b. Maryland 15 March 1865; m. 24 Feb. 1886, **Lulu Ash (Asch),** res. Oneonta & Philadelphia, PA.

v. **Fenton**, b. 12 Dec. 1868, d. 2 June 1869.

HERBERT EUGENE SPENCER[5] b. on family farm Town of Maryland, NY 3 May 1853. Studied law in the office of his cousin Gen. S. S. **Burnside**. **Herbert** m. at Oneonta at Gen. Burnside's house 27 June 1874 to **Jeannie M. Robinson, d/o Dwight and Mary Eliza (Babcock) Robinson**. They had two daus. A cousin of **Jeannie's** was the wife of Hon. **Daniel Longfellow Plummer**, an Otsego Co. man who had removed to Wausau, WI; banker, railroad man and lumberman. At his urging the Spencers removed to MN to learn the lumber business. They later returned to Oneonta, where **Herbert** worked for the Briggs Lumber Co.

URIAH SPENCER[6] b. 29 May 1798; d. Maryland, NY 10 Oct. 1872 and bur. in Amos Spencer Cemetery. He m. at Maryland in Nov. 1823, **Esther Worden**, b. at Middletown, Greene Co., NY 3 Aug. 1798, d. 15 May 1867. Children:
- i. **Philip D.**
- ii. **Israel.**
- iii. **Martha A.**, m. **Sanders Gurney.**
- iv. **George M.**
- v. **John U.**
- vi. **Joseph.**

[GBW; A:176; OB; A:176; *The American Genealogist* v. 27-30; DARPI; Haddam Vital Records; BR: 598-99; *Herbert E. Spencer, His Ancestors & Descendants* by F. M. Shumway, NY City, 1964. Typescript found in LDS records; BR:724; *Herbert E. Spencer, His Ancestors and Descendants* by Floyd Mallory Shumway, NY, 1964. A typescript found in the LDS collection; UNA:107]

SPENCER, WILLIAM[3] (*William*[2], *Gerard*[1]) (see above for **Nathaniel**[2] family, brother to **William**[2], father of our **William**[3] here). **William**[3] was b. at Haddam, CT 16 Sept. 1699; res. East Haddam in 1747. He m. **Lydia** ---.
Children:
4
- i. **Matthias.**
- ii. **Jeremiah**, b. c. 1725.
- iii. **Margaret** "probably," b. c. 1727; m. 23 June 1746 **John Stewart II.**
- iv. **Mary**, b. 27 Sept. 1736; d. 3 Oct. 1736.

MATTHIAS SPENCER[4] b. c. 1723, d. East Haddam, CT 18 March 1812. He m. 1st at East Haddam on 23 June 1746 **Mercy Rowley**, b. 1729, d/o **Moses** and **Mehitabel (Weeks) Rowley**; **Matthias** m. 2nd c. 1787 **Sarah (Stewart) Hungerford** who was bapt. 1732 and d. at Millington 17 Dec. 1817, aged 86; d/o **John** and **Elizabeth Stewart**, and widow of **Lemuel Hungerford**. Children by 1st wife:
- i. **Deborah**, d. young.
- ii. **Reuben**, b. 7 Dec. 1748; m. **Hannah** ---.
- iii. **Deborah**, b. 11 April 1750, d. Millington 29 Nov. 1833; m. 12 May 1791 **John Annable**, s/o **John** and **Hannah Annable** of Millington.

	iv.	Amaziah, b. 14 April 1753; d. 22 Oct. 1830; m. 13 July 1780 Eleanor Harvey of East Haddam.
	v.	Dorcas, b. 2 Jan. 1755; d. by 1812; m. --- Paddleford.
5	vi.	Timothy.
	vii.	Dau, b. 2 March 1759, d. young.
	viii.	Mehitabel, b. 22 Feb. 1760; m. --- Metcalf.
	ix.	William, b. 31 Dec. 1762. In 1812 res. Butternuts, NY; perhaps m. Thankful Gardner.
	x.	Sarah, b. 23 July 1767; d. before 1812.
	xi.	Daniel, b. 16 Sept. 1770.

TIMOTHY SPENCER[5], b. 6 Nov. 1756; d. at Springfield, NY in 1815. He m. 9 July (1779?) [sic], Sarah Arnold, b. 22 March 1762, d. Spencerport, NY 27 Oct. 1823. She was d/o **Joseph** and **Lucy (Barnes) Arnold**.
Children:

    i.   Daniel, b. 22 Feb. 1780; d. at Spencerport, Monroe Co., NY, 12 Jan. 1835. He m. 1st after 1804, **Anne Willey**, b. c. 1780, d. 17 Sept. 1825, d/o **Benajah Willey** of Ogden, NY. No issue. Daniel m. 2nd **Polly Foster** who was b. 11 Jan. 1798, d. 22 March 1864, d/o **Lebbeus** and **Polly Foster**.

    ii.   Arnold, b. c. 1780; d. in Washington Twp., Macomb Co., MI in 1840. He m. c. 1806 **Lavinia** ---, b. 1789, d. 1852.

    iii.   Austin, b. 24 July 1783; d. at Spencerport, NY 8 Jan. 1868; m. at Otsego Co., 6 Feb. 1806, **Polly F. Elwood**, b. 6 July 1788, d. at Spencerport 30 Jan. 1866.

    iv.   Nancy.
    v.   Sarah.
    vi.   Achsah.
    vii.   Emily.

[*The American Genealogist* v. 27-30.]

STEWART, ALVIN b. Washington, NY ["a Green Mountaineer"] in 1790; it is said that he was one of the most notable trial lawyers of the country in its early years. He early studied medicine and anatomy at Westfield, VT; entered Burlington College in 1809, went to Canada in 1811 and became a professor at St. Armand, Province of Quebec. In 1812 he returned to NY, presumably on account of the War. He went to Cherry Valley to teach in the academy; reading law. In 1815 he taught in KY, later returned to NY and settled again at Cherry Valley, forming a law partnership with **James O. Morse**, which he continued until c. 1832. "His appearance, manners and actions were peculiar, almost ludicrous. . . . His greatest power lay in that he could be humorous or pathetic, acrimonious or conciliating, denouncing the theories, testimony and pleas of the opposition in lofty declamation, and almost in the same breath convulsing his audience, the court and jury included, by the most laughable exhibitions of ridicule or burlesque." He had no personal enmities and no enemies. Later in life he became an anti-slavery agitator and temperance lecturer "pledged to total abstinence, the latter a much needed measure of reform in his case." He was a tall, large boned man, of sallow complexion . . . He

m. a **Miss Holt** and had four daus., two of whom fell victims to the scarlet fever. Those named:
- i. **Mrs. Marsh**; immortalized as "**Jennie Marsh** of Cherry Valley" by the poet **Morris**.
- ii. Dau., m. **Judge Dean** of Poughkeepsie.
- iii. **Alvin**, d. young.

[CH1:142; CENT:77]

SWEET, JONATHAN[1] (*Francis*[5], *Benjamin*[4], *Henry*[3], *John*[2], *John*[1] *RI*) was b. 29 April 1761. In the 3rd quarter of the 18th century his branch of the family removed to Cambridge, NY (then Albany Co., now Washington Co.) with his father. [From Greenwich, RI to Milford area and settled on Outhout Patent 1794.] One of the earliest families in the Town of Milford. At Burlington he united with others in the organization of the Second Baptist Church. He was ordained in 1812 and remained pastor of the church until 1822 when he removed to Diamond Grove, near Jacksonville, Morgan Co., IL. [Removed to Oneida Co. & res. there until his death.] His marriage register, kept from 1812 to 1820, was reproduced in the *New York Genealogical & Biographical Register*, Vol. 61, p. 39 (1930). Children:

2 i. **Amos**.
 ii. **Abel**, to Oneida Co., NY.
 iii. Dau., m. **Asa Eddy**, who came from Hoosick, Rensselaer Co. in 1805 to Milford area. [See Eddy family entry.]

AMOS SWEET[2], b. RI 15 March 1784, to Otsego Co. at age 4. He m. 1807 to **Patience Eldred**, who was b. in RI 15 Nov. 1783. Purchased a tract of land in Milford; farmer. **Amos** d. 23 Jan. 1863 at the home of his son **George W.** as did his wife; **Patience** d. in April 1857. **Amos** and **Patience** had 13 children, four yet living (in 1893). Those named:
- i. **Mary Ann**, b. 15 March 1813. She m. at age 19, **Anson C. Knapp**, who was b. in Danbury CT 5 June 1808. His father was **Salmon Knapp**, who was, so far as is known, a res. of Danbury all his life. When **Anson** was four, his father was drowned, and when he was nine he came to Otsego Co. with his uncle **Levi Stuart**. They settled on a farm in the Susquehanna Valley, one mile east of the village of Milford. In 1877 he removed to the village of Milford, where he d. in 1890 and where **Mary Ann** now lives (1893) with her dau. **Betsey**. Children of **Anson C.** and **Mary Ann (Sweet) Knapp**:
  - a. **Betsey**.
  - b. **Rowena**.
  - c. **Hannah**.
  - d. **Albert S.**, dentist at Cooperstown.

3 ii. **George W.**
3 iii. **John**.

GEORGE W. SWEET[3] b. in Town of Milford, 29 April 1814, on the farm the family first settled on upon coming into the county. He m. 23 Jan. 1868 to **Mary L. Sargent**, b. in village of Milford 15 Nov. 1844. She is

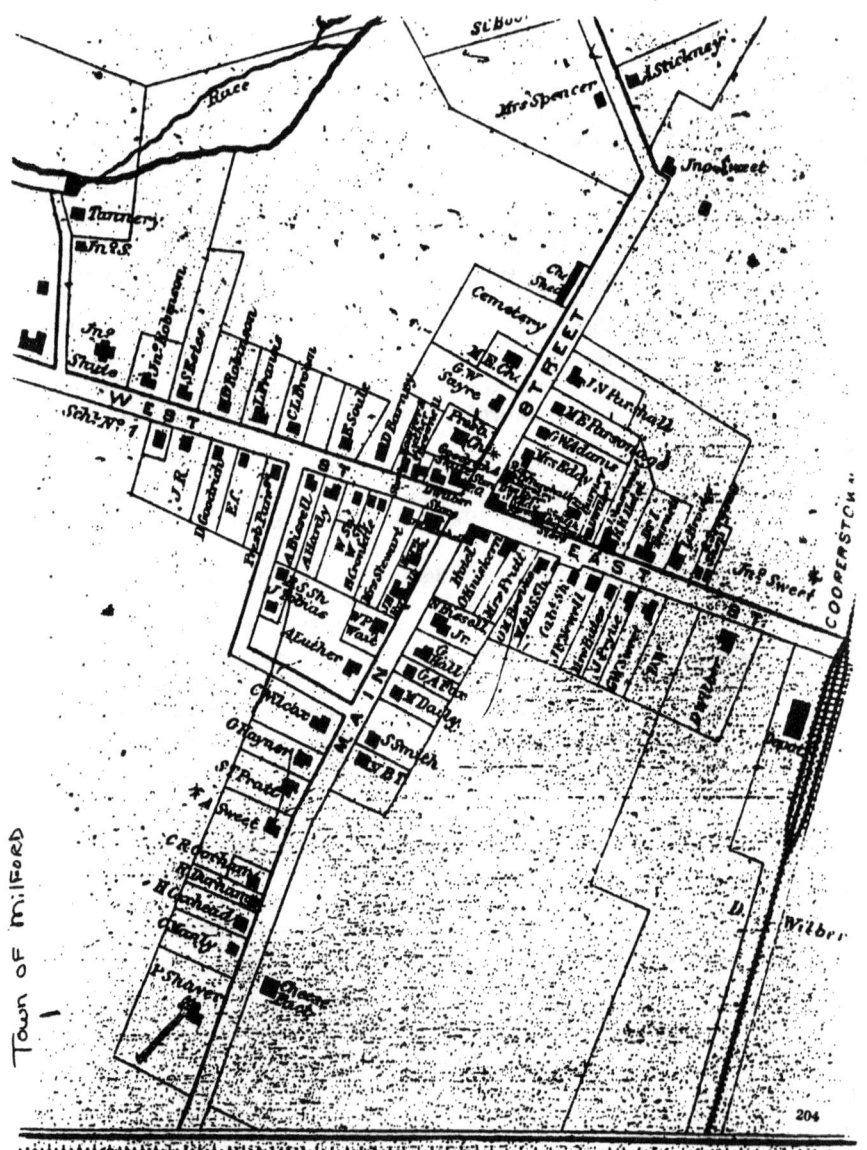

a d/o **Hiram** and **Sally M. (Lyon) Sargent**, her father b. in Otsego Co. 28 Nov. 1809 & d. in Delaware Co. while on a visit to some of his children, 16 March 1888. **Sally Lyon** was b. in Otsego Co. 5 July 1822 & d. in village of Milford 15 Oct. 1864. **Hiram** was a shoemaker and a pioneer tavern keeper in the village of Milford. **George** & wife have one child:
  i.   **George R.**, b. village of Milford 7 May 1870. A printer & Clerk of the Village Board of Trustees. He is mar. & the family attend the Presbyterian Church.

JOHN SWEET[3] b. Town of Milford, NY 10 March 1820; d. there 18 April 1890; farmer. He m. **Adeline Morris** who d. at the age of 75. Members Methodist Episcopal Church. Children, all college graduates:

4 i.   **Dorr R.**
   ii.   **Mary.**
   iii. **Grace.**

DORR R. SWEET[4] b. Town of Milford 11 Nov. 1867; always lived at home with his parents and after their deaths took on management of the family homestead.
[A:193; BR:425 & 661]

SWEET, JOSEPH [P] b. in Coventry, Tolland Co., CT 11 April 1822. He was s/o **Chester Sweet**, b. in Tolland Co., CT and s/o **Capt. Joseph Sweet**. **Chester** moved to Mt. Pleasant, Westmoreland Co., PA for many years, and returned to Tolland Co., where he d. aged 75. **Chester's** wife was **Eliza Peck**. **Joseph** came with his parents to town of Sidney, Delaware Co., NY with his parents when he was 12. Attended the Delaware Literary Institute, and afterward read medicine with Dr. **G. L. Hansley** of Unadilla. He then went to Delhi and continued his studies with Dr. **Jacobs** in 1845 and later took a course of lectures at Pittsfield, MA. He also studied in NY City and at the University of PA, grad. in spring of 1847. He first practiced medicine in Sidney, and in 1850 removed to Unadilla. Physician and surgeon. He m. in Sidney to **Melissa McMullen**, d/o **Archibald** and **Lucretia (Crawford) McMullen**, natives of NY who were m. in Delaware Co. Children:
  i.   **Gaius**, farmer in Town of Sidney, Delaware Co.
  ii.   **Mary**, m. **Dr. Martin** of Otego.
  iii. **Jennie**, m. **Walter Rutherford** of Franklin, Delaware Co.; he dealer in agricultural implements.
[BR:259-60]

TENNANT, JOHN, s/o **Daniel** of RI, m. **Elizabeth Loomis** in CT in 1788, to Springfield in 1788 or 1789. **Elizabeth** d. at their home in Middle Village in 1808, and was buried in the old town cemetery without a durable marker. [See Loomis family entry.] **John** was described as "a man of sterling qualities, great physical strength, a good neighbor and a loyal citizen." He served in both the Revolution and the War of 1812. The death of his wife and son, and the failure of a friend to pay a note that he had signed, caused him to flee to the wilds of MI. After some years he

married again and had a daughter. After the death of his second wife he removed to Ripley, Chautauqua Co., NY and lived with his daughters. He was a cabinet maker. He d. there 20 Feb. 1840 and was bur. in the cemetery at Ripley village. John and Elizabeth's children:
- i. **Alfred**, bur. Springfield.
- ii. **Betsey**, m. **Rev. George Sawin** of Starkville, Herkimer Co., NY, 19 March 1812; bur. Springfield.
- iii. **Orrel**, m. **Rev. John Sawin**, Springfield Center 25 June 1813; bur. Springfield.
- iv. **Alfred Loomis**, bur. Springfield.
- v. **Oliver**, bur. Springfield.
- vi. **Elizabeth**, bur. Springfield.
- vii. **Clarissa**, bur. Springfield.
- viii. **Olive E.**
- ix. **Alvin.**
- x. **Delinda.**

[SPR:215, 235; GBM; *Descendants of Joseph Loomis In America And His Antecedents In the Old World*, by Elisha S. Loomis, 1908]

THATCHER, JOSIAH (CAPT.)[7] (*Daniel*[6] *CT, Josiah*[5] *MA & CT, Deacon Josiah*[4] *MA, Hon. Col. John*[3] *MA, Anthony*[2] *England & MA, Rev. Peter*[1] *England*) b. in Aug. 1764 at Norwalk, CT, s/o **Daniel Tha[lt]cher** and wife **Mary Street**. He was a farmer and a soldier of the Revolution from NY state, and a pensioner. He d. 22 May 1850 at Sidney, NY, and was bur. at Unadilla. **Josiah** m. at Norwalk on 12 Oct. 1782 to **Anna Reed**, also of Norwalk. **Josiah** made his will on 2 March 1841 and it named his wife; a codicil to his will 1 Nov. 1847 states that **Anna** at that time was dec'd. She d. 26 Aug. 1842 at the age of 78. She was a d/o **Matthew Reed** of Norwalk and his wife **Elizabeth Kellogg**. **Josiah** was a founder of St. Mathew's Episcopal Church, where he is bur. in the churchyard. Children:
- i. **Polly Street**, b. 5 Aug. 1786; m. **Capt. Isaac (or William) Smith.**
- ii. **George O.**, b. 6 Oct. 1788 [1789]; d. 21 Feb. 1889; m. **Mary Hughston** who d. 30 Aug. 1888, aged 98 years. They are bur. with his parents at Unadilla.
- iii. **Esther**, b. 20 April 1791; m. **Uriah Seymour.**
- iv. **Harriet**, b. 23 Dec. 1792; m. **Henry Beach.**
- v. **Ann (Nancy) Reed**, b. 28 April 1795; d. 6 April 1868; m. **John Munson Betts.**
- vi. **Amelia**, b. 20 March 1799; m. **Don Carlos Hurd.**
- vii. **Sally**; m. **George Tansley.**
- viii. **Frances**, b. 6 Jan. 1802; d. Dec. 1902; m. 1st **Samuel Betts**, 2nd **Sheldon Griswold.**

[*NYG&B* Vols. 41, 42 +; *At Rest in Unadilla* by Shirley B. Goerlick, 1933; UNA:73; E: 83-4, 58; NYB&G, Vol. 41.]

TILSON, CEPHAS[6] (*Stephen*[5] *MA, Stephen*[4] *MA, Edmund*[3] *MA, Ephraim*[2] *MA, Edmond*[1] *England & MA*), s/o **Stephen** and **Hopestill (Shaw) Tilson**, was b. 15 Dec. 1775 at 6 o'clock A.M. in Greenwich, MA; m. 13 June 1799, **Elizabeth Converse** of Stafford, CT by Rev. **John Willard** of Stafford.

A family Bible gives her name as **Elizabeth C. Hyde**, of Stafford, with no marriage date. They soon moved to Morris, NY. She d. 11 March 1822, aged 41; **Cephas** d. 4 July 1849. Children, all b. Morris, NY:

	i.	**Azuba**, b. 29 Nov. 1799; m. **Rufus Platt** 23 May 1820. Res. Campbell, Stubens [sic] Co., NY.
7	ii.	**Stephen**.
	iii.	**Betsey**, b. 10 April 1803.
	iv.	**Sarah**, b. 3 Oct. 1805.
	v.	**Levina**, b. 11 Sept. 1807.
	vi.	**Alvin Hyde**, b. 30 Aug. 1809.
	vii.	**Mortimer R.**, b. 24 Feb. 1818.
7	viii.	**Cephas S.**

STEPHEN TILSON[7], b. 30 April 1801; m. 2 June 1825 **Phebe M. Platt** of Morris who was b. 18 March 1801. **Stephen** d. 25 June 1876. Children, all b. Butternuts:

i. **Jane E.**, b. 28 May 1828.
ii. **Ansel C.**, b. 2 April 1830; d. 1842.
iii. **Mary L.**, b. 21 July 1832.
iv. **Emily A.**, b. 20 Oct. 1834.
v. **Lewis**, b. 7 Feb. 1837.

CEPHAS S. TILSON[7], b. 24 Feb. 1818 in Morris, m. **Lydia Niles** of Morris who d. 20 July 1846 and **Cephas** m. 2nd **Sylvana Pickens** who d. 18 Dec. 1873, aged 45, and he m. 3d **Paulena McKeon** 19 June 1878. Children of 1st wife:

i. **Henry H.**, b. 30 Jan. 1841; served in the Union Army; d. 4 June 1864 at Pine Bluff, AR.
ii. **Angelia A.**, b. 10 March 1845; d. 19 Jan. 1880.

Children of 2nd wife:

iii. **DeEtta**, b. 28 Dec. 1850; m. **Alfred Winton** 16 July 1891.
iv. **Frank**, b. 22 Oct. 1852; m. 23 Dec. 1872, d. 15 April 1905. [Wife not named.]
v. **Fred**, b. 21 April 1855, m. 2 April 1892, **Lura M. Tilson**; d. 20 Dec. 1908.
vi. **Florence M.**, b. 30 April 1858; unm.
vii. **Charles C.**, b. 9 May 1862; m. 15 Sept. 1887 **Eliza Buell**.
viii. **Elizabeth**, b. 20 May 1867; m. 27 Nov. 1890, **Major R. Stenson**.

[*The Tilson Genealogy from Edmond Tilson at Plymouth, N.E. 1638 to 1911* . . ., Mercer V. Tilson; OB]

TILSON, MOSES[6] (*Stephen*[5] *MA, Stephen*[4] *MA, Edmund*[3] *MA, Ephraim*[2] *MA, Edmond*[1] *England & MA*), brother to **Cephas** above, also s/o **Stephen** and **Hopestill (Shaw) Tilson**, was b. 6 July 1778, at 4 o'clock A.M. in Greenwich, MA. He m. **Mary Young** of Richfield, NY and moved to Butternuts. **Moses** d. 17 Jan. 1845; **Mary** d. 18 Jan. 1869, aged 83. Children, all b. Otsego Co.:

i. **Polly**, b. 22 May 1803; d. 1 Aug. 1882.

| 7 | ii. | **Hopestill**, b. 10 July 1805. |
7	iii.	**Asa**.
	iv.	**Nancy**, b. 23 March 1810.
	v.	**Elizabeth**, b. 7 Sept. 1812.
	vi.	**Julia M.**, b. 3 May 1827.

HOPESTILL TILSON[7], b. 10 July 1805; m. 11 March 1827 **Bennett B. Hull** who was b. 1 Feb. 1799; d. 23 Dec. 1868. In 1888 she was res. Hawleyville, CT. Children (HULL):

i.	**John D.**, b. 3 Jan. 1828.
ii.	**Mary E.**, b. 17 May 1829.
iii.	**Robert E.**, b. 9 June 1832.
iv.	**Ezra M.**, b. 21 May 1835; unm.
v.	**James D.**, b. 23 Sept. 1837.
vi.	**Elizabeth M.**, b. 2 Oct. 1841; d. 27 Jan. 1843.
vii.	**Abel**, b. 8 Jan. 1843.
viii.	**Andrew C.**, b. 27 June 1845.
ix.	**Maranda E.**, b. 20 Jan. 1848; d. 9 Jan. 1855.

ASA TILSON[7], b. 23 Jan. 1808; m. **Camilla A. Pierce** b. c. 1812 in Otsego Co. Children, all b. Otsego Co.:

i.	**Louisa A.**, b. 14 Oct. 1832.
ii.	**Rosalie Mary**, b. 11 Dec. 1834; m. **James Albert Hunt** who was b. 24 March 1825 at Columbia, NY. They had 3 children, all b. Livermore, Humboldt Co., IA.
iii.	**Marcia M.**, b. 30 March 1837.
iv.	**Josiah Pierce**, b. 17 April 1839.
v.	**Hiram E.**, b. 21 May 1841.
vi.	**Ruth A.**, b. 27 April 1843.
vii.	**Marcella E.**, b. 24 April 1843.
viii.	**Sidney M.**, b. 27 Jan. 1848.
ix.	**Albert P.**, b. 24 March 1850.
x.	**Hiram A.**, b. 3 Oct. 1852.
xi.	**Ezra Warren**, b. 2 Dec. 1854.

[*The Tilson Genealogy from Edmond Tilson at Plymouth, N.E. 1638 to 1911* . . ., Mercer V. Tilson; OB; LDS Ancestral File]

WATSON, ARNOLD BEACH [P], b. Rensselaerville, Albany Co. on 12 Aug. 1798. He was the s/o **Josiah Watson** and **Mary Beach** his wife. When Arnold was aged 2 1/2 his mother died, he her only surviving child. When he was aged 4 1/2 his father m. a 2nd wife, who is not named in this source. Arnold removed to Unadilla at age of 23 in 1821 to take charge of a classical school in the town and after two years entered the employ of **Roswell Wright**, and became a partner. He later established the Unadilla Bank. His res. was later part of Bishop's Hotel, after being acquired by **Erastus Kingsley**. Arnold Watson was senior warden and treasurer of St. Matthew's Church for thirty years. He m. 1st **Susan Emily**, d/o **Isaac Hayes**, his partner on 2 Sept. 1827 at Unadilla. She d. 16 July 1863. His 2nd wife was **Augusta Hayes**, sister of his first wife. She d. 20 Dec. 1891,

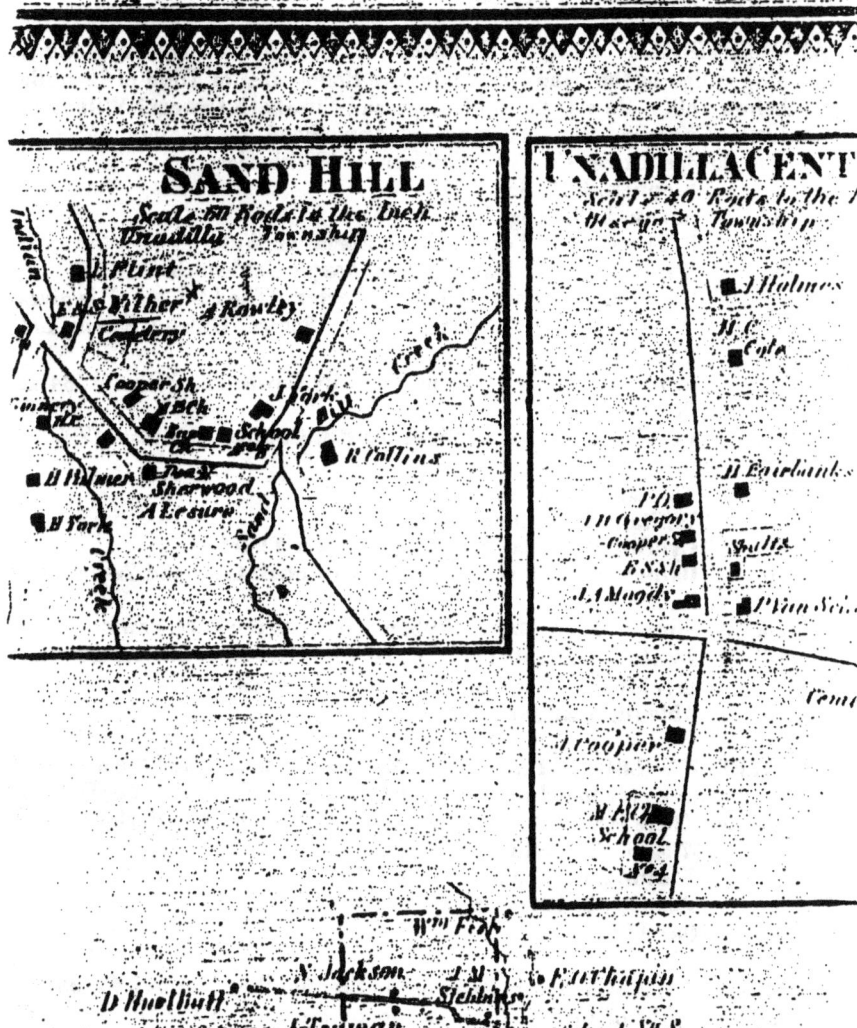

aged 73. **Arnold** was Master of Freedom, Masonic Lodge in Unadilla on the group's reorganization in 1854. He was bur. at St. Matthew's Episcopal Churchyard in Unadilla. Children, all by 1st wife:
- i. **Henry M.**, res. Buffalo.
- ii. **Julia N.**, d. in her youth.
- iii. **Sarah A.**, m. **Rev. E. Folsom Baker.**
- iv. **Susan H.**, m. **Frederick T. Sherman** of Brooklyn.
- v. **William H.**, res. Buffalo.

[UNA:89, 113-16; GBM; A:349-50]

WILBUR, THOMAS[5] (*George*[4] *RI, Thomas*[3] *RI, Joseph*[2] *RI, John*[1] *England & Ma*) settled in the Sand Hill-Hampshire Hollow area of Town of Unadilla before 1800. He was the s/o **George** and **Elizabeth (Sweet) Wilbur** of Little Compton, RI. **Thomas** m. **Ann Wood** b. 17 July 1753 at Wellsbridge, Otsego Co., NY. Children, b. Wellsbridge:

6 i. **Stephen**, b. 12 Jan. 1775.
- ii. **Sarah**, b. 30 Aug. 1776.
- iii. **Rebecca**, b. 17 Feb. 1778; m. **Ebenezer Wait.**
- iv. **Elizabeth**, b. 11 May 1780; m. **Asaph Goldsmith.**
- v. **Susanna**, b. 9 Dec. 1781; m. --- **Porter.** [The LDS Anc. File gives three husbands for **Susanna**: **Mr. Porter, Gideon Sisson** and **Eben Waite.**]
- vi. **Anna**, b. 11 July 1783; m. **Timothy Cowles**, b. 9 Sept. 1784 at Brookfield, VT.
- vii. **Phoebe**, b. 6 Oct. 1785; m. **Austin Cowles**, b. 3 May 1792 at Brookfield, VT.
- viii. **Thomas**, b. 15 Nov. 1787.
- ix. **William**, b. 30 June 1789.
- x. **Cynthia**, b. 1 March 1791; m. **Parker Fletcher.**
- xi. **Daniel**, b. 10 April 1793; m. 1st **Hannah Carr** and 2nd **Sarah Babcock.**
- xii. **Simeon**, b. 24 March 1795; m. **Rebecca Barbara Lewis.**
- xiii. **Judith**, b. 2 Sept. 1797; m. 1st **Asa Cowles**, b. 23 July 1794 at Brookfield, VT and m. 2nd **Chester Cowles.**
- xiv. **Abigail**, b. 22 Jan. 1799.

STEPHEN WILBUR [WILBOUR][6] m. **Martha Goldsmith** and the births of their children are found recorded in the Duanesburgh (Butternuts) Quaker records. There is an obituary for **Stephen Wilber** who d. at Burlington 28 Nov. 1847 aged 68. Children so far identified:
- i. **Susanna**, b. 17th of 11th mo., 1811.

7 ii. **Thomas**, b. 4th of 8th mo., 1814.
- iii. **Daniel G.**

THOMAS WILBUR[7] [assumed to be s/o **Stephen**[6]] m. **Hannah Freeman** and the births of their children are found recorded in the Duanesburgh (Butternuts) Quaker records. He was a farmer of the town of Unadilla. **Thomas'** birth is recorded in BR as May 1814 and his wife in NY state 30 Jan. 1820. They were mar. 4 Nov. 1844. **Thomas** d. aged 73 and **Hannah**

aged 39. Children so far identified:
i. **Jesse**, b. 25th of 10th mo., 1846.
ii. **Jane**, b. 11th of 8th mo., 1848; m. **David Porter Chapman** 7 Sept. 1870 in Otsego Co. [See Chapman family entry.]
iii. **Mary**, b. 6th of 12th mo., 1854.
[LDS Ancestral File; UNA:99; BQ; BR:770-71]

WILLIAMS, DANIEL[1] b. In Johnstown, Providence Co., RI was a direct descendant of **Rev. Roger Williams**, the famous divine of early Colonial days, who founded RI. **Daniel** was a farmer & res. his whole life in RI. His son:
LUTHER WILLIAMS[2], an early settler of Otsego Co., was b. in Johnstown, RI 2 June 1778. "Before attaining his majority" he migrated from his New England home with his brother **Silas** and family and settled in the town of Otsego. He d. there in Jan. 1853. He m. **Phebe Davidson** who d. 27 Dec. 1855 at Fly Creek. She was b. in the town of Kingsbury, 28 Oct. 1787, the d/o **Richard Davidson** of New England birth. **Richard** removed early to Kingsbury, NY and later moved to Otsego, where he bought land adjoining the **Williams**' homestead, where he died. His wife was **Elizabeth Beach** who is thought to have been b. at Sandy Hill, Washington Co. Children:
i. **Thomas**.
ii. **Timothy**.
iii. **Calvin**.
iv. **Elizabeth**.
v. **Edmund**, b. 24 May 1813; bapt. 16 July 1815 at Cooperstown.
vi. **Harriet**, b. 16 July 1815; bapt. 16 July 1815 at Cooperstown.
vii. **Chauncey**, b. 16 Dec. 1817; bapt. 24 May 1818.
viii. **Hannah E.**
ix. **Sherman**.
x. **Phebe**.
[BR:733; NASH 1]

INDEX

Abbott, Albert 99
  Ann Amanda (Griggs) 99
  Caleb 99
  Danford 27
  Dimis 111
  Hannah 27
  Hannah (Wheet) 99
  Harriet 99
  Harriet (Griggs) 99
  Leverette 99
  Mary (Allen) 27
  Melancthon 99
  Olive Miranda (Griggs) 99
  Sally (Sarah) 100
  Samuel 99
Abel, Daniel 48
  Sarah (Crane) 48
Abell, Ann Lucinda (Rockwell) 1, 171
  Eleanor Bryant 1
  Frances H. 1
  Mary 48
  Robert A. 1, 171
Adams, Abner 1, 7
  Almira 116
  Asahel 1
  Asenath 1
  Clarissa 2
  Clarissa (Smith) 2
  David 1
  Desire (Ashcraft) 1
  Dorcas (Paine) 1
  Ezra 2
  Fannie (Lee) 2
  Hannah 2
  Hannah (Pettingall) 2
  Henry 1
  Jared S. 171
  Jennie A. (Rockwell) 171
  Joanna 1
  John 1, 2
  Jonathan 1
  Levi 1, 2
  Lucy 1, 2, 7
  Lydia 1
  Margaret 1
  Margaret (Perkins) 1

Adams, Oren 2
  Ores 2
  Orrin 2
  Polly 2
  Richard 1
  Robert 1
  Ruby 2
  Sarah (Lane) 2
  Thomas 1
Adkins, Sopheria 166
Ainsworth, --- 3
  Alice 3
  Cyril 2
  Darius 2, 3
  Deborah (Bolton) 2
  Edward 2
  Eliza 3
  Elizabeth (Hayward) 3
  Elizabeth (Howard) 3
  Huldah (Peake) 2
  Ira 3
  Levi 3
  Lois 2
  Luther 3
  Mary (Child) 2
  Mary (Westcott) 3
  Mary Ann 3
  Nathan 2
  Polly 3
  Sarepta 2
  Stephen 2
  Stephen Howard 3
  Uldah 2
Alby, Mary 158
Aldin, Julius T. 84
  Roxy A. (Emmons) 84
Alexander, Almira 3
  Amanda 3
  Amanda (Alexander) 3
  Asenath (Foote) 3, 87
  Caleb 3
  Eliphas 3
  Eliphaz 87
  Francis Elizabeth 3
  Laura 3
  Lydia 3
  Mary Ann 3

Alexander, Sarah 3
  Sarah (Howe) 3
  Simeon 3, 87
  William Henry 3
Allen, --- 103
  Amasa 27
  Daniel 160
  Ella 114
  George Clyde 114
  Harriet (Huntington) 114
  Hezekiah 44
  Lorena 114
  Marcy (Mercy) (Spencer) 196
  Margaret (Hardy) 103
  Mary 27
  Melvia (Platt) 160
  Mnetriphantham 42
  Phineas 38
  Polly (Carroll) 38
Almy, Alice Elizabeth (Bowdish) 5
  Augusta Maria (Todd) 4
  Christopher 4
  Edmund James 4
  Elizabeth (Green) 4
  Frances Janet 5
  Henrietta Jeanette 4
  Henry Augustus 4
  Henry Beekman 5
  Joanna Maria 4
  John 4
  Juliana 4
  Maria Sophia 4
  Mary Linn 5
  Mary Louise (Shull) 5
  Walter 4
  Walter Duryea 5
  Wanton 4
  William 4, 5
  William Hoffman 5
  William Walton 4
Alverson, Hannah 78
  Jonathan 78
  Ursula (Church) 78
Ames, A. S. 123
  Albert 152
  Arabella 152
  Ceylon D. 152
  Cheney 152
  Coman Cheney 152

Ames, Eliza (Jarvis) 123
  Emily 152
  Emily (North) 152
  Helen 152
Andrews, Eunice 127, 130
  Rhoda 27
Andrus, Elizabeth 86, 167
  Mary 24
Angel, Ansel 17
  Betsey 18
  Betsy 17
  Jonathan 17
  Maria (Backus) 17
Annable, Deborah (Spencer) 201
  Hannah 201
  John 201
Applebee, Ella Melissa 8
Armstrong, Amy 138
  Avis 6
  Avis (Wing) 5
  Azariah 5
  Charles 159
  Charles H. 6
  Clara B. 6
  David M. 5
  Edith 6
  Elizabeth (Taylor) 5
  Farrand S. 5
  Floyd 5
  Gethro Gray 5
  Hannah (Eldred) 5
  Hopestale 5
  Hopestill 5
  Iris 5
  James 5
  Jethro Gray 5
  Louisa M. (Taylor) 6
  Lydia (Haynes) 5
  Margaret (Washburne) 5
  Maria 134
  Martha (Platt) 159
  May 6
  Minnie (Goodyear) 6
  Morey E. 5
  Morey W. 5
  Nellie 5
  Ominda 5
  Patience (Clark) 5
  Prudence M. (Bailey) 5

Armstrong, Sarah (Wilcox) 5
  Solomon 5, 6
  Solomon Eugene 6
Arnold, --- 3
  Clara M. (Sands) 180
  Frank B. 180
  Gideon 42, 44
  Joseph 202
  Lucy (Barnes) 202
  Mary (Church) 42
  Polly (Ainsworth) 3
  Sarah 202
Asch, Lulu 200
Ash, Lulu 200
Ashcraft, Desire 1
Aspenwall, Caleb 10
  Martha (Aylesworth) 10
Atkinson, John W. 100
  Martha Ann (Staples) 100
Augur, --- 9
  Abner Adams 8
  Abner E. 7
  Adaline 6, 7
  Adeline 7
  Adeline Jeanette 8
  Amelia Maria 8
  Austin Henry 7
  Bessie Caroline 8
  Betsey (Temple) 7
  Charles M. 7
  Charles Morrell 7
  Charlotte Janette 10
  Chlorana (Blakeslee) 6
  Diana (Upham) 7
  Dora (McKennan) 10
  Edward Blakeslee 6, 8
  Elenora (Reynolds) 8
  Elizabeth 6
  Elizabeth (Barney) 7
  Ellen L. (Chase) 7
  Elsie 6
  Emeline (Bowdish) 8
  Ernest Wells 10
  Frank Allen 8
  Frederick Linn 10
  Frederick T. 8
  Frederick Taylor 8
  George M. 1, 6
  George McClellan 7

Augur, George Milton 8, 10
  George Morrell 7
  Gideon 7
  Hannah Elizabeth 8
  Harriet 6
  Harvey 6
  Henry Dorr 8
  Irene (Comstock) 8
  Jane Maples (Wells) 10
  John 6
  John Wells 7
  Leverett 6
  Lorana 6
  Lorena 6
  Lorenel 6
  Lucinda 6
  Lucy (Adams) 1
  Maria Janette 8
  Marion Amelia 10
  Mary (Farmer) 7
  Mary Ellen (Ward) 8
  Mary Ruth 7
  Matty (Latin) 6
  Maurice Edwin 8
  Minerva 7
  Monroe Farmer 7
  Peter 6, 7
  Phebe C. (Hunter) 8
  Rachel (Barnes) 6
  Reuel 6
  Robert 6
  Ruth (Rogers) 6
  Samuel Henry 8
  Sophia (Hoadley) 6
  William Henry 8
Austin, Edward A. 168
  Elizabeth (Rockwell) 168
  Sarah 58
  T. R. 31
Avery, Barsheba 31
  Clusey 69
  Samuel 69
  Sarah 68
Aylesworth, Abigail (Hardy) 103
  Amy 10, 130
  Arthur 10
  Benjamin 10
  Edgar 103
  Isaac Clark 10

Aylesworth, James 10
  Justin 10
  Justis 10
  Lois 10
  Lois (Harrington) 10
  Lovina 10
  Margaret (Harrington) 10
  Martha 10
  Mercy 10
  Philip 10
  Polly 10
  Theodosia (Billings) 10
Babbitt, --- 13
  Albert 11, 14
  Alice (Doty) 14
  Amanda 12
  Amber Melinda 12
  Amy L. 15
  Andrew J. 14
  Ann Elizabeth (Brown) 14
  Anna 12, 14
  Anna (Woodward) 14
  Annis 11
  Bertha 14
  Blanche 14
  Catherine (Popple) 14
  Charles 14
  Charles H. 15
  Chester 11, 12
  Chester Harvey 12
  Clarissa 12
  Cora 14
  Daniel 12, 14
  David 11
  Delia (Trowbridge) 14
  Edward 10
  Elkanah 10
  Ella 14
  Ellen Lydia 14
  Emma Blanche 15
  Emma Charlotte 14
  Emma Wentworth (Luce) 15
  Emogene (Field) 12
  Eunice 14
  Eva Jane (Bailey) 12
  Fannie (Bliss) 12
  Frank A. 15
  Franklin Henry 14
  Frederick D. 15
  Babbitt, Grace May 12, 15
  Harriet A. 15
  Harry D. 14
  Hattie 14
  Herman Albert 12
  Horace 11
  James F. 15
  Jane (Barrs) 14
  Josiah 11
  Lemyra 11
  Linda 11
  Lorena E. 15
  Lucian 15
  Lucien Emory 14
  Lucy (Shipman) 11
  Lucy Ann 11
  Margaret 11
  Marian E. 15
  Mary 11
  Mary (Field) 12
  Mary (Putnam) 14
  Maude 11
  Melinda (Baker) 11
  Milo 11
  Morton L. 15
  Nancy (Luther) 11
  Nancy Maria 14
  Naomi 11
  Noyes Reuben 12
  Obedience (Pringle) 10
  Orlin Holmes 12
  Orrin 14
  Otis E. 15
  Otis H. 15
  Rachel 10
  Reuben 11, 12
  Roswell 14
  Sally 11
  Sally (Delano) 12
  Sally (Head) 11
  Sarah 12
  Sarah A. (Verry) 15
  Semi 11
  Stephen 10, 11, 12
  Susan 14
  Truman 11
  Warren 11, 12, 14
  William 11, 14
  William H. 11

Babcock, Adrian 16
  Alexander Hamilton 17
  Almira 15
  Alva 16
  Amelia Augusta 15
  Anna 16
  Artemas 17
  Betsey 15, 16
  Charles B. 16
  Chester 15, 16
  Clarissa 170
  Cornelia A. (Rockwell) 17
  Cornelia Ann (Rockwell) 170
  Cyrus 17
  Daniel 16
  Desire (Spencer) 200
  Ebenezer 16
  Electa 17
  Eliza Marie 17
  Elizabeth 16
  Enoch 15
  Erastus 16
  Fannella 15
  Francis Ray 16
  Frank Ruggles 17
  Grove L. 16
  H. H. 117
  Harrison Grey Otis 17
  Harvey 16, 17
  Hattie 134
  Hiram 15
  Hobart 16
  Isabelle Foote (Pratt) 16
  Joanna (Low) 16
  John Barton 15
  John Hervey 17
  Jonas 15
  Joshua 170
  Josiah 15
  Julia 123
  Julia Ann Frances 17
  Laura (Huntley) 117
  Lavina (Campbell) 37
  Linn 16
  Lorin 37
  Louisa 15
  Lucia M. (Gregory) 17
  Mary Eliza 201
  Mary Elizabeth 17

Babcock, Mary Jane 17
  Olive 15
  Onill 15
  Pamela 15
  Rebecca (Hubbell) 16
  Richardson 17
  Robert 16
  Roger 16
  Russell Prentice 17
  Samuel 15, 16
  Sandford 200
  Sarah 200, 210
  Sarah Adell 17
  Sarah G. (Fox) 16
  Semantha 15
  Sindey Smith 16
  Sylvina 16
  Thankful 16
  William 16
  William Delos 17, 170
Backus, --- (Buck) 17
  Allen 18
  Betsey (Angel) 18
  Betsy (Angel) 17
  Clara (Wing) 18
  Eunice 118
  Harriet 17
  Harrison 17
  Heman 17
  Heman W. 18
  Hiram 17
  John 17
  Julia 17
  Laura (Goodrich) 17
  Leonard 17
  Lisetta 17
  Maria 17
  Mary 18
  Ora O. 18
  Rebecca 17
  Sally 17
  Solomon 17, 18
  Stanley S. 18
  Timothy 1
  Walter A. 18
Bailey, --- (Dr.) 125
  Eva Jane 12
  Lena D. 74
  Mary (Cole) 126

Bailey, Olive 158
  Prudence M. 5
Baker, Barry J. 19
  Betsy (Rose) 18
  Charles H. 18
  Clarence A. 19
  E. Folsom 210
  Emma (Birdsall) 18
  Enos 18
  Fred M. 19
  Gideon 18
  Harvey 18
  Helen 18
  Hollister 18
  John 145
  Joshua 18
  Lois (Munson) 18
  Looe 145
  Loos 145
  Louise M. 19
  Melinda 11
  Merton H. 19
  Sarah A. (Watson) 210
  Sarah Sabina (Morris) 145
  Tabitha 127
  Thomas 18
  William 22
Balcom, George Webster 44
  Lucy (Church) 44
  Webster 44
Baldwin, Anna 191
  Aschsah 135
  Elizabeth (Patty) (Luce) 135
  Hannah (Luce) 135
  Joseph 135
  Josiah 191
Ballard, Mary 63
  Tryphosia 98
Ballcom, --- 102
  Ann (Hall) 102
  Elizabeth 102
  Isabele 102
Bangs, Hannah 52
Barber, Deborah 196
  Lois 189
Bard, Abeyriene S. (Rockwell) 173
  Carrie (Gosse) 173
  Chester M. 173
  William 173

Barger, Sarah Mustin 5
Baringer, Hannah 91
Barnes, Aaron 19
  Asa 38
  Charles P. 19
  Demas S. 119
  Dennison R. 19
  Elizabeth A. (Hemingway) 101
  Ellen Amanda 101
  Esther (Richardson) 38
  Frank Leslie 19
  Helen Amelia 19
  Jane T. (Wallace) 19
  Jennie L. 19
  Jerry F. 19
  Julia 19
  Lucy 202
  Margaret J. (Platt) 19, 20
  Mary 39
  Mary (Polly) 38
  Mary Elvira 19, 200
  Mary Frances (Hyde) 119
  Mary S. (Spencer) 19
  Pembroke S. 19
  Philip 19
  Rachel 6
  Rebecca R. 19
  S. R. 20
  Sarah 39
  Simeon R. 19
Barney, Ann Elizabeth (Farmer) 7
  Catherine 39
  Elizabeth 7
  Mary (Babbitt) 11
  Rossell 11
  William 7
Barnum, Abiah 21
  Abram C. 21
  Betsey D. 21
  Catherine 21
  Clarinda (Lent) 21
  Cora (Smith) 21
  Daniel A. 21
  Evander W. 21
  Harry E. 21
  Harry G. 21
  Henry C. 21
  Isabella 21
  Jane 21

Barnum, Jonas 21
  Lewis 21
  Lucy 21
  Lucy (Jones) 21
  Orpha (Hamilton) 21
  Sarah 21
  Sibel 21
  Sylvester 21
  Syvil R. 21
Barrett, Almira 22
  Ann E. T. (Henchman) 24
  Anna (Fiske) 22
  Benjamin 22
  Betsey (Gerish) 22
  Betsy 22
  Celia 102
  Clara R. (Griffin) 24
  Elizabeth O. (Gilchrist) 22, 24
  Esther 185
  Fiske 22, 24
  George 22, 24
  Gerrish 22
  Humphrey 22
  James 102
  Joseph 22
  Lucinda (Fancher) 102
  Mabel H. 24
  Oliver 22
  Samuel 22
  Samuel G. 24
  Thomas 22
  William 22
Barrows, Salome 75
Barrs, Jane 14
Barstow, Charles 116
  Dolly 30
  Eunice (Huntley) 116
Bartlett, Daniel 2
  Ezra 2
  Lois (Ainsworth) 2
  Sarah (Cutler) 2, 3
Barton, Lois (Aylesworth) 10
  William 10
Basinger, Daniel 81
  Eliza (Ely) 81
  Hannah 91
  Jacob 81
  Lydia (Ely) 81
Bassett, Emma 131

Bassett, Ida May 26
  Ruth 172
Batchelder, Harriet N. 88
Bates, --- 164
  Betsey (Southworth) 128
  Betsey C. (Whitney) 124
  Catherine (Quackenbush) 164
  Clarissa 157
  Delos A. 128
  Jerusha (Kelsey) 128
  LeRoy 128
  Thomas J. 124
Beach, Elizabeth 211
  Ellen 74
  Harriet (Thatcher) 206
  Henry 206
  Mary 208
  Timothy 123
Beal, Betsey (Jewell) 123, 124
  Reuben 123, 124
Beale, Ann 165
  Hannah 165
  William 165
Beals, --- 134
  Jamima (Knapp) 134
Beardsley, Abbie 145
  Eunice (Moore) 153
  Fanny 119
  Levi 77, 119
  Mary (Polly) Moon 153
  Obadiah 119, 153
  Samuel 119
  Sarah 77
Beatty, Lucinda R. 148
Becker, Elizabeth (Church) 88
Beckley, Clarissa (Dart) 7
  Horace 7
  Jason 7
  Minerva (Augur) 7
Bedent, Phebe 167
Bedicut, Phebe 167
Bedient, Phebe 142
Beebe, Lucretia (Huntley) 115
  Silas 115
  Thankfull 78
Beekman, Maria 4
Belcher, Moses 176
  Susan M. (Roseboom) 176
Belden, Mary (Spencer) 194

Belden, Samuel 194
Bell, Henry 27
  Rosalinda E. 27
Bellamy, Esther 185
Bemiss, Chloe (Spencer) 196
  Ephraim 196
Bemus, Helen Olivia (Morris) 154
  William P. 154
Benedict, Abel 24
  Ada A. 26
  Amiel 26
  Asahel 24
  Betsey 26
  Caroline 28
  Carrie 87
  Clara (Woolson) 161
  Clarissa 26
  Clarissa C. 26
  David 24, 26
  David E. 26
  Deborah (Dibble) 26
  Dorcas 24
  Elijah 24
  Elvira B. 26
  Emily 26
  George S. 161
  Hannah 24
  Hannah (Benedict) 24
  Hannah (Judd) 24
  Hezekiah 24
  Huldah (Hall) 24
  James 24
  Jemima 24
  John 24
  Lizzie B. (Burlbutt) 117
  Lydia (Dibble) 24
  Mary (Andrus) 24
  Mary A. (Murphy) 26
  Obadiah 24, 26
  Philor 26
  Philor T. 26
  Rebecca (Chase) 26
  Rhoda (Dibble) 24
  Sarah 147
  Sarah A. 26
  Solon 117
Benjamin, Sophronia 45
Bennett, Abigail 128
  Addie (Ely) 81

Bennett, Charlotte (Luce) 140
  Phebe (Moisier) 128
  Prince 128
  R. Perry 81
  Sheffield 140
Benson, Frances Augusta (Rockwell) 170
  H. W. 170
  Lucy (Church) 46
Bentley, Charles H. 148
  Hannah (Main) 148
  Oliver C. 148
  Phebe Ann (Nash) 148
Benton, Lovina 136
  Medad 136
Berger, Fanny (Brooks) 151
Betts, Ann (Nancy) Reed (Thatcher) 206
  Frances (Thatcher) 206
  John Munson 206
  Mary Ann (Noble) 150
  Peter J. 150
  Samuel 206
Bevins, Martha 198
  Mary 198, 199
  Thomas 198
Bigelow, Aborn T. 113
  Dorothy Jennett (Huntington) 113
  Elisha 78
  Fanny 78
  Martha Irene 114
  Polly Josephine 113, 114
  Thankfull (Beebe) 78
  Uriah Huntington 114
Billings, Jalleal 195
  Theodosia 10
Bilyea, Ann Elizabeth (Hess) 26
  Carl Thompson 26
  Deborah Ann (May) 26
  Foster Harmon 26
  Harriet Louise (Roberts) 27
  Homer C. 26
  Ida May (Bassett) 26
  J. Glenn 27
  John 26
  Mina (Thompson) 26
Birch, Jeremiah 195
Birdsall, Elizabeth 191
  Emma 18

Birdsall, Harvey 18
  Jane 18
  Sophia 31
Birdsey, Hannah 72
Birdseye, Hannah 72
Bishop, --- 11
  Anna 173
  Elizabeth (Ballcom) 102
  Margaret (Babbitt) 11
  Samuel 102
  Thiray (Ruggles) 177
Black, Elizabeth 180
  Phebe A. (Willey) 46
Blackman, James 93
  Jane 93
Blakeslee, Asher 6
  Chlorana 6
  Gad 6
  Oliver 6
  Ruth 6
Blakslee, Amelia 151
Blanchard, Clarissa (Luce) 136
  Thomas 136
Blelock, Sarah L. 47
Bliss, Clarissa (Boardman) 12
  Eleazer 12
  Fannie 12
  Jennie 56
Blonk, Ann 36
Bloomfield, Allen 27
  Anna 27
  Annette (Ford) 27
  Charles W. 27
  David C. 27
  Elizabeth (Wood) 27
  Eunice (Dunham) 27
  Hannah (Abbott) 27
  Jonathan 27
  Joseph 27
  Libie (McCready) 27
  Rosalinda E. (Bell) 27
  Russell 27
  Samuel 27
Boardman, Abel 28
  Amanda 27
  Annis 27
  Anson 28
  Anson Philetus 28
  Caroline (Benedict) 28

Boardman, Charlotte (Brown) 28
  Clarissa 12
  Clarissa C. (Benedict) 26
  Edward 28
  Edward Y. 28
  Eliza 27, 29
  Eliza (Gunn) 28
  Eliza (Hill) 28
  Elizabeth 27
  Elizabeth (Parks) 28
  Elizabeth (Yale) 26, 27
  Elkanah 26, 28
  Ephraim 26, 27, 28
  Hannah (Wright) 28
  Isaac 27
  L. E. (Hartwell) 29
  Leafy (Seaver) 28
  Levi 27, 29
  Levi Yale 28
  Lois 27
  Mary E. (Perry) 29
  Maryette (Chamberlain) 28
  Mattie E. (Warner) 28
  Philetus 28
  Polly 27
  Ransom Jerome 28
  Rhoda (Andrews) 27
  Samuel 27
  Submit E. (Leach) 28
  Triphena 27
  Verus Nelson 28
  William 28, 29
  Yale 29
Boies, Harriet Lucretia 135
Boles, Hannah 135
Bolles, Julia Ann (Cone) 59
Bolton, Albert Sumner 44
  Deborah 2
  Lemuel 155, 156
  Nancy (Church) 44
  Ruth 155, 156
  Susanna 155
  Susannah 156
Bonner, Caroline C. (Spencer) 200
  Elizabeth 181
  Hiram 200
Bosh, Phoebe J. 100
Bostwick, Clarissa (Benedict) 26
  Jehannah 150

Bostwick, Johannah 150
  Nathaniel 150
  Sarah 195
Botsford, Amos 29
  Amos S. 29
  Annie R. (White) 29
  Annis 29
  Caleb Baldwin 29
  Caroline E. 29
  Caroline L. (Rockwell) 29
  Charles Granderson 29
  Daniel 29, 173
  Elisha 29
  Ezra V. 29
  Frances A. (Brown) 29
  Gideon 29
  Helen Eliza 29, 64
  Henry 29
  Jerusha 29
  Jerushann 29
  Marcus D. 29
  Marcus R. 29
  Martha 29
  Martin 29
  Phebe (Rockwell) 29, 173
  Vine 29
Bottsford, Caroline L. (Rockwell) 171
  Ezra V. 171
  Mary Ann (Upham) 123
  William 123
Bourne, Albert L. 193
  Jessie 193
Bovee, Sarah 164
Bowdish, Alice Elizabeth 5
  Betsey (Keynon) 8
  Emeline 8
  John R. 8
Bowen, Abbie (Cole) 54
  Abby (Cole) 54
  Charles Montague 54
  Esther M. (Jewell) 185
  Jeannie 52
  Mary 85
  Mehitable 45
  Olive 7, 8
  Rose 40
  William M. 185
Bowne, Charles A. 70

Bowne, Elle 70
  Maria 122
  Mary C. 70
Boynton, Sophronia 75
Bradford, Betsey 121
Bradley, Louisa 101
  Mary (Munson) 101
  Titus 101
Brainard, Hannah (Spencer) 194
  Isaac 196
  Josiah 194
  Laura Almira (Huntington) 114
  Lucy (Day) 114
  Lucy (Swaddle) 126
  Mary Almira 114
  Othniel 126
  William 114
  William Orrin 114
  Zeruah (Spencer) 196
  Zipporah 197
Brainerd, Lois 126
Branch, Anna (Franklin) 91
  Leon W. 91
  Sarah M. 63
Brayton, Charles D. 36
Brewer, Adeline 58
  Benjamin 30
  Deborah (Brown) 30
  Ezra B. 167
  John 167
  P. 30
  Sarah (Brown) 30
  Theodosia (Rockwell) 167
Briggs, Amy (Church) 46
  Julia May 137
  Lydia 158
  Mary 172
Brockett, Harriet (Augur) 6
Brockway, Lucy 138
Bromley, Nelson 158
  Ruama H. (Peck) 158
Bronner, Elizabeth 181
Bronson, Charles 99
  Hermon 154
  Mary (O'Connor) 154
Brooks, Amelia (Blakslee) 151
  Benjamin 69
  Esquire 139
  Fanny 151

Brooks, Lemuel 151
  Lucinda 151
  Mary 69
  Thankful (Hickox) 69
Brown, --- (Gen.) 127
  Albert R. 87
  Ann Elizabeth 14
  Anna 127
  Asa 30, 127, 166
  Benjamin 30
  Charlotte 28
  David 27
  Deborah 30
  Diana (Foote) 89
  Dolly (Barstow) 30
  Emeline 30
  Frances A. 29
  George S. 27
  Harriet A. (Fleming) 87
  Harriet E. 146
  Louisa (Wilbur) 30
  Lovina 62
  Lucy (Dow) 30, 166
  Lucy A. (Merchant) 30
  Lucy D. 30
  Maria 30, 122, 166
  Martha 30
  Mary Frances (Jewell) 125
  Mercy 30
  Oliver 30
  Polly (Boardman) 27
  Rebecca 30
  Sarah 30, 127
  Wheeler 30
  William 125
Browning, --- 163
  Charlotte Derbyshire (Prentiss) 163
Brush, Alexander 53
  Mary E. (Cole) 53
Bryam, Frances Rebecca 63
Bryan, Alexander 30
  Amanda (Giddings) 30
  Esther 30
  Fowler P. 30
  Richard 30
  Samuel 30
  Sarah (Platt) 30
Bryant, Anita C. 53

Bryant, Charles H. 53
  Harriet Catherine (Gilbert) 92
  Jennie M. (Cole) 53
  John 92
  William C. 53
Buck, --- 17
Buckley, Elil 143
  Zelpha (Merriman) 143
Bucklin, Patience 54
Buckston, Martha 149
Buell, Adaline M. (Rockwell) 171
  Annie E. 171
  Eliza 207
  Frederick 171
  Porter F. 171
  William R. 171
Bugbee, Elizabeth (Franklin) 2
  Sarepta (Ainsworth) 2
  Willard 2
  William 2
Bulson, Libbie B. (Multer) 147
  Merrill 147
Bundy, Abigail (French) 30
  Barsheba (Avery) 31
  Bertha 33
  David S. 31
  Delilah 33, 191
  Elisha 30
  Emma (Coonley) 31
  Ephraim 31
  Eunice 31
  Gilbert S. 31
  Greeley 33
  Henry 30
  Herman S. 33
  James 31
  James L. 33
  John L. 33
  Julia 31
  Levi 31
  Marilla 31
  Menzo 31
  Moses 31
  Myron H. 33
  Peter 30, 31, 77, 191
  Polly (Oberheiser) 31
  Priscilla (Prentice) 30, 191
  Rebekah 31
  Sally 31

Bundy, Sarah 31
  Sophia (Birdsall) 31
  Stephen A. 31
Burbanks, Hannah 51
Burdick, Amos 33
  Clark 158
  Cyrena 33
  David 33
  Elizabeth (Nichols) 33
  Ida 74
  Jacob 67
  Lois 33
  Lucy (Green) 33
  Marilla 33
  Mary Caroline 67
  Nancy 33
  Phebe 33
  Ruama H. (Peck) 158
  Samuel Hubbard 33
  Sarah 67
  Sarah (West) 67
  Thomas 33, 74
Burgess, Allen 17
  Rebecca (Backus) 17
  Serena 145
Burk, Eliza 56
  James 56
  Maria (Freeland) 56
Burlbutt, Lizzie B. 117
Burlingham, Elizabeth B. 10
Burnside, Adeline Jeanette (Augur) 8
  Catherine Dorcas (Spencer) 200
  Catherine M. (Spencer) 200
  Claude Alexander 8
  Ella Melissa (Applebee) 8
  Ephraim 8
  Everett Sigsbee 200
  Gloud 199
  Gloud T. 159
  Margaret (Wilson) 159
  Nancy 159
  Nellie 188
  Rhoda (Spencer) 199
  S. S. 201
Burr, Abigail (Smith) 191
  Robert H. 191
  Sarah 107
Burras, Mary 188

Burrell, David 123
  Sally (Jewell) 123
Burroughs, Freelove 153
Burton, Relief (Jewell) 124
  Stephen 124
Bush, Harriet 45
  Martha 56
Bushnell, Abisha 46
  Anna 46
  E. W. 27
  Elizabeth (Boardman) 27
  Triphena (Boardman) 27
Butler, Charles A. 93
  Martha D. (Gilbert) 93
  Patty (Luce) 136
Butters, Betsey 64
Cadwalder, Bassett 172
  Gertrude V. (Moody) 172
Cady, Abigail 42
  James 42
Caldwell, Betsey S. 182
  Mary S. 182
Calkins, Clarissa (Church) 42
  Lydia 116
Cambpell, Brayton Allen 36
  Clarence 36
  Deborah 36
  Ellen 36
  Eugene Milton 36
  Frederick 36
  Howard 36
  Icynthia (Meeks) 36
  Josephine 36
  Matilda 36
  Matthew 36
  Rachel (Pomeroy) 36
  Robert 36
  Robert Pomeroy 36
  Samuel 36
  Sarah 36
  Sarah Meeks 36
Campbell, --- (McClean) 33
  Aaron Putnam 35
  Ada C. 37
  Alfred E. 34
  Almira 34
  Alonzo 34
  Alonzo S. 72
  Amy (Dunham) 75

Campbell, Augustus 35
  Bessie B. 35
  Betsey (Hughs) 34
  Caroline 37
  Catherine 35
  Charles Henry 33
  Daniel 157
  Deborah (Putnam) 35
  Dewitt Clinton 35
  Dudley M. 37
  Eleanor 34
  Elizabeth 35
  Elizabeth (Church) 42
  Elizabeth (Griffin) 34
  Ephraim 42, 44
  Evelina Coleman (Stone) 33
  George W. 35
  Gilbert E. 37
  Henry James 35
  James 33
  James L. 35
  James S. 34
  Jane 34, 35
  Jane (Cannon) 33
  Jane Ann 35
  Jeanette 33
  John 37
  John Cannon 35
  Judith Sabrina 34
  Julia C. 36
  Lavina 37
  Loomis J. 37
  Lovina (Lindsley) 37
  Margaret 51
  Margaret (Shannon) 33
  Mariah (Starkweather) 35
  Marion 35
  Martha 51
  Martha (Marsh) 37
  Mary (Jones) 35
  Mary Ann 34
  Mary L. 37
  Matthew 34, 35
  Polly (Peck) 157
  Robert 33, 34
  Sabrina 34
  Sabrina (Crafts) 34
  Sally (DeForest) 72
  Samuel 33, 34, 35

Campbell, Samuel B. 35
  Samuel G. 34
  Samuel R. 33
  Samuel S. 34
  Sarah 33, 34, 35
  Sarah (Elderkin) 34
  Sarah (Mynderse) 33
  Sarah (Simpson) 33
  Sarah M. 35
  Sarah M. (Campbell) 35
  Sylvanus 37
  William 33, 34, 35
  William W. 34
Campfield, Mary 138
Canfield, Amos 134
  Eleanor (Knapp) 134
Cannon, Jane 33
  Matthew 33
Cantwell, Mary A. 172
Carey, --- 149
  Jane (Nash) 149
Carleton, --- 101
Carley, Alanson 38
  Bartholomew 37
  Ebenezer 37
  Eleanor 38
  Ellen 38
  Hannah 38
  Henry 37
  Hepsibath 38
  Joanna (Swift) 38
  Joseph 37
  Orrin 38
  Peter 37
  Polly 38
  Rachel 38
  Sally (Cortright) 38
  Sarah (Washburn) 37
  William 37
Carlisle, Fanny 97
Carlton, Eliza 88
  Moses 88
  Susan 88
Carpenter, Ada 14
  Clarence 14
  Daniel 14
  Ervin 14
  Eunice (Babbitt) 14
  Jane (Wheeler) 14

Carpenter, Maria 14
Carr, Almira (North) 152
  Daniel 152
  Hannah 210
  Huldah 76
Carrick, Amos G. 96
  Evah Martha (Gilbert) 96
Carroll, Amos 38
  Betsey S. 182
  Davis 38, 182
  Ezra 38
  Hannah (Thayer) 38
  John 38
  Lucinda 38
  Mary S. 182
  Nancy 38
  Nathaniel 38
  Phebe 182
  Polly 38
  Robert 38
  Seneca 38
  Watyl 38
  Wotey 38
Carter, Emma Clark (Woolson) 161
  L. 161
Caryl, Alvira C. 40
  Ann (Clark) 38
  Anne 39
  Benjamin 38
  Catherine (Barney) 39
  Catherine (VanAlstyne) 40
  Catherine M. 40
  Christina Ann (Smith) 39
  Clarissa 39
  Eliza (Chase) 40
  Elizabeth Crippen 40, 80
  Ella 40
  Ellen 40, 80
  Emily 39
  Frank B. 40
  Hannah (Lampman) 39
  Helen 40
  Isaac 38, 39
  Joel 38, 39, 40
  John 39
  John Gibson 39
  Jonathan 38
  Joseph 38
  Julius Henry 40

Caryl, Leonard 39, 40, 80
  Lillian 40
  Louisa 39
  Mary 39
  Mary (Barnes) 39
  Mary (Crippen) 40, 80
  Mary (Polly) (Barnes) 38
  Mary Jane 40
  Moses 38, 39
  Nathaniel 38
  Rose (Bowen) 40
  Sarah (Barnes) 39
  Susan 39, 40
  Susan (Snell) 38
Cass, Anson B. 27
  Byron 27
  David O. 27
  Lois (Boardman) 27
  Samuel 27
Casterline, Mary 53
Caswell, Levi N. 98
Caulder, Fannie 154
Chaffin, Abigail (Rogers) 42
  Abigail C. 42
  Charles N. 42
  George Rogers 42
  Hannah 42
  Hannah (Mirick) 42
  Lucy A. (Guild) 42
  Mary 42
  Robert 42
  Samuel 42
  Samuel H. 42
  Tilla 42
  William 42
Chalmers, Edith H. 80
Chamberlain, Addie 160
  Alvin 160
  Delia (Platt) 160
  Hattie V. 163
  Louise 160
  Maryette 28
  Permillia 160
Chapin, Sephe 138
Chapman, Abigail (Church) 44
  Caroline 92
  Catherine 165
  Daniel 197
  Dwight 14

Chapman, Emma Charlotte (Babbitt) 14
  Hattie 66
  Jane (Wilbur) 211
  Lucy 197
  N. C. 93
  Nellie May 14
  Sarah Beth 14
  Susan (Babbitt) 14
  William 92
  Zenas 44
Chase, Benjamin Comfort 8
  Buffum 66
  Comfort 8
  Daniel H. 21
  Eliza 40
  Ellen L. 7
  Hannah (Goddard) 26
  Hannah Elizabeth (Augur) 8
  Jemima 66
  Jemima (Chase) 66
  Josiah 26, 194
  Julia A. (Houghton) 108
  Louisa Prudence (Crandall) 66
  Mary 22
  Mercy (Murdock) 8
  Nathan 7, 8
  Nelson 40
  Olive (Bowen) 7, 8
  Rebecca 26
  Reuben C. 108
  Russell C. 66
  Sarah A. (Benedict) 26
  Seth H. 26
  Syvil R. (Barnum) 21
Chawgo, Catherine 62
Cheney, Amey (Cole) 54
  Arnebua (Knapp) 134
  John 134
  Jonathan 54
  Matilda 152
Cheny, Mary 131
  William 131
Chessbro, Margaret 97
Child, Keziah (Hutchings) 2
  Mary 2
  Samuel 2
Childs, Phoebe 143
Church, Abigail 42, 44, 119

Church, Abigail (Cady) 42
  Alena 47
  Almira (Gere) 44
  Alonzo 45
  Amasa 42, 44
  Amy 46
  Anna (Bushnell) 46
  Anna Maria 46
  Avolin 45
  Caroline 46
  Charles 44
  Clara Emily (Conant) 45
  Clarissa 42
  Cornelia A. 44
  E. A. (Miller) 46
  Eber Ferris 46
  Edward 46
  Eli 42
  Elizabeth 42, 45, 88
  Ellen (Fisher) 45
  Emily 44
  Eunice 46
  Fred L. 46
  Harriet (Bush) 45
  Henrietta 46
  Herbert B. 47
  Huldah 45
  James Cady 42, 44
  Jane (Ealick) 45
  Jane Ann (Hicks) 45
  Jane H. 114
  Jane Hannah 113
  John 42
  John W. 46
  Jonathan 42, 44
  Joseph 42
  Lafayette 45
  Leroy 45
  Lorenzo 45
  Lorinda (Osborn) 44
  Lucinda 72
  Lucy 44, 46
  M. D. 47
  Mari (Putnam) 45
  Mary 42, 44, 46
  Mary (Lowell) 46
  Mary (Porter) 42
  Mary Violet 47
  Mnetriphantham (Allen) 42

Church, Nancy 44
  Origen 44
  Pharcellus 45
  Polly (Mary) 46
  Richard 42, 46
  Samuel 46
  Sarah (Davis) 45
  Sarah (Smith) 44
  Sarah L. (Blelock) 47
  Simeon 46
  Sophronia (Benjamin) 45
  Susan 45
  Susan (Halleck) 45
  Theodore Huntley 46
  Theodosia 46
  Titus 46
  Ursula 78
  Volney 45
  Willard 42, 44, 45
  Willard O. 47
  William 44
Churchill, Sophara 159
Cilley, Polly 78
Clapp, Agnes (Cruttenden) 70
Clark, --- 6
  --- (Nichols) 47
  Abel 48
  Abel H. 84
  Abiah 96
  Ada A. (Benedict) 26
  Alfred Corning 47
  Ambrose 48
  Ambrose Jordan 47
  Ann 38
  Ann (Fitch) 48
  Anna (Whitcomb) 111
  Arthur P. 33
  Bertha (Bundy) 33
  Betsey (Loomis) 48
  Caroline (Jordon) 47
  Clarissa 120
  Cyrus 48
  Daniel 48
  Edward 47
  Edward L. 47
  Edward Severin 47
  Eliza 48
  Elizabeth (Ernst) 84
  Elizabeth (Severin) 47

Clark, Elvira B. (Benedict) 26
  F. Ambrose 47
  Hannah (Kellogg) 48
  Harry 48
  Helen 77
  Israel 48
  James W. 178
  Jared 48
  Jehiel 46
  John 193
  Jonathan 66
  Joseph 48
  Justin 48
  Lorana (Augur) 6
  Lorena (Augur) 6
  Lorenel (Augur) 6
  Lucy (Williams) 48
  Luke 64
  M. M. 26
  Maria 67
  Marsha 48
  Mary 48, 111
  Mary (Abell) 48
  Melinda 66
  Nathan 26, 47
  Nathaniel 48
  Patience 5
  Philotha 48
  Polly (Mary) (Church) 46
  Prudence 64
  Rebecca (Porter) 193
  Robert Sterling 47
  Sarah 12
  Sherman 48
  Simon 48
  Solomon 48
  Stephen Carlton 47
  Susan 48
  Susan (Vanderpoel) 48
  Susannah 58
  Thomas 128
  William 111
Clemmons, Hannah 67
  John 67
Cleveland, Almira (Barrett) 22
  Betsey 139
  George W. 22
  Mary Jane 153
  Moses 198

Cleveland, Tabitha (Spencer) 198
Clinton, Aurelia 102
  George 34
Clyde, Catharine (Wasson) 49
  Catherine 51
  Catherine V. S. (Dorr) 49
  Daniel 49
  Eloise C. 51
  Esther (Rankin) 49
  Frances A. (Crafts) 51
  George C. 49, 51
  James D. 49, 51
  Joseph 49, 51, 80
  Julia 51
  Lafayette 51
  Margaret 51
  Margaret (Campbell) 51
  Martha (Campbell) 51
  Samuel 34, 49
Coard, Clara Adelia 185
  Ella J. (Shaw) 185
  James A. 185
  Josephine Ella 185
Cobb, Charles 44
  Lucy (Church) 44
Colby, Adaline 157
Cole, Abbie 54
  Abby 54
  Abel 51
  Achsah (Pearl) 52
  Ada 52
  Albert B. 51
  Alice A. 53
  Amey 54
  Benjamin 51, 52
  Blanch V. 52
  Byron 52
  Calvin 54
  Caroline (Miller) 52
  Carrie 53
  Carrie M. 52
  Charity (Hazen) 52
  Clayton 52
  Clyde 52
  David 52
  Ebenezer 51
  Eli 52
  Elisha 52
  Eliza 54

Cole, Elizabeth 54
  Elizabeth (Hunter) 53
  Elizabeth (Rockwell) 53, 170
  Elizabeth (Ross) 52
  Emeline O. (Faulkner) 54
  Emerson 52
  Emily 53
  Emma L. 53
  Ernest B. 52
  Eseck 54
  Florence 52
  Hannah (Bangs) 52
  Hobart H. 53
  Hugh 51, 53
  Ida M. 53
  James 51, 53, 54
  Jane (Sisson) 53
  Jeannie (Bowen) 52
  Jennie M. 53
  Joseph 52
  Lee 52
  LeRoy 54
  Lillas 54
  Lovina 54
  Lucinda 54
  Lucretia 54
  Lucy 54
  Marcus 126
  Mary 117, 126
  Mary (Casterline) 53
  Mary E. 53, 54
  Menzo S. 54
  Merton 52
  Nancy 54
  Nancy (Davis) 54
  Nehemiah 54
  Patience (Bucklin) 54
  Paulina 54
  Phebe (Scoville) 126
  Rebecca (Hopkins) 52
  Richard 53, 170
  Sarah E. (Dunn) 52
  Saray (Tobey) 53
  Sisson 53, 54
  Syson 54
  Thomas 54
  William 52, 54
  William J. 52
  William R. 53

Cole, William Rappleye 52
Coleman, Abigail (Nabby) (Dole) 55
  Anson 55
  Arthur 56
  Asaph 56
  Blanche 56
  Caroline 55, 56
  Carrie (Lewis) 56
  Catherine Kimball (Rochester) 55
  Charles Darwin 55
  Clara 56
  Clarissa Harlow (Porter) 55
  Edward 56
  Eliza (Burk) 56
  Elizabeth 56
  Elizabeth (Martin) 55
  Ella S. 56
  Floyd 56
  Franklin 55
  Gertrude 56
  Gertrude (Hines) 56
  Grace 56
  Hamilton 55, 56
  Harriet Cornelia 55
  Homer 55
  Horace 55
  Horatio 56
  James 55
  Jennie (Bliss) 56
  Job 55
  John E. 56
  Laura Kate 55
  Lester 55, 56
  Maria 56
  Marietta (Fake) 56
  Nancy (Sprague) 55
  Nelson 55
  Noah 56
  Noah T. 56
  Norman J. 55
  Polly (Tunnicliff) 56
  Samuel 55
  Sophia 55
Colerton, Bridget 176
Colgrove, Sarah 157
Collier, John A. (Mrs.) 146
Colt, Elizabeth (Gilbert) 93
  James 93
Coman, Fred Lynn 67

Coman, Jennie May (Crandall) 67
Comstock, Albert L. 170
  Albert Ruggles 170
  Catharine Louise 170
  Catharine V. (Rockwell) 170
  Hannah (Taylor) 8
  Irene 8
  Martin Luther 8
Conant, Clara Emily 45
  Rufus 62
  Susanna (Cook) 62
Cone, Adeline (Brewer) 58
  Adonijah (Adanijah/Nijah) 58
  Albert Gallatin 58
  Barbara Fowler 59
  Bertha (McKay) 59
  Caroline 58
  Daniel 58, 59
  David 58, 59
  Elizabeth (More) 59
  Frederick 58
  Frederick Lewis 59
  Gardner 58
  Gilbert 58
  Hannah (Taylor) 59
  Harriet 58, 59
  Hubbell 58
  Ira 128
  Jared 58
  Julia Ann 59
  Julia E. (Fowler) 60
  Julia Eleanor (Fowler) 58
  Katherine Sarah 59
  Lewis G. 59
  Lucy (Williamson) 58
  Lydia (Taylor) 59
  M. S. 60
  Margaret (Hall) 59
  Mary 58
  Mary (Gilbert) 58
  Mary (Skilton) 58
  Mercy A. 58, 60
  Mercy A. (Cone) 58, 60
  Molly 58
  Montie Fowler 59
  Montie S. 60
  Nathaniel K. 58
  Nijah (Adonijah/Adanijah) 59
  Salmon Gardner 58, 60

Cone, Samuel 58
  Sarah 58
  Sarah Alaska 59, 60
  Sarah Ann (Robertson) 59
  Solomon Fowler 59, 60
  Stephen 58
  Susannah (Clark) 58
  Susannah (Hutchinson) 58
  Walter 58
  Wealthy 58
  Wealthy (Kingsbury) 58, 60
  Zachariah 58, 60
Conine, Mary (Cook) 62
Conklin, Eugene 139
  Henry 62
  Mary (Luce) 139
  Phebe (Cook) 62
Conkling, Ernestine 193
Converse, Elizabeth 206
Cook, Abner 60, 62
  Amanda 62
  Amasa 87
  Amasa G. 170
  Ann M. 62
  Anna 63
  Augustus Paul 63
  Benjamin 60
  Catherine (Chawgo) 62
  Catherine Cornelia 63
  Catherine Hamilton (Nichols) 63
  Charles 60
  Clara (Genter) 62
  Clarissa 62, 159
  Clarissa (Hatch) 60
  Constant 60
  Daniel 62
  David 62
  Elizabeth 62
  Frances Rebecca (Bryam) 63
  Hannah 60
  Hannah (Peabody) 60
  Henry 63
  Ira 62
  Isabel (Devol) 60
  Isaiah 62
  James Hamilton 63
  Jerusha (Hatch) 60
  John 60, 62
  Joseph 60

Cook, Joseph Russell 60
  Lovina (Brown) 62
  Lucy 62
  Maria (Kemp) 63
  Martha Frances 63
  Mary 62, 125
  Mary (Elliott) 60
  Mary (Picard) 60
  Mary Ann 62
  Mary Ann (Riley) 62
  Mary Dorothea (Foote) 87
  Mercy 60
  Molly 60
  Nellie 148
  Nelson 60
  Paul 60, 62
  Peabody 60
  Phebe 62
  Philip 60
  Sarah (Mitchell) 60
  Sarah J. (Rockwell) 170
  Sarah M. (Branch) 63
  Susan 62
  Susanna 62
  Susanna (Mattison) 62
  Thomas 60, 62
  William 60, 176
  William Nichols 63
Cooke, Emma Waldron 98
  Fanny G. (Graves) 98
  Howard DeW. 98
  Lionel 98
  Samuel 98
  Samuel W. 98
Cooley, Catharine (Niles) 149
  Mary 120
  William 149
Coolidge, Elizabeth (Coleman) 56
  John H. 56
Coon, Hannah 159
  Keziah 117
Coonley, Emma 31
Cooper, Ann 160
  Elizabeth (Fenimore) 160
  Jacob Morris 145
  James Fenimore 120, 161
  Mary Ann (Morris) 145
  William 30, 120, 160
Cope, Allen Wood 64

Cope, Anne M. (Quincy) 64
 Belle (Morgan) 64
 Benjamin 63
 E. Chalmers Botsford 64
 Edward 63
 Elizabeth 63
 Emily (Kilbourne) 63
 Emma Ballard 64
 Helen Eliza (Botsford) 29, 64
 James 145
 John 63, 145
 Judith 63
 Mary 63
 Richard 63
 Sophia 63
 Thomas 63
 Thomas K. 29
 Thomas Kilbourne 64
 Walter Russell Rockwell 64
Corning, Alexander B. 88
 Alexander Foote 88
 Benjamin T. 88
 Erastus 88
 Erastus B. 88
 Harriet (Foote) 88
 Harriet W. 88
Cornish, Aaron B. 124
 Aaron R. 124
 Abigail C. (Jewell) 124
 Angeline 124
 Ann E. 124
 Elisha 124
 Elvira 124
 Rhoda Jane 124
 Sally T. (Jewell) 124
 Sylvania 124
 Sylvester 124
 Thompson 124
Cornwall, Mary 80
Cortright, Hester 38
 Sally 38
 Thomas 38
Cortwright, --- 138
 Anna (Luce) 138
Cosseler, Elias 191
 Julia (Sleeper) 191
Cotton, Lucy (Gilbert) 92
 Mary (Gilbert) 92
 Samuel 92

Countryman, Eve 106
 John 106
Courter, Grace 80
 Stanton 80
Courwright, Anna (Luce) 138
 George C. 138
Cowen, Chester 5
 Finnet 5
 Ominda (Armstrong) 5
Cowles, --- 143
 Anna (Wilbur) 210
 Asa 210
 Austin 210
 Chester 210
 Judith (Wilbur) 210
 Phoebe (Merriman) 143
 Phoebe (Wilbur) 210
 Timothy 210
Cox, Delilah (Foote) 89
 Mary 145
 Ransom 89
Coye, Esther 145
 Hannah F. 1, 171
Crafts, Alfred 51
 Erastus 34
 Frances A. 51
 Hannah (Burbanks) 51
 Mary Ann (Campbell) 34
 Sabrina 34
Craig, Andrew 44
Crandall, --- 149
 Alcha 187
 Almira 66
 Avery Clinton 64, 67
 Bethiah 64
 Byron Manning 66
 Carrie (Clara) Phebe 66
 Charles L. 67
 Charles W. 66
 Daniel Stanton 64
 Dolly Ann 67
 Eber 64
 Edward 147
 Eliza 67
 Eliza M. 66
 Emily E. 147
 Esther 66
 Esther (Hall) 64
 Esther S. 64

Crandall, Flora L. 67
  Francis E. 64
  Francis O. 67
  Freelove (Niles) 149
  Freeman 66
  George Van Renssalaer 64
  George Van Rensselaer 67
  Hattie (Chapman) 66
  Henry Clark 66
  Henry Denison 64, 66
  Henry Duane 67
  Henry Francis 64
  Henry T. 66
  Jennie May 67
  John 64
  Joseph 64
  Joseph (Rosy Top) 66
  Joseph Hiram 64, 66
  Lewis J. 66
  Loren Burdick 67
  Louisa Jane 66
  Louisa Prudence 66
  Lurana 66
  Lurana Bethiah 64
  Maria (Clark) 67
  Marian Elnora 66
  Marian Elnora (Manning) 66
  Martha L. (Green) 67
  Mary (Dye) 66
  Mary (Todd) 147
  Mary Caroline (Burdick) 67
  Melinda (Clark) 66
  Mercy (Rogers) 67
  Nancy Maria 66
  Phebe (Dye) 66
  Polly (Dennison) 64
  Polly (Webb) 64
  Polly Maria 64
  Polly Marie 66
  Prudence (Clark) 64
  Samuel 187
  Samuel D. 66
  Sarah (Burdick) 67
  Sarita 66
  Truman 66
  William 67
  William B. 66
  William Henry 67
  William Riley 64, 67
Crane, Ellen 36
  Sarah 48
Cranston, Albert D. 69
  Almira (Maltby) 68
  Anne C. 69
  Barzillai K. 68
  Betsey 68
  Eliza (Maltby) 68
  Elizabeth 68
  Elizabeth K. 68
  Elizabeth R. 69
  Eva (Ellis) 69
  Eva M. (Wheeler) 69
  Florence (Small) 68
  George 68
  George Clemmons 68
  George Maltby 68
  Hannah (Clemmons) 67
  Hannah Jane 69
  Hannah Thedasia 68
  Helen 68
  Isah 68
  Janet 68
  Jeremiah M. 69
  John 67
  John C. 69
  John Clemmons 68
  Julia Lambert 68
  Mary 68
  Mary (Quigley) 68
  Mary L. 69
  Mayo A. 69
  Melissa (Newell) 68
  Myron 68
  Peleg 67, 68
  Phebe Ann 67
  Sally (Davis) 68
  Samuel 67
  Samuel J. 68
  Sarah (Avery) 68
  Sarah A. 68
  Sarah E. (Gardner) 69
  Sarah M. 69
  Thomas 67
  William 68
  Zilpha Maria 68
Crapsher, Mary A. (Multer) 147
  Wallace 147
Craw, Joseph 194

Crawford, Lucretia 205
Crippen, Catherine (Barney) 39
  Elizabeth 39
  Emily (Wilsey) 39
  Lucinda 192
  Mary 40, 80
  Moses Henry 39
  Philip 40
  Silas 39, 40
Cromwell, --- 145
Crosby, Enoch 52
  Ruth 198
Cross, Ameail M. 68
  Mary (Cranston) 68
Crozer, Samuel Aldrich 171
Cruttenden, Abraham 69
  Agnes 70
  Albert 70
  Alexis H. 69
  Annotte 70
  Casandana (Noble) 70
  Daniel 69
  Edward 70
  Edway N. 70
  Elle (Bowne) 70
  Ellen 70
  Evoline 70
  Hannah 69
  Harriet (Noble) 69
  Harry Lee 70
  Harvey 69
  Henry L. 70
  Hopestill 69, 70
  Jeremiah 69
  Julia 69
  Julia M. (Stephenson) 69
  Lee B. 70
  Lizzie K. 70
  Lyman 69, 70
  Mary 69, 70
  Mary (Brooks) 69
  Mary C. 70
  Mary G. 70
  Sarah 70
  Sarah (Sally) 69
  William Hubbard 69
Cuer, John 128
Cullinan, Margaret 174
Cully, Anna (Sleeper) 190

Cully, John 190
Cummings, Elias 70, 72
  Esther 120
  Harriet (Smith) 72
  Harris 72
  Leman 72
  Lemon 72
  Lucinda (Church) 72
  Moses 70
  Moses D. 72
  Moses Vanness 72
  Patty 70
  Theresa 72
Curtin, Ella M. (Rogers) 174
  Thomas J. 174
Curtis, --- 111
  Anna (Lull) 74
  Anna W. (Luce) 140
  Caroline (Hudson) 111
  Enoch Arnold 154
  Lottie 74
  Lysander 74, 140
  Mary Jane Elizabeth (Norton) 154
Cushman, Elizabeth (Babcock) 16
  Minerva 16
Cutler, Flora L. (Crandall) 67
  Leo 67
  Leslie 67
  Levi 67
  Levi C. 67
  Llewellyn 67
  Nancy (Miller) 67
  Sarah 2, 3
Cutting, Abby 158
  Clara 185
Daggett, Aseneth 58
Dairy, Sarah 118
Dally, Ana 168
Dante, Mary 40
Darbe, Chester 46
  Theodosia (Church) 46
Darby, Julia (Clyde) 51
Dart, Clarissa 7
Davenport, Caroline B. (Tuller) 125
  Harriet (Tuller) 125
  Helen M. 125
  James S. 125
  Lemuel 27
  Polly (Boardman) 27

Davidson, Phebe 211
  Richard 211
Davis, Benjah 93
  Charles 172
  Delia (Platt) 160
  Elizabeth 85
  Elizabeth A. 93
  Emeline (Rockwell) 172
  Eugene 172
  Francis 88
  Inez (Webster) 172
  John 33
  John A. (Mrs.) 146
  Jonathan 45
  Margaret (Peggy) 133
  Martha 93
  Mary 88
  Mehitable (Bowen) 45
  Nancy 54
  Patty 70
  Sally 68
  Sarah 45
  Sarah (Southern) 193
  Solomon 70
  Syllia 33
  Turner (Mrs.) 140
  Waring 193
  Waterman 160
  William J. 85
Day, --- 109
  Emily V. 133
  Fanny A. (Sisson) 187
  Joseph S. 187
  Levina (Hubbard) 109
  Lucy 114
Dayger, Blanch V. (Cole) 52
  Carrie 52
  William H. 52
De Pomeroy, Ralph 160
Dean, --- (Stewart) 203
  Abbyrene S. (Rockwell) 168
  Catherine 199, 200
  Delos W. 168
  Mary 77
Declems, Mattie 172
DeForest, Abel 72, 74
  Abel Birdseye 72
  Anna 74
  Betsy (Rodgers) 74

DeForest, Charles Augustus 72
  Clark E. 74
  Cora (Slade) 74
  Cyrus Hawley 72
  David 72
  Deborah (Barber) 196
  Eber 196
  Effie 74
  Ellen (Beach) 74
  Eunice (Sweet) 74
  George 74
  Gideon 72, 74
  Hannah (Birdsey) 72
  Hannah (Birdseye) 72
  Harriet 72, 196
  Homer 74
  Ida 74
  Ida (Burdick) 74
  Isaac 72
  J. N. 74
  Jesse 72
  Joseph 72
  Lee 72
  Lottie (Curtis) 74
  Lyman 74
  Maria 72
  Mary (Nutter) 74
  Mason 74
  Mills 72
  Nelletje (Quackenbush) 72
  Sally 72
  Samuel 72
  Susanna (Mills) 72
  Tracy Robinson 72
DeGroat, Mary Adelia 7
  Mary Ruth (Augur) 7
  William H. 7
Delaney, Rebecca 199
Delano, Benjamin 12
  Sally 12
  Sarah (Clark) 12
Denio, Elon 12
  Eunice (Thompson) 12
Denman, Emma Blanche (Babbitt) 15
  George 15
Dennison, Bethiah (Crandall) 64
  George 64
  Polly 64

Denny, Arthur B. 93
Devol, Hannah 60
  Isabel 60
  Joseph 60
  Margaret (Potter) 60
Dewey, Alexander 158
  Elias 171
  Helen Augusta 171
  Isabel Starr 171
  Laura Mayo 171
  Lucretia (Peck) 158
  Mary Rockwell 171
  Priscilla Augusta (Rockwell) 171
  Winifred Coye 171
Dibble, Deborah 26
  Jerusha 159
  Lydia 24
  Maria 142
  Rhoda 24
  Samuel 24
Dickson, Eleanor (Campbell) 34
  Julanna H. (O'Connor) 154
  Mary 154
  Samuel 34
  William H. 154
Diel, John 181
  Margaretha 181
Dietz, Jacob 114
Dimmick, Lucinda 151
Dix, Maggie 187
Dixson, Charles Henry 74
  Emert Monroe 74
  Grace Lillian 74
  Lena D. (Bailey) 74
  Leon Edward 74
  Mary Amelia (Monroe) 74
Doane, Rebecca 1
Dockstander, David A. 182
  Martha (Shaul) 182
Dodge, Catherine Lucretia (Prentiss) 162
  John C. 162
Dole, Abigail (Lawrence) 55
  Abigail (Nabby) 55
  Lawrence 55
  Parker 55
Doliver, Henry 30
Donaldson, Adelia 117
  Kezia (Rockwell) 168

Donaldson, N. 168
Doolittle, Augustus 81
  Harriet (Ely) 81
  Oliver 87
  Sibbil 87
  Susanna 62
Dorman, Syvil 102
Dorr, Catherine V. S. 49
  Russell 49
Dorrill, Lois 154
Doty, Alice 14
  George W. 14
  George Washington 14
  Katherine (Monmouth) 14
Doubleday, Eloise C. (Clyde) 51
Doud, Betsey (McGraw) 192
  Polly Betsey 192
  Reuben Griffin 192
Douglas, John 1
  Mary 115
Douglass, Charles Thomas 154
  Eunice Gertrude (Norton) 154
  Lucy Ann 177
Doun, Helen Louisa (Franchot) 90
  Volkertde Peyster 90
Douw, Elizabeth 174
  Helen Louisa (Franchot) 90
  Volkertde Peyster 90
Dow, Lorenzo 30, 166
  Lucy 30, 166
Dowd, Esther 103
Drake, Dimmis (Kelsey) 130
  Francis 130
Drew, Lorena (Lull) 140
  Samuel 140
Dunbar, Harriet (Luce) 139
  R. H. 139
Dunham, Abigail (Kneeland) 75
  Abigail (Neland) 75
  Abner 75
  Amy 75
  Angeline (McCollum) 75
  Ann 159
  Candice (Irons) 75
  Eber 75
  Eunice 27
  Ferdinand 75
  Gratis (Griffin) 75
  Jabez 75

Dunham, Joanna 75
  John 75
  Joseph 75
  Lois (Hendricks) 75
  Lois (Hendryx) 75
  Lucy (Gillett) 75
  Lucy (Jewett) 75
  Melissa 159
  Obadiah 75
  Obediah 75
  Salome 75
  Sophronia (Boynton) 75
Dunn, Sarah E. 52
Dupee, Charles 76
  E. Elvira (Sewell) 76
  Elsie M. (Greene) 76
  Evaline 76
  Grace Greenwood 76
  Hannah (Williams) 76
  Huldah (Carr) 76
  Imogene 76
  James 76
  Lucius James 76
  Nancy (Turner) 76
  William J. 76
  William James 76
Durrell, Esther 124
Durry, Robert M. 98
  Robey 98
  Sarah Ann (Gray) 98
Dye, Daniel 128
  Eliza (Prosser) 66
  Mary 66
  Phebe 66
  Rhoda 128
  Rhoda (Taft) 128
  Samuel 66
Ealick, Jane 45
Earl, Maria 188
Eastbrook, Haley 134
Eaton, Drucilla 100
  William 100
Eckler, Christina 182
Ecob, James 93
Eddy, --- (Sweet) 203
  Asa 203
  Betsey 85
  Mary (Bowen) 85
  Mathewson 54

Eddy, Noah 85
  Rupel 54
Edgcomb, Isaac 200
Edson, Abigail (Smith) 78
  Anna (Johnson) 76
  Asahel 79
  Aurora (Higgins) 78
  Benjamin 76, 77
  Caroline 76
  Dinah 76
  Dinah (Washburn) 76
  Dorcas 76
  Edna 76
  Elam 76
  Elizabeth 79
  F. (Stetson) 79
  Fanny 79
  Fanny (Bigelow) 78
  Fanny Aurora 78
  Fanny Ursula 78
  Freeman Willard 76, 77
  Hannah 78
  Hannah (Alverson) 78
  Henry Sheldon 77
  Irene 76
  Irene (Howard) 76
  Isaac 31, 77
  Jesse 77
  Joanna 77
  John Milton 78
  Joseph 76
  Julia 76
  Keturah 77, 78
  Keturah (Willis) 77
  Lewis 77
  Lucy 78
  Lydia 77
  Lydia (Wells) 79
  Martha (Thomas) 77
  Martin 76
  Martin Austin 77
  Mary (Dean) 77
  Mary (Jarvis) 79, 120
  Mary (Polly) 79
  Nancy (Mead) 77
  Obed 76, 77, 78, 79
  Olive 78
  Oramel 79
  Orenell 79

Edson, Polly (Fairchild) 79
  Prudence 78, 79
  Prudence (Howe) 78
  Sally (Noble) 150
  Samuel 76, 77
  Sarah (Sally) 79
  Sarah (Sheldon) 77
  Seth 76
  Silence 77
  Stephen Fiske 78
  Theodatus 79
  Theodorus 79
  Thomas 77, 79, 120
  William (Billy) 79
  William Jarvis 79
  Willis 150
  Wyllys 78
Edwards, George 102
  Jeannette (Hall) 102
Eldbree, Martha (Knapp) 134
  Nathan 134
Elderkin, Ella S. (Coleman) 56
  Jennie M. 56
  Mary 56
  Sarah 34
  Sheldon H. 56
Eldred, --- 116
  Andrew 138
  Hannah 5
  Mary (Luce) 138
  Patience 203
  Roxana (Huntley) 116
  Roxy Ann (Huntley) 116
Ellinwood, Sarah (Thompson) 12
  Truman 12
Elliott, --- 162
  Elizabeth 102
  Isabele (Ballcom) 102
  John 102
  Mary 60
  William 102
Ellis, Eva 69
Ellsworth, Mariah 155
  Marla 155
  Marla (Mariah) 155
Elmer, Jemima (Benedict) 24
Elmore, Amos 39
  Louisa (Caryl) 39
Elwood, Arthur Hyde 119

Elwood, Augustus R. 119
  Elizabeth (Cook) 62
  Hannah (Holt) 107
  Joseph 62
  Olive Beardsley (Hyde) 119
  Peter P. 107
  Polly F. 202
Ely, Addie 81
  Adriel 80
  Adriel Gilbert 80
  Adriel S. 80
  Alanson 79
  Benjamin 40
  Benjamin C. 40
  Benjamin Caryl 80
  Benjamin Cornwall 80
  Caroline (Tennant) 81
  Daniel Dana 79
  Edith H. (Chalmers) 80
  Eliza 81
  Elizabeth 80
  Elizabeth Crippen (Caryl) 40, 80
  Ella Louise 80
  Ellen (Caryl) 40, 80
  Eunice Smith 80
  Fitz-James 81
  Frances Amanda 79
  Gertrude Elizabeth 80
  Grace (Courter) 80
  Hannah King (Gilbert) 80
  Hannah Knapp 80
  Harriet 81
  James Edward 79
  Jennie Carlotta 80
  Lorenzo Smith 79
  Lusia (Smith) 79
  Lydia 81
  Lydia Amanda 80
  Margaret 81
  Maria Louisa 79
  Marian Hortense 79
  Martha (Wikoff) 81
  Mary Ann (Snyder) 80
  Mary Lola 80
  Menso White 79
  Nathaniel 79, 81
  Noah 80
  Richard 80, 81
  Samuel 79, 80, 81

Ely, Sarah (Stowe) 80
  Simeon 79
  Smith 81
  Sumner 40, 80, 156
  Sumner Stow 80
  Susan Sophia 79
  Tabitha 156
  Theodore Dwight 80
  Theodore Julius 80
  Warren 81
  William 80
  William Caryl 80
  William Frederick 80
  William H. 38, 40
  William Horace 40, 80
Emmons, Asa 81
  Carlton 81
  Delos W. 84
  Elizabeth 53, 170, 185
  Eunice (Prentice) 81
  Maria (Fairchild) 81
  Mary (Stoddard) 84
  Olive 158
  Roxey Ann 81
  Roxy A. 84
Enderlin, John J. 31
Engell, Mary M. (Seeber) 181
  Oliver G. 181
Ensign, Frances Janet (Almy) 5
  William O. 5
Ernst, Catherine 84
  Elizabeth 84
  Florence A. 84
  George W. 84, 98
  Henry 84
  Henry B. 84
  John Frederick 84
  Louisa 84
Evens, Amy (Kelley) 127
  Simeon 127
Fairchild, Charles Stone 151
  Eunice (Prentice) 81
  Louesa 151
  Lucy Ann (Starkey) 151
  Maria 81
  Polly 79
  William 81
Fake, Barbara 56
  Joseph 56

Fake, Marietta 56
Fancher, Lucinda 102
Farmer, Ann (Whitewell) 7
  Ann Elizabeth 7
  Francis Ford (Miller) 144
  Mary 7
  Richard H. 144
  William 7
Farnsworth, Josiah 194
  Patience 194
Farwell, Almeda 11
  Darius 11
  Florence 11
  Henry 11
  Lowell 11
  Milo 11
  Sally (Babbitt) 11
Fashouris, Maria 106
Faulkner, Emeline O. 54
  Joseph 54
  Judson G. 54
  Mary (Reynolds) 54
  Prudence 154
Fay, T. P. 40
Felkins, Fannie 144
Fellows, Christopher D. 178
Felton, Lucinda 98
  Skelton 98
  Tryphosia (Ballard) 98
Fenimore, Elizabeth 160
Fenner, Deane K. 4
  Juliana (Almy) 4
Fenton, Harriet (Gilbert) 96
  Samuel 96
Ferguson, Eliza 84, 85
  Elizabeth (Davis) 85
  Elizabeth (McClellan) 84
  Fannie 85
  Hannah (Howe) 85
  Isabella 85
  James 85
  James G. 85
  James I. 84
  Jennie (McGowan) 84
  John 84, 85
  Joseph 85
  Margaret 84
  Mary E. 85
  Robert 85

Ferguson, Samuel 84
  Sanford 84
  Thomas 84
  William 84, 85
Ferry, Oliver 101
  Phila 101
Field, Amorett (Yates) 12
  Betsey (Eddy) 85
  Charles 85, 86
  Elisha 86
  Emogene 12
  Esther 86
  George 85
  Hannah 85, 86
  Henry 86
  Huldah 86
  James 85
  Lewis 86
  Marcus 85
  Martha 86
  Mary 12, 86
  Mary (Pearce) 85
  Mary A. 85
  Melinda 88
  Nancy 85
  Nathan 85, 86
  Silas 86
  Stephen 85, 86
  Susan 86
  William 12, 86
  William S. 86
Filkins, Alexander 118
  Andrew 118
  Clarence 118
  Delia (Hyde) 118
  Elizabeth (Hyde) 118
  George 118
  John 118
  Mary 118
  Orson 118
  Timothy 118
Finch, D. O. 86
  Daniel 86
  Daniel A. 86
  David 86
  Elizabeth 86
  Marcus A. 86
  Maria T. 86
  Mary A. 86

Finch, Ruth (Mallery) 86
  Sarah Ann 86
  William T. 86
Fish, Betsey (Cleveland) 139
  Hamilton (Mrs.) 145
  Perlina 139
  Reuben 139
Fisher, Ellen 45
Fisk, Charles 190
  Henrietta 190
Fiske, Anna 22
  Beneezer 22
  Bethia (Muzzy) 22
Fitch, --- (VanHouser) 143
  Ann 48
  Harry 48
  Joanna Maria (Almy) 4
  Justa Maria 152
  Lucy 134
  Lucy G. 178
  Maria 143
  Maria (Vaughn) 178
  Maurice 4
  Prosper 178
  William 143
Flaty, Domenick 36
  Mary 36
Fleming, Alice 87
  Andrew M. 87
  Bishop A. 87
  Caroline I. 87
  Carrie (Benedict) 87
  Catharine (Russell) 87
  Darius S. 87
  Elizabeth A. 87
  Fanny C. 87
  George 86, 167
  George W. 87
  Harriet A. 87
  John F. 87
  Julia (Rockwell) 86, 167
  Lottie 87
  May 87
  Millard A. 87
  Seymour 87
  Willie 87
Fletcher, Cynthia (Wilbur) 210
  Parker 210
Fling, David 136

Fling, Lydia (Luce) 136
Flint, Calista (Holt) 107
  Christopher L. 107
  Elizabeth (Campbell) 35
  Hiram 35
Foot, Clarissa (Sisson) 188
  George 188
Foote, --- (Parker) 87
  Abigail (Kirkland) 88
  Albert 89
  Amelia 89
  Ann G. (Walpole) 88
  Asenath 3, 87
  Augustus 89
  Bernice 87, 88
  Chloe 87
  Cynthia 89
  Daniel 89
  Delilah 89
  Diana 89
  Electa W. (Harwood) 88
  Elias 123
  Eliza (Carlton) 88
  Elizabeth (Church) 88
  Elizabeth (Taylor) 89
  Erastus 88
  Feronia 88
  Harriet 88
  Harriet M. 125
  Harriet N. (Batchelder) 88
  Henry D. 89
  Hiram 88
  Horace 88
  Horatio 88
  Louisa 89
  Lucius 88, 89
  Lydia 87
  Marilla (Ives) 125
  Mary 88
  Mary (Todd) 3, 87
  Mary Ann 89
  Mary Dorothea 87
  Melinda (Field) 88
  Moses 87, 89
  Nathaniel 87
  Obed 3, 87, 88
  Orange 125
  Philena 88
  Reuben 89
  Rhoda Ann 88
  Robert 87
  Sally (Jarvis) 123
  Samuel 87
  Sedate 87, 89
  Sibbil (Doolittle) 87
  Stephen Augustus 89
  Susan (Carlton) 88
  Terressa 89
  Violetta (Mayham) 89
  William 89
  Zephaniah 89
Forbes, James 144
  Mary (Miller) 144
Ford, Annette 27
  Catherine 146
  Isaac 27
  Lydia 27
  Lydia (Reed) 189
  Samantha 189
  Sylvester 189
Forrester, John 60
Foster, B. W. 115
  Jonah 167
  Lebbeus 202
  Polly 202
  Rachel 77
Fowler, Hiram 58
  Julia E. 60
  Julia Eleanor 58
  Sarah (Austin) 58
Fox, Candace 157
  H. I. 147
  Martha A. (Multer) 147
  Sarah G. 16
Franchot, --- 89
  A. C. (Powell) 90
  Antoinette 90
  Auguste 90
  Catharine (Hansen) 90
  Charles F. 91
  Deborah (Hansen) 90
  Francis G. 90
  Helen Louisa 90
  Joanna 90
  Julia A. 90
  Julia Agnes 90
  Lewis 90, 91
  Louis 90, 91

Franchot, Marie Augusta 91
  Meeta 90
  Paschal 90
  Richard 91
Francke, Keno 93
Franklin, Aaron 91
  Amelia (Walrath) 91
  Ann (Kelly) 91
  Anna 91
  Benjamin 91
  Daniel 91
  Elizabeth 2
  Euphenia (McGar) 91
  Hannah (Baringer) 91
  Hannah (Basinger) 91
  Henry 91
  Jabez 91
  James 91
  Jessie 91
  Margaret (Luther) 91
  Moses 91
  Philip 91
  Sarah (Starr) 91
Frazee, Hannah 168
Freeland, James 56
  Maria 56
Freeman, Hannah 210
  Maria E. 192
Freman, Ann 166
French, Abigail 30
  Eunice (Bundy) 31
  Harriet 101
  James 31
  Wyram 31
Frey, Augustus 152
  Henrietta (Swift) 152
Frisbee, Greckson 190
  Irene 190
Frisbie, Deborah 6
Fuller, Elijah 72
  Harriet (DeForest) 72
  Lovinia 96
  Ruth (Robinson) 72
  Sally (Backus) 17
  Thomas 17
  Thomas A. 72
Funston, David F. 187
  Julia W. (Sisson) 187
Furman, Agnes (Scott) 181

Furman, C. 17
  Elizabeth (Scott) 181
  Julia (Backus) 17
  Walter 181
  William 181
Galpin, Abigail 152
  Hepzibah (North) 152
  Horace 152
  Judson 152
  William 152
Gambrill, Ione 172
Gano, Benjamin 92
  Caty 92
  Garratt 92
  Isaac 92
  James 92
  James H. 92
  John 91
Gardineir, W. H. 155
Gardiner, Catherine 164
Gardner, --- 126
  Abram 155
  Amy (Aylesworth) 10
  Hannah 187
  Harriet (Hollister) 106
  Jared 106
  Joanna 155
  Mary J. 106
  Nathaniel 10
  Robert R. 69
  Sarah 69, 155
  Sarah E. 69
  Thankful 202
  William 106
Garland, Helen 173
Garnet, David 117
  Hannah (Hyde) 117
Garratt, Elizabeth (Russell) 177
  John R. 177
  Richard 177
Garrett, Elizabeth 166
  Marcia 177
  Robert 139, 177
  Sarah 177
Gates, Armenia 134
  Azel 134
  Esther 111
  Esther (Smith) 111
  Harriet 114

Gates, Margaret (Holbrook) 134
Genter, Clara 62
George, Grace May (Babbitt) 15
  Hannah 172
  Robert 15
Gere, Almira 44
Gerish, Betsey 22
  Harriet 22
  Samuel 22
Getman, Betsey (Nellis) 106
  Carrie M. (Cole) 52
  Catherine 106
  Clark 52
  George 106
  John 106
  Lynn 52
  Mary 106
Geutier, --- 103
  Mary (Hardy) 103
Gibson, Mary A. 160
Giddings, Amanda 30
Gilbert, --- 146
  Abigail 96
  Abijah 92
  Ann Elizabeth (Lathrop) 93
  Asenath 96
  Benjamin 80
  Butler 93, 96
  Caroline (Chapman) 92
  Catharine Winter 93
  Edwin W. 96
  Elizabeth 92, 93
  Elizabeth A. (Davis) 93
  Eunice A. 96
  Evah Martha 96
  Fitch 93
  Hannah (Thorp) 92
  Hannah King 80
  Harriet 96
  Harriet Catherine 92
  Henry L. 93
  James B. 93
  James L. 93
  Jane (Blackman) 93
  Jay 96
  John 92
  John H. 93
  John T. 92
  Joseph T. 92, 93

Gilbert, Julia Agnes 93
  Kate (Harrington) 96
  Levi 96
  Lloyd 96
  Louis 96
  Louisa 96
  Lucy 92
  Lydia (Smith) 92
  Marietta 96
  Martha (Green) 96
  Martha D. 93
  Mary 58, 92
  Mary (Cornwall) 80
  Mary (Hill) 92
  Morris 93
  Robert W. 93
  Roy Butler 96
  Samuel C. 93
  Sarah 96, 142
  Sylvester 96
  Walker 96
  William 93, 96
  William Butler 96
Gilchrist, Daniel F. 22
  Elizabeth O. 22, 24
  Martha Malvina 182
  Mary (Chase) 22
Gilday, Mary Ellen 8
Gillett, Joel 75
  Lucy 75
  Mary (Kelsey) 75
  Selina 182
Goddard, Edward 27
  Hannah 26
  Hannah (Mann) 27
Goff, Diana (Foote) 89
  Loren 89
Goldsmith, Asaph 210
  Elizabeth (Wilbur) 210
  Martha 210
Goodale, Job 87
  Lydia (Foote) 87
  Nathan 87
Goodman, Dora 100
Goodrich, Almira 97
  Amelia (Foote) 89
  Anna (Strong) 96
  Calvin 96
  Calvin Ripley 97

Goodrich, Chauncey 97
  Cornelia (Winslow) 97
  David 96, 97
  Harriet S. (Norwood) 97
  Josiah H. 97
  Laura 17
  Lovinia (Fuller) 96
  Lucinda 97
  Lydia C. 97
  Margaret (Chessbro) 97
  Martha (Young) 97
  Matilda 97
  Matilda (Young) 97
  Parthena 97
  Polly 97
  Reuben A. 97
  Ruanna 97
  William 96
Goodsell, Frederick E. 35
  Sarah (Campbell) 35
Goodyear, Minnie 6
Goss, Keziah 198
Gosse, Carrie 173
Gott, Irene (Luce) 135
  Isaac 39
  John 135
  Mary D. 39
  Susan (Caryl) 39
  William 39
  William L. 39
Gould, Elizabeth 59
Grace, Lydia E. 121
Graham, Amos 158
  Anna G. (Peck) 158
Graves, Aaron 97
  Abner 97
  Asenath 198
  Benjamin 97
  Calvin 97
  Fanny (Carlisle) 97
  Fanny G. 98
  Frances R. 97
  George C. 97
  Harriette M. 97
  John 97
  John C. 97, 98
  Jonah 198
  Mary 97
  Mary (Graves) 97

Graves, Mary L. (Keyes) 98
  Nelson 97
  Ruth (Crosby) 198
Gray, Alfred 98
  Charles M. 98
  Dorcas (Nash) 148
  Eliza J. (Pratt) 99, 162
  Elizabeth (Rockwell) 53, 170
  George M. 98
  Harmon 86
  John Felton 98, 99, 162
  John Hudson 98
  Lucinda (Felton) 98
  Maria T. (Finch) 86
  Mary (Olmstead) 98
  Nathan 148
  Sarah (Hudson) 98
  Sarah (Sally) Ann 98
  Sarah Ann 98
  William E. 170
Green, --- 142
  Ann 180
  Calvin G. 97
  Eliza (Cole) 54
  Elizabeth 4, 97
  Frances R. (Graves) 97
  Francis 97
  George 97, 181
  Horace D. 67
  Isaac N. 158
  Lois (Johnson) 67
  Lois (Peck) 158
  Lucy 33
  Martha 96
  Martha L. 67
  Rebecca 181
  Robert 97
  Ruth (Lull) 142
  William 97
  Woodward 97
Greene, Elsie M. 76
Gregory, Cyrenius 45
  Elizabeth (Church) 45
  Lucia M. 17
Grey, Eunice 118
Griffin, Annie 29, 173
  Clara R. 24
  Dellia Tidd 100
  Elizabeth 34

Griffin, Gratis 75
Griggs, --- (Smith) 100
  Adeline 100
  Albert 100
  Albert Gurley 100
  Alonzo Melancthon 100
  Ann Amanda 99
  Bertha 100
  Caroline 100
  David 100
  David G. 99
  Dellia Tidd (Griffin) 100
  Dora (Goodman) 100
  Drucilla (Eaton) 100
  Electa G. 99
  Esther 100
  Esther Gurley 99
  Harriet 99
  Harriet Drusilla 100
  Ichabod 99, 100
  Ichabod Newton 100
  Jerusha 99, 100
  Jerusha (Gurley) 99
  John Albert 100
  John Allen 100
  Jonathan G. 99
  Joseph 99
  Julia Ann 100
  Leontia 99
  Levantia 99
  Marilla Duerer 100
  Marilla Mary 100
  Martha Ann (Staples) 100
  Martha Miranda 100
  Mattie Louise 100
  Mercy (Hatch) 99
  Olive A. 157
  Olive Miranda 99
  Phoebe J. (Bosh) 100
  Rhoda P. (Smith) 100
  Sally (Sarah) (Abbott) 100
  Sarah 100
  Sylvester 100
  Thomas 99
Griswold, Abigail 121
  Frances (Thatcher) 206
  Sheldon 123, 206
Grogan, Joanna Maria (Almy) 4
  Richard 5

Grosbeck, Margaret 21
Gross, Anna (Kelsey) 127
  Crowell 127
  Dorothy 127
  Fannie (Ferguson) 85
  Jebez 127
Grover, Abigail 124
Guild, Lucy A. 42
Gunn, Eliza 28
Gurley, Jerusha 99
  Jonathan 99
Gurney, Clara 159
  Eliza (Boardman) 29
  Martha A. (Spencer) 201
  Patience 29
  Samuel H. 29
  Sanders 201
Hacker, Hoysteed 60
Haden, Ambrosia (Rockwell) 172
  Benjamin 172
Haines, Hannah 190
Hale, Abigail (Warner) 101
  Abigail M. (Newton) 102
  Daniel 101
  Elam 101
  Elam W. 102
  Eleazer 101
  Elias E. 101
  Eliza 102
  Elizabeth A. (Hemingway) 101
  Ellen Amanda (Barnes) 101
  Emma (Robinson) 102
  Esther Blake (Jones) 101
  Frederick 101
  Grace Angeline (Todd) 102
  Harriet (French) 101
  Henry 101, 102
  Hiram 102
  James 101
  Joan 101
  Joanna 101
  Joanna (Hale) 101
  John 101
  Katherine 102
  Laura 101
  Louisa (Bradley) 101
  Mary Angeline (Sanford) 102
  Mehitable 101
  Mehitable (Knowlton) 101

Hale, Nehemiah 101
  Orrin 101
  Persis 101
  Philia 101
  Robert 101
  Samuel 101, 102
  Stephen 101
  Warner E. 101
  William H. 102
Hall, --- 116
  --- (Roseboom) 176
  Andy 102
  Ann 102
  Celia (Barrett) 102
  Dorothy (Turnbull) 102
  Ebenezer 24
  Edward 102
  Elizabeth (Elliott) 102
  Esther 64
  George 102
  Hannah Sarah 107
  Huldah 24
  Jeannette 102
  John T. 102
  Lany 133
  Lydia (Huntley) 116
  Margaret 59
  Perry 133
  Phineas 116
  Polly 107
  Samuel 107
  William 176
  William W. 102
Halleck, Susan 45
Hamilton, Orpha 21
  Silas 21
Haner, Nancy 52
Hanford, Harriet (Cone) 59
  Thomas 59
Hannay, Ella 123
  J. Ella 122
  John 123
  Julia (Babcock) 123
Hansen, Catharine 90
  Deborah 90
  Derrick 90
Hansley, G. L. 205
Hard, Lovina 168
Hardenburg, Rebecca 133

Hardy, Abigail 103
  Albert 103
  Charles 103
  David 103
  Elbridge G. 103
  Elizabeth 103
  Esther 103
  Esther (Dowd) 103
  Fidelia 103
  George W. 103
  James 103
  Jeremiah 103
  John 103
  Joshua 103
  Maline 103
  Margaret 103
  Margaret (Low) 103
  Mary 103
  Mary (Pembleton) 103
  Oscar 103
  W. R. 104
  William 102, 103
  William Henry 103
  William R. 103, 105
Harkness, Harriet N. (O'Connor) 154
  James 154
Harp, Albert 153
  Susan (North) 153
  Susie 153
  William C. 153
Harrington, Allen B. 180
  Caroline 142
  Daniel 10
  Elizabeth (Scott) 180
  Kate 96
  Lois 10
  Margaret 10
  Mary S. 180
  Polly (Aylesworth) 10
Harris, Daniel 107
  Julia 117
  Phebe (Holt) 107
Harrison, Freeman 190
  John Sleeper 190
  Mary (Sleeper) 190
Hart, --- (Deacon) 152
  Anna Mena (Moore) 161
  Jacob 161

Hart, Mercy (North) 152
  Phebe 161
Hartshorn, Samuel 27
  Silence 27
Hartwell, L. E. 29
Harvey, Eleanor 202
  Ellen Maria (Nash) 148
  Eva May 148
  Flora Belle 148
  Robert Henry 148
  William B. 148
Harwood, Electa W. 88
  Nathan 88
Haskell, Keziah (Goss) 198
  Sarah 196, 198, 199
  Zachariah 198
Hastings, Alice 107
  Jane (Toles) 130
Hatch, Clarissa 60
  Elizabeth (Jarvis) 120
  Jerusha 60
  Malatiah 120
  Mercy 99
Hathaway, Francis 193
  Jennie M. (Southern) 193
Hatheway, King J. 31
Havens, Abigail 81
Hawks, Mary 143
Hayden, J. Lasell 40
  Louis O. 40
  Mary (Dante) 40
  Mary Jane (Caryl) 40
Hayes, Anna 150
  Augusta 208
  Isaac 123, 150, 208
  Susan Emily 208
Haynes, Lydia 5
Hayward, Elizabeth 3
Hazen, Caroline Rebecca 187
  Charity 52
Head, Sally 11
Heath, Sybil 152
Heaton, --- (Niles) 149
  Jacob 149
Hebbard, Linden 58
  Wealthy (Cone) 58
Hemingway, Elizabeth A. 101
Henchman, Ann E. T. 24
  David 22, 24

Henderson, Alonzo W. 99
Hendricks, Lois 75
Hendryx, Lois 75
Herkimer, Clarissa (Cook) 62
Herring, Hannah (Carley) 38
  James 193
  Mary 193
  Nathan 38
Herrington, Mary L. (Campbell) 37
  Matthew 37
Hess, Ann Elizabeth 26
Hewell, Jane (Southern) 193
  John 193
Hewlett, Edna (Edson) 76
  James 76
  Lewis 89
  Terressa (Foote) 89
Hickox, Frances A. 168
  Thankful 69
Hicks, --- 158
  Caroline H. (Peck) 158
  Jane Ann 45
Higby, Emily (North) 152
  William 152
Higgins, Aurora 78
  Mehitable (Youngs) 196
  William 196
Hill, Burdick 27, 28
  Caroline (Edson) 76
  Eliza 28
  Mary 92
Hillman, Hannah 53
Himrod, Mary (Cruttenden) 70
Hines, Gertrude 56
Hisbis, --- 149
  Hannah M. (Nash) 149
Hitchcock, Arthur 29
  Caroline E. (Botsford) 29
  Miranda 159
  Robert B. 29
  William B. 29
Hoadley, Deborah (Frisbie) 6
  Ralph 6
  Sophia 6
Hoag, Amy 150
  Caleb 128
Hodges, Darius 45
  Susan (Church) 45
Hoke, Catherine (Getman) 106

Hoke, Clara C. 106
  Earl 106
  Ella (Nellis) 106
  Eve (Countryman) 106
  Flora 106
  Frederick 106
  Frrederick 103
  Hattie 106
  Margaret (Shaver) 103
  Margaret (Shaves) 103
  Maria (Fashouris) 106
  Mary J. (Gardner) 106
  Melvin 106
  Menzo 106
  Morris 106
  Philip 103, 106
  Richard 106
Holbrook, Margaret 134
Holdridge, Austin 158
  Betsey Ann (Peck) 158
Holl, Betsy 144
  Edward 144
  Susanna 144
Hollenbeck, Andrew 182
  Viola (Shaul) 182
Hollis, Marie Antoinette (Luce) 138
  Richard 138
Hollister, Harriet 106
Holman, Thomas S. 177
Holmes, John 163
  Lucretia 162, 163
Holt, --- 203
  Calista 107
  Camilla 107
  George 106, 107
  Hannah 107
  Hannah (Holt) 107
  Hannah Sarah (Hall) 107
  Joseph 135
  Joshua 107
  Lovisa 107
  Lucy 107
  Nathan 107
  Nathaniel 106
  Patty (Luce) 135
  Phebe 107
  Phebe (Lay) 106
  Polly (Hall) 107
  Sarah 107

Holt, Sarah (VanBenschoten) 107
  Sarah (VanScoten) 107
  Walter 107
  William 106
Hone, Fannie 125
Hoose, Amanda (Boardman) 27
  Anna Maria 185
  Richard 27
Hopkins, Abigail 103
  Alice (Hastings) 107
  Benjamin S. 107
  Celia Aurelia (Kelsey) 129
  Charles J. 107
  Cornelius 107, 160
  Elizabeth (Townsend) 52
  Henry Brown 129
  J. Belle 107
  Jane (Platt) 107
  Joseph 52
  Kate A. 107
  L. Jane (Platt) 160
  Rebecca 52
  Sarah (Burr) 107
Houghton, Abigail 108
  Alva 108
  Angeline 108
  Anna (Spencer) 108
  Anna H. 108
  Anna S. 108
  Caroline Matilda 199
  Daniel 108
  Daniel E. 108
  Eliphalet E. 108
  Eunice (Wilder) 108
  Israel 108
  Jacob 108
  Jerehamel 108
  John 108
  Josephine E. 108
  Jotham 108
  Julia A. 108
  Lester 108
  Lydia 108
  Lydia D. 108
  Madison 108
  Martha (Wheelock) 108
  Mildred 108
  Milton W. 108
  Rhoda 108

Houghton, Sarah (King) 108
  Tomason 108
  William A. 108
  William H. 108
House, Mary 55
Hovey, E. O. 117
  Ellen Maria (Nash) 148
  Eva May 148
  Flora Belle 148
  Julia (Huntley) 117
  Robert Henry 148
  William B. 148
Howard, Clarence C. 35
  David 27
  Eliza (Boardman) 27
  Elizabeth 3
  Irene 76
  Mary 153
Howe, Artemas 187
  Dorcas (Edson) 76
  Fanny (Parker) 187
  Hannah 85
  James Cole 81
  Joseph 76
  Keturah (Edson) 78
  Mary Ann 187
  Prudence 78
  Sarah 3
  Willis 78
  Wyllys 78
Hoxie, --- (Slade) 100
  Ezra 100
  John 100
  Martha Miranda (Griggs) 100
Hoyt, Rebecca 170
Hubbard, Abigail 109
  Asena 109
  Beulah 109
  Bridget 108
  Daniel 194
  Drusilla 109
  Ebenezer 108, 109
  Elijah 109
  Eri 109
  Finnet (Cowen) 5
  George 108
  Jared 109
  John 108
  John Lester 109

Hubbard, Julia 109
  Levi 109
  Levina 109
  Lydia 109
  M. (Lester) 109
  Molly (Simons) 108
  Phebe 109
  Polly 109
  Reuben 109
  Samuel 109
  Selinda 109
  Serena 109
  Simon 5
  Susanna (Spencer) 194
  William 109
Hubbell, Rebecca 16
Hubby, John 80
  L. 80
Hudson, --- 111
  Ann E. 111
  Caroline 111
  Cyril 111
  Cyrus 109
  Eliza (Toby) 109
  George 109
  Henry 111
  Horace 111
  M. Lavintia 111
  Mary (Clark) 111
  S. T. 110
  Sally (Windsor) 109
  Samuel 109
  Sarah 98
  Sarel 111
  Stephen T. 109
  William 111
Hughs, Betsey 34
Hughston, Mary 206
Hull, Abel 208
  Andrew C. 208
  Bennett B. 208
  Elizabeth 197
  Elizabeth M. 208
  Ezra M. 208
  Hopestill (Tilson) 208
  Jacob 46
  James D. 208
  John D. 208
  Maranda E. 208

Hull, Mary (Church) 46
  Mary E. 208
  Nathaniel 197
  Polly 197
  Robert E. 208
Hun, Marcus T. 48
Hungerford, Lemuel 201
  Sarah (Stewart) 201
Hunt, James Albert 208
  Ransom 31
  Rosalie Mary (Tilson) 208
Hunter, Elizabeth 53
  Lucinda 151
  Lucinda (Dimmick) 151
  Peter 151
  Phebe C. 8
Huntington, --- 111, 115
  Adaline Julia (Parmalee) 114
  Adeline Julia (Parmale) 113
  Agnes Church 114
  Alice Parmalee 114
  C. P. 114, 115
  Caroline D. 115
  Delia 111
  Dimis (Abbott) 111
  Dorothy Jennett 113
  Edwin Wells 111
  Eliza (Stillman) 111
  Ephraim 158
  Esther Elvira 114
  George Mason 114
  H. E. 115
  Harriet 114
  Harriet (Gates) 114
  Harriet (Saunders) 114
  Helen Wilson 114
  Jane H. (Church) 114
  Jane Hannah (Church) 113
  Jennet (Mosley) 111
  Jonas Gates 114
  Laura Almira 114
  Martha Adeline 111
  Mary A. 113
  Mary Amelia 113
  Mary Ann (Walker) 114
  Mason Coggswell 111, 114
  Olive L. (Peck) 158
  Royal 111, 114
  S. G. 112, 113

Huntington, Samuel 111, 113, 114
  Samuel Gates 113, 114
  Simon 111
  Solon 114
  W. V. 115
  William Stillman 114
Huntley, Aaron 115
  Albert Phineas 115
  Alonzo 116
  Anna 115
  Betheul 46
  Betsey 115
  Calvin 115, 116, 117
  Carlos 117
  Caroline (Lord) 115
  Charles 116
  Charles Russell 116
  Clorinda (Talbot) 116
  Daniel 115
  Elisha 116
  Eliza 116
  Elknah 115
  Enoch 115
  Esther (McKnight) 115
  Eunice 116
  Eunice (Church) 46
  Experience 116
  Ezekiel 115
  Florus 116
  George 117
  Hannah 115
  Ira 115
  Irene 115
  Isaac 116
  Jack 116
  James 115, 116
  James Calkins 116
  James Floras 117
  Jerusha (Mack) 115
  John 115
  Julia 117
  Laura 117
  Laura (Wood) 116
  Lester 116
  Loring 116
  Lucretia 115, 116
  Lucretia (Smith) 115
  Lydia 116, 117
  Lydia (Calkins) 116

Huntley, Lyman 116
  Marvin 115
  Mary (Douglas) 115
  Mary (Wallbridge) 115
  Olive 117
  Olive (Huntley) 117
  Phineas 115
  Polly (Lee) 115
  Porter 116, 117
  Porter Calkins 116
  Reny 115
  Reynold 115
  Roxana 116
  Roxy Ann 116
  Ruamah 158
  Ruhamah 115
  Russell 116
  Seth 115
  Silas 115
  Washington 116
Hurd, Amelia (Thatcher) 206
  Don Carlos 206
  Mary A. 117
Hurlbutt, Adelia (Donaldson) 117
  Caroline (Rockwell) 117, 173
  Charles A. 117
  David 96
  Ezra B. 117
  Francis D. 117
  Frank L. 117
  Gould L. 117
  Henry R. 117
  John 117, 173
  Louis (Gilbert) 96
  Mary A. (Hurd) 117
Husbands, Anna Maria Blackman (Miller) 144
  Joseph D. 144
Hutchings, Keziah 2
Hutchins, Camilla (Holt) 107
  Hiram 107
Hutchinson, Susannah 58
Hyde, Abel 118
  Adeline Amanda (Lewis) 117
  Adolphus 117
  Almira (Singleton) 118
  Alonzo 119
  Ambrose 118
  Anne Bennet (Keith) 119

Hyde, Charles Backus 118
  Delia 118
  Delina 118
  Eli 118
  Eliza (Tracy) 119
  Elizabeth 118, 119
  Elizabeth (Betsey) (Starr) 118
  Elizabeth C. 207
  Eugene 119
  Eunice (Backus) 118
  Eunice (Grey) 118
  Fanny (Beardsley) 119
  George W. 117
  Gustavus 117
  Hannah 117
  Hannah (Pember) 117, 118
  Hannah (Shoots) 117
  Ira 117, 118
  Isaac 117
  James 117, 118, 119
  Jay 119
  John 117, 118
  Julia (Harris) 117
  Keziah (Coon) 117
  Laura (Williams) 118
  Laura Emily 119
  Louisa 117
  Lucinda 118
  Maria 117
  Marinda (Risley) 117
  Martha (Jamison) 119
  Mary (Cole) 117
  Mary (Shumway) 118
  Mary Frances 119
  Matthew 117, 118
  Nathaniel 119
  Nathaniel S. 119
  Olive Beardsley 119
  Parley 117
  Robert T. 119
  Roswell 118
  Samuel 117, 118
  Sarah 118
  Sarah (Dairy) 118
  Susannah (Torrey) 118
  Wealthy 118
  William 117, 118
Ingalls, Sally 136, 137
  Sarah 114

Ingalls, Stephen 137
Ingersoll, Ellen (Fisher) 45
Irish, Hugh M. 139
Irons, Candice 75
Ives, Marilla 125
Jamison, Martha 119
Jarvis, Abigail (Church) 119
  Abigail (Griswold) 121
  Abigail (Preston) 120
  Alfred 120
  Alma 121
  Annie (Rice) 121
  Asahel 120, 121
  Asahel Amos 122
  Ashel Hatch 120
  Aurel Content 122
  Aurelia Content (Morris) 121
  Bill 119, 120
  Cath. (Williams) 123
  Chester 121, 122
  Chester B. 122
  Chloe 120
  Clarissa (Clark) 120
  Clarissa (Jennnings) 123
  Daphany (Taylor) 120
  Dwight 121
  Edwin 121
  Elijah 119
  Eliza 123
  Elizabeth 120
  Ella (Hannay) 123
  Eloise 121
  Emma Bowne 123
  Emma E. 121
  Erastus 120
  Euretta M. (Williams) 121
  Fran. Griswold 121
  Frances (Upham) 121
  Frank G. 122
  Frederick Tiffany 121
  G. L. Bowne 123
  George 123
  Griethene 120
  Hannah 123
  Harriet 121
  Henry Kent 121, 122
  Horace Benjamin 121
  Ira S. 122
  J. Ella (Hannay) 122
  Jarvis, J. Wilson 122
  James White 120
  Jerta Maria 121
  Joseph 119
  Joseph Sidney 121
  Kent 120, 121
  Lena E. 122
  Loren Taylor 120
  Lorenzo Taylor 120
  Lydia E. (Grace) 121
  Maria (Bowne) 122
  Maria (Brown) 122
  Maria (Perry) 122
  Marietta Taylor 121
  Mary 79, 120
  Mary (Cooley) 120
  Mary (White) 120
  Mary (Wright) 79, 119
  Mary Ann 121
  Mary White 121
  Melancthon Bryant 123
  Minerva J. (Steere) 122
  Polly 120
  Poly (Smith) 123
  Rufus 120
  Rufus P. 121
  Sally 120, 123
  Thomas 119
  William 79, 119
  William Cooper 120
  William Hamilton 123
Jaycox, Adelbert 39
  Amanda 39
  Anna Eliza 39
  Chester 39
  Clarissa (Caryl) 39
  John 39
  John Henry 39
  Leonard 39
  Lorenzo 39
  Sally Jane 39
  Samuel 39
Jenkins, Allen Carroll 66
  Carrie (Clara) Phebe (Crandall) 66
  Jay Stewart 66
  Jay W. 66
  Joseph 157
  Sarah Ann (Peck) 157
Jennings, Clarissa 123

Jerome, Sarah 27
Jewell, --- 125
  Abigail (Salisbury) 124
  Abigail C. 124
  Adonijah 123
  Betsey 123, 124
  Betsey C. 124
  Betsey C. (Jewell) 124
  Charlotte 123
  E. M. 125
  Edward 123
  Edward B. 125
  Edward Vernon 125
  Electra (Russell) 124
  Emerald F. 125
  Esther 124
  Esther (Barrett) 185
  Esther (Durrell) 124
  Esther M. 185
  Ezra 124
  Fannie (Hone) 125
  Harriet M. (Foote) 125
  Harvey C. 124
  Helen M. (Davenport) 125
  James 124
  Jared 123, 124, 185
  John 123
  John M. 123
  Jonathan 124
  Joseph 123
  Josephine 125
  Lemuel 124
  Mary Ann 124, 185
  Mary Frances 125
  Myron 124
  Myron D. 125
  Nathaniel 123
  Niles Demoresse 125
  Niles Harry 125
  Norman D. 125
  Oliver 124
  Osborn 124
  Paschal A. 124
  Relief 124
  Sally 123
  Sally T. 124
  Sarah (Pratt) 123
  Sophia (Tyalor) 124
  Susan 123
  Jewell, Susan Beyoux 125
  Thomas 123
  Whitney 123, 124
  William 123
Jewett, Lucy 75
Johnson, --- 109, 142
  --- (Gardner) 126
  Abigail (Tefft) 125
  Alonzo G. 126
  Anna 76, 125
  Anna (Babbitt) 12
  Anna (Johnson) 125
  Anna (Parmelee) 126
  Caleb 125
  Charlotte 142
  Elisha 126
  Eliza 142
  Enos 126
  Ginnett (Lull) 142
  Harris 126
  Ira 126
  Jack 139
  James 12, 125
  Jane L. (Pierce) 126
  Jared 126
  John 125, 126
  John Jewett 126
  Joseph 125
  Julia 126
  Latia 142
  Liva 126
  Lois 67, 126
  Lois (Brainerd) 126
  Lois Louisa 126
  Lucy 126
  Lucy Ann 126
  Marquis D. 130
  Martha 126
  Mary 126, 177, 196
  Mary (Cole) 126
  Mary (Cook) 125
  Mary (Johnson) 196
  May (Kelsey) 130
  Nancy 126
  Phebe Brainard 126
  Phila 126
  Rosamond (Porter) 130
  Serena 126
  Serena (Hubbard) 109

Johnson, Thankful 151
  Thomas 196
  Verta Vern 130
  Vesta 130
Jones, Cornelius 196
  Esther Blake 101
  Israel 88
  Josiah 87
  Louisiana 185
  Lucy 21
  Mary 35
  Philena (Foote) 88
  Sarah 21
  Sedate (Foote) 87
  Thomas 21
Jordan, Ambrose L. 47
Jordon, Caroline 47
Joslyn, Martha 149
  Myron 124
  Sylvania (Cornish) 124
Josslyn, Daniel 116
  Eliza (Huntley) 116
Judd, Hannah 24
  Phila 168
Kaner, Lydia Ann 140
Kean, Peter 145
  Sarah Sabina (Morris) 145
Keech, Martha 195
Keeler, Eldred 177
  George 177
  Huldah (Ruggles) 177
  Mary 177
  William 177
Keese, George Pomeroy 161
  Georgianna (Pomeroy) 161
  Theodore 161
Keith, Anne Bennet 119
  Israel 119
Kelley, Amy 127
  Emily (Benedict) 26
  Ezekiel 127
  Hannah (Wells) 127
  John 127
  Joseph 127
  Lysander W. 26
  Phoebe 127
  Stephen 127
  Tabitha (Baker) 127
Kellog, Giles 39

Kellogg, Elizabeth 206
  Ezekiel 48
  Hannah 48
  Philotha (Clark) 48
Kelly, Ann 91
  John 62
  Sarah 59
Kelsey, Abigail (Bennett) 128
  Anna 127
  Anna (Brown) 127
  Asa 128
  Benedict 127
  Calvin 128
  Celia Aurelia 129
  Daniel 127, 128, 130
  Daniel Dye 128, 129, 130
  Dimmis 130
  Elias 130
  Ellen (Whitmore) 130
  Ephraim 130
  Erastus 130
  Eunice (Andrews) 127, 130
  Fred 128
  Helen Arlina (Monroe) 128
  Henry H. 128
  James 127, 130
  Jane (Toles) 130
  Jerusha 128
  John 127, 130
  Joseph 127, 128
  Julia Ann 128
  Lucy (Thayer) 128
  Martha Augusta 129
  Martha Jane Johnson 129
  Martin 130
  Mary 75, 127
  Mary (Pope) 129
  Mary Elizabeth 129
  May 130
  Patience 127
  Phebe 127
  Polly 127
  Rachel 128
  Rebecca 128
  Rhoda (Dye) 128
  Robert 128
  Roswell 128, 129
  Sarah 128
  Silas 128

Kelsey, Solomon 127
  Solomon D. 128
  Stephen 127
  Susan (White) 130
  Susanna Mary 127
  William 127, 128, 130
  William Henry 129, 130
Kemp, Maria 63
Kennedy, --- 107
  Lucy (Holt) 107
Kent, Lois (Dorrill) 154
  Olivia 154
  Warren 154
Kenyon, Harvey 131
Kessler, Anne Eva 181
  John 55
  Thomas 181
Ketchum, Ephraim 198
  Mary (Spencer) 198
  Polly 200
Keyes, --- 133
  Adeliza (Lane) 131
  Anna 131
  Annie K. 131
  Betsey 131
  DeForest 131
  Diantha 131
  Emily 131
  Emily V. (Day) 133
  Emma (Bassett) 131
  Eva 131
  Franklin C. 131
  Harey 131
  Helena (Pruine) 131
  Hervey 131, 132
  Hiram 131
  Irvin 131
  Irvin J. 133
  Irving 131
  James 131
  James H. 131
  Jennie (Monfort) 131
  John 130
  John T. 131
  Josiah 130
  Josiah D. 131, 133
  Laverne 133
  Maggie A. (Wellman) 133
  Marcus L. 131

Keyes, Margaret 131, 132
  Margaret (Lane) 133
  Margaret (Marlette) 131
  Maria 131
  Marquis L. 131
  Marvin 131
  Mary 130, 131
  Mary (Cheny) 131
  Mary (Lane) 130
  Mary L. 98
  Melville 131
  Omar 131
  Paul 62
  Ralph 131
  Thomas B. 131
  Thompson 130
  Victor 131
  Washington B. 131
  Washington T. 131
  Webster C. 98
Keynon, Betsey 8
Kibby, --- 11
  Electa (Rexford) 11
  Marcia 11
  Nancy 11
Kidder, George 193
Kilbourne, Emily 63
  Mary (Ballard) 63
  Thomas 63
Kimball, Joanna 136
King, Sarah 108
Kingsbury, Aseneth (Daggett) 58
  Nathaniel 58
  Wealthy 58, 60
Kingsley, Erastus 208
Kinne, J. Belle (Hopkins) 107
  John J. 107
  Jonathan 107
  Lucy (Holt) 107
Kirkland, Abigail 88
Kitchell, Esther (Peck) 157
  John 157
Klumph, Alexis 133
  Almond 133
  Arch C. 133
  Augustine 133
  Catharine 133
  Cornelius 133
  Dorr 133

Klumph, Fayette 133
  Gustavus 133
  Ida 133
  Jacob 133
  Jeremiah 133
  John 133
  Laura Adelia (Slayton) 133
  Lester R. 133
  Margaret 133
  Margaret (Peggy) (Davis) 133
  Mary 133
  Morton 133
  Pattie 133
  Sally 133
  Thomas 133
Knap, Charles 80
Knapp, --- 123
  Albert S. 203
  Anson C. 203
  Armenia (Gates) 134
  Arnebua 134
  Augusta 134
  Azel 134
  Betsey 203
  David 134
  Ebenezer 139
  Eleanor 134
  Elizabeth 139
  Emily Margaret 134
  Fannie 134
  Fanny (Temple) 134
  Frederick Jerome 134
  Haley (Eastbrook) 134
  Hannah 203
  Hannah (Jarvis) 123
  Hattie (Babcock) 134
  Hiram 134
  Isaac 134
  Isabelle (Taylor) 134
  Jamima 134
  Jerome 134
  Lucy (Fitch) 134
  Maria (Armstrong) 134
  Martha 134, 139, 140
  Mary 139
  Mary Ann (Shackleton) 134
  Mary Ann (Sweet) 203
  Mary Gates 134
  Pamelia R. 172

Knapp, Patty (Martha) (Liscom) 134
  Patty (Martha) (Liscum) 134
  Rowena 203
  Salmon 203
  Sarah (Sayre) 134
  Sylvester 134
  William 134
Kneeland, Abigail 75
Knowlton, --- 101
  Daniel 101
  Joan (Hale) 101
  Mehitable 101
  Zerviah (Watkins) 101
Lammon, Jane 136
Lampman, Hannah 39
Lane, Abagail 151
  Abigail 70
  Adeliza 131
  Cornelius 130, 133
  Elizabeth 130
  Margaret 133
  Mary 130
  Rebecca (Hardenburg) 133
  Sarah 2
Lansing, --- 103
  Elizabeth (Hardy) 103
  Everet 33
  Jeanette (Campbell) 33
LaSalle, Elizabeth 135
Lasell, Elizabeth 135
Lathrop, Ann Elizabeth 93
  William 93
Latin, Matty 6
Lattin, Luke 7
Lawrence, Abigail 55
  Joseph William 152
  Penthesiler 135
  Susan (North) 152
  Sybil (Heath) 152
Lay, Frederick (Mrs.) 128
  Phebe 106
Layton, Harvey 118
  Wealthy (Hyde) 118
Leach, Submit E. 28
Leavitt, Jonathan 87
  Mary (Todd) 87
Lee, Charles 145
  Clarissa (Adams) 2
  Elizabeth 194, 195

Lee, Fannie 2
  Harry 134
  Joseph 194, 195
  Lois (Plumb) 194, 195
  Mortimer M. 2
  Polly 115
Leland, Aaron 38
Lent, Abram 21
  Christina (Storms) 21
  Clarinda 21
  Daniel 21
  Margaret (Grosbeck) 21
Leonard, Elizabeth 153
Lester, M. 109
LeSuer, Lewis P. 42
  Mary (Chaffin) 42
Lewis, --- 115
  Abbie (Beardsley) 145
  Adeline Amanda 117
  Anna (Huntley) 115
  Carrie 56
  Charles 115
  Cornelia 137
  Edward Rockwell 171
  Frank Filmore 171
  Isaac 160
  Jeremiah 137
  Lydia 59
  Mabel B. 171
  Maria Victorine (Rockwell) 171
  Mary (Proctor) 137
  Rebecca Barbara 210
Lidell, Don F. 99
Liggett, Laura Kate (Coleman) 55
Lillie, Emeline (Peck) 157
  Francis 138
  Jared 138
  Mary 138
  Roger Ferdinand 138
  Susan (Tuckerman) 138
  William O. 157
Lindsay, --- (Dr.) 81
Lindsley, Joseph 37
  Lovina 37
Lines, Julius 128
  Laura 128
  Laura M. 128
  Louisa (Tubbs) 129
  Mary Elizabeth (Kelsey) 129

Lines, Rufus 129
  Sarah (Kelsey) 128
  William 129
Linnedoe, Isaac 176
Lippett, Esther (Field) 86
Liscom, Patty (Martha) 134
Liscum, Patty (Martha) 134
Livingston, --- (Mrs.) 128
  Cornelia Rutgers 176
  Susan (Field) 86
Loomis, --- 6
  Albert 44
  Betsey 48
  David P. 174
  Eliza Ann (Morris) 189
  Elizabeth 205, 206
  Henry 189
  Mary (Church) 44
  Mary Eliza 189
Lord, Caroline 115
Low, Abigail (Hopkins) 103
  Joanna 16
  John 103
  Margaret 103
  Peter 174
Lowell, Mary 46
Luce, --- 14, 138
  Adelia (Tedrick) 138
  Adolphis Skinner 137
  Alfred John 139
  Alonzo Boiles 135
  Anna 138
  Anna W. 140
  Artimassa 136
  Artimessa 136
  Asa 135, 136
  Caroline 136, 137
  Carrie 139
  Catherine E. 135
  Catherine Ella 137
  Charles 136
  Charlotte 140
  Chauncy P. 137
  Clarissa 136
  Cora (Babbitt) 14
  Cornelia (Lewis) 137
  Cynthia 139
  Cynthia P. 137
  Daniel 138

Luce, Dolphus Skinner 137, 138
   Dora 138
   E. Byram 138
   Elizabeth (Betsey) (Pierce) 138
   Elizabeth (Knapp) 139
   Elizabeth (LaSalle) 135
   Elizabeth (Lasell) 135
   Elizabeth (Patty) 135
   Eloisa 135
   Elthea 135
   Emily Grace (Shumway) 138
   Emma (Wentworth) 137
   Emma Wentworth 15
   Eunice 136
   Frances Ellen 138
   Frederick 136
   George 135, 136
   George Henry 138
   George Torry 137
   Hannah 135
   Hannah (Boles) 135
   Harriet 139
   Harriet E. 138
   Harriet Lucretia (Boies) 135
   Harry P. 138
   Henry 135
   Henry J. 136
   Henry James 137
   Henry Winters (Harry) 138
   Horace 136, 139
   Huldah Eliza (Peters) 136, 137
   Ira 136, 139
   Irene 135
   Jacob M. 137
   James 135, 136
   Jane (Lammon) 136
   Joanna (Kimball) 136
   John 136
   John H. 137
   John LaSalle 135
   John Lasell 136, 137
   John Lassell 135, 139
   John Stephen 138
   John Wentworth 138
   Josiah 135
   Julia May (Briggs) 137
   Kate 139
   Kate (Richardson) 138
   Lavinia 139

Luce, Levi 138
   Lois 135
   Lovell Bernard 137, 138
   Lovina (Benton) 136
   Lucinda 139
   Lydia 136
   Marie Antoinette 138
   Marilla 139
   Martha 136
   Mary 138, 139
   Mary (Campfield) 138
   Mary (Lillie) 138
   Mary (Polly) 135
   Mary (Prentice) 135
   Mary (Prentiss) 135
   Mary Etta 139
   Morgan 136
   Nancy 136
   Nancy A. (Robinson) 139
   Nancy May 136
   Nathan 135
   Nathaniel 135
   Orrin C. 139
   Othniel 135
   Patty 135, 136
   Penthesiler (Lawrence) 135
   Perlina (Fish) 139
   Richard O. 137
   Robert Lee 137
   Rufus 135, 136
   Rufus P. 136
   Rufus Peters 137
   Sally (Ingalls) 136, 137
   Sally (Walker) 137
   Samuel Dickson 135
   Sarah P. 138
   Sophia 136
   Stephen Ingalls 137, 138
   Stephen M. 138
   Theron J. 139
   Torrey J. 136
   Torry James 137, 138
   Tresa (Shoemaker) 138
   Uriah 135, 136
   VanRensalear Williamson 138
   Willard 136
   Winifred 136
   Zabad 136
   Zabine 136

Luce, Zadoc 136
Lull, Abigail (Gilbert) 96
  Alexid 96
  Anna 74
  Benjamin 139
  Caleb 139, 142
  Caroline (Harrington) 142
  Charlotte (Moore) 142
  Clarissa 140
  Cyrus 140
  Ebenezer 140
  Ezra 139
  Ginnett 142
  J. K. 141
  Jacob K. 140
  Joel 142
  Jonathan M. 140
  Joseph 139, 140, 141
  Laura 140
  Lorena 140
  Louisa (Gilbert) 96
  Lucy 140
  Luther 140
  Lydia Ann (Kaner) 140
  Martha 140, 141
  Martha (Knapp) 139, 140
  Mary 140
  Nathan 139, 140
  Nathaniel 142
  Nathaniel W. 140
  Oliver F. 140
  Orphson 140
  Pascal F. 140
  Perry 96
  Rachel 140
  Rodwick 142
  Ruth 142
  Ruth (Moore) 140
  Sarah 140
  William 139, 140, 142
Lummis, Albert 44
  Ella 44
  Mary (Church) 44
Luther, Arthur 123
  Clarissa (Upham) 123
  Margaret 91
  Nancy 11
Lye, Charles 66
  Polly Marie (Crandall) 66

Lyman, Dolly Ann Frances 153
  Harry 152
  Sarah (North) 152
Lyon, Sally M. 205
Lyons, Marion 130
Mabey, Peggy 36
Mack, Abner 149
  Harriet (Griggs) 99
  Jerusha 115
  John 99
Mackey, Joanna (Dunham) 75
Macy, William Henry 35
Main, Hannah 148
Mallery, Ruth 86
Mallory, Adelbert 106
  Flora (Hoke) 106
Maltby, Almira 68
  Eliza 68
  Jacob 68
Manchester, Deborah T. (Peck) 158
  Welcome 158
Mann, Hannah 27
Manning, Marian Elnora 66
Maples, Lucinda 10
Marble, Henry D. 200
  Henry L. 200
  Olive R. (Spencer) 200
Marchant, Gurdon 142
  Sarah (Gilbert) 142
Markley, Charles Edward 185
  Frances Elizabeth (Shaw) 185
  George H. 185
  George Herman 185
Marlette, Elizabeth (Pattengille) 131
  Margaret 131
  Peter 131
Marsh, Betsey (Huntley) 115
  Elisha 115
  Ely T. 115
  Henry L. (Mrs.) 160
  Ira 115
  Jacob 115
  Jennie (Stewart) 203
  Martha 37
Martin, --- 149
  Abigail (Nash) 149
  Elizabeth 55
  John 55
  Mary (Sweet) 205

Martin, Nathaniel 88
  Rhoda Ann (Foote) 88
Marvin, Daniel 177
  I. C. 79
  Mary 115
  Mary (Polly) (Edson) 79
  Sarah (Russell) 177
Mather, Georgiana Pomeroy
    (Woolson) 161
  S. L. 161
Matheson, --- 116
  Lucretia (Huntley) 116
Mathewson, Amanda (Babbitt) 12
  Amos 12
Matteson, Isabella (Ferguson) 85
Mattison, Susanna 62
  Susanna (Doolittle) 62
  Thomas 62
Maxson, Daniel 66
  George W. 66
  Louisa (Tellvie) 66
  Marian Elnora (Crandall) 66
Maxwell, Mary 157
May, Deborah Ann 26
  Harmon 26
  Sarah (Monroe) 26
Mayham, Violetta 89
McCall, Henry S. 180
  John M. 180
McClean, --- 33
McClellan, Elizabeth 84
McClintock, Alexander 142
  Charles 142
  David 142
  James 142
  Jane 142
  John 142
  Joseph 142
  Margaret Ann 142
  William 142
McCollum, Angeline 75
McCready, Libie 27
McCullen, L. 30
  Mercy (Brown) 30
McFee, Sarah (Shaul) 182
  William 182
McGar, Euphenia 91
McGowan, Jennie 84
McGraw, Betsey 192

McKay, Bertha 59
  Sarah (Kelly) 59
  Thomas 59
McKennan, Dora 10
  Elizabeth B. (Burlingham) 10
  John 10
McKenney, Albert 14
  Ellen Lydia (Babbitt) 14
McKeon, Paulena 207
McKinley, Elizabeth 59
McKnight, Esther 115
McLean, Emma Bowne (Jarvis) 123
  Walter 123
McLellan, Charaldine (Peck) 159
  William 159
McManus, Mary (Rogers) 174
  Patrick 174
McMullen, Archibald 205
  Lucretia (Crawford) 205
  Melissa 205
Mead, Charles 14
  Elizabeth (Finch) 86
  Nancy 77
  Nancy Maria (Babbitt) 14
  Rufus G. 86
Meade, Catherine 176
  Mary 176
Meeks, Icynthia 36
Merchant, Andrew Percival 142
  Betsey (Elizabeth) (Rockwell) 142
  Betsey (Rockwell) 167
  Eleanor 143
  Eliza A. 148
  Eliza Ann 143
  Emma Harris 143
  Gurdon 142
  Helen Maria 142
  Jane Elizabeth 142
  John 142
  Lemuel 142, 148, 167
  Lucy A. 30
  Maria (Dibble) 142
  Mary Eveline 142
  Niram Rockwell 142
  Olive 143
  Orrin Gilbert 142
  Paschal 143
  Sally L. (Smith) 142
  Sarah (Gilbert) 142

Merchant, Susan (Smith) 143
Merrick, Lucy 171
Merrill, Helen (Cranston) 68
  Howard 68
  Mary Moore (Norton) 153
  Myron 68
  Robert J. 153
Merriman, Eunice (Severy) 143
  George 143
  Mary 143
  Mary (Hawks) 143
  Nathaniel 143
  Phoebe 143
  Phoebe (Childs) 143
  Sally 188
  Samuel 143
  Sarah 143
  Sylvanus 143
  Thankful 143
  Theophilus 143
  Theopolis 143
  Zelpha 143
Merritt, Caleb 143
  Daniel W. 143
  Ella (Reed) 143
  Hiram 143
  Maria (Fitch) 143
  Martin 143
  Melissa (Pierce) 143
  Nathan 143
Metcalf, Huldah (Field) 86
  Mehitabel (Spencer) 202
Metcalfe, Mary (Abell) 48
  Zebulon 48
Michael, Lucy 189
Mickle, Miranda 142
Mickler, Eleanor 182
Miles, --- (Rogers) 174
  Chloe (Jarvis) 120
  John 120
Millard, Gustavius 107
  Kate A. (Hopkins) 107
Miller, Adelia 67
  Adeline 144
  Alice 67
  Anna 144
  Anna Maria Blackman 144
  Caroline 52
  Chester 67

Miller, Clement 144
  E. A. 46
  Edward 144
  Eliza (Crandall) 67
  Eliza C. 67
  Elizabeth 144
  Fannie (Felkins) 144
  Fannie M. 144
  Francis Ford 144
  George 144
  Harriet P. (Roach) 144
  Henry L. 178
  John 144
  Joseph Richard 144
  Katherine Martha 144
  Margaret 144
  Mary 144
  Mary Margaret 144
  Nancy 67
  Nancy (Haner) 52
  Samuel M. 67
  Susanna 144
  Susanna (Holl) 144
  William J. 52
Mills, Lafayette 142
  Sarah Ann 142
  Susanna 72
Mirick, Abbie (Beardsley) 145
  Elisha 42
  Esther (Coye) 145
  Hannah 42
  James 144, 145
  John 144
  Lucy 145, 171
  Persis (Moore) 42
  Willard 145
Mitchell, Harmon 146
  Patta 146
  Polly 146
  Sarah 60
Moeller, Henry 4
  John C. 4
  Julia Ann (Ritter) 4
  Juliana 4
Moisier, Phebe 128
Monfort, Jennie 131
Monk, Libbie 167
  Susan (Cook) 62
Monmouth, Katherine 14

Monroe, Edward N. 74
　Helen Arlina 128
　Jane (Weatherhead) 74
　Lydia 163
　Mary Amelia 74
　Sarah 26
Montague, Henry O. 171
　Mary Stewart (Rockwell) 171
Moody, Annetta J. (Rockwell) 172
　Augustus 172
　Gertrude V. 172
　Ione (Gambrill) 172
　Seeley R. 172
Moor, Irene (Huntley) 115
　William 115
Moore, Anna 140
　Anna Mena 161
　Charlotte 142
　Eunice 153
　John 34
　Jonathan 140
　Persis 42
　Ruth 140
More, David 59
　Elizabeth 59
　Elizabeth (Gould) 59
Morehouse, Deborah 18
Morgan, Belle 64
Morris, --- (Gilbert) 146
　--- (Upton) 145
　Adeline 205
　Aurelia Content 121
　Betsey (Bradford) 121
　Catherine (Ford) 146
　Catherine Cox 146, 162, 163
　Charles 145, 146
　Charles Lee 146
　Charles Valentine 146
　Eliza Ann 189
　Elizabeth (Gilbert) 92
　George 145
　Hannah (Winter) 146
　Harriet E. (Brown) 146
　Helen Olivia 154
　Jacob 145, 163
　Jacob Walton 145
　James Elliott 146
　John Cox 145, 146
　Lewis 92, 145, 146

Morris, Lewis Lee 92, 145, 146
　Martha E. (Wright) 146
　Mary (Cox) 145
　Mary Ann 145
　Mary Cox 146
　Richard 92, 145
　Robert Hunter 146
　Samuel 121
　Sarah Sabina 145
　Serena (Burgess) 145
　Sophia (Pringle) 145
　William 146
　William Augustus 146
　William Pringle 146
Morse, Caroline 6
　Charlotte (Jewell) 123
　James O. 202
　Mary (Backus) 18
　Samuel 18
　William 123
Moseley, Rachel 160
Mosley, Esther (Gates) 111
　Jennet 111
　Josiah 111
Moss, Rachel 160
Mudge, Lucy (Spencer) 197
　Micah 197
　Ruth 195, 197
Multer, Alice 147
　Catharine 146
　Christian 146
　John D. 146
　Libbie B. 147
　Martha A. 147
　Mary 146
　Mary A. 147
　Philip 146
　Polly (Mitchell) 146
　Rose H. 147
Mumford, Joseph 2
　Polly (Adams) 2
Munro, --- 149
　Olive L. (Nash) 149
Munson, George Gilvert 102
　Julia 18
　Lois 18
　Mary 101, 165
　Mary Angeline (Sanford) 102
　Moses 18

Murdock, Martha (Field) 86
  Mercy 8
Murphy, Mary A. 26
  Timothy 26
Murray, Ann 99
  Ella 99
  Hattie 172
  Henry 99
  James 99
  Joseph 99
  Leontia (Griggs) 99
  Levantia (Griggs) 99
Musson, Amelia Lucy (Rockwell) 171
  Robert Rockwell 171
  Theodore H. 171
  W. A. 171
  Winifred D. 171
Muzzy, Bethia 22
Mygatt, Clarissa A. 178
  Henry R. 178
Mynderse, Sarah 33
Myrick, Charles Rockwell 147
  Emma (Storey) 147
  Frank H. 147, 171
  George A. 147
  Helen Tryphena (Rockwell) 147, 171
  Kate Evelyn 147
Nash, Aaron S. 147
  Abiah 147
  Abigail 149
  Abraham 147, 148
  Alphonso DeMortimer 147
  Alphonso Nelson 147
  Amber Melinda (Babbitt) 12
  Barbara (Weber) 149
  Bina (Thompson) 148
  Charles Gould 148
  Daniel 78, 148, 149
  David 148
  Dorcas 148
  Edward 148, 149
  Edward Lewis 147
  Eliakim 148
  Eliza A. (Merchant) 148
  Eliza Ann (Merchant) 143
  Elizabeth 149
  Elizabeth Olive 148

Nash, Ellen Maria 148
  Emily E. (Crandall) 147
  Erumett 12
  Eva 148
  Gould Merchant 148
  Grace 148
  Hannah M. 149
  Harvey Olmstead 143, 148
  Henry C. 147
  Jane 149
  Jared 147
  John 148
  John F. (Mrs.) 149
  John Frederick 149
  Josephine 12
  Lena 148
  Lewis F. 147
  Lucinda R. (Beatty) 148
  Marcia Irene (Winsor) 148
  Martin Marion 148
  Mary 149
  Mary E. 147
  Mary Elizabeth 148
  Nellie (Cook) 148
  Olive 148, 149
  Olive (Nash) 148
  Olive L. 149
  Phebe Ann 148
  Sally 147
  Samuel 147
  Sarah 148
  Sarah (Benedict) 147
  Sarah (Olmstead) 148
  Silas A. 147
  Sophia (Shipman) 147
  Sophia S. 147
  William C. 149
  William Olmstead 148
  William Penn 12
  Willis Winsor 148
Neland, Abigail 75
Nellis, Betsey 106
  Ella 106
  Mary (Getman) 106
  William 106
Newboro, Ruth 100
Newell, Melissa 68
Newman, Abraham 192
  Betsey 192

Newton, Abigail M. 102
  J. S. 159
  Jeduthan 102
  Martha Maria (Smith) 102
  Viola (Platt) 159
Nicholas, John 47
Nichols, --- 47
  Catherine Hamilton 63
  Catherine Hamilton (Wood) 63
  Elizabeth 33
  John 47
  Meribah 130
  William 63
Nicklas, Caroline 36
Niles, --- 149
  Alpha 150
  Amy (Hoag) 150
  Asenath 149
  Catharine 149
  Deborah 150
  Elizabeth 149, 150
  Freelove 149
  Hannah 149
  Hanson 149, 150
  Henry 149
  Jane 149, 190
  Julian 149
  Lydia 207
  Martha (Buckston) 149
  Martha (Joslyn) 149
  Mary 150
  Nathaniel 149, 190
  William 77, 149
Noble, Abagail (Lane) 151
  Abigail 149
  Abigail (Lane) 70
  Adelia 151
  Anna (Hayes) 150
  Bostwick 150
  Casandana 70
  Charles C. 59, 151
  Charles Curtis 150
  Curtis 123, 150, 151
  Cyrenus 150
  Edward 151
  Eli 75
  Elizabeth B. 151
  Elnathan 150
  Fanny (Brooks) 151
  Noble, George 151
  George H. 59
  George Hayes 150
  George Weston 150
  Guaradus 150
  Hannah 149
  Hannah (Edson) 78
  Harriet 69, 150
  Henry Carrington 150
  Henry M. 151
  Jehannah (Bostwick) 150
  Johannah (Bostwick) 150
  John 150
  Julia Sophia 150
  Lay 151
  Lewis Leonard 151
  Louesa (Fairchild) 151
  Lucinda (Brooks) 151
  Lucinda (Hunter) 151
  Martin 70, 149, 151
  Martin William 151
  Mary 150
  Mary Ann 150
  Nathaniel 150
  Pomeroy 78
  Prudence (Edson) 79
  Sally 150, 151
  Sally Jennette 151
  Sophia (Utley) 150
  Susan M. 170
  Sylvanus 150, 151
  Thomas 150
  William 150
North, --- 152
  Albert 152, 153
  Almira 152
  Amelia 152
  Ann H. 152
  Asahel 153
  Belle (Sands) 180
  Ceylina N. 152
  Ceylon 152, 153
  Ceylon Henry 153
  Charles Gilbert 153
  Dolly Ann Frances (Lyman) 153
  Edwin 153
  Emily 152
  Frances A. 153
  George Lyman 153

North, Hepzibah 152
  Irena (Taylor) 152
  Irene (Taylor) 152
  Isaac 151
  Jedediah 151
  John 151
  Justa Maria (Fitch) 152
  Linus 152
  Mary 152
  Matilda (Cheney) 152
  Mercy 152
  Patience (Spalding) 152
  S. S. 180
  Sarah 152
  Sarah (Wilcox) 151
  Stephen 151, 152
  Susan 152, 153
  Susannah (Savage) 151
  Thomas 151
Northrop, John 164
Northrup, Horace 177
Norton, --- 149
  Benjamin 153
  Elijah 153
  Elizabeth (Leonard) 153
  Elizabeth (Nash) 149
  Eunice Beardsley 153
  Eunice Gertrude 154
  Frances Malvina 153
  Freelove (Burroughs) 153
  Hannah (West) 153
  Jabez 153
  Levi Warren 153
  Lucy Beardsley 153
  Mary (Howard) 153
  Mary (Polly) Moon (Beardsley) 153
  Mary Jane (Cleveland) 153
  Mary Jane Elizabeth 154
  Mary Moore 153
  Merritt Milton 153
  Morris 153, 154
  Nicholas 153
  Olivia (Kent) 154
  Samuel Herman 153
  Sullivan Sedgwick 153
  Theressa M. 154
Norwood, Harriet S. 97
Nutter, Mary 74
Nye, John A. C. 5

Nye, Mary Linn (Almy) 5
O'Brien, Maria (Carpenter) 14
  Schuyler 14
O'Connor, Annie H. (Taylor) 155
  Charley 155
  Edward 154, 155
  Fannie 154
  Fannie (Caulder) 154
  Francis 154
  Harriet N. 154
  Harvey 155
  James 154
  Julanna H. 154
  Lindsay 155
  Mary 154
  Mary (Dickson) 154
  Milo 154
  Prudence (Faulkner) 154
Oberheiser, Conrad 31
  Mary (Story) 31
  Polly 31
Olmstead, Mary 98
  Sarah 148
Oothout, Volkert 177
Orderson, Thomas H. 144
Osborn, A. R. 187
  Belle (Platt) 160
  Elnathan 120
  Henry R. 160
  Lorinda 44
  Lydia (Sisson) 187
  Nancy (Cole) 54
  Sally (Jarvis) 120
Packard, Asahel 30
Paddleford, Dorcas (Spencer) 202
Page, Almeron 66
  Eliza M. (Crandall) 66
  Maria 178
  Marie E. 168
  Sherman 178
  Stephen 66
Paine, Dorcas 1
  Elisha 1
  Rebecca (Doane) 1
Parker, --- 87
  Abraham 155
  Alexander 155
  Betsey 155
  Charles 155

Parker, David 155
  David G. 155, 156
  Dexter A. 156
  Elisha 60, 155
  Ella M. 155, 156
  Fanny 187
  Ira 155
  Isaac B. 155, 156
  Joanna 156
  Joanna (Gardner) 155
  John 155
  Mariah (Ellsworth) 155
  Marla (Ellsworth) 155
  Marla (Mariah) (Ellsworth) 155
  Mehitible 155
  Mercy (Cook) 60
  Norman 156
  Otis M. 156
  Patience 155
  Polly 155
  Ruth H. J. 156
  Sally 155
  Sarah 155
  Sarah (Gardner) 155
  Susanna (Bolton) 155
  Susannah (Bolton) 156
  Willis D. 155
Parks, David J. 118
  Delina (Hyde) 118
  Elizabeth 28
Parlin, Cutler 160
  E. Ophelia (Platt) 160
  Marcus 160
Parmale, Adeline Julia 113
  Alvin 113
  Viletto 113
Parmalee, Adaline Julia 114
  Alvin 114
  Violetta 114
Parmelee, Anna 126
  John 126
Parsons, Augustus 152
  James 152
  Mary (North) 152
  Sarah (North) 152
Partridge, Theressa M. (Norton) 154
  William W. 154
Pattengille, Elizabeth 131
  Sarah 133

Peabody, Hannah 60
  Jireh 200
  Nancy 200
Peake, Huldah 2
Pearce, Mary 85
Pearl, Achsah 52
Peck, --- 115
  Abby (Cutting) 158
  Abel 157
  Adaline (Colby) 157
  Adaline (Randall) 158
  Albert E. 159
  Almira (Taft) 157
  Amanda (Richmond) 157
  Anna 157
  Anna G. 158
  Asa 158
  Benjamin 158
  Betsey Ann 158
  Calvin 115
  Calvin H. 158
  Candace (Fox) 157
  Caroline H. 158
  Charaldine 159
  Clarissa 157
  Clarissa (Bates) 157
  Dan 158
  David W. 157
  Deborah T. 158
  Elijah 156, 157, 158
  Elisha 157, 158
  Elisha Erwin 159
  Eliza 205
  Elizabeth (Betsey) L. 158
  Elizabeth L. 159
  Emeline 157
  Erastus 157
  Esther 157
  Fannie M. (Miller) 144
  Hepsibah 156
  Hepzibah 156
  Jedediah 156, 157, 158
  Jedediah W. 158
  Joseph 156, 158
  Joseph H. 158, 159
  Julia A. (Smith) 157
  Lois 158, 199
  Lovinia 158
  Lucretia 158

Peck, Luther P. 158
  Lydia (Briggs) 158
  Mary (Alby) 158
  Mary (Maxwell) 157
  Mary (Rappler) 158
  Mary (Taft) 157
  Olive (Bailey) 158
  Olive (Emmons) 158
  Olive A. (Griggs) 157
  Olive L. 158
  Ozias W. 144
  Peter 157
  Polly 156, 157
  Richard E. 157
  Ruama H. 158
  Ruamah (Huntley) 158
  Ruhamah (Huntley) 115
  Samuel 156, 158
  Sarah 157
  Sarah (Colgrove) 157
  Sarah (Tyler) 157
  Sarah Ann 157
  Silas 158
  Sophara (Churchill) 159
  Tabitha E. 157
  William 156, 158
  William E. 158
Peckham, Joanna 77
Pember, Hannah 117, 118
Pembleton, Mary 103
Penny, John 127
  Polly (Kelsey) 127
Perkins, Margaret 1
Perry, H. M. 122
  Maria 122
  Mary E. 29
Peters, Amasa 136, 137
  Caroline (Cone) 58
  Huldah Eliza 136, 137
  Jonathan 58
  Sarah (Swift) 136, 137
Pettingall, Hannah 2
Phelps, Harriet (Cone) 58
  William 58
Phillips, Sarah 166
Picard, Mary 60
Pickens, Sylvana 207
Pier, Abner 118
  Sarah (Hyde) 118

Pierce, Abram 126
  Alfred 128
  Aschsah (Baldwin) 135
  Betsey (Cranston) 68
  Camilla A. 208
  Catherine Cornelia (Cook) 63
  Chloe (Foote) 87
  Elizabeth (Betsey) 138
  Emeline (Woodward) 143
  Hiram 143
  Isaac 87
  Jane L. 126
  Julia Ann (Kelsey) 128
  Melissa 143
  Milo 138
  Nathaniel 135
  Sarah (Satterlee) 126
  Thomas Wentworth 63
  William 139
  Winfield 68
Pitcher, James 159
  Mary (Platt) 159
  Nathaniel 131
Platner, John 36
Platt, Abigail (Smith) 160
  Andrew H. 159
  Ann (Dunham) 159
  Azuba (Tilson) 207
  Belle 160
  Benjamin S. 160
  Caroline (Tyler) 160
  Clara (Gurney) 159
  Clarissa (Cook) 159
  Daniel 159
  Delia 160
  E. Ophelia 160
  Elizabeth (Thomas) 160
  George 159
  Grace 160
  Hannah (Coon) 159
  Horatio N. 160
  Jane 107
  Jerusha (Dibble) 159
  Julia 160
  Kezia (Rockwell) 168
  Keziah (Rockwell) 107, 159
  L. Jane 160
  L. Juliette 160
  L. Paschal 160

Platt, Leroy R. 160
  Margaret J. 19, 20
  Martha 159
  Mary 159
  Mary A. (Gibson) 160
  Melissa (Dunham) 159
  Melvia 160
  Merlin J. 159
  Minnie 160
  Miranda (Hitchcock) 159
  Nancy 19
  Nancy (Burnside) 159
  Nathan E. 160
  Nelson H. 159
  Peter 107, 159, 168
  Phebe M. 207
  Rachel (Moss) 160
  Rufus 207
  Rufus H. 159
  Sarah 30
  Slawson M. 160
  Sophrona (State) 160
  Stephen 19, 159
  Viola 159
  William 160
Plum, Dorothy 10
Plumb, Lois 194, 195
Plummer, Daniel Longfellow 201
Pomeroy, Ann (Cooper) 160
  Anna 161
  Catherine 161
  Daniel 160
  Ebenezer 160
  Edgar Cooper 161
  Elizabeth 161
  Ellen Cooper 161
  Eltweed 160
  Fenimore Cooper 161
  Francis 161
  George 160
  George Quartus 161
  Georgianna 161
  Hannah 161
  Helen 161
  Helen (Starkweather) 36
  Isaac Hart 161
  Laura Cornelia 161
  Mary 161
  Medad 160

Pomeroy, Phebe (Hart) 161
  Phebe Hart 161
  Phoebe (Sheldon) 160
  Quartus 160
  Rachel 36, 160
  Rachel (Moseley) 160
  Rachel (Pomeroy) 160
  Robert 36
  Seth 160
  Stella (Woolson) 161
  Theodore Keese 161
  Walter 161
  William 160, 161
  William Cooper 161
Pope, Catherine 172
  Marcus 130
  Mary 129
  Meribah (Nichols) 130
Popple, Catherine 14
Porter, Anne (White) 193
  Clarissa Harlow 55
  David 198
  John 193
  Kate Evelyn (Myrick) 147
  Lewis C. 147
  Mary 42
  Rebecca 193
  Rosamond 130
  Susanna (Wilbur) 210
Potter, --- (Dr.) 153
  Elizabeth (Severin) 47
  Fanny Aurora (Edson) 78
  Frances Malvina (Norton) 153
  Henry C. 47
  Horace 78
  Margaret 60
Powell, A. C. 90
Pratt, Caroline 162
  Catherine E. (Luce) 135
  Daniel 99, 162
  Eliza 99, 162
  Eliza J. 99, 162
  Frederick 135
  George 162
  Henry 162
  Isabelle Foote 16
  Louisiana (Jones) 185
  Lucy J. 185
  Mary 162

Pratt, Sarah 123
  Thomas 185
Prentice, Blanch Lydia 164
  Byrah Henrietta 164
  Eunice 81
  George Henry 163
  George William 163
  Hattie V. (Chamberlain) 163
  Henry Josiah 163
  John A. 160
  John H. 163
  Julia Florena 164
  L. Juliette (Platt) 160
  Lydia (Monroe) 163
  Mary 135
  Neil Leslie 163
  Pearl Anna 163
  Priscilla 30, 191
  Ruth Edna 163
  Samuel 162, 163
Prentiss, Alexander S. 162
  Ann Lucretia 162
  Catherine Cox (Morris) 146, 162, 163
  Catherine L. 146
  Catherine Lucretia 162
  Charlotte Derbyshire 163
  Daniel S. 163
  George H. 162
  George L. 163
  Hannah 163
  Henry 163
  John 146
  John H. 162, 163
  John Holmes 162
  Jonas 163
  Lucretia (Holmes) 162, 163
  Mary 135
  Mary M. 146
  Mary Margaret 162
  Mary Martha 162
  Phoebe 163
  Rachel A. 163
  Samuel 162, 163
  Thomas 162, 163
  Truman 163
  Urilla (Shankland) 162
  Valentine 162
  William L. P. 163

Prescott, Benjamin 116
  Experience (Huntley) 116
Preston, Abigail 120
  Daniel 120
  Esther (Cummings) 120
  Rufus 120
Price, --- 136
  Elizabeth (Edson) 79
  Harriet E. (Luce) 138
  J. 79
  Leonard H. 138
  Ruanna (Goodrich) 97
Pride, Eunice A. (Gilbert) 96
  Palmer 96
Prindle, Dorothy (Plum) 10
  Samuel 10
Pringle, John 145
  Obedience 10
  Sophia 145
  William Augustus 145
Proctor, Mary 137
Prosser, Eliza 66
Pruine, Helena 131
Puletreau, John 180
Pulletreau, Clara L. 180
Putman, Eleanor 181
Putnam, Deborah 35
  Hannah 36
  Mari 45
  Mary 14
  Ruth 36
Quackenbush, --- 164
  Ann Eliza (Woolf) 165
  Betsy 164
  Caroline 164
  Catherine 164
  Catherine (Gardiner) 164
  David 164
  Elizabeth 165
  Emma 165
  Garret 164
  Isaac 164
  Jacob 164
  John 164
  Mariah 164
  Nancy Maria 164
  Nelletje 72
  Nicholas 164
  Orlando 164

Quackenbush, Peter 164
  Rachel 164
  Sarah (Bovee) 164
Quaif, Clara (Coleman) 56
  Norman J. 56
Quail, Atcheson 165
  Luke 165
  Robert 165
  William 165
  William C. 165
Quigley, Mary 68
Quimby, Anna (DeForest) 74
  Heman 74
Quincy, Anne M. 64
Randall, Adaline 158
Rankin, Esther 49
Ransom, Miles 38
  Polly (Carley) 38
Rappler, Mary 158
Rathbun, Caroline (Griggs) 100
  George 100
  George A. 100
  Jane 100
  John A. 100
  Marilla Duerer (Griggs) 100
Rawlings, Ann (Beale) 165
  Isaac H. 165
  John H. 165
  Mary (Munson) 165
Ray, Eunice (Luce) 136
  William 136
Reed, Anna 206
  Elizabeth (Kellogg) 206
  Ella 143
  Lydia 189
  Matthew 206
  Mehitable (Hale) 101
  Shubael 101
  Thurlow 48
Reese, Laney 181
Reeve, Ellis 193
  Harriet L. 193
Remington, Caroline (Campbell) 37
  George 37
Reniff, Hannah 189
Rexford, Annis (Babbitt) 11
  Electa 11
  Ensign 11
Reynolds, Elenora 8

Reynolds, Elizabeth Ann (Roselle) 8
  James Henry 8
  Mary 54
  Sarah 4
Rice, Annie 121
  Ebenezer 164
  Eliza 79
  Mary (Webster) 121
  Michael 121
Rich, Edward Blakeslee 8
  Maria Janette (Augur) 8
  Michael 8
Richardson, Esther 38
  Kate 138
Richmond, Amanda 157
Rider, Aaron 77
  Adda (Town) 166
  Adelbert J. 166
  Catherine (Chapman) 165
  George L. 166
  Gracie A. 165
  Harriet A. (Turner) 166
  Helen (Clark) 77
  Joanna (Edson) 77
  John 165
  John J. 165
  Mary 165
  Nathan 166
  Polly 166
  Rachel (Foster) 77
  Silas 77
  Sophia 165
  Sophia (Summer) 165
  Sophia (Sumner) 165
  Stephen 165, 166
Riggs, Catharine Winter (Gilbert) 93
  Thomas 93
Riley, Alice 168
  Mary Ann 62
Risley, Marinda 117
Ritter, Julia Ann 4
Roach, Harriet P. 144
Robbins, --- 139
  Marilla (Luce) 139
Roberts, Asahel B. 168
  Harriet Louise 27
  Laura (Rockwell) 168
Robertson, Sarah Ann 59

Robinson, Albert D. 166, 167
  Alice (Schooley) 167
  Alice A. 167
  Ann 166
  Ann (Freman) 166
  Annie B. 167
  Asenath (Gilbert) 96
  Bruce M. 74
  Carrie 167
  Charles 166
  Charles Nelson 166
  Christabel 167
  Claude 167
  David 166
  David G. 166
  Dwight 201
  Earl A. 167
  Elisha 96
  Elizabeth (Garrett) 166
  Emma 102
  Frances M. (Rockwell) 172
  Garrett 167
  George 166
  George W. 166
  Grace Lillian (Dixson) 74
  Irving 167
  Jeannie M. 201
  Jennie 167
  John 166
  John Garrett 166, 167
  Joseph 30, 166
  Josie 167
  Libbie (Monk) 167
  Lucy Maria 166
  Mabel 167
  Malcolm Bruce 74
  Maria (Brown) 30, 166
  Mary Ann 166
  Mary Eliza (Babcock) 201
  Matilda 166
  Myrtle 167
  Nancy A. 139
  Ruth 72
  Sarah (Phillips) 166
  Thomas 172
  Vera 167
  Wallace B. 166
  William 166
  Willie 167

Rochester, Catherine Kimball 55
  Nathaniel 55
Rockwell, A. Starr 168
  Abareen 173
  Abbyrene S. 168
  Abeyriene S. 173
  Adaline M. 171
  Albert 168
  Alice (Riley) 168
  Alice Adelia 170, 185
  Almon 145, 168, 171, 172
  Almon Ferdinand 171
  Alphonzo P. 172
  Ambrosia 172
  Amelia Lucy 171
  Amos 53, 168, 170, 172, 185
  Ana (Dally) 168
  Andrew 168
  Ann Lucinda 1, 171
  Anna (Bishop) 173
  Annetta J. 172
  Annie (Griffin) 29, 173
  Anson 1, 168, 171
  Ard S. 168
  Asahel 168
  Ashbel R. 17, 168, 170
  Ashbel Ruggles 170
  Benjamin 167, 168
  Benjamin Albert 170
  Benjamin S. 168
  Betsey 167, 172
  Betsey (Elizabeth) 142
  Betsey (Shaw) 168
  Caroline 117, 173
  Caroline L. 29, 171
  Catharine V. 170
  Catherine (Pope) 172
  Caty (Shaw) 17, 170
  Charles D. 173
  Charlotte A. (Sage) 172
  Cornelia A. 17
  Cornelia Ann 170
  David Henry 168
  David Shaw 170
  Edward B. 170
  Edward Brewer 170
  Edward S. 172
  Eli 167, 172
  Elizabeth 53, 168, 170

Rockwell, Elizabeth (Andrus) 86, 167
Elizabeth (Emmons) 53, 170, 185
Elizabeth (Sperry) 167
Elizabeth (Wellman) 173
Emeline 172
Eva 168
Ezra 29, 117, 173
Ezra Bedent 167
Florence A. 171
Florence S. 170
Frances A. 168
Frances A. (Hickox) 168
Frances Augusta 170
Frances M. 172
George 168
George A. 170
George Albion 170
George S. 172
H. Donnell 171
Hannah (Frazee) 168
Hannah (George) 172
Hannah F. (Coye) 1, 171
Hattie (Murray) 172
Helen (Garland) 173
Helen Tryphena 147, 171
Henry B. 173
Ida E. 172
Jabez 86, 142, 167
James 170, 171
James S. 171
Jane A. (Shaw) 171
Jennie A. 171
Jenny (White) 173
John 167, 168, 173
John S. 168
Julia 86, 167
Kate Augusta 170
Kezia 168
Keziah 107, 159, 167
Laura 168
Legrand 168
Lester R. 168
Levi 167, 172
Levi Clark 172
Lizzie S. 171
Lovina (Hard) 168
Lucy (Merrick) 171
Lucy (Mirick) 145, 171

Rockwell, Mahalia (Van Dusen) 172
Malcolm V. 172
Maria Victorine 171
Marie E. (Page) 168
Mary 168, 173
Mary (Briggs) 172
Mary A. (Cantwell) 172
Mary Ann 168
Mary Laura 170
Mary Stewart 171
Mattie (Declems) 172
Oscar B. 172
Pamelia R. (Knapp) 172
Percy 173
Phebe 29, 173
Phebe (Bedent) 167
Phebe (Bedicut) 167
Phebe (Bedient) 142
Phila (Judd) 168
Priscilla Augusta 171
Rachel 168, 170
Rachel (Rockwell) 170
Rebecca (Hoyt) 170
Robert M. 171
Ruth (Bassett) 172
Sarah J. 170
Seeley 172
Sperry 168, 172
Starr A. 170
Susan (Van Deuson) 172
Susan M. (Noble) 170
Theodosia 167
Thomas 167
Tryphena (Starr) 168
Victoria 168
Wallace H. 172
William Noble 170
Rodgers, Betsy 74
Rogers, --- 152, 174
Abigail 42
Amelia (North) 152
Charles S. 174
Ebenezer 6
Edward 174
Edward R. 174
Elisha 39
Eliza A. 189, 190
Ella M. 174
Emma C. 174

Rogers, Gustavus 174
  Hannah (Reniff) 189
  Henry W. 174
  Jabez 173
  Jabez J. 174
  James 174
  John J. 174
  Joseph 173
  Joshua 189
  Margaret (Cullinan) 174
  Mary 174
  Mary (Caryl) 39
  Mercy 67
  Perry P. 173
  Rose M. 174
  Ruth 6
  Ruth (Blakeslee) 6
  Samuel 173
  Sarah (Skinner) 173
  Sherman S. 174
  Thomas F. 174
Ronan, J. L. 174
  Rose M. (Rogers) 174
Root, Edwin 31
Rose, --- (Mrs.) 80
  Betsy 18
  Deborah (Morehouse) 18
  Lovina (Spencer) 199
  Nathan 18, 196, 198, 199
  Nathaniel 199
  Sally 196
  Sarah (Haskell) 196, 198, 199
Roseboom, --- 176
  Abraham 176
  Abram 176
  Abram (Abraham) 174
  Abram Hendrick 176
  Catharine 176
  Catherine 176
  Catherine Augusta 176
  Cornelia 176
  Cornelia Livingston 176
  Cornelia Rutgers (Livingston) 176
  Elizabeth 176
  Henry 176
  Henry Hyndert 176
  Henry Myndert 176
  Jacob 174
  Jacob Livingston 176

Roseboom, John 174, 176, 177
  John I. 176
  John J. 176
  Laracha Livingston 176
  Levantia Livingston 176
  Lucy 176
  Marietta 176
  Mary Elizabeth 176
  Myndert 176
  Ruth 174, 176
  Sarah Ely 176
  Susan M. 176
  Susannah (Vedder) 174
  Susannah (Veeder) 174
  William Campbell 176
Roselle, Elizabeth Ann 8
Ross, Elizabeth 52
Rotch, Francis 93
Rowan, Ellen T. (Sisson) 187
  Theodore W. 187
Rowe, George 19
  Grace 19
  Mary S. (Spencer) 19
  Spencer 19
Rowland, Mary Ann (Robinson) 166
  Thomas 166
Rowley, Mary (Cone) 58
  Mehitabel (Weeks) 201
  Mercy 201
  Mosts 201
  Reuben 58
Ruggles, Eldred 177
  Eli 177
  Huldah 177
  Huldah (Wakelee) 177
  Isaac W. 177
  Lucinda 177
  Marcia 177
  Samuel 177
  Thiray 177
Russell, Arthur D. 178
  Catharine 87
  Dorr 178
  Electra 124
  Elizabeth 177
  Hannah (Devol) 60
  Harriet 178
  John 177
  Joseph 177

Russell, Lucie 178
  Lucy Ann (Douglass) 177
  Lucy G. (Fitch) 178
  Mary 177
  Mary (Johnson) 177
  Minnie 178
  Phebe 177
  Rensselaer 178
  Richard 178
  Robert E. 177
  Sarah 177, 178
  Sarah (Garrett) 177
  Thomas 177
  William 177
Rutherford, Jennie (Sweet) 205
  Walter 205
Ryan, Irene (Huntley) 115
  James 115
  Joseph 115
  Lucretia 115
  Polly 115
  Reny (Huntley) 115
Sage, --- 136
  Charlotte A. 172
  Nancy (Luce) 136
Salisbury, Abigail 124
Sammons, Francis 38
  Watyl (Carroll) 38
  Wotey (Carroll) 38
Sands, Ada (Wilson) 180
  Belle 180
  Benjamin 178
  Clara L. (Pulletreau) 180
  Clara M. 180
  Clarissa A. (Mygatt) 178
  Elizabeth (Teed) 178
  Florence 180
  Frederick A. 180
  Frederick Augustus 178
  Henry 180
  J. Frederick 180
  James 178
  John 178
  Maria (Page) 178
  Obadiah 178
Sanford, Ann E. (Hudson) 111
  J. C. 111
  Mary Angeline 102
  Perit Merriman 102

Sanford, Sarah 177
  Syvil (Dorman) 102
Sargent, Hiram 205
  Mary L. 203
  Sally M. (Lyon) 205
Satterlee, Sarah 126
Saunders, Almira (Crandall) 66
  Dell 66
  Harriet 114
  Henry 114
  James 66
Savage, Elisha 151
  Susannah 151
  Thankful (Johnson) 151
Sawdy, Benjamin 60
  Hannah (Cook) 60
Sawin, Betsey (Tennant) 206
  George 206
  John 206
  Orrel (Tennant) 206
Saxbury, B. 76
  Dorcas (Edson) 76
Sayre, Sarah 134
Schall, Bastian 182
  Johannes 182
  Lena 182
Schierholz, Florence Madeline
    (Shaw) 185
  Herman 185
Schnerr, Elizabeth 181
Schooley, Alice 167
Schrierrin, Elizabeth 181
Scott, Agnes 180, 181
  Ann (Green) 180
  Catherine M. (Strong) 180
  Elizabeth 180, 181
  Elizabeth (Black) 180
  George M. 180
  Henry 180
  Horace 117
  Jane 180
  John 180
  Maria (Hyde) 117
  Mary 180
  Mary Ann 180
  William 180
Scoville, Phebe 126
Seaver, Daniel 27
  Leafy 28

Seeber, Adam 181
  Adolphus 181
  Alvin 181
  Anne Eva (Kessler) 181
  Caroline 181
  David 181
  Eleanor (Putman) 181
  Elizabeth (Schnerr) 181
  Elizabeth (Schrierrin) 181
  Heinrich 181
  Johannes 181
  Margaretha (Diel) 181
  Maria C. (Walbrathin) 181
  Martha A. 181
  Mary M. 181
  Sally (Yates) 181
  Waldo 181
  Wilhelm 181
  William 181
Severin, Elizabeth 47
Severy, Eunice 143
Sewell, Almon 76
  E. Elvira 76
  Eliakim 76
  Lucinda 76
Seymour, Abiah (Nash) 147
  Esther (Thatcher) 206
  Thaddeus 147
  Uriah 206
Shackleton, Mary Ann 134
Shankland, Thomas 162
  Urilla 162
Shannon, Luch 176
  Margaret 33
Shark, Elizabeth (Southern) 193
  Loren 193
  Nettie (Southern) 193
  Ransom 193
Shaul, Adolph 182
  Albert 182
  Betsey S. (Caldwell) 182
  Betsey S. (Carroll) 182
  Christina (Eckler) 182
  Cornelius 182
  Daniel 181, 182
  Elizabeth (Bonner) 181
  Elizabeth (Bronner) 181
  Gershom Smith 182
  Henrietta 182

Shaul, Henry 182
  John 181
  John A. 182
  John C. 182
  John D. 182
  Laura L. 182
  Libbie 182
  Margaret (Yule) 182
  Martha 182
  Martha Malvina (Gilchrist) 182
  Mary 182
  Mary S. (Caldwell) 182
  Mary S. (Carroll) 182
  Menzo 182
  Merzie 182
  Norman 182
  Rachel (Smith) 181
  Sarah 182
  Selina (Gillett) 182
  Sylvia 182
  Viola 182
Shaver, Margaret 103
Shaves, Margaret 103
Shaw, --- 138
  Alice Adelia (Rockwell) 170, 185
  Allen D. 185
  Betsey 168
  Caty 17, 170
  Clara (Cutting) 185
  David 138
  Dora (Luce) 138
  Ella J. 185
  Ferdinand 138
  Florence Madeline 185
  Frances Elizabeth 185
  Frances Ellen (Luce) 138
  George Valentine 185
  Hopestill 206, 207
  James Henry 185
  James Rockwell 185
  Jane A. 171
  Mary E. (Wood) 185
  S. Valentine 170, 185
  Samuel Charles 185
  Samuel S. V. 185
  Sephe (Chapin) 138
Sheldon, Abigail (Church) 44
  Henry 77
  Irene (Edson) 76

Sheldon, Joanna (Peckham) 77
  Jonathan 44
  Joseph 76
  Phoebe 160
  Sarah 77
Shepard, David B. 31
  Rebekah (Bundy) 31
Shepherd, Edith (Spencer) 197
  Silas 197
Sherman, Frederick T. 210
  Susan H. (Watson) 210
Shevlin, Frank 155
Shipman, Lucy 11
  Maria 125
  Sophia 147
Shoemaker, Tresa 138
Shoots, Hannah 117
Shove, Henry 131
  Hiram 131
  Mary (Keyes) 131
  Melville 131
Shull, Frederick Augustus 5
  Mary Louise 5
  Sarah Mustin (Barger) 5
Shumway, Emily Grace 138
  Mary 118
Sibley, Aaron 185
  Anna Maria (Hoose) 185
  Caroline Rebecca (Hazen) 187
  Eber 187
  Esther 187
  Esther (Bellamy) 185
  Frederick O. 185
  Hezekiah 185
  James 185
  Jared 185
  Jerusha (Griggs) 100
  John 185, 187
  John F. 100
  Laura 185
  Lucy J. (Pratt) 185
  Mary Ann (Jewell) 124, 185
  Mary J. (Teachant) 185
  Orin 187
  Orrin 124, 185
Sill, Hepzibah (Peck) 156
  Jedediah Peck 156
Simmons, Annis (Boardman) 27
  Evaline (Dupee) 76

Simmons, Roswell 76
Simons, Molly 108
Simpson, Sarah 33
Sinclear, Fanny (Bigelow) 78
  Samuel 78
Singleton, Almira 118
Sinkker, Isaac Watts 3
  Mary Ann (Alexander) 3
Sinkler, Polly (Cilley) 78
  Richard 78
Sisson, Aaron 188
  Alanson 188
  Alcha (Crandall) 187
  Alvin 188
  Amos 187
  Ann 188
  Benjamin F. 188
  Catherine 189
  Christopher 188
  Clarissa 188
  Delmar F. 188
  Edwin 188
  Elbert N. 187
  Elizabeth K. (Cranston) 68
  Ella Mae 189
  Ellen T. 187
  Fanny 189
  Fanny A. 187
  Frances A. 189
  Francis M. 188
  George 187
  George W. 187
  Gideon 210
  Giles 187
  Hannah (Gardner) 187
  Harriet A. 189
  Harriett 188
  Hattie Maud 189
  Henry 188
  Henry E. 187
  Henry Spencer 189
  James 187
  Jane 53, 188
  John 187
  John E. 187
  Joshua C. 189
  Joshua G. 189
  Julia E. 187
  Julia W. 187

Sisson, Kathryn L. 189
  Laura (Stiles) 188
  Leila Agnes 189
  Leo 188
  Lucy Ann 187
  Luther S. 189
  Luther Spencer 189
  Lydia 187
  Maggie (Dix) 187
  Maria (Earl) 188
  Mary 187
  Mary (Burras) 188
  Mary A. (Stephens) 187
  Mary Ann (Howe) 187
  Mary Eliza 189
  Mary Eliza (Loomis) 189
  Melville C. 187
  Myrtle (Youmans) 188
  Nellie (Burnside) 188
  Polly (Mary) 188
  Polly (Mary) (Sisson) 188
  Putnam 188
  Richard 187
  Rosemund 188
  Sally (Merriman) 188
  Sally Ann 188
  Samuel 187, 188
  Sarah 187, 188
  Susanna (Wilbur) 210
  Tacy L. 189
  Theodore 188
  Thomas 187
  Uriel 68
  William H. 188
Siver, Hannah 128
Skilton, Mary 58
Skinner, Mary Amelia (Huntington) 113
  Sarah 173
Slade, --- 100
  Aaron 189
  Alfred 189
  Cora 74
  Eliza A. (Rogers) 189, 190
  Elvina 189
  Hamilton Ford 189
  Henrietta (Fisk) 190
  James 189
  Lewis Sherrill 189
  Lois (Barber) 189
  Lucy (Michael) 189
  Lumon Reed 189
  Mabel A. 190
  Melvin E. 190
  Orville F. 190
  Samantha (Ford) 189
  Sherman Winslow 189
  Theron Ford 189
Slater, Eliza (Hale) 102
  John 102
Slayton, Alonzo H. 137
  Caroline 137
  Caroline (Luce) 137
  Charles 137
  Grace 137
  Laura Adelia 133
  Ruth 137
  Torry 137
Sleeper, Anna 190
  Benjamin 190
  Caroline Eliza 191
  Charlotte 191
  Cynthia 190
  Ephraim 149, 190
  Hannah 190, 191
  Hannah (Haines) 190
  Hiram 190, 191
  Hudson 190, 191
  Irene (Frisbee) 190
  Jane (Niles) 149, 190
  John 190
  Jonathan 190
  Joseph 190
  Julia 191
  Lucy 190
  Lydia 191
  Manda (Weller) 191
  Mary 190
  Morris 191
  Nehemiah 190
  Phebe 190
  Reuben 190
  Samuel 190
Sloat, Phoebe (Kelley) 127
  Robert 127
Small, Florence 68
Smart, Philena (Foote) 88
  Sarah (Alexander) 3

Smart, William 3, 88
Smead, Lucy (Church) 46
Smith, --- 100
  Abigail 78, 160, 191
  Abraham Newman 192
  Alfred James 192
  Anna (Baldwin) 191
  Anteneta 191
  Archaleus 191
  Austin 72
  Betsey (Newman) 192
  Caroline E. 192
  Caroline I. (Fleming) 87
  Christina Ann 39
  Clarissa 2
  Collins G. 72
  Cora 21
  Cornelia Betsey 192
  Daniel 81, 191
  David 190
  Delilah (Bundy) 191
  Della 191
  Deloss 191
  Ejesta 191
  Eleanor (Carley) 38
  Elijah 191, 194
  Elisha S. 191
  Elizabeth (Birdsall) 191
  Ephraim 191
  Esther 111
  Frederick N. 192
  George C. 192
  George Henry 192
  George Warden 192
  Gersham 181
  Gilbert 191
  Harriet 72
  Ira 194
  Isaac 206
  James F. 119
  Jesse 194
  John 38, 191
  Joseph 177
  Josiah 127
  Julia A. 157
  Kittie M. 192
  Laney (Reese) 181
  Laura Emily (Hyde) 119
  Leon D. 29
  Lois (Spencer) 194
  Lucinda (Crippen) 192
  Lucinda Crippen 192
  Lucretia 115
  Lucy (Stevens) 191
  Lusia 79
  Lydia 92, 193
  Margaret (Ely) 81
  Maria E. (Freeman) 192
  Martha Maria 102
  Martha Ritta 192
  Mary 191
  Mary (Marvin) 115
  Mary A. 192
  Melania 191
  Melvina 191
  Moses Gage 192
  Patience (Gurney) 29
  Polly Betsey (Doud) 192
  Polly Street (Thatcher) 206
  Poly 123
  Rachel 181
  Reuben M. 72
  Rhoda P. 100
  Richard 133
  Rossiter P. 192
  Rufus C. 87
  Sally L. 142
  Samuel 39, 115
  Sarah 44
  Seth 194
  Squier 191
  Susan 143
  Sybil (Stevens) 191
  Thomas 193
  Ursula 191
  Welcome W. 192
  Willard A. 192
  William 206
  William Potter 192
  Zabiah C. (Stone) 192
Snell, Susan 38
Snyder, Augusta (Knapp) 134
  B. F. 134
  Betsey 80
  George 80
  Henry 72
  Maria (DeForest) 72
  Mary Ann 80

Southerland, John 118
  Lucinda (Hyde) 118
Southern, Adelbert 193
  Edgar 193
  Edward 193
  Elizabeth 193
  Ernestine (Conkling) 193
  George R. 193
  Harriet L. (Reeve) 193
  James 193
  James L. 193
  Jane 193
  Jennie M. 193
  Jessie (Bourne) 193
  Mary (Herring) 193
  Nelson 193
  Nettie 193
  Richard 193
  Sarah 193
  William 193
Southworth, Betsey 128
Spalding, Jacob 152
  Jedediah 152
  Patience 152
  Sarah (North) 152
Spangler, Alice (Multer) 147
  Thomas 147
Spencer, --- (Gen.) 125
  A. Lincoln 200
  Abner 194
  Abram 200
  Achsah 202
  Ahimaaz 197
  Alexander 194
  Almeron 199
  Amaziah 202
  Amos 194, 195, 198, 199, 200
  Amos Daniel 19, 200
  Amos P. 200
  Anna 108, 198
  Anna (Babbitt) 14
  Anne (Willey) 202
  Arnold 202
  Asa 198
  Asenath (Graves) 198
  Asher 196
  Austin 202
  Barsilla 195
  Barzilla 195, 196

Spencer, Billa 197
  Brinton 196
  Calvin 200
  Caroline C. 200
  Caroline Matilda (Houghton) 199
  Catherine (Dean) 199, 200
  Catherine Dorcas 200
  Catherine M. 200
  Chloe 196
  Daniel 194, 202
  Deborah 200, 201
  Desire 198, 200
  Dorcas 198, 199, 202
  Dorcas (Spencer) 198, 199
  Dorcas (Woodcock) 199
  Dorothy 194
  Edith 197
  Eleanor (Harvey) 202
  Eleazer 194, 196, 197
  Eliphas 194
  Eliphaz 194
  Elisha 194, 195
  Elisha H. 197
  Elizabeth 193, 194, 196, 198
  Elizabeth (Hull) 197
  Elizabeth (Lee) 194, 195
  Emily 202
  Enoch 200
  Enos J. 196
  Esther (Worden) 201
  Eugene S. 197
  Eunice 198
  Experience 198
  Fenton 201
  Francis 196
  Francis U. 195
  George L. 197
  George M. 201
  Gerard 193, 201
  Hannah 193, 194, 196, 201
  Harriet 199
  Harriet (DeForest) 196
  Harvey H. 197
  Helen R. 200
  Henry 194
  Herbert Eugene 200, 201
  Irving S. 197
  Isaac 200
  Israel 194, 198, 201

Spencer, Ithmar 198, 199
  Ithmar A. 199
  Jabez 194
  Jane B. 200
  Jeannie M. (Robinson) 201
  Jennie L. (Barnes) 19
  Jeremiah 201
  Jerusha 198
  Jesse 194
  Joel 197, 198, 199
  John 194, 197, 198, 199, 200
  John U. 201
  Jonathan 194, 195, 197
  Jonathan Lee 195
  Joseph 201
  Lavinia 202
  Lois 194, 195
  Lois (Peck) 199
  Louanna 199
  Lousanna 199
  Lovina 196, 199
  Lovina (Todd) 196
  Lucretia 194
  Lucy 197
  Lulu (Asch) 200
  Lulu (Ash) 200
  Lydia 193, 194, 196, 198, 201
  Lydia (Smith) 193
  Marcy (Mercy) 196
  Margaret 201
  Martha 197
  Martha (Keech) 195
  Martha A. 201
  Mary 194, 196, 197, 198, 201
  Mary (Bevins) 198, 199
  Mary (Johnson) 196
  Mary (Wetmore) 197
  Mary Elvira (Barnes) 200
  Mary S. 19, 200
  Maryette 199
  Matthias 201
  Mehitabel 202
  Mercy (Rowley) 201
  Mica (Micah) 195
  Nancy 202
  Nancy (Peabody) 200
  Naomi 199
  Nathan 199, 200
  Nathaniel 193, 194, 195, 197, 201
  Nehemiah 198
  Olive R. 200
  Orange 195, 196
  Orrangh 195
  Patience (Farnsworth) 194
  Peggy 197
  Philip 199
  Philip D. 201
  Phinehas 194
  Polly (Foster) 202
  Polly (Ketchum) 200
  Polly F. (Elwood) 202
  Rachel (St. John) 197
  Rebecca 198, 199, 200
  Rebecca (Delaney) 199
  Rebecca (Porter) 193
  Rebecca (Spencer) 198, 199
  Reuben 201
  Rhoda 199
  Ruth (Mudge) 195, 197
  Sally (Rose) 196
  Sarah 202
  Sarah (Arnold) 202
  Sarah (Babcock) 200
  Sarah (Bostwick) 195
  Sarah (Haskell) 198
  Sarah (Stewart) 201
  Seth 195, 196
  Seth J. 194
  Simeon 197, 199
  Solomon 196
  Susanna 194
  Susannah 197
  Tabitha 198
  Thankful (Gardner) 202
  Thomas 194
  Timothy 202
  Uriah 200, 201
  William 201, 202
  William C. 197
  William D. 195
  Zeruah 196
  Zipporah (Brainard) 197
Sperry, Elizabeth 167
Sprague, Nancy 55
St. John, Almira (North) 152
  J. R. 152

St. John, Rachel 197
  Sally (Nash) 147
  Silas 147
Stacy, Charles P. 1
  Frances H. (Abell) 1
Stanton, --- 149
  Elizabeth (Niles) 149
  Lovina (Aylesworth) 10
  Nathan 10
Staples, Martha Ann 100
  Ruth (Newboro) 100
  Samuel 100
Stark, Jonathan 195
Starkey, Lucy Ann 151
Starkweather, George A. 47
  Helen 36
  Mariah 35
Starr, Comfort 91
  Elizabeth (Betsey) 118
  Sarah 91
  Tryphena 168
State, Sophrona 160
Stebbins, E. Winchester 170
  Mary Laura (Rockwell) 170
Steere, Minerva J. 122
  Nicholas 122
Steinburg, Abbie 12
Stenson, Elizabeth (Tilson) 207
  R. 207
Stephens, Mary A. 187
Stephenson, Julia M. 69
Sterline, Abigail C. (Chaffin) 42
  Isaac 42
Stetson, F. 79
Stevens, Lucy 191
  Sybil 191
Stewart, --- 203
  --- (Holt) 203
  Alvin 202, 203
  Ann M. (Cook) 62
  Elizabeth 201
  Horatio 168
  Jennie 203
  John 201
  Laura 168
  Margaret (Spencer) 201
  Rachel (Rockwell) 168
  Sarah 201
  William 168

Stewart, William C. 62
Stiles, Laura 188
Stillman, Eliza 111
Stocker, Clara (Genter) 62
  David 62
Stoddard, Mary 84
Stone, Augustus L. 192
  Benjamin 139
  Clinton 17
  Evelina Coleman 33
  Harriet (Backus) 17
  Loammi 3
  Lucinda (Goodrich) 97
  Polly (Ainsworth) 3
  Zabiah C. 192
Storey, Emma 147
Storms, Christina 21
Storr, Experience 115
Story, Mary 31
Stoughton, Abigail 77
Stowe, --- (Capt.) 145
  Sarah 80
Stowell, A. B. 134
  James 178
Straight, Calvin 190
  Phebe (Sleeper) 190
Stranahan, --- (Col.) 156
Street, Mary 206
Strong, Abiah (Clark) 96
  Anna 96
  Caleb 96
  Catherine M. 180
Stuart, Levi 203
Summer, Sophia 165
Sumner, Sophia 165
Swaddle, Lucy 126
Sweet, --- 203
  Abel 203
  Adeline (Morris) 205
  Amos 203
  Benjamin 203
  Chester 205
  Dorr R. 205
  Eliza (Peck) 205
  Elizabeth 210
  Eunice 74
  Francis 203
  Gaius 205
  George R. 205

Sweet, George W. 203, 205
  Grace 205
  Henry 203
  Jennie 205
  John 203, 205
  Jonathan 203
  Joseph 74, 205
  Mary 205
  Mary Ann 203
  Mary L. (Sargent) 203
  Melissa (McMullen) 205
  Patience (Eldred) 203
Sweeting, Clarissa (Luce) 136
  Eliphalet 136
  Whitney 136
Swift, --- (Gen.) 137
  Ceylina N. (North) 152
  Charles 152
  Elizabeth (Hyde) 119
  Henrietta 152
  Joanna 38
  Judah 119
  Rufus C. 152
  Sarah 136, 137
Swinnerton, H. U. 176
  Laracha Livingston (Roseboom) 176
  Levantia Livingston (Roseboom) 176
Taft, Almira 157
  Mary 157
  Rhoda 128
Talbot, Almira (Adams) 116
  Clorinda 116
  John 116
Talmadge, John M. 200
  Mary S. (Spencer) 200
Tanner, James 117
  Lydia (Huntley) 117
Tansley, George 206
  Sally (Thatcher) 206
Taylor, Annie H. 155
  Caroline (Morse) 6
  Daphany 120
  Elizabeth 5, 89
  Epaphras 6
  Erastus 120
  Hannah 8, 59
  Irena 152

Taylor, Irene 152
  Isabelle 134
  Jerusha (Spencer) 198
  John 198
  Louisa M. 6
  Lydia 59
  Lydia (Lewis) 59
  Noadiah 59
  Sophia 124
  Stephen 89
  Timothy 24
Teachant, Mary J. 185
Tedrick, Adelia 138
  Amy (Armstrong) 138
  John 138
Teed, Elizabeth 178
Tefft, Abigail 125
Tellvie, Louisa 66
Temple, Betsey 7
  Fanny 134
  Jemima 134
  William 134
TenEyck, Harmon Hoffman 4
  Joanna Beekman 4
  Maria (Beekman) 4
Tennant, Abigail (Havens) 81
  Alfred 206
  Alfred Loomis 206
  Alvin 206
  Anson 81
  Betsey 206
  Caroline 81
  Clarissa 206
  Daniel 205
  Delinda 206
  Elizabeth 206
  Elizabeth (Loomis) 205, 206
  John 205, 206
  Olive E. 206
  Oliver 206
  Orrel 206
Thatcher, Amelia 206
  Ann (Nancy) Reed 206
  Anna (Reed) 206
  Anthony 206
  Daniel 206
  Esther 206
  Frances 206
  George O. 206

Thatcher, Harriet 206
  John 206
  Josiah 123, 206
  Mary (Hughston) 206
  Mary (Street) 206
  Peter 206
  Polly Street 206
  Sally 206
Thayer, Hannah 38
  Hannah (Siver) 128
  Hattie (Hoke) 106
  Henry C. 106
  Lemuel 128
  Levi 128
  Lucy 128
  Rachel (Kelsey) 128
Thomas, --- (Capt.) 166
  Daniel 68
  Elizabeth 160
  Enoch 68
  Fanny C. (Fleming) 87
  George 87
  George W. 68
  Hannah Thedasia (Cranston) 68
  Julia Lambert (Cranston) 68
  Martha 77
  Zilpha Maria (Cranston) 68
Thompson, Anna (Cook) 63
  Bina 148
  Clarissa (Babbitt) 12
  Eunice 12
  Ira 14
  James M. 63
  John 12
  Mamie 12
  Mina 26
  Nellie May (Chapman) 14
  Sarah 12
  Sarah (Simpson) 33
Thornton, James 49
  Jeremiah 195
  Matthew 49
Thorp, Hannah 92
  John 92
Thorpe, --- 12
  Abbie (Steinburg) 12
  Clarissa (Babbitt) 12
  Earl 12
Thrall, Freeborn Garretson 4

Thrall, Maria Sophia (Almy) 4
  Roger 4
  Sarah (Reynolds) 4
Throop, Enos T. 131
  Montgomery H. 35
Thurston, Edward 148
  Elizabeth Olive (Nash) 148
  Gould 148
  Increase 139
  Joseph 148
  Moses 139
Tiffany, DeWitt Clinton 40
  Lillian (Caryl) 40
  Marietta (Gilbert) 96
  Olive (Edson) 78
  Salome 75
  Seth 78
Tilson, Albert P. 208
  Alvin Hyde 207
  Angelia A. 207
  Ansel C. 207
  Asa 208
  Azuba 207
  Betsey 207
  Camilla A. (Pierce) 208
  Cephas 206, 207
  Cephas S. 207
  Charles C. 207
  DeEtta 207
  Edmond 206, 207
  Edmund 206, 207
  Eliza (Buell) 207
  Elizabeth 207, 208
  Elizabeth (Converse) 206
  Elizabeth C. (Hyde) 207
  Emily A. 207
  Ephraim 206, 207
  Ezra Warren 208
  Florence M. 207
  Frank 207
  Fred 207
  Henry H. 207
  Hiram A. 208
  Hiram E. 208
  Hopestill 208
  Hopestill (Shaw) 206, 207
  Jane E. 207
  Josiah Pierce 208
  Julia M. 208

Tilson, Levina 207
  Lewis 207
  Louisa A. 208
  Lura M. 207
  Lura M. (Tilson) 207
  Lydia (Niles) 207
  Marcella E. 208
  Marcia M. 208
  Mary (Young) 207
  Mary L. 207
  Mortimer R. 207
  Moses 207
  Nancy 208
  Paulena (McKeon) 207
  Phebe M. (Platt) 207
  Polly 207
  Rosalie Mary 208
  Ruth A. 208
  Sarah 207
  Sidney M. 208
  Stephen 206, 207
  Sylvana (Pickens) 207
Tobey, Elisha 53
  Emily (Cole) 53
  Emma L. (Cole) 53
  Hannah (Hillman) 53
  Joseph E. 53
  Saray 53
  Stephen 53
Toby, Eliza 109
Todd, Adeline (Augur) 7
  Almira (North) 152
  Andrew 8
  Andrew H. 4
  Ann 7
  Augusta Maria 4
  Aurelia (Clinton) 102
  Benjamin 152
  Bessie Caroline (Augur) 8
  Charles N. 8
  Grace Angeline 102
  Henrietta Jeanette (Almy) 4
  Ira 4
  James E. 7
  Joanna Beekman (TenEyck) 4
  Lemuel 4
  Lovina 196
  Mary 3, 87, 147
  Nancy (Wentworth) 8

Todd, Orange 7
  Orrin 102
  Samuel 87
  Sarah 4
Toles, Amy (Aylesworth) 130
  Jane 130
  Myron 130
Tomlinson, Lucinda (Ruggles) 177
Torrey, Lucy 118
  Michael 118
  Susannah 118
Tount, Eleanor Bryant (Abell) 1
  George L. 1
Town, Adda 166
Townsend, Elizabeth 52
  James 166
  John 166
  Matilda (Robinson) 166
Tracy, Eliza 119
  Philotha (Clark) 48
Trowbridge, Delia 14
Trupwell, James 77
  Silence (Edson) 77
Tubbs, Louisa 129
Tucker, George 182
  Mary (Shaul) 182
Tuckerman, Susan 138
Tuller, Caroline B. 125
  Harriet 125
  Henry 125
  Horace 125
  Josephine (Jewell) 125
  Maria (Shipman) 125
Tunnicliff, --- (Mr.) 177
  John 56
  Polly 56
Turnbull, Dorothy 102
Turner, Harriet A. 166
  James 166
  Julia C. (Campbell) 36
  Levi C. 36
  Nancy 76
  Sopheria (Adkins) 166
Tyler, Caroline 160
  Sarah 157
Upham, Clarissa 123
  Diana 7
  Frances 121
  Joseph 123

Upham, Lucy (Adams) 7
  Mary Ann 123
  Susan (Jewell) 123
  Sylvanus 7
Upton, --- 145
Usher, Elizabeth Olive (Nash) 148
  William S. 148
Utley, Andesus 135
  Antepus 135
  Mary (Polly) (Luce) 135
  Sophia 150
Vail, Abraham 59
  Clarence Ernest 59
  Elizabeth (McKinley) 59
  Sarah Alaska (Cone) 59
Van Deuson, Susan 172
Van Dusen, Mahalia 172
VanAlstyne, Catherine 40
VanBenschoten, Sarah 107
Vanderpoel, Susan 48
VanHouser, --- 143
VanName, William 31
VanRensselaer, Henry R. 90
  Joanna (Franchot) 90
VanScoten, Sarah 107
VanValkenbrugh, Herbert 40
Vaughn, Maria 178
Veber, Israel 165
  Mary (Rider) 165
Vedder, Elizabeth (Douw) 174
  Myndert 174
  Susannah 174
Veeder, Elizabeth (Douw) 174
  Myndert 174
  Susannah 174
Velie, Adelia (Noble) 151
  J. C. 151
Vermilyea, Fannie (O'Connor) 154
  Noah 154
Verry, Sarah A. 15
Vibbard, Elizabeth 133
  Leonard 133
Wait, Ebenezer 210
  Rebecca (Wilbur) 210
Waite, Eben 210
  Lucretia (Spencer) 194
  Philip 194
  Susanna (Wilbur) 210
Wakelee, Huldah 177

Walbrathin, Maria C. 181
Waldo, Albigence 2
Walker, --- 108
  Angeline (Houghton) 108
  John 108
  Mary Ann 114
  Sally 137
  Sarah (Ingalls) 114
  William 114
Wallace, Jane T. 19
Wallbridge, Ebenezer 75
  Mary 115
Wallin, Alice A. (Cole) 53
  George H. 53
  Ida M. (Cole) 53
  Theodore 53
Walling, Fannie (Knapp) 134
  Jeremiah 134
Walpole, Ann G. 88
Walrath, Amelia 91
Ward, Leonard 8
  Mary Ellen 8
  Mary Ellen (Gilday) 8
  Milton 164
  Phebe Ann (Cranston) 67
  Rachel (Quackenbush) 164
  Samuel 67
Warner, Abigail 101
  Eleazer 101
  Joanna (Hale) 101
  Laura (Hale) 101
  Mattie E. 28
  Zachariah 101
Warren, Darius 48
  Julius 48
  Mary (Clark) 48
Washbon, Zenas 63
Washburn, Dinah 76
  Sarah 37
Washburne, Margaret 5
Washington, George 103
Wasson, Catharine 49
Watkins, Zerviah 101
Watson, --- (Mr.) 178
  Arnold 210
  Arnold Beach 208
  Augusta (Hayes) 208
  Henry M. 210
  Josiah 208

Watson, Julia N. 210
  Mary (Beach) 208
  Sarah A. 210
  Susan Emily (Hayes) 208
  Susan H. 210
  William H. 210
Weatherhead, Jane 74
Weaver, Almira (Goodrich) 97
Webb, Polly 64
Weber, Barbara 149
Webster, Inez 172
  Mary 121
Weeks, J. E. 139
  Kate (Luce) 139
  Mehitabel 201
  Parthena (Goodrich) 97
Welch, Betsey (Butters) 64
  Charles 64
  Lurana Bethiah (Crandall) 64
  Marquis Alvah 64
Weller, Daniel 191
  Manda 191
Wellman, Alfred 133
  Elizabeth 173
  Maggie A. 133
  Sarah (Pattengille) 133
Wells, Edwin A. 10
  Elizabeth A. (Fleming) 87
  Gideon 127
  Hannah 127
  Harvey 87
  Jane Maples 10
  Lewis 157
  Lucinda (Maples) 10
  Lydia 79
  Meeta (Franchot) 90
  Robert 90
  Sarah Ann (Peck) 157
Wentworth, Elisha 137, 138
  Emma 137
  Lucy (Brockway) 138
  Nancy 8
Wesley, --- (Mrs.) 128
West, Hannah 153
  Sarah 67
Westcote, Lydia C. (Goodrich) 97
  Moses A. 97
Westcott, Mary 3
Wetmore, Mary 197

Wheat, Martha Miranda (Griggs) 100
  Samuel 100
Wheeler, Abigail 2
  Charles 30
  Emeline (Brown) 30
  Eva M. 69
  James 2
  Jane 14
  John 30
  John R. 168
  Martha (Brown) 30
  Mary (Rockwell) 168
  Rebecca (Brown) 30
  Russell 146
  Uldah (Ainsworth) 2
Wheelock, Martha 108
Wheet, Hannah 99
Whitcomb, Anna 111
White, Anne 193
  Annie R. 29
  Delos 98
  Jenny 173
  John Edward 130
  Joseph 176
  Marietta (Roseboom) 176
  Mary 120
  Susan 130
Whiteman, Ann (Green) 180
Whitewell, Ann 7
Whitman, Gerry 181
Whitmore, Alfred D. 130
  Ellen 130
  Marion (Lyons) 130
Whitney, Betsey C. 124
Wickham, Caroline (Quackenbush) 164
  Henry 164
Wiggins, Mehitable 196
Wikoff, Garret 133
  Martha 81
Wilbur, Abigail 210
  Ann (Wood) 210
  Anna 210
  Cynthia 210
  Daniel 200, 210
  Daniel G. 210
  Elizabeth 210
  Elizabeth (Sweet) 210

Wilbur, George 210
  Hannah (Carr) 210
  Hannah (Freeman) 210
  Jane 211
  Jesse 211
  John 210
  Joseph 210
  Judith 210
  Louisa 30
  Martha (Goldsmith) 210
  Mary 211
  Phoebe 210
  Rebecca 210
  Rebecca Barbara (Lewis) 210
  Sarah 210
  Sarah (Babcock) 200, 210
  Simeon 210
  Stephen 210
  Susanna 210
  Thomas 210
  William 210
Wilcox, Betsey (Keyes) 131
  Charles 44
  Cornelia A. (Church) 44
  Emily (Church) 44
  Hiram 44
  Lucy (Cook) 62
  Owen 131
  Sarah 5, 151
Wilder, Eunice 108
  Rachel (Carley) 38
  Silas 38
Willard, David 156
  John 206
  Louanna (Spencer) 199
  Lousanna (Spencer) 199
  Polly (Peck) 156
Willey, Anne 202
  Benajah 202
  Caroline (Church) 46
  Hiram 46
  Norman B. 46
  Phebe A. 46
  T. L. 46
Williams, Amos 177
  Calvin 211
  Cath. 123
  Chauncey 211
  Daniel 211

Williams, Edmund 211
  Elizabeth 211
  Elizabeth (Beach) 211
  Elpihalet 121
  Euretta M. 121
  Halsey 17
  Hannah 76
  Hannah E. 211
  Harriet 211
  John 48
  Laura 118
  Lisetta (Backus) 17
  Lucy 48
  Luther 211
  Marcia (Ruggles) 177
  Phebe 211
  Phebe (Davidson) 211
  Polly (Jarvis) 120
  Roger 211
  Sherman 211
  Susan 48
  Thomas 211
  Timothy 211
  William 120
Williamson, Cyrus 91
  James 91
  Lucy 58
Willis, Abigail (Stoughton) 77
  Elam 78
  Jonathan 77
  Keturah 77
  Lucy (Edson) 78
Wilsey, Charles 188
  Elizabeth (Cranston) 68
  Emily 39
  Henry 68
  Jane (Sisson) 188
Wilson, Ada 180
  Frank B. 97
  George B. 97
  Harriette M. (Graves) 97
  Margaret 159
Windsor, Sally 109
Wing, Avis 5
  Clara 18
  Walter A. 18
Winslow, Cornelia 97
Winsor, Marcia Irene 148
Winter, Hannah 146

Winton, Alfred 207
  Amasa 89
  Cynthia (Foote) 89
  DeEtta (Tilson) 207
Withey, Erastus 89
  Mary Ann (Foote) 89
Witt, Frances 39
  John 39
  Samuel 39
  Susan (Caryl) 39
Wood, Abigail (Church) 42
  Ann 210
  Catherine Hamilton 63
  Elizabeth 27
  Huldah (Church) 45
  John 42
  Laura 116
  Mary E. 185
  Zebina 45
Woodbeck, Henrietta (Shaul) 182
Woodbrom, Eliza 176
Woodcock, Dorcas 199
Woodward, Abijah 14
  Anna 14
  Emeline 143
Woolf, Ann Eliza 165
  Elizabeth (Quackenbush) 165
  Isaac 165
Woolson, Alida 161
  Annie 161
  Charles Jarvis 161
  Clara 161
  Constance Fenimore 161
  Emma Clark 161
  Georgiana Pomeroy 161
  Gertrude 161
  Hannah (Pomeroy) 161
  Julia 161
  Stella 161

Worden, Clara B. (Armstrong) 6
  Edwin 6
  Esther 201
  Esther (Jewell) 124
  James 124
Wright, Ezra H. 200
  Hannah 28
  Helen R. (Spencer) 200
  Marietta (Gilbert) 96
  Martha E. 146
  Mary 79, 119
  Roswell 208
  Thomas 96
Wyman, Jonas 188
  Sally Ann (Sisson) 188
Yale, Abel 27
  Elizabeth 26, 27
  Sarah (Jerome) 27
Yates, Amorett 12
  Emily Margaret (Knapp) 134
  Sally 181
  Thomas 134
York, Effie (DeForest) 74
  Mahlon 74
Youmans, Myrtle 188
Young, Martha 97
  Mary 207
  Matilda 97
Youngs, Elizabeth (Spencer) 196
  John 196
  Lovina (Spencer) 196
  Mehitable 196
  Mehitable (Wiggins) 196
  William Fitz 196
Yule, Catharine 182
  George 182
  Margaret 182
Zetwitz, Julia Ann (Ritter) 4

Other Heritage Books by Martha and Bill Reamy:

Erie County, New York Obituaries as Found in the Files of The Buffalo and Erie County Historical Society

Genealogical Abstracts from Biographical and Genealogical History of the State of Delaware

History and Roster of Maryland Volunteers, War of 1861-1865, Index

Immigrant Ancestors of Marylanders, as Found in Local Histories

Pioneer Families of Orange County, New York

Records of St. Paul's Parish, [Baltimore, Maryland], Volume 1

Records of St. Paul's Parish, [Baltimore, Maryland], Volume 2

St. George's Parish Register [Harford County, Maryland], 1689-1793

St. James' Parish Registers, 1787-1815

St. Thomas' Parish Register, 1732-1850

The Index of Scharf's History of Baltimore City and County [Maryland]

Other Heritage Books by Martha Reamy

1860 Census Baltimore City: Volume 1, 1st and 2nd Wards (Fells Point and Canton Waterfront Areas)

Abstracts of South Central Pennsylvania Newspapers Volume 2, 1791-1795

Early Families of Otsego County, New York, Volume 1

Early Church Records of Chester County, Pennsylvania, Volume 2
Martha Reamy and Charlotte Meldrum

Abstracts of Carroll County Newspapers, 1831-1846
Martha Reamy and Marlene Bates

www.ingramcontent.com/pod-product-compliance
Lightning Source LLC
Chambersburg PA
CBHW070724160426
43192CB00009B/1306